5.00 ✓

THE DAWN OF LIBERATION

The King entertains the Dominion Prime Ministers at Buckingham Palace. (*Left to right*) The Right Hon. Peter Fraser; the Right Hon. John Curtin; the Right Hon. Winston S. Churchill; The King; the

THE DAWN OF LIBERATION

War Speeches by the
RIGHT HON. WINSTON S. CHURCHILL
C.H., M.P.
1944

Compiled by
CHARLES EADE

CASSELL AND COMPANY LTD.
LONDON, TORONTO, MELBOURNE AND SYDNEY

THIS BOOK IS PRODUCED IN
COMPLETE CONFORMITY WITH THE
AUTHORIZED ECONOMY STANDARDS

First Published 1945

MADE AND PRINTED IN GREAT BRITAIN
AT THE CHAPEL RIVER PRESS
ANDOVER, HANTS
F.345

CONTENTS

v

Contents

vii

CONTENTS

LIST OF ILLUSTRATIONS

INTRODUCTION

ON January the first, 1944, Mr. Winston Churchill was at Marrakesh, in Morocco, recovering from his second attack of pneumonia in a year. As he surveyed the world war from his sick bed he had much to cheer him on the way to complete good health. In a New Year message he spoke of the year ahead as " this year of decision." He laid emphasis on the formidable tasks of war and the problems of the peace which would follow, but he also expressed a glowing confidence which was shared by millions throughout the Allied countries.

There was much to justify that confidence. The year which had just closed had been one of almost unbroken success for the United Nations, and there were high hopes that the war or at least, the war in Europe, would be brought to a triumphant conclusion in 1944.

Everywhere the Allied forces were on the offensive. First among them stood the Russians. At the opening of the year the Red Army held the initiative along the whole Eastern Front. During the past few months they had pushed back the Germans as much as 500 miles in some sections. They had out-fought and out-generalled them. Now they faced the still formidable enemy in 1944 with superiority in man-power and equipment. A desperate German counter-offensive against the Kiev salient had recently been smashed, and the dawn of New Year's Day saw the Red Army pressing out from the threatened salient, closing in on Berdichev, and menacing the whole of the enemy's right centre. Farther south in the Ukraine they were assaulting Novigrad Volynsk and the main Kiev-Warsaw railway, only 15 miles from the 1939 Polish frontier. Zhitomar, with 150 smaller places on that section of the front, had just fallen. All along the line the Russians were on the move, or poised ready to strike a new blow. The German people were prepared for more bad news and the continuation of large-scale withdrawals from Russian territory. The Eastern scene was very bright for the United Nations.

In Italy progress was slow but persistent. After rapid advances following the Allied landing on the Italian mainland on September 3rd, an unduly early winter, with torrents of rain in mid-November, had bogged-down the forward march of General Alexander's Fifth and Eighth Armies. For nearly a month the Fifth had been trying to open the Liri Valley, " the road to Rome ; " but the enemy contested every mile, and was making full use of the defensive strength of the mountainous country. Bad weather, too, prevented the Allies exploiting their air power. Their supremacy in the skies was undisputed, but conditions denied them full use of this advantage in co-operation with ground forces. The front in Italy ran in a north-easterly direction from Garigliano, about 40 miles north of the Bay of Naples, to Ortona, roughly midway between Venice and Brindisi. Even on this front, despite the hold-up, hopes ran high that better weather would bring another great surge forward.

The hard winter could not check the great British-American air assault on Germany and Occupied Europe. Raids of ever-increasing weight brought devastation to the enemy's cities, factories and communications. Half of Berlin lay in ruins, and with relentless intensity the bombers continued their task of destroying the Germans' capacity to wage war.

At sea, too, the news was still holding fair. The U-boat menace had been conquered, and the sinking of the *Scharnhorst* on Boxing Day had been a fitting finale to a year of solid naval success.

And, while the war against Germany was moving to its climax, in the Far East the Japanese were, in their turn, feeling the growing might of the British Empire and the United States.

In the South Pacific General MacArthur's forces in New Guinea, New Britain and the Solomons were pressing on steadily. Progress was not spectacular, but it was effective, and Japs were being killed. In the North the enemy had been swept from the Aleutian Islands, and in the Central Pacific powerful U.S. naval forces, which in the preceding months had attacked the Marshall Islands and the Gilbert Islands, were a constant menace to the outer ring of Japan's defences. In Burma, British and American forces under the newly-created Supreme Command of Admiral Mountbatten, were holding the enemy from India. The American-trained Chinese forces of General Stilwell were pushing ahead with the Ledo road, which was planned to link the railways of India with the old Burma road into China. In China itself the hard-pressed forces of General Chiang Kai-shek still fought on. Ill-equipped, cut off from all but the smallest supplies, they retained the will and the courage to battle desperately until their Allies could open up other routes into their sorely-tried country.

But far transcending all these mighty events in the minds of the people of the Allied nations was—the Invasion of Europe from the West, still known, despite the many campaigns that were being waged, as the Second Front. Huge forces of British and American soldiers, sailors and airmen, trained and equipped as none had ever been before, were massed in Southern England awaiting D Day, while their leaders, General Eisenhower, Air Chief Marshal Tedder, and General Montgomery, perfected their final plans. Across the Channel the Germans stood ready for the assault, their concrete and steel defences manned and gunned.

This was the war scene at the opening of 1944. Well might the Prime Minister look forward to it as a " year of decision "—and a year of Liberation.

CHARLES EADE

THE DAWN OF LIBERATION

"PREFARATION, EFFORT, RESOLVE"

A Speech to the House of Commons on the Progress of the War
February 22, 1944

January 1.	*Victorious Russian troops made further advances to the Polish frontier.*
	R.A.F. dropped a thousand tons of bombs on Berlin in the ninth major assault in six weeks.
January 3.	*General Montgomery arrived in Britain to take up his appointment as Commander-in-Chief of the armies under General Eisenhower.*
	R.A.F. made another thousand-tons attack on Berlin.
January 6.	*Russians captured Kokitno, 15 miles inside Polish border.*
	It was revealed that Britain was using a jet-propelled fighter aeroplane, invented by Group-Captain Whittle.
January 7.	*Russians launched new offensive, surrounded Kirovograd, and routed five German divisions.*
January 9.	*Fifth Army troops captured San Vittore on the road to Rome.*
January 11.	*Russians established a 40-miles front in Poland and advanced on Kovno.*
	Americans made big daylight air-raid on Germany, destroying 152 enemy fighters for the loss of 60 bombers and five fighters.
January 12.	*Russians captured Sarny, first big town in Poland to fall into their hands.*
January 14.	*Mozyr and Kalinkovichi were captured by the Russians.*
January 16.	*Announced that Mr. Churchill had met General de Gaulle at Marrakesh.*
January 17.	*Germans strengthened their resistance to the Russian offensive on the railway running from Novo-Sokolniki to Leningrad.*
	Fifth Army troops advanced on Rome and reached the River Rapido.
January 18.	*Russians launched a new offensive on the Leningrad front.*
	Mr. Churchill arrived in London fully recovered from his illness.

1

January 19.	Russian troops pressing on in the new Leningrad offensive captured many 16-in. guns which had been bombarding the city for months.
January 20.	R.A.F. dropped 2,300 tons of bombs on Berlin, the city's heaviest raid of the war.
January 21.	In retaliation for Berlin raid the German air force attacked London and S.E. England in strength.
January 22.	Allied troops with sea and air support landed at Anzio south of Rome, taking the Germans by surprise.
January 23.	Fifth Army troops penetrated several miles inland following the landings south of Rome.
	Russian offensive in the Leningrad region developed into a general attack on a 50-miles front.
January 24.	Fifth Army advanced another four miles inland and captured Nettuno.
January 25.	Forward troops from the landing south of Rome reached the Appian Way.
January 27.	Russians captured Tosno on the Leningrad-Moscow railway.
	Troops of the Hermann Göring Panzer Division were repulsed by the Fifth Army near Littoria.
January 29.	Russians captured Novo Sokolniki, Chudovo and Smyela.
	U.S. bombers dropped more than 1,800 tons of bombs in daylight raid on Frankfort.
January 31.	Fifth Army launched offensive from the Nettuno-Anzio bridgehead.
February 1.	U.S. forces, it was announced, had landed on the Marshall Islands, the biggest Pacific operation so far.
	Russians crossed the Estonian frontier.
February 2.	Fifth Army troops broke through the Gustav Line in Italy.
February 3.	Russians announced their greatest victory since Stalingrad —encircling of 100,000 Germans west of the Middle Dnieper.
February 5.	British troops in the Anzio beachhead held off heavy counter-offensive.
February 6.	Russians broke through German defences on the Lower Dnieper and routed seven enemy divisions.
February 7.	Enemy forces assembled for a major attack on the Anzio beachhead were dispersed by artillery fire.
February 8.	Russians captured Nikopol.
February 9.	Germans announced that a general attack had been launched against the Anzio beachhead. Fifth Army encountered bitter fighting in Cassino.

2

February 11.   *Heavy bombers called in to smash German counter-attack on Anzio beachhead.*

February 12.   *It was announced that reports from General Wilson and General Alexander expressed confidence that the battle for Rome would be won.*

February 15.   *R.A.F. made its biggest attack so far on Berlin, dropping well over 2,500 tons of bombs in 20 minutes.*

February 16.   *Fifth Army repulsed a tank attack on Anzio beachhead.*

        Bombing of the Monte Cassino Abbey destroyed the strongest German defence on the road to Rome.

February 17.   *Powerful U.S. naval task force attacked Truk, Japanese stronghold in the Caroline Islands.*

        Allies directed heaviest air assault ever against the Germans attacking the Anzio beachhead.

        Russians announced that 52,000 Germans had been trapped and wiped out in a pocket at Kanyev.

February 18.   *German air force attempted a reprisal fire blitz on London.*

February 19.   *Allies held German attacks on the Anzio beachhead and inflicted heavy casualties.*

        U.S. Marines captured Japanese air base at Engebi.

February 20.   *R.A.F. dropped more than 2,300 tons of bombs on Leipzig.*

        It was announced that in the attack on Truk 19 Japanese ships were sunk and 201 aircraft destroyed.

February 21.   *R.A.F. dropped nearly 2,000 tons of bombs on Stuttgart and another great force of U.S. bombers also joined in the attack on Germany.*

February 22.   *Mr. Churchill reviewed the war in a speech to the House of Commons.*

        Marshal Stalin announced the capture of Krivoi Rog.

[*February* 22, 1944.

THIS is no time for sorrow or rejoicing. It is a time for preparation, effort and resolve. The war is still going on. I have never taken the view that the end of the war in Europe is at hand, or that Hitler is about to collapse, and I have certainly given no guarantees, or even held out any expectations, that the year 1944 will see the end of the European war. Nor have I given any guarantees the other way. On the whole, my information—and I have a good deal—goes to show that Hitler and his police are still in full control, and that the Nazi party and the Generals have decided to hang together. The strength of the German Army is about 300 divisions, though many of these are substantially reduced in numbers. The fighting quality of the troops is high. The German General Staff system, which we failed to liquidate after the last war, represents an Order comprising many thousands of highly-trained officers and a school of doctrine of long, unbroken continuity. It possesses great skill, both in the handling of troops in action and in their rapid movement from place to place. The recent fighting in Italy should leave no doubt on these points.

It is true that the results of our bombing have had a noteworthy effect upon Germany's munitions production. In the people they have produced a dull apathy, which also affects munitions production and all A.R.P. services. The splendid victories of our Soviet Allies on the Eastern front are inflicting immense losses upon the enemy. The fact that so many of the enemy's divisions have been drawn into Italy and into Yugoslavia, while other large bodies of his troops are held in France and the Low Countries by the fear of invasion, has been a help to these victories. Moreover, the Anglo-American bombing of Germany, absorbing, as it does, above three million Germans, has drawn, together with other British and American activities, four-fifths of the German fighter force to the British and American front; and I believe a large proportion of their bombers are employed against us and our American Allies.

This also has been of assistance to the Soviet Union. I think these statements should be made in justice to the Western Allies. They in no way detract from the glory of the Russian arms. It must also be be borne in mind, in surveying the general foundations of the scene as we see it to-day, that as the German troops retreat westwards they will find many opportunities of narrowing their front, and that if they choose to cut their losses in the Balkans or in the Italian peninsula at any time, a considerable number of divisions can be made available for the purpose of strengthening their central reserve. It is far from my wish to make any boastful statements about the part which this island is playing in the war. It has, however, been borne in on me that the interests of the Alliance as a whole may be prejudiced if its other members are left in ignorance of the British share in the great events which are unfolding. The Dominions also have the right to know that the Mother Country is playing its part.

I think it is therefore my duty to state a few facts which are not perhaps generally realized. For instance, since January 1st, 1943, up to the present time, the middle of February, ships of the Royal Navy and aircraft of the Royal Air Force, that is to say the Forces of the Mother Country only, have sunk more than half the U-boats of which we have certain proof in the shape of living prisoners, and they have also destroyed 40 per cent. of the very large number of other U-boats of which either corpses or fragments provide definite evidence of destruction. Again, on the naval side, apart from enemy U-boats we

4

have sunk by British action alone since January 1st, 1943, 19 enemy warships and also a large number of E-boats, escort vessels, mine-sweepers and other auxiliaries. British action has been predominantly responsible for sinking during this period 316 merchant ships aggregating 835,000 tons. In that same period, 7,677 officers and men of the Royal Navy and about 4,200 Merchant Navy officers and men have lost their lives in British ships. This last, however, does not at all represent the total war sacrifice to date of our merchant seamen, because matters have improved so much lately. Since the beginning of the war the proportion of merchant seamen hailing from these islands alone who have been lost at sea on their vital duty has been about one-fifth of the average number engaged in this service. The total of personnel, officers and men, of the Royal Navy lost since the war started is just over 30 per cent. of its pre-war strength, the figures being 41,000 killed out of 133,000, which was its total strength on the outbreak of war. Since January 1st, 1943, ships of the Royal Navy have bombarded the enemies' coasts on 716 occasions. In the same period we have lost in action or had disabled for more than a year—serious disablement—95 ships of war.

Turning to the air, the honour of bombing Berlin has fallen almost entirely to us. Up to the present we have delivered the main attack upon Germany. Excluding Dominion and Allied squadrons working with the Royal Air Force, the British islanders have lost 38,300 pilots and air crews killed and 10,400 missing, and over 10,000 aircraft since the beginning of the war—and they have made nearly 900,000 sorties into the North European theatre. As for the Army, the British Army was little more than a police force in 1939, yet they have fought in every part of the world—in Norway, France, Holland, Belgium, Egypt, Eritrea, Abyssinia, Somaliland, Madagascar, Syria, North Africa, Persia, Sicily, Italy, Greece, Crete, Burma, Malaya, Hong Kong. I cannot now in this speech attempt to describe these many campaigns, so infinitely varied in their characteristics, but history will record how much the contribution of our soldiers has been beyond all proportion to the available man-power of these islands. The Anglo-American air attack upon Germany must be regarded as our chief offensive effort at the present time. Till the middle of 1943 we had by far the larger forces in action. As the result of the enormous trans-portations across the Atlantic which have been made during 1943 the United States Bomber Force in this Island now begins to surpass our own, and will soon be substantially greater still, I rejoice to say.

The efforts of the two forces fit well together, and according to all past standards each effort is in itself prodigious. Let me take the latest example. During the 48 hours beginning at 3 a.m. on February 20th, four great raids were made upon Germany. The first was against

Leipzig on the night of 19–20th by the Royal Air Force, when nearly 1,000 machines were dispatched, of which 79 were lost. On Sunday morning a tremendous American raid, nearly 1,000 strong, escorted by an even greater number of fighters, American and British, but mostly American, set out for German towns, including Leipzig, in broad daylight. The losses in this raid were greatly reduced by the fact that the enemy fighters had been scattered beforehand by the British operations of the night before. The fighters descend at bases other than their own and cannot be so readily handled on a second rapidly-ensuing occasion, and the full effect of the American precision bombing could therefore be realized.

Following hard upon this, on the night of 20–21st another British raid was delivered, this time on Stuttgart, in very great strength—about 600 or 700. The effect of the preceding 24 hours' bombing relieved this third raid to a very large extent. Finally, the American force went out on Monday, again in full scale, and drove home in the most effective manner our joint air superiority over the enemy. Taking them together, these four raids, in which over 9,000 tons of bombs were dropped by the two Allied and complementary air forces, constitute the most violent attacks which have yet been made on Germany, and they also prove the value of saturation in every aspect of the air war. That aspect will steadily increase as our forces develop and as the American forces come into their full scope and scale.

The Spring and Summer will see a vast increase in the force of the attacks directed upon all military targets in Germany and in German-occupied countries. Long-range bombing from Italy will penetrate effectively the southern parts of Germany. We look for very great restriction and dislocation of the entire German munitions supply, no matter how far the factories have been withdrawn. In addition, the precision of the American daylight attack produces exceptional results upon particular points, not only in clear daylight, but now, thanks to the development of navigational aids, through cloud. The whole of this air offensive constitutes the foundation upon which our plans for overseas invasion stand. Scales and degrees of attack will be reached far beyond the dimensions of anything which has yet been employed or, indeed, imagined. The idea that we should fetter or further restrict the use of this prime instrument for shortening the war will not be accepted by the Governments of the Allies. The proper course for German civilians and non-combatants is to quit the centres of munition production and take refuge in the countryside. We intend to make war production in its widest sense impossible in all German cities, towns and factory centres.

Retaliation by the enemy has, so far, been modest, but we must expect it to increase. Hitler has great need to exaggerate his counter-attacks in order to placate his formerly deluded population ; but besides these air attacks there is no doubt that the Germans are preparing on the French shore new means of assault on this country, either by pilotless aircraft, or possibly rockets, or both, on a considerable scale. We have long been watching this with the utmost vigilance. We are striking at all evidences of these preparations on occasions when the weather is suitable for such action and to the maximum extent possible without detracting from the strategic offensive against Germany. An elaborate scheme of bombing priorities, upon which a large band of highly skilled American and British officers are constantly at work, in accordance with the directions given by the combined Chiefs of Staff in Washington, has governed our action for some time past and is continually kept up to date and in relation to our strategic needs and aims. I do not believe that a better machinery could be devised. It is always flexible enough to allow us to turn aside for some particularly tempting objective, as, for instance, Sofia, the capital of hated Bulgaria. The weather, of course, remains the final factor in the decision where each day's or night's activities shall be employed. That leaves very great responsibility in the hands of the officers who actually handle these enormous masses of aircraft. The use of our air power also affects the general war situation by the toll which it takes of the enemy's fighter aircraft both by day and night, but especially the Americans by day, because they have fought very great actions with their formations of Flying Fortresses against enemy fighter aircraft.

Already we have seen the German air programme concentrated mainly on fighters, thus indicating how much they have been thrown on to the defensive in the air. Now this new German fighter strength is being remorselessly worn down, both in the air and in the factories, which are the objectives of the continuous attack. Every opportunity is and will be sought by us to force the enemy to expend and exhaust his fighter air strength. Our production of aircraft, fighters and bombers, judged by every possible test, already far exceeds that of the Germans. The Russian production is about equal to ours. The American production alone is double or treble the German production. When I speak of production, I mean not only that of aircraft, not only of the machines, but of all that vast organization of training schools and ancillary services which minister to air power, and without whose efficiency air power could not manifest itself. What the experiences of Germany will be when her fighter defence has been almost completely eliminated, and aircraft can go all over the country, by day or night, with nothing to fear but the flak—the anti-aircraft defences—has yet to be seen.

The same is true of the air power of Japan. That also is now being over-matched and worn down, and the production is incomparably small compared with that of the great Powers whom Japan has assailed. Whereas on former occasions when I have addressed the House and tried to give a general picture of the war in its structure and proportion, I have always set in the forefront the war against the U-boat menace, I deliberately, on this occasion, give the primacy to the great developments in air power which have been achieved and which are to be expected. This air power was the weapon which both the marauding States selected as their main tool of conquest. This was the sphere in which they were to triumph. This was the method by which the nations were to be subjugated to their rule. I shall not moralize further than to say that there is a strange, stern justice in the long swing of events.

Our other great joint Anglo-American offensive is in Italy. Many people have been disappointed with the progress there since the capture of Naples in October. This has been due to the extremely bad weather which marks the winter in those supposedly sunshine lands, and which this year has been worse than usual. Secondly, and far more, it is because the Germans, bit by bit, have been drawn down into Italy and have decided to make extreme exertions for the retention of the city of Rome. In October, they began to move a number of divisions southwards from the Valley of the Po and to construct a winter line south of Rome in order to confront and delay the advance of the Fifth and Eighth Armies under General Alexander. We were, therefore, committed to a frontal advance in extremely mountainous country which gave every advantage to the defence. All the rivers flow at right angles to our march, and the violent rains, this year above the normal, often turned these rivers into raging torrents, sweeping away all military bridges which had been thrown across them, and sometimes leaving part of the assaulting force already committed to the attack on the far side and beyond the reach of immediate reinforcements or support.

In addition to the difficulties I have mentioned, there has been the need to build up a very large supply of stores and vehicles of all kinds in Italy. Also, the strategic air force which is being developed for the attack on Southern Germany, has made extremely large priority inroads upon our transportation especially upon those forms of transportation which are most in demand. An immense amount of work has, however, been done, and the results will become apparent later on. Among the Allies we have, of course, much the largest army in Italy. The American air force in the Mediterranean, on the other hand, is larger than the British, and the two together possess an enormous superiority, quantitative and also, we believe, qualitative, over the enemy. We have also, of course, the complete command of the seas, where an American squadron is actively working with the British Fleet. Such being the position, many people wondered why it was not possible to make a large amphibious turning movement, either on the Eastern or Western side of Italy, to facilitate the forward advance of the army.

The need for this was, of course, obvious to all the commanders, British and American, but the practicability of carrying it into effect depended upon this effort being properly fitted-in with the general Allied programme for the year. This programme comprises larger issues and forces than those with which we are concerned in Italy. The difficulties which had hitherto obstructed action were, I am glad to say, removed at the Conferences which were held at Carthage at Christmas and at Marrakesh in January. The conclusions were approved, step by step, by the President of the United States and the combined Chiefs of Staff. All that the Supreme War Direction could do was done by the first week in January. Preparations had already been begun in anticipation of the final surmounting of difficulties, and January 22nd was fixed as the zero day by General Alexander, on whom rests the responsibility for fighting the battle. It was certainly no light matter to launch this considerable army—40,000 or 50,000 men—in the first instance with all the uncertainty of winter weather and all the unknowable strength of enemy fortifications—to launch it out upon the seas.

The operation itself was a model of combined work. The landing was virtually unopposed. Subsequent events did not, however, take the course which had been hoped or planned. In the upshot, we got a great army ashore, equipped with masses of artillery, tanks and very many thousands of vehicles, and our troops moving inland came into contact with the enemy. The German reactions to this descent have been remarkable. Hitler has apparently resolved to defend Rome with the same obstinacy which he showed at Stalingrad, in Tunisia, and, recently, in the Dnieper Bend. No fewer than seven extra German divisions were brought rapidly down from France, Northern Italy and Yugoslavia, and a determined attempt has been made to destroy the bridgehead and drive us into the sea. Battles of prolonged and intense fierceness and fury have been fought. At the same time, the American and British Fifth Army to the southward is pressing forward with all its strength. Another battle is raging there.

On both fronts there has been in the last week a most severe and continuous engagement, very full accounts of which have been given every day in the Press and in the official *communiqués*. Up to the present moment the enemy has sustained very heavy losses, but has not shaken the resistance of the bridgehead army. The forces are well matched, though we are definitely the stronger in artillery and armour, and, of course, when the weather is favourable our air power plays an immense part. General Alexander, who has probably seen more fighting against the Germans than any living British commander—unless it be General Freyberg, who is also in the fray—says that the bitterness and fierceness of the fighting now going on both in the bridgehead and at the Cassino front surpass all his previous experience. He even used in one message to me the word " terrific." On the southern front, the Cassino front, British, American, Dominion, Indian, French and Polish troops are fighting side by side in a noble comradeship. Their leaders are confident of final success. I can say no more than what I have said, for I would not attempt to venture on a more sanguine prediction, but their leaders are confident ; and the troops are in the highest spirit of offensive vigour.

On broad grounds of strategy, Hitler's decision to send into the South of Italy as many as 18 divisions involving, with their maintenance troops, probably something like a half a million Germans, and to make a large secondary front in Italy, is not unwelcome to the Allies. We must fight the Germans somewhere, unless we are to stand still and watch the Russians. This wearing battle in Italy occupies troops who could not be employed in other greater operations, and it is an effective prelude to them. We have sufficient forces at our disposal in Africa to nourish the struggle as fast as they can be transported across the Mediterranean. The weather is likely to improve as the Spring approaches, and as the skies clear, the Allied air power will reach its fullest manifestation.

This time last year, to a day—February 22nd—when, I remember, I was ill in bed, I was deeply anxious about the situation in Tunisia, where we had just sustained an unpleasant check at the Kasserine Pass. But I placed my confidence then in General Alexander and in the British, American and French troops who were engaged in the battle—and that is how I feel about it now.

In the discussions at Cairo, and during my enforced stay amid the ruins of Carthage, I was able, by correspondence, to settle with the President and with the War Cabinet here the remodelling of the commands for our joint operations in the Mediterranean and elsewhere. The principle which should obviously be followed between two Allies working together as closely as we and the United States is that the nationality of the commander should generally follow the majority of the troops in any theatre. In General Maitland Wilson and General Alexander, we have at once the supreme commander in the Mediterranean and the fighting head of the Army in Italy. We and our American Ally have full confidence in these officers, under whom the United States General Devers and General Clark, the most daring and gallant leader of the Fifth Army, are the corresponding

American chiefs. In Great Britain, on the other hand, where forces are being assembled for future operations of the greatest magnitude, General Eisenhower, with whom we have worked for so long, so happily and so successfully, has been placed at the summit of the war direction, with Air Chief Marshal Tedder as his deputy and with his brilliant United States Chief of Staff, the trusty General Bedell Smith—these are the central figures of this command under whom many distinguished commanders, British and American, are serving, including General Montgomery; and these officers will, when the time comes and in accordance with the arrangements which have been made, lead our Armies to the liberation of Europe.

As certain statements have been made in America—unofficial statements—about the relative strengths of the Armies to be employed from here, I think it necessary to state that the British and American Armies at the outset of the struggle will be approximately equal, but that if its duration is prolonged, the continuous inflow of the American build-up at an enormous rate will naturally give them that superiority of numbers which would be expected from the great resources of man-power which they dispose of, and which they desire above all things to bring into contact as speedily as possible with the enemy. Hence, it is right that the supreme command should go to the United States. I would turn aside for one moment just to emphasize how perfect is the co-operation between the commanders of the British and the American Armies. Nothing like it has ever been seen before among allies. No doubt language is a great help, but there is more in it than that. In all previous alliances the staffs have worked with opposite numbers in each department and liaison officers, but in Africa General Eisenhower built up a uniform staff, in which every place was filled with whoever was thought to be the best man, and they all ordered each other about according to their rank, without the slightest regard to what country they belonged to. The same unity and brotherhood is being instituted here throughout the Forces which are gathering in this country, and I cannot doubt that it will be found most service-able, and unique also in all the history of alliances.

I must now turn from the actual military operations to the European scene, which influences all military affairs so vehemently. In this present war of so many nations against the Nazi tyranny, there has, at least, been a common principle at work throughout Europe, and among the conquered peoples there is a unity of hatred and a desire to revolt against the Germans such as has never been known against any race before. The penalties of defeat are frightful. After the blinding flash of catastrophe, the stunning blow, the gaping wounds, there comes an onset of the diseases of defeat. The central principle of a nation's life is broken, and all healthy normal control vanishes. There are few societies that can withstand the conditions of subjugation. Indomitable patriots take different paths; quislings and collaborationists of all kinds abound; guerrilla leaders, each with their personal followers, quarrel and fight. There are already in Greece and Yugoslavia factions engaged in civil war one with another, and animated by hatreds more fierce than those which should be reserved for the common foe. Among all these varied forces the German oppressor develops his intrigues with cynical ruthlessness and merciless cruelty.

It is hard enough to understand the politics of one's own country; it is almost impossible to understand those of foreign countries. The sanest and the safest course for us to follow is to judge all parties and factions dispassionately by the test of their readiness and ability to fight the Germans and thus lighten the burden of the Allied troops. This is no time for ideological preferences for one side or the other, and certainly we, His Majesty's Government, have not indulged ourselves in this way at all. Thus, in Italy we are working for the present through the Government of the King and Badoglio; in Yugoslavia we give our aid to Marshal Tito; in Greece, in spite of the fact that a British officer was murdered by the guerrilla organization called E.L.A.S., we are doing our best to bring about a reconciliation, or at least a working agreement, between the opposing forces. I will say a word, if the House will permit me, about each of these unhappy countries, and the principles which should govern us, and which we are certainly following.

We signed the Italian Armistice on the basis of unconditional surrender with King Victor Emmanuel and Marshal Badoglio, who were, and up to the present are, the legitimate Government of Italy. On their authority, the Italian Navy, not without risk and loss, surrendered to us, and practically all Italian troops and airmen who were not dominated by the Germans also obeyed the orders they received from the Crown. Since then these Italian forces have co-operated with us to the best of their ability, and nearly 100 Italian ships of war are discharging valuable services in the Mediterranean and the Atlantic. Italian troops have entered the front line in Italy, and although on one occasion they suffered severe casualties they continue to fight alongside our men. Very much larger numbers are engaged in indispensable services to the Allied Armies behind the front. Italian airmen are also fighting at our side.

The battle in Italy, for reasons which I have already explained, will be hard and long. I am not yet convinced that any other Government can be formed at the present time in Italy which would command the same obedience from the Italian Armed Forces. Should we succeed in the present battle and enter Rome, as I trust and believe we shall, we shall be free to discuss the whole Italian political situation, and we shall do so with many advantages that we do not possess at the present time. It is from Rome that a more broadly based Italian Government can best be formed. Whether a Government thus formed will be so helpful to the Allies as the present dispensation, I cannot tell. It might, of course, be a Government which would try to make its position good with the Italian people by resisting, as much as it dared, the demands made on them in the interests of the Allied Armies. I should be sorry, however, to see an unsettling change made at a time when the battle is at its climax, swaying to and fro. When you have to hold a hot coffee-pot, it is better not to break the handle off until you are sure that you will get another equally convenient and serviceable, or, at any rate, until there is a dishcloth handy.

The representatives of the various Italian parties who assembled a fortnight ago at Bari are, of course, eager to become the Government of Italy. They will certainly have no elective authority, and certainly no constitutional authority, until either the present King abdicates himself or his successor invites them to take office. It is by no means certain that they would have any effective authority over the Italian Armed Forces now fighting with us. Italy lies prostrate under her miseries and disasters. Food is scarce ; shipping to bring it is voraciously absorbed by our ever-expanding military operations. I think we have gained 12,000,000 tons this year increase to the Allies, yet the shortage continues, because our great operations absorb every ship as it comes, and the movement of food is difficult.

It would be a mistake to suppose that the kind of political conditions or forces exist in Italy which work so healthily in unbeaten lands, or in countries which have not been shattered by war or stifled by a long period of Fascist rule. We shall see much more clearly how to proceed, and have much more varied resources at our disposal, if and when we are in possession of the capital city. The policy, therefore, which His Majesty's Government have agreed provisionally with the Government of the United States is to win the battle for Rome and take a new view when we are there. On the other side of the Adriatic, in the vast mountain regions of Yugoslavia, Albania and Greece, an area of perhaps 800 miles from north to south and 300 or 400 miles from East to West, a magnificent resistance to the German invaders is in full and violent progress.

With the surrender of Italy—with which I think Great Britain had something to do, having fought the Italians since the summer of 1940 —62 Italian divisions ceased to be a hostile fighting factor. Forty-three were disbanded and enslaved, apparently without any of the safeguards which attach to prisoners of war, by the Germans. Ten were disbanded by the guerrillas in the Balkans, and nine, which were stationed in the South of Italy, or in Corsica and Sardinia, came over to

the Allies. Confronted with this situation, Hitler decided to reinforce
the Balkan Peninsula heavily, and, at the present time, no fewer than
20 German divisions are engaged in the Balkans. That is to say, there
are 25 German divisions in Italy, of which 18 are in the present battle
south of Rome, and another 20 are spread over the vast area of the
Balkans. Well, they might be worse employed.

In Yugoslavia, in spite of the most ferocious and murderous cruelties
and reprisals perpetrated by the Germans, not only against hostages,
but against the village populations, including women and children,
the Partisan forces have the upper hand. The Germans hold the
principal towns and try to keep the railways working. They can
march their columns of troops hither and thither about the country.
They own the ground they stand on, but nothing else. All the rest
belongs to the valiant Partisans. The German losses have been very
heavy, and, so far as actual fighting is concerned, greatly exceed
the losses of the Partisans ; but the killing of hostages and civilians
in cold blood adds to the German score—and to our score against the
Germans. In Yugoslavia, two main forces are in the field. First, the
guerrilla bands under General Mihailovitch. These were the first to
take the field, and represent, to a certain extent, the forces of old
Serbia. For some time after the defeat of the Yugoslav army, these
forces maintained a guerrilla. We were not able to send them any aid
or supplies, except a few droppings from aeroplanes. The Germans
retaliated for any guerrilla activities by shooting batches of 400 or 500
people together in Belgrade. General Mihailovitch, I much regret to
say, drifted gradually into a position in which some of his commanders
made accommodations with the Italian and German troops, which
resulted in their being left alone in certain mountain areas, and, in
return, doing very little or nothing against the enemy.

However, a new and far more formidable champion appeared on
the scene. In the autumn of 1941, Marshal Tito's Partisans began a
wild and furious war for existence against the Germans. They wrested
weapons from the Germans' hands, they grew rapidly in numbers ;
no reprisals, however bloody, whether upon hostages or the villages,
deterred them. For them, it was death or freedom. Soon they began
to inflict heavy injury upon the Germans and became masters of wide
regions. Led with great skill, organised on the guerrilla principle,
they were at once elusive and deadly. They were here, they were
there, they were everywhere. Large scale offensives have been
launched against them by the Germans, but in every case the
Partisans, even when surrounded, have escaped, after inflicting great
losses and toil upon the enemy. The Partisan movement soon out-
stripped in numbers the forces of General Mihailovitch. Not only
Croats and Slovenes, but large numbers of Serbians, joined with

Marshal Tito, and he has at this moment more than a quarter of a million men with him, and large quantities of arms taken from the enemy or from the Italians, and these men are organized, without losing their guerrilla qualities, into a considerable number of divisions and corps.

The whole movement has taken shape and form, without losing, as I say, the guerrilla quality without which it could not possibly succeed. These forces are, at this moment, holding in check no fewer than 14 German Divisions, out of the 20 in the Balkan Peninsula. Around and within these heroic forces, a national and unifying movement has developed. The Communist element had the honour of being the beginners, but, as the movement increased in strength and numbers, a modifying and unifying process has taken place, and national conceptions have supervened. In Marshal Tito, the Partisans have found an outstanding leader, glorious in the fight for freedom. Unhappily, perhaps inevitably, these new forces came into collision with those under General Mihailovitch. Their activities upset his commanders' accommodations with the enemy. He endeavoured to repress them, and many tragic fights took place and bitter feuds sprang up between men of the same race and country, whose misfortunes were due only to the common foe. At the present time, the followers of Marshal Tito outnumber many times those of General Mihailovitch, who acts in the name of the Royal Yugoslav Government. Of course, the Partisans of Marshal Tito are the only people who are doing any effective fighting against the Germans now.

For a long time past, I have taken a particular interest in Marshal Tito's movement, and have tried, and am trying, by every available means, to bring him help. A young friend of mine, an Oxford don, Captain Deakin, now Lieut.-Colonel Deakin, D.S.O., entered Yugoslavia by parachute nearly a year ago and was for eight months at Marshal Tito's headquarters. On one occasion, both were wounded by the same bomb. They became friends. Certainly, it is a bond between people, but a bond which, I trust, we shall not have to institute in our own personal relationships. From Colonel Deakin's reports we derived a lively picture of the whole struggle and its personalities. Last Autumn, we sent a larger Mission under the hon. and gallant Member for Lancaster (Brigadier Fitzroy Maclean). Having joined the Foreign Secretary and myself at Cairo to report, he has now re-entered Yugoslavia by parachute. I can assure the House that every effort in our power will be made to aid and sustain Marshal Tito and his gallant band. The Marshal sent me a message during my illness, and I have since been in constant and agreeable correspondence with him. We intend to back him with all the strength we can draw, having regard to our other main obligations.

What, then, is the position of King Peter and the Royal Yugoslav Government in Cairo ?   King Peter, as a boy of 17, escaped from the clutches of the Regent, and, with the new Royal Yugoslav Government, found shelter in this country. We cannot dissociate ourselves in any way from him. He has undoubtedly suffered in the eyes of the Partisans by the association of his Government with General Mihailovitch and his subordinate commanders. Here, in these islands, we are attached to the monarchical principle, and we have experienced the many blessings of constitutional monarchy, but we have no intention of obtruding our ideas upon the people of any country. Greece, Yugoslavia, Italy—all will be perfectly free to settle what form their governments shall take, so far as we are concerned, once the will of the people can be ascertained under conditions of comparative tranquillity. In the meantime, the position is a somewhat complicated one, and I hope to have the confidence of the House in working with my right hon. Friend the Foreign Secretary to unravel it, as far as possible, in concert with our Russian and United States Allies, who both, I am glad to say, are now sending Missions to Marshal Tito. Our feelings here, as everywhere else, I should like the House to see, follow the principle of keeping good faith with those who have kept good faith with us, and of striving, without prejudice or regard for political affections, to aid those who strike for freedom against the Nazi rule and thus inflict the greatest injury upon the enemy.

I have now given the House the fullest account in my power of this difficult, and in some ways delicate, situation in Yugoslavia, and I do not desire to add to it in any way at the present time. I have to pick my words with care because the situation is complicated. The saddest case of all, of what I may call the diseases of defeat, is Greece. Everyone can recall the sentiments of admiration which the heroic defence of Greece, first against the Italian and then against the German invader, aroused throughout the civilized world.   It is indeed painful to see the confusion and the internecine strife which has broken out in Greece, attended as it is by so many incidents of treachery and violence, all of which has been to the advantage of the German invaders, who watched with contemptuous complacency Greeks killing Greeks with ammunition sent to them to kill Germans. There is also present the idea that powerful elements among the guerrillas are thinking much less of driving out the foreign enemy than of seizing the title deeds of their country and establishing themselves as the dominant party, irrespective of the views of the masses of the nation, after the war is over. Here the situation, like that in Yugoslavia, is also most obscure and changing, but it can be said beyond all doubt that the great mass of the Greek people wait with fortitude and longing the hour of their liberation from the cruel servitude and bondage into which they have been thrown; and, so far as we are concerned, they shall not wait in vain.

A very full account was given to the House in December by my right hon. Friend the Foreign Secretary of the meeting of the heads of governments in Cairo and Teheran, and also of the meetings of the Foreign Secretaries which he had previously attended in Moscow. Things move so fast nowadays that this already seems ancient history, and I have little to add to what he said or to what has since been published. It was a great advantage and pleasure to me to meet for the first time Generalissimo Chiang Kai-Shek and his wife. The Generalissimo is a world figure, and the main hope and champion of China. Madame Chiang Kai-Shek is also a most remarkable and fascinating personality. Her perfect command of English, and complete comprehension of the world struggle as a whole, enable her to be the best of all interpreters in matters in which she herself plays a notable part.

Most of our time in Cairo, before we visited Teheran, was taken up in discussing the strategy and policy to be pursued against Japan ; the best means of pressing forward the war in the Indian and Pacific theatres with the utmost energy ; and, of course, the fitting of these plans into the requirements of the Atlantic and Mediterranean theatres. At Teheran the long-desired triple meeting between President Roosevelt, Marshal Stalin and myself was, at length, achieved. The personal contacts which we established were, and will, I am convinced, prove to be, helpful to the common cause. There would be very few differences between the three great Powers if their chief representatives could meet once a month. At such meetings, both formal and informal, all difficulties could be brought out freely and frankly, and the most delicate matters could be approached without the risk of jars or misunderstandings, such as too often arise when written communications are the only channel. But geography imposes its baffling obstacles, and though I trust it may be possible to hold further meetings as the war proceeds, I have no definite suggestions to make to the House at the moment.

The question is asked, I have heard, " Have the good relations established at Moscow and Teheran proved durable, or have they failed during the weeks that have passed ? " Does the *Pravda* statement, for instance, it is asked, or do the articles which are appearing in various organs of the Soviet Government, imply a cooling-off in Anglo-Russian or American-Russian friendship and a rebirth of suspicion of Western Allies on the part of Russia ? [An hon. Member : " On the British side."] On either side. I feel fully entitled to reassure the House on that all-important point. None of the ground made good at Moscow and Teheran has been lost. The three great

Allies are absolutely united in their action against the common foe. They are equally resolved to pursue the war, at whatever cost, to a victorious conclusion, and they believe that a wide field of friendly co-operation lies before them after the destruction of Hitlerite Germany. It is upon such a prolonged, intimate and honourable association that the future of the world depends.

I took occasion to raise personally with Marshal Stalin the question of the future of Poland. I pointed out that it was in fulfilment of our guarantee to Poland that Great Britain declared war upon Nazi Germany; that we had never weakened in our resolve, even in the period when we were all alone; and that the fate of the Polish nation holds a prime place in the thoughts and policies of His Majesty's Government and of the British Parliament. It was with great pleasure that I heard from Marshal Stalin that he, too, was resolved upon the creation and maintenance of a strong integral independent Poland as one of the leading Powers in Europe. He has several times repeated these declarations in public, and I am convinced that they represent the settled policy of the Soviet Union.

Here I may remind the House that we ourselves have never in the past guaranteed, on behalf of His Majesty's Government, any particular frontier line to Poland. We did not approve of the Polish occupation of Vilna in 1920. The British view in 1919 stands expressed in the so-called Curzon line, which attempted to deal, at any rate partially, with the problem. I have always held the opinion that all questions of territorial settlement and re-adjustment should stand over until the end of the war, and that the victorious Powers should then arrive at formal and final agreements governing the articulation of Europe as a whole. That is still the wish of His Majesty's Government. However, the advance of the Russian armies into Polish regions in which the Polish underground army is active makes it indispensable that some kind of friendly working agreement should be arrived at to govern the war-time conditions and to enable all anti-Hitlerite forces to work together with the greatest advantage against the common foe.

During the last few weeks the Foreign Secretary and I together have laboured with the Polish Government in London with the object of establishing a working arrangement upon which the Fighting Forces can act, and upon which, I trust, an increasing structure of goodwill and comradeship may be built between Russians and Poles. I have an intense sympathy with the Poles, that heroic race whose national spirit centuries of misfortune cannot quench; but I also have sympathy with the Russian standpoint. Twice in our lifetime Russia has been violently assaulted by Germany. Many millions of Russians have been slain and vast tracts of Russian soil devastated as a result of repeated German aggression. Russia has the right of reassurance against future attacks from the West, and we are going all the way with her to see that she gets it, not only by the might of her arms but by the approval and assent of the United Nations. The liberation of Poland may presently be achieved by the Russian armies after these armies have suffered millions of casualties in breaking the German military machine. I cannot feel that the Russian demand for a reassurance about her Western frontiers goes beyond the limits of what is reasonable or just. Marshal Stalin and I also spoke and agreed upon the need for Poland to obtain compensation at the expense of Germany both in the North and in the West.

Here I may point out that the term "unconditional surrender" does not mean that the German people will be enslaved or destroyed. It means, however, that the Allies will not be bound to them at the moment of surrender by any pact or obligation. There will be, for instance, no question of the Atlantic Charter applying to Germany as a matter of right and barring territorial transferences or adjustments in enemy countries. No such arguments will be admitted by us as were used by Germany after the last war, saying that they surrendered in consequence of President Wilson's fourteen points. Unconditional surrender means that the victors have a free hand. It does not mean that they are entitled to behave in a barbarous manner, nor that they wish to blot out Germany from among the nations of Europe. If we are bound, we are bound by our own consciences to civilization. We are not to be bound to the Germans as the result of a bargain struck. That is the meaning of "unconditional surrender."

It may be that I shall have a further statement to make to Parliament about Poland later on. For the present, what I have said, however incomplete, is all that His Majesty's Government are able to say upon the subject, and I hope that we shall not be pressed further in the Debate, because matters are still under discussion.

I thank the House very much for giving me their attention and so much consideration. There are many dangers and difficulties in making speeches at this moment ; first, it is a time for deeds and not words ; secondly, I must find the narrow line between reproof of complacency at home and encouragement of the enemy abroad. One has to confront the grave times through which we are still passing without depressing the soldiers who will have to fight and win the battles of 1944. Moreover, this should be remembered. There was a time when we were all alone in this war and when we could speak for ourselves, but now that we are in the closest relation on either side with our great Allies, every word spoken has to be considered in relation to them. We have lived through periods of mortal danger, and I cannot say that the dangers are mortal now. They are none the less very serious, and we need all the support and good will that attended us at the time when everyone felt that our national existence was at stake.

There is, I gather, in some quarters the feeling that the way to win the war is to knock the Government about, keep them up to the collar, and harry them from every side; and I find that hard to bear with Christian patience. Looking far abroad, it is also election year in the United States, and this is the time when, naturally, a lot of rough things have to be said about Great Britain, and when popularity is to be gained in that vast community by demonstrating Americanism in its highest forms. We are ourselves well accustomed to the processes of elections, and I think we should not allow ourselves to be unduly concerned at anything that may be said or written there in the course of a great constitutional process which is taking place. All this, however, accords none too well—this atmosphere and mood at home—with the responsibilities and burdens which weigh upon His Majesty's Ministers, and which, I can assure the House, are very real and heavy. We are in the advent of the greatest joint operations between two Allies that have ever been planned in history. There is the desire in this country in many quarters to raise the old controversies between the different parties. There is also a mood in the Anglo-American alliance to awaken slumbering prejudices and let them have their run; yet Liberals, Labour men and Tories are at this moment fighting and dying together at the front, and working together in a thousand ways at home, and Britons and Americans are linked together in the noblest comradeship of war under the fire and flail of the enemy. My hope is that generous instincts of unity will not depart from us in these times of tremendous exertions and grievous sacrifices, and that we shall not fall apart, abroad or at home, so as to become the prey of the little folk who exist in every country and who frolic alongside the Juggernaut car of war, to see what fun or notoriety they can extract from the proceedings.

There is one thing that we agreed at Teheran, above all others, to which we are all bound in solemn compact, and that is to fall upon and smite the Hun by land, sea and air with all the strength that is in us during the coming Spring and Summer. It is to this task that we must vow ourselves every day anew. It is to this ordeal that we must address our minds with all the moral fortitude we possess. The task is heavy, the toil is long, and the trials will be severe. Let us all try our best to do our duty. Victory may not be so far away, and will certainly not be denied us in the end.

A TRIBUTE TO THE PHYSICIANS

A Speech in Proposing the Toast of "The College" at the
Luncheon of the Royal College of Physicians in London
March 2, 1944

February 23. *U.S. aircraft based on Britain and Italy made a two-way attack on targets in Germany.*
A U.S. carrier task force raided the Mariana Islands, in the Pacific.

February 24. *R.A.F. and U.S. bombers continued day and night attacks on Germany.*

February 26. *Duel between big guns waged on the Anzio beachhead.*
Tokio reported that U.S. naval formations had struck at Guam.

February 27. *More than 50,000 Japanese were cut off in New Britain and New Ireland by the Allied sea and air blockade, in the Pacific.*

February 28. *A British victory on the Burma front was secured when a Japanese force of 6,000 which attacked the rear of the 7th Indian Division was wiped out.*

February 29. *Moscow announced the terms on which Finland would be granted an armistice.*

March 1. *Russians launched a new offensive south of Narva and crossed the river.*
Greek guerrillas led by a British officer wrecked a train packed with hundreds of German troops.

March 2. *British and American troops counter-attacked in Anzio beachhead and recovered all lost ground.*
R.A.F. in a raid on an aircraft factory at Albert used the biggest bomb ever—$5\frac{1}{2}$ tons.

[*March 2, 1944.*

I AM very grateful to my cherished friend, Lord Moran, for all the kind expressions he has used, in commending this toast to you, about me and about the conclusions which his naturally close and intimate investigations have enabled him to form. He has been my companion on the various journeys I have had to take in the course of public business about the world during this war, and always a devoted and comforting friend. We get on very well together. As you can see

C
21

from the excellent speech to which you have just listened, we divide our labours; he instructs me in the art of public speaking, and I teach him how to cure pneumonia.

But, close as our relations are, I must confess that it was not without compunction, and even misgiving, that I accepted his hospitable invitation to-day. I do not profess to be very deeply acquainted with the science of medicine. I am a surgeon myself. My experiences in medicine have been vivid and violent, and completely absorbing while they were going on. Nevertheless, I cannot claim that they have given me that broad, detached, general experience which, I believe, is the foundation for all correct scientific action.

Moreover, to address so distinguished a company on topics with which one is necessarily not profoundly acquainted is an ordeal. But the most serious part of my misgivings arose from the fact that I should have to leave my patient for a while. I have a patient whom I have been looking after for some years, as you may know, and I am glad to be able to assure you that she is no longer in mortal danger. On that I can give you an absolute assurance. You must not suppose that this has in any way reduced my work; on the contrary, now that the greatest danger is passed, my patient has reached a stage where restiveness, fretfulness, the impatience of convalescence, the weariness of a long prolongation of the disease, while they do not excite the same anxiety in one's breast, nevertheless require a very full measure of one's personal attention.

The recent advances in medicine are most remarkable and inspiring. Human inventiveness has been fanned by the fierce wings of war. New drugs of a remarkable healing potency are becoming common-places of science, and even the latest text-books on many diseases require to have very considerable annotations and additions made to them. I personally have never failed to pay my tribute of respect and gratitude to M and B; although I am not competent to give you an exact description of how it works, it certainly has in my case always been attended by highly beneficial results. Then there is penicillin, which has broken upon the world just at a moment when human beings are being gashed and torn and poisoned by wounds on the field of war in enormous numbers, and when so many other diseases, hitherto insoluble, cry for treatment. It is a great satisfaction to be able to congratulate St. Mary's Hospital on their association with penicillin.

The discoveries of healing science must be the inheritance of all. That is clear. Disease must be attacked, whether it occurs in the poorest or the richest man or woman, simply on the ground that it is the enemy; and it must be attacked just in the same way as the fire brigade will give its full assistance to the humblest cottage as readily as to the most important mansion. His Majesty's Government have adopted the policy outlined in the remarks of Lord Beaconsfield on health and the laws of health, and that is the course upon which we have embarked. Our policy is to create a national health service in order to ensure that everybody in the country, irrespective of means, age, sex, or occupation, shall have equal opportunities to benefit from the best and most up-to-date medical and allied services available.

The plan that we have put forward is a very large-scale plan, and in ordinary times of peace would rivet and dominate the attention of the whole country ; and even during this war it deserves the close study and thought of all who can spare themselves from other duties for that purpose. It is not a rigid or arbitrary plan. We welcome constructive criticism, we claim the loyal and active aid of the whole medical profession. Any health service must rest on two arches ; the first, the general practitioner, the rank and file of the profession ; the second, the hospital service, depending upon the staffs of the hospitals, sustained and guided by the consultants.

The fact that many more consultants will be needed in the future than there are now must not result in dilution or in the lowering of the standard of consultant work. There is a new gap to be filled, and it is essential that in this new effort the Colleges should play their great part. We ask your aid. We invite your counsel. If we work together, these vast problems may take a forward move which will be notable and permanent in its effects long after the roar of the cannonade has died away.

We have to-day announced the names of the Royal Commission on Population. There is no branch of human knowledge in which we can pierce the mysteries of the future so clearly as in the trend of population. Here you have prophecies which rest on certainty ; here the searchlight of statistics ranges with accuracy for 30 or 40 years ahead. The destiny of our country, which after all has rendered notable services to mankind in peace and latterly in war, depends upon an ever-flowing fountain of healthy children, born into what we trust will be a broader society and a less distracted world. Science, now so largely perverted to destruction, must raise its glittering shield not only over the children but over the mothers, not only over the family, but over the home. In all this field again you must be active. Your services will be given with devotion, and your voice will be heard with respect.

This College, on whose past you, Lord Moran, have descanted, on whose past you have opened some windows which cast a view upon its former glories, was, I am assured, founded by a man of wide experience of human nature—and of both sexes—King Henry VIII, in 1518. It is claimed that he thus created medicine as a profession, and cast a stern Tudor frown upon quackery of all kinds. However, the Ministry of Health are of opinion that the suppression of quackery dates not from 1518, but from the Medical Act of 1588. I would not for worlds plunge into a new controversy in a world which is already sufficiently filled with strife, but certainly this College was famous, and its career was remarkable, for many long periods of history, during some of which it has been a veritable pillar of the State. Certainly, if appeal is made to antiquity, the honours rest with the Royal College of Physicians. The Ministry of Health, I remember well, is quite a newcomer in the field, for I can recollect myself having at one time been offered by Mr. Asquith the Local Government Board—it sounds a very modest affair—carrying with it only a salary of £2,000 a year as a minor Ministry, but which has blossomed out quite recently into the full-blown majesty of the Ministry of Health.

As between the old and the new, you have undoubtedly the advantage of antiquity. This College must play its part in keeping alive the historic tradition of the medical profession, and must ever foster those high standards of professional behaviour which distinguish a profession from a trade. This is what you have tried to do as an institution, for nearly 400 years. I confess myself to be a great admirer of tradition. The longer you can look back, the farther you can look forward. This is not a philosophical or political argument—any oculist will tell you this is true. The wider the span, the longer the continuity, the greater is the sense of duty in individual men and women, each contributing their brief life's work to the preservation and progress of the land in which they live, the society of which they are members, and the world of which they are the servants.

With these few thoughts, or remarks—for I would not rate them too high—with these few remarks I will invite this great company, and with no apprehension of refusal on your part, to drink the health of the Royal College of Physicians, and to wish them all prosperity and success in the great part they have to play in the unfolding evolution of our nation.

BASIC ENGLISH

[*March* 9, 1944.

THE Committee of Ministers on Basic English, after hearing a considerable volume of evidence, have submitted a Report which has been approved in principle by His Majesty's Government. The Committee, in their report, distinguish between the use of a system such as Basic English as an auxiliary international language, and as a method for the teaching of ordinary English. In this latter field, several very promising methods, other than Basic, have been developed in recent years, which make use of progressively increasing vocabularies based on analysis of the words most frequently used in conversational and literary English. In foreign countries, the method used in the teaching of English will naturally be a matter for the decision of the Departments of Education in those countries, and, where teaching is conducted in British Institutes, it will be a matter for the free decision of those who direct the teaching of English, whether they shall employ any of these methods or the Basic method. There is no reason why His Majesty's Government should support one method rather than another. So far, however, as concerns the use of Basic English as an auxiliary international language, His Majesty's Government are impressed with the great advantages which would ensue from its development, not in substitution for established literary languages, but as a supplement thereto. The usefulness of such an auxiliary language will, of course, be greatly increased by its progressive diffusion.

His Majesty's Government have, therefore, decided on the following steps to develop Basic English as an auxiliary international and administrative language :—

(1) The British Council will include among its activities the teaching of Basic English, so far as may be practicable, in any area where there may be a demand for instruction in Basic for its specific purpose as an auxiliary medium of international communication. This will be in addition to, and not in substitution for, the Council's more general activities in promoting the teaching of English for its own sake.

(2) Diplomatic and commercial representatives in foreign countries will be asked to do all they can to encourage the spread of Basic English as an auxiliary language.

(3) It is also intended to arrange for the translation into Basic

English of a wider range of literature—scientific, technical and general —than is at present available, both from ordinary English and from foreign languages, and also to increase the supply of manuals of instruction in Basic English.

(4) Some Colonial Governments will be invited to experiment by the issue in Basic English of handbooks for colonial peoples on agriculture, hygiene, etc. and by the use of this simplified language as the medium for some administrative instructions issued by the Government.

(5) The British Broadcasting Corporation has been asked to consider a recommendation to include the use and teaching of Basic English in appropriate overseas programmes. The Corporation has already expressed its willingness to make experiments on these lines within the limits imposed by special war-time responsibilities and conditions. It is recognized that such developments as may be practicable must proceed in parallel with the steps to be taken by other agencies.

It will be seen that several Departments are concerned in these measures. It has been decided, however, that primary responsibility for questions affecting Basic English, and for giving effect to the recommendations of the Committee of Ministers, should rest with the Foreign Office, through the British Council. The British Council will, of course, keep in close contact with the Foreign Office and with the other Departments concerned, and an inter-Departmental committee has been established for this purpose, under a chairman who will be nominated by the British Council.

FUTURE OF THE ITALIAN FLEET

A STATEMENT TO THE HOUSE OF COMMONS
MARCH 9, 1944

[*March* 9, 1944.

A S President Roosevelt has said, the question of the future employment and disposal of the Italian Fleet has been the subject of some discussion. In particular, consideration has been given to the immediate reinforcement of the Soviet Navy either from Anglo-American or Italian resources. On these discussions, I have no statement to make other than to say that at present no change is contemplated in the arrangements with the Italian naval authorities under which Italian ships and their crews take part in the common struggle against the enemy in the theatres where they now operate. It may well be found that the general question of enemy or ex-enemy fleet disposal would best be left over till the end of the war against both Germany and Japan, when the entire position can be surveyed by the victorious Allies, and what is right and just can be done.

WAR DECORATIONS

March 3.	American planes made their first daylight raid on Berlin.
March 5.	Russians broke through strong enemy defences in the Ukraine.
March 6.	U.S. bombers made another great daylight raid on Berlin, destroying 173 enemy aircraft.
March 8.	Continuing their daylight assault on Berlin, 1,100 American bombers dropped 2,000 tons.
March 10.	Russians defeated 14 enemy divisions on the Ukraine front and captured the towns of Uman and Kristinovka.
	Mr. de Valera refused the U.S. request for the expulsion of Axis representatives from Eire.
March 11.	Entire enemy front of over 350 miles in Southern Ukraine reported to be in a state of collapse.
March 12.	British Government suspended travelling to Eire "for military reasons."
March 13.	Russians captured Kherson, German stronghold at the mouth of the Dnieper.
March 14.	Russians driving for Rumania crossed the River Bug in force.
March 15.	Heaviest air blow on record was struck at Germany when R.A.F. dropped 3,000 tons of bombs with Stuttgart as the main target.
March 16.	Allied tanks in Italy reported to be advancing along the main road from Cassino to Rome.
	R.A.F. bombers dropped 12,000-lb. bombs on the Michelin works at Clermont-Ferrand.

[*March 22, 1944.*

THE object of giving medals, stars and ribbons is to give pride and pleasure to those who have deserved them. At the same time a distinction is something which everybody does not possess. If all have it, it is of less value. There must, therefore, be heartburnings and disappointments on the border line. A medal glitters, but it also casts a shadow. The task of drawing up regulations for such awards is one which does not admit of a perfect solution. It is not possible to satisfy everybody without running the risk of satisfying nobody. All that is possible is to give the greatest satisfaction to the greatest number and to hurt the feelings of the fewest. But that is a most difficult task, and it is easy to err on one side or the other. One must be careful in the first place to avoid profusion. The tendency to expand, shall I say inflate, and dilute the currency through generous motives, is very strong. When the Order of the Golden Fleece was founded its first motto was " I will have no other " (" *autre n'aurai* "). But this proved too austere an ordinance for the Emperors, Kings and heroes concerned, and the motto was very rapidly changed to a much less self-denying and non-committal form, " I have accepted it " (" *Je l'ai empris* ").

The German distinctions have usually been very lavishly bestowed. When Voltaire was invited to visit the Prussian Court he stipulated that all expenses should be paid, and that the Order of Merit should be thrown in. Both were forthcoming. So there were, before 1914, as is well known, very many German medals and orders. Nevertheless, during the last war the Germans created about 80 different crosses, medals and decorations, including various kinds for the different Duchies and Principalities, and about 20 different distinctive badges of a similar character. At the start of the last war the Iron Cross was a highly prized decoration, but by 1918 it had been granted so freely that it was little valued except, I believe, by Herr Hitler, who it is alleged gave it to himself some time later. After the Armistice, the Germans, who are a most adaptive people, manufactured large numbers of Iron Crosses for sale to the French troops as souvenirs. In the present war they have already some 15 new medals and 29 new distinctive badges. They have not yet reached the stage of manufacturing them for sale to the Allies.

The French, in the last war, were wiser than the Germans, but even they were inclined to err slightly on the side of generosity. When, after the termination of hostilities, they instituted a war medal for the troops, they got drawn beyond the line which limited it to the armed forces. It was granted, for instance, to hospital staffs generally, and then to the police, park-keepers, Customs officers and so on. The result was that very soon after the war it was impossible to tell whether an individual had actually fought in the real fighting zones or not. And ten years later the French found it necessary—and this also gave pleasure—under the pressure of the ex-Service men to reopen the whole question and create a distinction called the Croix du Combattant.

A similar process, though much more dignified, sedate and tardy, took place in this country after the Napoleonic wars; but it was not until 1851 that the services rendered between 1793 and 1814 by the veterans who still survived were recognized. Queen Victoria took a great interest in this, and the Duke of Richmond, who led the public agitation, was given by the grateful recipients of the long overdue awards plate worth about 1,500 guineas. I hope that this example will encourage my hon. Friends in their zeal and activities in this matter, and assuage any temporary dissatisfaction they may feel with the announcements which I have to make.

It would have been very much easier to leave all this matter on one side until more leisurely times shall have come. On the other hand, this war has now raged for 54 months. Many famous campaigns have been fought, several have been brought to a successful conclusion. Devoted, valiant service has been rendered in many parts of the world on land, on the sea, in the air. Several million soldiers, sailors and airmen have been sent abroad, where they have remained for long periods, enduring severe hardships, rendering faithful service, and achieving splendid results. They greatly value the distinction which a ribbon gives them.

I know of the satisfaction which has been given to our battalions of troops which have been authorized to mount the Africa Ribbon or the 1939–43 Ribbon, and I felt myself bound to try to attempt at any rate a partial solution of the problem which I could submit to His Majesty, with whom these matters rest, subject to advice. Accordingly, the Committee on the Grant of Honours, on which all Services are represented, was directed in March last year to frame Regulations governing the grant of the Africa Star—this was to commemorate the expulsion of the enemy from the African continent—and also the 1939–43 Star, with a different ribbon, covering service in other theatres of war, including, of course, the oceans and the air. The Africa Star has already been awarded to 1,500,000 officers and men, and the latter decoration, the 1939–43 Star, to 1,600,000 officers and men, a total of 3,100,000 of our warriors in all spheres ; and with the other cases that are now under consideration I am told the two ribbons together may ultimately cover nearly 4,000,000 men.

In considering the qualifications for the grant of the 1939–43 Star, the question arose of what period of service would be required. There are some forms of service which are measured by time and others by the episode itself. We have adopted both conditions. Six months is taken as the qualifying period of time, but in special operations in which individual combatants would not have the opportunity of serving six months, actual presence with the Forces will be sufficient. Naturally, in drawing up a list of such episodes it was necessary to consult the Dominion and Indian Governments. The final list is now complete and will be made public immediately. Indeed, my right hon. Friend the Secretary of State for Air, who will deal with any points raised in the Debate, will, if he thinks fit and the House desires it, be in a position to read out the list as we have so far devised it. It had been hoped that it would be published two days ago, but I am perhaps to blame for having somewhat delayed its publication. Additions can be made to this list in accordance with well-informed opinion. I am very anxious that Service opinion should fix and focus on these different points, and that we can profit by it as we get to hear of it, so that we can make submissions to the Crown in respect of these matters, for this is a Royal Prerogative.

I hope that even in its present form the list may meet some of the many questions which are asked about this episodic aspect of the qualifications for the 1939–43 Star. Among the Naval Forces who served for a long time afloat and ashore in the Mediterranean, and played a vital part in the victories there by cutting off the German reinforcements, there has been, I am told, a discernible preference shown for the Africa Star as against the 1939–43 Star, and the suggestion has been made that an officer or man whose service qualifies him for either award should be permitted to choose one or the other. I am advised that such an option would be very difficult to work. It might also seem to reflect upon the 1939–43 Star if people, on account of local associations, chose the Africa Ribbon instead of the General Service Ribbon, which must be considered as the primary, the senior ribbon. I am still studying this question. The same kind of doubt occurs again in the case of those who served both in the First and Eighth Armies, where there is an emblem. I have not finally closed the discussion of this difficult problem. I would like to see, on all these subjects, how opinion shapes. One thing is clear, however, that no one can have both stars or both ribbons, nor can they have both the two emblems, 1 and 8. To this last rule there is one exception. His Majesty has approved of both the Emblems 1 and 8 being mounted on the ribbons of General Eisenhower and General Alexander, these being the only two officers who did, in fact, command the whole of the First and Eighth Armies.

I ought not to overlook two other forms of reward of merit which have been approved. First, there is the King's Badge, about which a discussion was promised. The issue of the King's Badge is at present restricted to those invalided from the naval, military and air forces and the Merchant Navy and fishing fleets through wounds or war disablement attributable to service since September 3rd, 1939. The question has arisen, Should it not be extended to those discharged through disability not due to service ? Against this, as the House will see, it may be urged that a considerable number of those eager to join the Fighting Forces have to be rejected on medical grounds, and it would be argued that those whose disabilities escape notice until after they have been enlisted ought not to have an advantage over those who are rejected at the outset. Under National Service all men and women in this country are doing the work which renders best service to our nation.

All forms of faithful service are honourable, but we do not propose at present to extend the King's Badge beyond those whose disabilities are attributable to their service. The matter must, however, be considered in conjunction with chevrons, about which I will say a word in a minute or two. The only ex-soldiers who will not be able shortly to wear any token of their service will be those who have not qualified for either the Africa Star or the 1939-43 Star, and who were discharged for non-attributable reasons with less than one year's war-time service; and these may be eligible in due course for any awards which may be granted later in respect of military service, such as a general medal. But only those I have specified who do not qualify for either of the stars or who were discharged for non-attributable reasons and who have less than one year's service, will not have some record of their connection with our Armed Forces, be it by chevrons or some other form.

Even greater complications would arise if men and women invalided from the Civil Defence general services, including the National Fire Service, were made eligible for the badge. There is no fixed minimum medical standard for discharge, and there are those who have been discharged on account of reductions. I can, however, announce to-day that the official chevrons for war service are to be extended to certain further Civil Defence organizations, including the Rest Centre, the Emergency Food (including the Queen's Messenger Convoy Service), the Canteen, the Emergency Information and the Mortuary Services, which have been up to the present excluded. We are also on the point of expanding the chevron scheme so that some 227,000 additional members of the Women's Voluntary Services engaged in Civil Defence will also be eligible.

At this point I must explain that medals are struck at the end of wars, and stars are given for particular episodes or periods during their course. I must also explain that the manufacture of medals or stars cannot possibly be undertaken during the war, and therefore all that we can do is to issue ribbons.

Apart from the right to wear particular ribbons, certain emblems have been approved under conditions which have been set forth in the White Paper. These emblems are a very highly-prized feature of these awards. There are the Arabic numerals 1 and 8 for service in the First and Eighth Armies, which played the main part in liberating North Africa. These are valid from the period of the Battle of Alamein in October—perhaps, I am not sure, from the final repulse of Rommel in the month before, I may be in error as to which. They served from that period to the complete surrender or destruction of all the German and Italian forces, upwards of 300,000 prisoners being taken in Tunis in May. There is also the Silver Rose, which is worn as a special emblem for the Royal Navy and Royal Air Force, with the 1939–43 Ribbon. Those emblems, of which there can only be a few, can be worn on their respective ribbons. They are undoubtedly a super-distinction and are intended to be so. It will not be physically possible to add to them indefinitely, because there is no more room on the little slip of ribbon for a multiplicity of emblems without producing a confused impression.

The question of clasps, or bars as they are sometimes called—in my opinion miscalled—on medal ribbons will not come up till after the war. Then, when all the events can be seen in their true perspective and proportion, it must be carefully considered. After the last war a large number of clasps were provisionally approved, but it was found impossible to make a general issue of them on account of the great number earned by individuals and of the vast number of persons whose claims had to be examined. This would have entailed enormous staffs at a time when, among many difficulties, the need for economy was considered to be important. I do not know what will happen after this war, when, of course, we are all going to be so rich, or we hope so. The clasps can only be worn on the long ribbon—the long length of ribbon which carries a medal or a star. There is no room for them on the ordinary narrow strips of ribbon which are all we have to give at the present time. However, this whole matter will be most attentively studied, bearing in mind, of course, that a clasp for a spectacular action may connote less sacrifice and endurance and daring than long service in the submarines, or in a series of bombing sorties, or hard service in the front line, or in going to-and-fro across the oceans for months and years on end.

There is another general principle which I will venture to commend to the House. It is always easy in these matters to widen the Regulation and to admit a new class. On the other hand, it is never possible to go back and take away what has been given unless it has been given in error. There is no need for us to take any final negative decision at the present time. I thought this Debate would be one for consultation, for sensing the feelings of the country through its best exponent, the House of Commons, rather than for the arbitrary laying-down of final awards. It is, however, necessary, while not taking negative decisions, to take every step with great caution and to examine carefully the consequences to other classes besides those newly benefiting.

The most difficult border-line case is, of course, the anti-aircraft battery, and especially the Dover coastal batteries, which are constantly engaged with the enemy's artillery across the Straits. I have been most anxious to include these batteries in the 1939-43 ribbon. Up to the present I have found no way of doing so without opening the door, successively, first to the whole of the Ack-ack Command, and, secondly, to the searchlights and predictors of all kinds, without which the guns cannot fire or cannot hit, and whose personnel were, and still often are, in equal danger to that of the gunners. In the next place you would immediately come to the National Fire Service, whose casualties have been at a much heavier rate than the ack-ack batteries. And, then, what about the Police, who stood around and kept order and rendered every assistance ? And what about the A.R.P. and the fireguards, so often in danger and discharging their work with so much efficiency, as we can see even from our recent minor experiences ? If the National Fire Service and others like them were included, how could the whole Regular Army which stood in Great Britain be excluded, or the Dominion Forces which performed here a vital strategic role ? If the Regular Army were included, why should not the Home Guards be eligible, who did their work without pay at the end of long days, who wore their uniforms and played an essential part in hurling back the danger of invasion from our shores ? There remain a number of other categories such as the training and maintenance personnel of the R.A.F., the bomb-disposal squads, which are, with the ack-ack batteries, one of the balancing cases. In many cases personal decorations have been won on a large scale by that heroic band of men, but, at the same time, I am admitting quite frankly the difficulties which these cases have created—the difficulty of denying, and the difficulty of opening the door to such a vast extent.

If we were to take the whole course I have indicated and open the door to class after class, as I have shown you would be asked to do and, I think, bound to do in logic, this would involve throwing the 1939-43 Star and Ribbon open to an additional 12,000,000 persons, and by doing this I am sure you would take away much of the distinction now attaching to the decoration. It would become so common as to be very nearly universal. I am sure the soldier, the sailor and the airman returning from prolonged active service abroad and wearing the Africa or 1939-43 Star would feel bewildered when he saw all around him 12,000,000, mostly adult, males who had not left the island but had got the same ribbon as himself. " Bewildered " is, I think, an instance of under-statement.

But if these grants were made so widespread, could you stop at the Services themselves ? Indeed, I think the civil population, the railwaymen, who bore with immense composure and unflinching fortitude the full fury of the blitz and went about their ordinary work with faithful diligence and punctuality under the most trying conditions, and those who continued at work in factories while the danger signals were going, would certainly have a moral claim to be considered. If danger is to be made the test, if proper and correct demeanour in the face of danger, and showing indifference to personal injury or death—if that is to be made the test, millions of civilian men and women in their small homes with nothing but the Anderson or Morrison shelters to shield them—not that I depreciate those admirable institutions—who all the time preserved so fine a spirit, would have a claim as compared with the men in uniform ; and there are many who have so far passed the war in districts unaffected by the blitz and have not been in action—had the honour to be in action—or come under the fire of the enemy.

I can assure the House I have given a great deal of thought to these questions, which I have been interested in all my life, and I have assumed the duty of giving the Committee on the grant of honours guidance from time to time and representing the results of their labours to His Majesty in respect to the use of his Royal Prerogative. I trust the House will see how very numerous the difficulties are, yet I do not at all repent that we have embarked on this, because I know the pleasure it has given the 3,000,000 men who already wear the ribbon on their breast. As at present advised, we cannot consent to widen the 1939–43 Ribbon in order to include the whole Army or all who took part in the Battle of Britain, and we could not take any step which would lead us or drag us into such a course, for the reasons I have tried to explain to the House.

The question then arises whether a third and different Ribbon for another Star should not be instituted for service in this country, whether it should not be issued to the ten or twelve million persons affected. This would not detract in the same way from the distinction of the 1939–43 decoration, and it would certainly be well deserved in several million cases. Well, I have asked that this should be examined and pondered over, and certainly, on this and other points, as I have said already, we shall be influenced by the opinions expressed and the feelings manifested in this Debate, and in general endeavour to sense the feelings of the House as a whole. I have not so far been able to reach any decisive conclusion myself—certainly not any negative conclusion—upon the point. All the same, there are important and substantial reasons for postponing to the end of the war this award, which would, of course, involve something similar for the Civil Defence in Malta and other British countries, islands and fortresses which have been subject to attack, and there are many other complications connected with it. Therefore, I say that I remain in a state of not being at all convinced that this step would be possible or desirable.

I may say, however, that at the end of the war, when medals are struck, every one who has worn the King's uniform and served in uniformed, disciplined Services, will, I presume—I say " presume " because the matter may not rest with His Majesty's present advisers— receive a Victory Medal to commemorate this great struggle for human freedom. There will also, very likely, be a United Nations or Allied war medal of the widest possible application, and it is upon the background of these general medals that the Stars, the issue of which His Majesty has already approved, will shine brightly forth.

"OUR GREAT AMERICAN ALLY"

A Speech Delivered at an Inspection of an American Force in Britain
March 23, 1944

[*March* 23, 1944.

IT is with feelings of emotion and of profound encouragement that I have the honour to review you here to-day. In these weeks that are passing so swiftly I see gathered here on English soil these soldiers of our great American Ally preparing themselves to strike a blow for a cause which is a greater cause than either of our two countries has ever fought for in by-gone days.

It is a world cause because though no one can tell how the future of the world will shape itself, we are determined that the dark tyrannies which have overclouded our lives and drawn our people from their homes shall be broken and battered down, and that an example shall be made of the guilty which will prevent such tyrannies being inflicted again upon the masses of the people.

You have a great part to play. You are specially trained. You are the most modern expression of war. Soon you will have the opportunity of testifying your faith in all those inspiring phrases of the American Constitution, and of striking a blow which, however it may leave the world, will, as we are determined, make it a better and a broader world for all.

You have come across the ocean. Here you are on this little Island wrapped in northern mist. I cannot give you any guarantee about the weather, but I can assure you that you are greeted with warm hearts on every side.

Our troops, British and American, are at this moment shedding their blood side by side in Italy, at Cassino, or in the Anzio bridgehead, fighting hard and losing heavily in the struggle. And now here this comradeship in arms is repeated, and I am confident that not only will the enemy feel the shock of our joint exertions, but that there will be left behind a core of good feeling and mutual understanding and a unity which will in itself be of priceless advantage to the good will which has united us now for so many years.

I thank God you are here, and from the bottom of my heart I wish you all good fortune and success.

"THE HOUR OF OUR GREATEST EFFORT IS APPROACHING"

A WORLD BROADCAST
MARCH 26, 1944

March 18. German 6th Army was routed in the battle of the Dnieper Bend and the Russians captured Jmerinka and Pomoshnaya.

March 19. Russians forced the Dniester on a 30-miles front and occupied 40 places on the right bank.

In Italy, New Zealand troops took the railway station at Cassino.

March 21. Russian troops deepened their bridgehead across the Dnieper and made good progress in the advance on Lvov.

March 22. German troops took over control of Hungary, and appointed a pro-Nazi, Sztojay, Prime Minister.

R.A.F. and American bombers kept up all-night attacks on Germany, and the R.A.F. dropped 3,000 tons on Frankfort in half an hour.

Enemy planes reached London and S.E. England and at least ten were destroyed.

March 24. Marshal Zhukov delivered a smashing blow to the Germans defending the approaches to the Northern Carpathians. Enemy lost 20,000 killed and 3,500 prisoners.

March 26. Advancing through Bessarabia, the Russians reached the Pruth, frontier of Rumania.

Broadcasting for the first time since his illness, Mr. Churchill said the hour of greatest effort was approaching.

[March 26, 1944.

I HOPE you will not imagine that I am going to try to make you some extraordinary pronouncement to-night, and tell you exactly how all the problems of mankind in war and peace are going to be solved. I only thought you would like me to have a short talk with you about how we are getting on, and to thank you for all the kindness with which you have treated me in spite of my many shortcomings.

It is a year almost to a day since I spoke to you on the broadcast here at home. This has been a time of disappointments as well as successes. But there is no doubt that the good news has far outweighed the bad, and that the progress of the United Nations towards their goal has been solid, continual, and growing quicker.

The long and terrible march which the rescuing Powers are making is being accomplished stage by stage, and we can now say, not only with hope but with reason, that we shall reach the end of our journey in good order, and that the tragedy which threatened the whole world and might have put out all its lights and left our children and descendants in darkness and bondage—perhaps for centuries—that tragedy will not come to pass.

He is a rash man who tries to prophesy when, how, and under what conditions victory will come, but come it will. That at least is sure. It is also certain that unity of aims and action and singleness of purpose among us all—Britons at home, Allies abroad—will make it come sooner.

A year ago the Eighth Army, which had marched 1,500 miles across the desert from Alamein, was in battle for the Mareth Line, and the First British Army and the American Army were fighting their way forward through Tunisia. We were all confident of victory, but we did not know that in less than two months the enemy would be driven with heavy slaughter from the African continent, leaving at one stroke 335,000 prisoners and dead in our hands.

Since then the successful campaign in Sicily brought about the fall of Mussolini and the heartfelt repudiation by the Italian people of the Fascist creed. Mussolini indeed escaped, to eat the bread of affliction at Hitler's table, to shoot his son-in-law, and help the Germans wreak vengeance upon the Italian masses whom he had professed to love, and over whom he had ruled for more than 20 years. This fate and judgment, more terrible than death, has overtaken the vain-glorious dictator who stabbed France in the back and thought his crime had gained him the empire of the Mediterranean.

The conquest of Sicily and Naples brought in their train the surrender of Sardinia and the liberation of Corsica, islands which had been expected to require for themselves a serious expedition and a hard campaign. We now hold one-third of the mainland of Italy. Our progress has not been as rapid or decisive as we had hoped. I do not doubt that we shall be victors both at the Anzio beachhead and on the main front to the southward, and that Rome will be rescued.

Meanwhile we have swept out of the struggle 66 Italian divisions, and we are holding in Italy, for the most part in close action, nearly 25 German divisions and a noteworthy part of the German air force, all of whom can burn and bleed in the land of their former ally while other even more important events which might require their presence are impending elsewhere.

We have been disappointed in the Aegean Sea and its many islands, which we have not yet succeeded in dominating, but these setbacks in the Eastern Mediterranean are offset and more than offset by the panic and frenzy which prevail in Hungary, Rumania, and Bulgaria, by the continued activities of the Greek guerrillas, and, above all, by the heroic struggles of the Partisans of Yugoslavia under the leadership of Marshal Tito.

In the Near and Middle East we have certainly travelled a long way forward from those autumn days of 1940 when we stood all alone, when Mussolini was invading Egypt, when we were driven out of British Somaliland, when all Ethiopia was in Italian chains, and when we wondered whether we could defend the Suez Canal, the Nile Valley, the Sudan, and British East Africa. There is much still to be done in the Balkans and the Eastern Mediterranean, but here again I do not doubt that the task will be finished in a workmanlike manner.

We who dwell in the British Isles must celebrate with joy and thankfulness our deliverance from the mortal U-boat peril, which deliverance lighted the year which has ended. When I look back upon the 55 months of this hard and obstinate war, which makes ever more exacting demands upon our life-springs of energy and contrivance, I still rate highest among the dangers we have overcome the U-boat attacks upon our shipping, without which we cannot live or even receive the help which our Dominions and our grand and generous American Ally have sent us.

But there are other deliverances which we should never forget. There was the mining peril, the sea-mining peril, which loomed so large in 1939, and which has been mastered by superior science and ingenuity, and by the often forgotten but almost unsurpassed devotion to duty of our minesweeper crews and the thousands of ships they work and man that we may eat and live and thus fight for the good cause. We have been delivered from the horrors of invasion at a time when we were almost unarmed.

We have endured without swerving or failing the utmost fury which Hitler could cast upon us from the air, and now the tables are turned, and those who sought to destroy their enemies by the most fearful form of warfare are themselves reeling and writhing under the prodigious blows of British and American air power. We had ourselves a large air force in these Islands this time last year. We have a larger one to-day.

Besides all that, our American Allies have now definitely overtaken and outnumbered us in the mighty air force they have established here. The combination in true brotherhood of these two air forces— either of which is nearly as large in numbers as, and in power is much greater than, the whole air force of Germany, aided as it will be by another Allied air force in Italy almost as large, now established there, will produce results in these coming months which I shall not attempt to measure in advance, but which will certainly be of enormous advantage to the cause of the Allies.

Not only have the British and Americans this great preponderance in numbers, which enables them to send 1,000 bombers as often as the enemy is able to send 100 against us, but also, by sharing all our secrets with one another, we have won the leadership in the marvels of Radar both for attack and defence.

Surveying these famous and massive events, land, sea, and air, in the war waged by the two western Allies, Britain and the United States, against Hitlerism, we are entitled—nay bound—to be encouraged, to be thankful, and to resolve to do better than we have ever done before.

It would be quite natural if our Soviet friends and Allies did not appreciate the complications and difficulties which attend all sea-crossing—amphibious is the word—operations on a large scale. They are the people of the great land spaces, and when they face a threat to the sacred soil of Russia it is by land that they march out to meet and attack their foes. Our tasks are different. But the British and American peoples are filled with genuine admiration for the military triumphs of the Russian Armies.

I have paid repeated tributes to their splendid deeds, and now I must tell you that the advance of their Armies from Stalingrad to the Dniester river, with vanguards reaching out towards the Pruth, a distance of 900 miles, accomplished in a single year, constitutes the greatest cause of Hitler's undoing. Since I spoke to you last not only have the Hun invaders been driven from the lands they had ravaged, but the guts of the German Army have been largely torn out by Russian valour and generalship.

The peoples of all the Russias have been fortunate in finding in their supreme ordeal of agony a warrior leader, Marshal Stalin, whose authority enabled him to combine and control the movements of armies numbered by many millions upon a front of nearly 2,000 miles, and to impart a unity and a concert to the war direction in the East which has been very good for Soviet Russia and for all her Allies.

I have now dealt with the progress of the war against Hitlerite Germany. But I must also speak of the other gigantic war which is proceeding against the equally barbarous and brutal Japanese. This war is waged in vast preponderance by the fleets, air forces, and armies of the United States. We have accepted their leadership in the Pacific Ocean just as they have accepted our leadership in the Indian theatre.

We are proud of the contribution made by Australia and New Zealand against Japan. The debt which the British Empire and Common-wealth of Nations owe to the United States for the fact that their operations against the Japanese shielded Australia and New Zealand from Japanese aggression and from mortal peril during a period when the Mother Country was at full stretch in the struggle against Germany and Italy, that, that is one that will never be forgotten in any land where the Union Jack is flown.

Remarkable success has attended the work of the American Navy and of the American, Australian, and New Zealand troops. The progress in New Guinea is constant. The American victories in the Pacific, and in particular their latest conquest and liberation of the Marshall Islands, constitute superb examples of the combination of naval, air, and military force.

It is possible that the war in the Pacific may progress more rapidly than was formerly thought possible. The Japanese are showing signs of grave weakness. The attrition of their shipping, especially their oil tankers, and of their air forces, on all of which President Roosevelt dwelt with sure foresight a year ago, has become not merely evident but obvious.

The Japanese have not felt strong enough to risk their fleet in a general engagement for the sake of their outer defence line. In this they have been prudent, considering the immense expansion of the United States naval power since the Japanese treacherous assault on Pearl Harbour. What fools the Japanese ruling caste were to bring against themselves the mighty, latent war-energies of the great Republic, all for the sake of carrying out a base and squalid ambuscade!

The British Empire and Commonwealth of Nations have pledged themselves to fight side by side with the United States against Japan, no matter what it costs or how long it lasts. Actually we have suffered from the Japanese injuries even greater than those which have roused the armed wrath of the American Union. In our theatre of war, in Burma and the Bay of Bengal, we shall strive our utmost to aid the Americans in their contacts with China and to add to our own.

The more we can fight and engage the Japanese, and especially wear down their air power, the greater the diversion we make from the Pacific theatre and the more help we give the operations of the United States.

In Burma those plans which were prepared last August at Quebec are now being put into practice. Young men are at the helm. Admiral Mountbatten has infused a spirit of energy and confidence into the heavy forces gathered to recover Burma and by that means to defend the frontiers of India and reopen the road to China. Our airborne operations enable us to attack the Japanese in rear. They for their part have also got behind our front by infiltration at various places, and fierce fighting is going on at many points.

It is too soon to proclaim results in this vast area of mountain and jungle, but in nearly every combat we are able to count three or four times more Japanese dead, and that is what matters, than we have ourselves suffered in killed, wounded, and missing.

Individual fighting superiority in the jungle has definitely passed to the British and Indian soldiers as compared with the Japanese. Farther to the North an American column of experienced jungle-fighters and a considerable Chinese army under General Stilwell, of the United States Service, are progressing with equal mastery. Later on I shall make to you or to Parliament a further report on all this hard fighting, which, mind you, is not by any means decided yet. Meanwhile we have placed a powerful battle-fleet under Admiral Somerville in Indian waters in order to face the main part of the Japanese Fleet should it turn westward after having declined battle against the Americans.

When I spoke a year ago I drew attention to the possibility that there would be a prolonged interval between the collapse of Hitler and the downfall of Japan. I still think there will be an interval, but I do not consider it will necessarily be as long an interval as I thought a year ago. But be it long or be it short, we shall go through with our American brothers with our utmost strength to the very end.

I have now tried to carry you as if in a Mosquito aircraft on reconnoitring duty over the world-wide expanse of this fell and ferocious war, and I trust you have gained not only some glimpses of particular scenes, but also a feeling of the relative size and urgency of the various things that are going on. There are, as you see, quite a lot of things going on.

Still, I remember that when I spoke to you on March 21st of last year, I gave up the main part of what I said to what we were planning to do to make our island a better place for all its people after the war was over, whenever that should be.

I told you there would have to be a General Election and a new House of Commons, and that if I were still thought fit to be of any further use, I should put to the country a Four-Years' Plan to cover the transition period between war and peace, and to bring the soldiers, sailors, and airmen back to a land where there would be food, work, and homes for all. I dwelt on how wrong it would be to make promises which could not be fulfilled, and for one set of politicians to try to outbid another in visionary scheming and dreaming. But I mentioned five or six large fields in which practical action would have to be taken.

Let me remind you of them. A reform and advance on a great scale in the education of the people and a nation-wide uplifting of their physical health. I spoke of the encouragement of agriculture and food production and the vigorous revival of healthy village life. I dwelt upon the importance of a national compulsory insurance scheme for all classes, for all purposes, from the cradle to the grave, and of a sound scheme of demobilization which would not delay the rebuilding of industry and would not seem unfair to the fighting men.

I also spoke about the maintenance of full employment, and about the rebuilding of our cities and the housing of the people, and I made a few tentative suggestions about economic and financial policy, and what one may well call the importance of making both ends meet. All this was to happen after the war was over. No promises were to be made beforehand; but every preparation that was possible, without impeding the war effort, including legislative preparation, was to be set on foot.

Now, my friends, as your unfailing kindness encourages me to call you, I am a man who has no unsatisfied ambitions except to beat the enemy and help you in any way I think right, and therefore I hope you will not suppose that in what I am going to say to you I am looking for votes or trying to glorify this party or that.

But I do feel I may draw your attention to the fact that several of these large measures, which a year ago I told you might be accomplished after the war was over, have already been shaped and framed and presented to Parliament and the public.

For instance, you have the greatest scheme of improved education that has ever been attempted by a responsible Government. This will soon be on the Statute-book. It involves a heavy cost upon the State; but I do not think we can maintain our position in the post-war world unless we are an exceptionally well-educated people, and unless we can handle easily and with comprehension the problems and inventions of the new scientific age.

Then there is the very far-reaching policy of a National Health Service, which has already been laid before Parliament in outline and has received a considerable measure of acceptance. Before this session is out we shall lay before you our proposals for the extension of National Insurance, upon which a vast amount of patient work has been done.

So here you have, or will have very shortly, three of the important measures which I thought would be put off till after the war, already fashioned and proclaimed at a time when no one can tell when the war will end, and all this has been done without relaxing the war effort or causing any party strife to mar the national unity.

But there are several other large problems upon which Ministers and their assistants have toiled and wrought which are far advanced, and, indeed, if this process continues and the war goes on long enough, the greater part of my Four-Years' Plan of a year ago may well be perfected and largely in operation before we reach the General Election and give the people a chance to say what they think about it.

Now I must say that one might have expected that His Majesty's Government would receive many compliments on the remarkable progress they have made, not only with the war, but with the preparations for social and domestic welfare at the armistice or peace. Last October I thought the time had come to ask the King to appoint Lord Woolton Minister of Reconstruction with a seat in the War Cabinet. His was a record which rightly commanded respect.

However, there is a large number of respectable and even eminent people, who are not at all burdened with responsibility, who have a lot of leisure on their hands, and who feel most sincerely that the best work they can do at this present time of hard effort and anxiety is to belabour the Government with criticism, and condemn them as un-profitable servants because they are not, in the midst of this deadly struggle, ready at any moment to produce fool-proof solutions for the whole future of the world as between nation and nation, as between victors and vanquished, as between man and man, as between Capital and Labour, as between the State and the individual, and so forth and so on.

The harshest language is used, and this National Government, which has led the nation and the Empire, and, as I hold, a large part of the world, out of mortal danger, through the dark valleys into which they had wandered largely through their own folly back to the broad uplands where the stars of peace and freedom shine, is reviled as a set of dawdlers and muddlers unable to frame a policy, or take a decision, or make a plan and act upon it.

I know you, around your firesides, will not forget that this Administration, formed in the hour of disaster by the leaders of the Conservative, Labour, and Liberal Parties banded together in good faith and good will, has brought the British Isles and the British Commonwealth and Empire " out of the jaws of death, back from the mouth of hell, while all the world wondered." I know you will not forget that.

There are two subjects of domestic policy which I mentioned last year on which we have not yet produced our course of action. The first is housing. We set before ourselves, as a prime responsibility, the provision of homes for all who need them, with priority for our service men as and when they come home from the war.

Let me first of all lay down this absolute rule. Nothing can or must be done in housing or rehousing which, by weakening or clogging the war effort, prolongs the war. Neither labour nor material can be diverted in any way which hampers the vast operations which are in progress or impending.

Subject to that, there are three ways in which the business of housing and rehousing the people should be attacked.

I do not take the view myself that we were a nation of slum-dwellers before the war. Nearly 5,000,000 new approved houses or dwellings were built in this small Island between the two wars, and the British people as a whole were better housed than almost any people on the continent of Europe or, I will add, in many parts of the United States of America.

But now about a million homes have been destroyed or grievously damaged by the fire of the enemy. This offers a magnificent opportunity for rebuilding and replanning, and, while we are at it, we had better make a clean sweep of all those areas of which our civilization should be ashamed.

However, I have given my word that, so far as it may lie in my power, the soldiers when they return from the war and those who have been bombed out and made to double up with other families shall be restored to homes of their own at the earliest possible moment.

The first attack must evidently be made upon houses which are damaged but which can be reconditioned into proper dwellings. This must go forward during the war, and we hope to have broken the back of it during this year. It is a war measure, for our Allies are here among us in vast numbers, and we must do our best for them.

The second attack on the housing problem will be made by what are called the prefabricated or emergency houses.

On this the Minister of Works, Lord Portal, is working wonders. I hope we may make up to half a million of these, and for this purpose not only plans but actual preparations are being made during the war on a nation-wide scale.

Factories are being assigned, the necessary set-up is being made ready, materials are being earmarked as far as possible, the most convenient sites will be chosen. The whole business is to be treated as a military evolution handled by the Government, with private industry harnessed to its service; and I have every hope and a firm resolve that several hundred thousand of our young men will be able to marry several hundred thousand of our young women and make their own four years' plan.

Now what about these emergency houses? I have seen the full-sized model myself, and steps are being taken to make sure that a good number of housewives have a chance of expressing their views about it. These houses will make a heavy demand upon the steel industry, and will absorb in a great measure its overflow and expansion for war purposes.

They are, in my opinion, far superior to the ordinary cottage as it exists to-day: not only have they excellent baths, gas or electric kitchenettes, and refrigerators; but their walls carry fitted furniture —chests of drawers, hanging cupboards, and tables—which to-day it would cost £80 to buy.

Moreover, for the rest of the furniture standard articles will be provided and mass-produced, so that no heavy capital charge will fall upon the young couples, or others who may become tenants. Owing to the methods of mass-production which will be used, I am assured that these houses, including the £80 worth of fitted furniture, will be available at a very moderate rent. All these emergency houses will be publicly owned, and it will not rest with any individual tenant to keep them in being after they have served their purpose of tiding-over the return of the fighting men and after permanent dwellings are available. As much thought has been and will be put into this plan as was put into the invasion of Africa, though I readily admit that it does not bear comparison in scale with the kind of things we are working at now. The swift production of these temporary houses is the only way in which the immediate needs of our people can be met in the four or five years that follow the war.

In addition to this and to the reconditioning of the damaged dwellings, we have the programme of permanent rebuilding which the Minister of Health has recently outlined and by which we shall have 200,000 or 300,000 permanent houses built or building by the end of the first two years after the defeat of Germany. For these, 200,000 sites are already owned by the local authorities.

Side by side with this comes the question of the employment of the building trade. We do not want a frantic splurge of building, to be followed by a sharp contraction of the trade. I have sympathy with the building trade and with the bricklayers. They are apt to be the first to be taken for the wars, and in time of peace they all know, as they work at their job, that when it is finished they may have to look for another. If we are to secure the best results, it will be necessary that our Twelve-Years' Plan for the building trade, on which Mr. Bevin and Lord Portal have spent so much time, shall guarantee steady employment for long periods and increased reward for increased efforts or superior skill, and this will be carried out. Then we are told by the busy wiseacres : " How can you build houses without the land to put them on ? When are you going to tell us your plans for this ? "

But we have already declared, in 1941, that all land needed for public purposes shall be taken at prices based on the standards of values of March 31st, 1939. This was a formidable decision of State policy which selected property in land for a special restrictive imposition. Whereas stocks and shares and many classes of real property have gone up in value during the war, and when agricultural land, on account of the new proposals and prospects open to farmers, has also risen in value, the State has the power, which it will on no account surrender, to claim all land needed *bona fide* for war industry or for public purposes, at values fixed before war-time conditions supervened.

There are certain hard cases which will be best adjusted by Parliamentary debate, but in the main, you may be sure that ample land will be forthcoming when and where it is needed for all the houses, temporary or permanent, required to house our people far better than they have ever been housed before.

Nobody need be deterred from planning for the future by the fear that they may not be able to obtain the necessary land. Legislation to enable local authorities to secure any land required for the reconstruction of our towns has been promised and will be presented to Parliament this session.

There are some comfortable people, of course, who want to put off everything until they have planned and got agreed in every feature a White Paper or a blueprint for the regeneration of the world, before, of course, asking the electors how they feel about it. These people would rather postpone building the homes for the returning troops until they had planned out every acre in the country to make sure the landscape is not spoiled. In time of war we have to face immediate needs and stern realities, and it surely is better to do that than to do nothing while preparing to do everything.

Here is my difficulty. I cannot take any step that will hinder the war—and no one except the very clever ones can tell when the war will end, or whether it will end suddenly or peter out. Therefore, there must be an emergency plan, and that is what Ministers concerned have been working at for some time past. But in spite of this and of all I have said, I cannot guarantee that everything will be perfect or that if the end of the war came suddenly, as it might do, there will not be an interval when things will be pretty rough. But it will not be a long interval, and it will be child's play compared to what we have gone through.

Nor need we be frightened about the scale of this task. It looks to me a small one—this housing—compared with some of those we have handled and are handling now. The value of the land involved is between one-twentieth and one-thirtieth of the cost of the houses to be built upon it, and our population itself is unhappily about to enter upon a period of numerical decline which can only be checked by the most robust treatment of housing and all its ancillaries.

There is one other question on which I should like to dwell to-night, but for a reason which I will mention later I only intend to utter a passing reassurance. I mean demobilization. Now I know as much about this as most people, because I was Secretary of State for War and Air at the time of the great demobilization after the last war, when in about six months we brought home from abroad, released from military service, and restored to their families, nearly 3,000,000 men.

Great plans had been prepared before the Armistice by the planners to bring home all the key men first, and any soldier who could get a telegram from someone at home saying that he was wanted for a key job had priority over the man who had borne the burden and heat of the war. The troops did not think this was fair, and by the time I went to the War Office a convulsion of indiscipline shook the whole of our splendid Army, which had endured unmoved all danger, slaughter, and privation. I persuaded the Cabinet to reverse this foolish and inequitable plan and substitute the simple rule " First out, first home," and the process of demobilization went forward in a smooth and orderly fashion.

Now my friend Mr. Bevin, the Minister of Labour, for whose deep sagacity and knowledge of the wage-earning masses I have high admiration, has devised a very much less crude, but equally fair and healthy scheme, in which I have the greatest confidence, in which all concerned may have the greatest confidence. Why am I not going to tell you all about it to-night, or why will Mr. Bevin not tell you about it in the near future ?

Here is the reason. This is no time to talk about demobilization. The hour of our greatest effort and action is approaching. We march with valiant Allies who count on us as we count on them. The flashing eyes of all our soldiers, sailors, and airmen must be fixed upon the enemy on their front. The only homeward road for all of us lies through the arch of victory. The magnificent Armies of the United States are here or are pouring in. Our own troops, the best trained and best equipped we have ever had, stand at their side in equal numbers and in true comradeship. Leaders are appointed in whom we all have faith. We shall require from our own people here, from Parliament, from the Press, from all classes, the same cool, strong nerves, the same toughness of fibre, which stood us in good stead in those days when we were all alone under the blitz.

And here I must warn you that in order to deceive and baffle the enemy as well as to exercise the forces, there will be many false alarms, many feints, and many dress rehearsals. We may also ourselves be the object of new forms of attack from the enemy. Britain can take it. She has never flinched or failed. And when the signal is given, the whole circle of avenging nations will hurl themselves upon the foe and batter out the life of the cruellest tyranny which has ever sought to bar the progress of mankind.

A TEST OF CONFIDENCE

THE GOVERNMENT WAS DEFEATED IN THE HOUSE OF COMMONS, ON MARCH 28, BY ONE VOTE ON A CLAUSE IN THE EDUCATION BILL. THE FOLLOWING DAY THIS STATEMENT WAS MADE TO THE HOUSE BY THE PRIME MINISTER

THE event of yesterday requires an alteration in Government business. It would not be possible for His Majesty's Government to leave matters where they stood when the Motion to Report Progress was accepted. At this very serious time in the progress of the war, there must be no doubt or question of the support which the Government enjoys in the House of Commons. Accordingly we have decided, as the first Business on the next Sitting Day, to resume the Committee Stage of the Education Bill, and to delete Clause 82, as amended, entirely from the Measure. This act of deletion will be regarded as a Vote of Confidence in the present Administration. If the Government does not secure an adequate majority, it will entail the usual constitutional consequences. Should the House agree to the deletion of the Clause, the Government propose to move to re-instate the original Clause, without the Amendment, on the Report Stage, and to treat its passage throughout as a matter of confidence.

It is really impossible to distinguish between votes on domestic policy and votes on the general policy of the war, in this country. His Majesty's Government are entirely in the hands of the House, which has the fullest authority of any legislative assembly in the world, and we trust it will use it with responsibility.

I cannot attempt to control the activities of hon. Members. I can offer them merely some suggestions as to the consequences which may attend their actions, but certain I am that we cannot go on on the present basis—with a Government which has been defeated after the language which was used from this bench, in spite of the very great task which lies immediately ahead of us—that we could not possibly do. As to the course which individual Members take on every Amendment, on every question, they must consult their consciences and their duty.

The Government obtained a vote of confidence, Clause 82 of the Education Bill, as amended, being carried by 425 to 23. In the course of the debate the Prime Minister said on March 30 :

I do not intend to detain the Committee because, owing to the Rulings that have been given as to what may be and may not be urged in this discussion—which I, of course, accept with the greatest respect —I do not feel that I should be justified in attempting to unfold the arguments which I should otherwise have put before the Committee on this particular Measure and the significance attaching to it. Therefore, I will not do so, and I rise only for the purpose of assuring the Committee that my not taking part in the Debate is not due to any want of respect for them or any desire to shirk my duty of laying before them arguments which I conceive would be likely to influence them on this occasion.

The position of the Government is, that until they are fortified by a Vote of Confidence from the House, taking the form of the deletion of this Clause, they do not feel entitled to embark upon promises for the future. I may say that I cannot conceive how anyone who cares about the equality of payment for equal work between men and women could feel damnified in presenting that case in the future, by the fact that they do not to-day wish to tack it on to the end of Clause 82. Their rights remain absolutely unimpeached. Everyone knows what opportunities there are in every Session. Everyone knows that it is the duty of the Government to give effect to what is known to be the general wish of the House, even if the particular Parliamentary moments do not occur. Therefore, I say there cannot be any question of conscientious clash upon that subject, but I do not wish to trespass beyond the strict limits to which it is our duty to confine ourselves in what we say, as I am sure it will be the desire of the Committee to expedite the proceedings on this Bill.

ANSWERS IN THE HOUSE OF COMMONS

IMPERIAL DEFENCE

Replying to a member who asked that there should be an annual report to Parliament by the Committee of Imperial Defence, setting out the country's responsibilities and weapons needed, the Prime Minister said on January 18:

THE Committee of Imperial Defence has no fixed membership. It consists of those persons, political and military, who are invited by the Prime Minister to take part in its deliberations. I certainly should not be prepared to support a system in which naval, military or air force officers would be invited to pronounce probably against the wishes of the Government of the day. That would conflict with the whole foundation of our Parliamentary system.

WOMEN AND THE V.C.

Asked whether women were eligible for the Victoria Cross and whether any had been recommended for the honour, the Prime Minister said on January 18:

No recommendation in favour of a woman has been made during the war so far for the Victoria Cross, which is given only for services in active operations against the enemy. The Naval, Military and Air Force Nursing Services and the Women's Auxiliary Services have been eligible for the award since the outbreak of war, with the exception that, owing to a change of status, the Auxiliary Territorial Service and the Women's Auxiliary Air Force became ineligible for a period during 1941–42. Women are also eligible for the George Cross for services not in active operations against the enemy, and Corporal J. D. M. Pearson of the Women's Auxiliary Air Force holds that decoration. I can, therefore, readily give my hon. Friend the assurance he desires, and I should like to take this opportunity of paying tribute to the courage and devotion to duty displayed by women in all walks of life and forms of service during the present war.

" NO CHANGE IN MY ROUTINE "

Asked what steps he was taking to relieve himself of some of his official burdens with a view to conserving his health, the Prime Minister said on January 18 :

I am obliged to my hon. and gallant friend for his solicitude, but I have no changes at present to propose in my routine.

When another member suggested that they should all drink the toast " Death to all Dictators and Long Life to All Liberators, among whom the Prime Minister is first," Mr. Churchill replied :

It is very early in the morning.

SERVICE M.P.s

Asked under what regulations, applicable to all the Forces of the Crown, the War Office forbade Lieut. Lawson, M.P. for Skipton, to address a meeting outside his constituency, the Prime Minister said on January 19 :

Paragraph 541 (a) of the King's Regulations is the one which is involved. I consider, however, that the question should be dealt with on broader grounds. It is the right of a member of Parliament to decide that his parliamentary duties must claim priority over any military obligations he has accepted or incurred. If he wishes, as many hon. members have done, to combine the dual function, he must observe a certain measure of restraint and discretion in his conduct. Should he fail to do this, the First Lord of the Admiralty or the Secretary of State for War or Air must be the judge of when to invite him to concentrate his attention exclusively upon his parliamentary duties. I am glad to think that in so many cases it has been found possible for members of this House to combine effective parliamentary service with an honourable part in the active defence of the country. I think very few things have been more successful than this system of having members both serving in the Fighting Forces, where so many have given their lives and others have won distinction, and at the same time continuing as active members of the House. It is a most remarkable achievement.

MINERS IN THE ARMY

Asked how much longer it was proposed to retain in the Army experienced miners under 36 years of age who were anxious to return to the mines and who were engaged on menial jobs, such as looking after wash-houses and feeding pigs and cleaning out their sties, the Prime Minister said on February 1 :

The word "menial " should not be applied in any disparaging sense to " looking after wash-houses and feeding pigs and cleaning out their

E

sties." All forms of duty required by the State in time of war are worthy of respect, and class or occupational prejudice about them should not be encouraged. If, however, the hon. Member will furnish me with the names of " experienced miners under 36 years of age who are anxious to return to the mines," but whose work in the Army consists wholly or even mainly in " looking after wash-houses and feeding pigs and cleaning out their sties," and who have no prospect of taking part in operations of war, I will give my personal attention to their cases.

When the member then said that the word " menial " had been used by the men themselves, Mr. Churchill replied :

I took the precaution, before answering this question, of looking up the word " menial " in the dictionary. I find that it is generally used in a contemptuous sense. But I am sure that is not what my hon. Friend intended, and my answer was framed in order to show how glad I was that he had not adopted that interpretation.

WAR CORRESPONDENTS' MESSAGES

Asked for information about his inquiries into the restrictions on messages from war correspondents in Italy, the Prime Minister said on February 22 :

My inquiries did not take me very long, as I myself sent the telegram asking for a stricter censorship on alarmist reports about the position in the bridgehead sent not by the correspondents there, but by persons in Naples and Algiers. Such words as " desperate " ought not to be used about the position in a battle of this kind when they are false. Still less should they be used if they were true. In the first case they needlessly distress the public ; in the second they encourage the enemy to attack. I am glad that radio facilities have been restored to the correspondents in the bridgehead. These were not the people who caused the trouble, but others far in rear. The liberty of the Press is of high consequence, and so also are the lives of the troops.

I take full responsibility for doing my best to see that these matters are conducted in a proper manner. I certainly thought, from some of the headlines and some of the telegrams coming from people at Algiers, and from many reports sent to the American Press, that a wrong impression was being given, both to our people and to the enemy, of the situation in the bridgehead. I therefore issued some reassuring statements myself, based on those of the commanders, and at the same time telegraphed asking that there should be a stricter censorship on alarmist phraseology. I take full responsibility for that. I did not in fact telegraph to General Alexander at all.

I thought he was much too busy with the battle. I telegraphed to General Wilson, who may have shown the telegram to General Alexander. With regard to giving a general certificate of blamelessness to all newspaper correspondents, wherever they have been at any time during the war, I should like to say that I think they have discharged their duties with very great discretion, and that is particularly true of the men who were nearest to the enemy and in the same danger as the troops. There is a general desire among newspaper correspondents to discharge their duties with discretion, and to help the troops in every way. At the same time, accidents will happen even in the best regulated families.

POST-WAR PLANS

Questioned about a speech by the Home Secretary on post-war plans, which, a member suggested, might disrupt national unity, the Prime Minister said on March 9:

I am quite sure that the Home Secretary has no desire to disrupt national unity. I gather that he was embarking on a purely philosophical disquisition on a hypothetical and conjectural situation which might arise after the war.

Asked if he would consider selecting a member of the Government to speak for the Government, the Prime Minister replied:

If the worst came to the worst I might have a shot at it myself.

SERVICE PAY

Answering a member who asked if a revision of Service pay could be considered and who referred to "the rest of the community picking the pockets of the Service man," the Prime Minister said on March 9:

Of course, it is always easy to get popularity by using an expression like "picking people's pockets," but when you consider the gravity of the times in which we live, it is a pity that these matters should be discussed otherwise than with a great sense of responsibility. I have nothing to add, because Question Time is not the time when the merits of these important matters, about which there is legitimate and keen interest in the House, should be discussed. Question Time is not the time when the merits of a large question can be threshed out.

AXIS AGENTS IN EIRE

Asked what action would be taken on the refusal of Eire to remove Axis representatives at the request of America, the Prime Minister said on March 14:

The initiative in this matter was taken by the United States, because of the danger to the American armed forces from the presence of Axis missions in Dublin. His Majesty's Government were however, of course, consulted throughout by the United States Government, and gave the American approach full support. We have for some time past taken a number of measures to minimize the dangers arising from the substantial disservice to the Allied cause involved in the retention by Mr. de Valera's Government of the German Minister and the Japanese Consul with their staffs in Dublin. The time has now come when these measures must be strengthened, and the restrictions on travel to Ireland announced in the Press yesterday are the first step in the policy designed to isolate Great Britain from Southern Ireland and also to isolate Southern Ireland from the outer world, during the critical period which is now approaching.

I need scarcely say how painful it is to us to take such measures in view of the large numbers of Irishmen who are fighting so bravely in our armed forces and the many deeds of personal heroism by which they have kept alive the martial honour of the Irish race. No one, I think, can reproach us with precipitancy. No nation in the world would have been so patient. In view however of the fact that both British and British Dominion lives and the lives of the soldiers of our Allies are imperilled, we are bound to do our utmost to obtain effective security for the forthcoming operations.

There is also the future to consider. If a catastrophe were to occur to the Allied armies which could be traced to the retention of the German and Japanese representatives in Dublin, a gulf would be opened between Great Britain on the one hand and Southern Ireland on the other which even generations could not bridge. His Majesty's Government would also be held accountable by the people of the United States if it could be shown that we had in any way failed to do everything in our power to safeguard their troops.

Asked whether the retention of Axis agents in Dublin was consistent with membership of the British Commonwealth of Nations, the Prime Minister replied:

The whole question of the position of Southern Ireland is anomalous from various points of view, and I can conceive that high legal authorities might have very great difficulty in defining the exact relationship which prevails. At any rate, I shall not attempt to do so at the end of Questions.

When another member suggested that in further approaches it should be suggested to Eire that the question of partition would be a subject for discussion when peace was being decided, the Prime Minister said :

I could hardly think of a more ill-conceived approach to the unity of Ireland.

WORK OF THE MINISTRY OF HEALTH

Asked to reduce the work of the Ministry of Health to enable it to deal with matters of prior importance, the Prime Minister said on March 16 :

The proposals which the Government will shortly be making in regard to social insurance will involve reconsideration of the respon-- sibilities of several Departments, including the Ministry of Health, but apart from this question and the possibility of minor adjustments in departmental boundaries, I am satisfied that the functions of the Ministry of Health cover a well-defined and manageable field of action.

This is a time when departmental boundaries are a little fluid, because of the many extraordinary problems with which we are endeavouring to grapple, but I have no doubt that the frontiers will be precisely delimited.

Asked to be careful not to increase the number of Ministries to such an extent that all M.P.s would be in official positions, the Prime Minister said :

I have several times deprecated the idea that difficult problems can be solved by making new Ministers. I gladly give the assurance asked for by the hon. Member that no attempt will be made to include all the House of Commons in the Ministry.

BRITISH TANKS

Asked by Mr. Stokes what action he proposed to take " in view of the unsatisfactory reports which he has received both as to the inadequacy of British tanks in the field and the waste in production in this country," the Prime Minister said on March 16 :

I repudiate the allegations of the hon. Member. The next time that the British Armies take the field, in country suitable for the use of armour, they will be found to be equipped in a manner at least equal to the forces of any other country in the world.

I have received an advance copy of the report of the Select Committee, and its various criticisms will be carefully considered. I am not interested to know from what sources the hon. Gentleman receives his information. I am sure it would have been gratifying to him if the information had been of an adverse character.

An opportunity will be found in a very short time—during the next series of Sittings—for a Debate in Secret Session, when anything can be said. And I should like to say that it is not part of my submission that no mistakes are ever made by this Government.

FOOD RATIONING AFTER THE WAR

Asked whether a speech by the Minister of Food, indicating that food-rationing would continue for years after the war, represented the Government's policy, the Prime Minister said on March 22 :

The full text of the speech of the Minister of Food shows clearly that he is no advocate of rationing for rationing's sake, and in particular that he is a firm believer in the fact that we are down, in this country, to the minimum ration diet which will enable it to realize its full war effort in the field and in the factory. It is obvious that rationing will have to continue for some time after the end of the war. I do not, therefore, consider that the speech raised any new issue.

I think that the whole business of food distribution during this war has been thought to be a pretty good show.

ATLANTIC CHARTER

Asked to make a clarifying statement regarding the Atlantic Charter, the Prime Minister said on March 22 :

It is evident that as the changing phases of the war succeed one another, some further clarification will be required of the position under the document which has now become honourably known as the Atlantic Charter, and that this must be a subject for renewed consultation between the principal Allies. I am not prepared to embark upon this subject at Question Time to-day further than to state that the Atlantic Charter stands as a declaration of the spirit and purpose in which its signatories are waging this war—not without success—and that it implies no pact or bargain with our enemies.

BRITISH AND GERMAN TANKS

Asked by Mr. Stokes, M.P. for Ipswich, to have a German Mark VI Tiger Tank and a British A22 brought to the yard of the House of Commons so that members could see the relative merits of the two weapons, the Prime Minister said on March 30 :

I think the trouble and expense involved, though not very great, is still more than is justified to satisfy the spiteful curiosity of my hon. Friend.

When another member suggested that the Prime Minister should take charge of a Churchill tank and allow Mr. Stokes to take charge of a Tiger tank, Mr. Churchill replied :

I think it might be one way of settling the difference.

MESSAGES

"THIS YEAR OF DECISION"

A message to Mr. Harry Riddiough, the National Government candidate in the Skipton by-election. January 2, 1944.

YOU have my best wishes for success in your contest. The National Government needs, and, on its record deserves, the nation's full confidence, as it enters upon the formidable tasks of war and peace that lie ahead of us in this year of decision. I hope and trust that Skipton electors will not hesitate to vote in full strength for a Skipton man who stands as a consistent supporter of the Government that it is my duty to lead.

TO THE ROYAL SOCIETY

A message read at a meeting of the Royal Society at New Delhi, India. January 3, 1944.

It is the great tragedy of our time that the fruits of science should, by a monstrous perversion, have been turned on so vast a scale to evil ends.

But that is no fault of science. Science has given to this generation the means of unlimited disaster or of unlimited progress. There will remain the greater task of directing knowledge lastingly towards the purposes of peace and human good.

In this task, the scientists of the world, united by the bond of a single purpose which overrides all bounds of race and language, can play a leading and inspiring part.

TO "SEAC"

A message published in the first issue of the newspaper for the troops of the South East Asia Command. January 10, 1944.

I am glad to know of the proposal to publish a daily newspaper for the officers and men of the South East Asia Command, and I send my best wishes for its success. Soldiers of the Fourteenth Army as well as sailors and airmen now serving under Admiral Mountbatten have already won for themselves distinction in battle. Ahead there lie even more dangerous and arduous tasks, but I know that with confidence in their Commander and comprehension of the great issues which lie in their hands, they will acquit themselves with the audacity, the valour and the resourcefulness which our country and the common cause now need.

THANKS TO THE ANTI-AIRCRAFT

A message to General Sir Frederick Pile, G.O.C. in C., Anti-Aircraft Command. January 28, 1944.

I am very glad to hear of the excellent work of the anti-aircraft batteries and searchlights in the latest minor raid of the Germans. The heavy barrages which were fired and the efficient co-operation of searchlights with fighters prevented the bulk of the enemy aircraft from entering the Metropolitan zone. Give my compliments to all ranks.

"MAGNIFICENT FRENCH TROOPS"

A message of congratulations to General de Gaulle on the performance of General Juin's French troops on the Fifth Army front in Italy. February 3, 1944.

Accept my compliments on the magnificent way in which your troops are fighting in the present battle. It is a comfort to have a strong French formation alongside the British and Americans in the line. It reminds us of old times, and heralds new times.

"A PROUD POLITICAL TRADITION"

A message to the Marquess of Hartington, National Government candidate in the West Derbyshire by-election. February 10, 1944.

10, Downing Street.

My dear Hartington,

I see that they are attacking you because your family has been identified for about 300 years with the Parliamentary representation of West Derbyshire. It ought, on the contrary, to be a matter of pride to the constituency to have such long traditions of constancy and fidelity through so many changing scenes and circumstances. Moreover, it is an historical fact that your family and the people of West Derby have acted together on every great occasion in this long period of our history on the side of the people's rights and progress. It was so in the Revolution of 1688 which finally established the system of Constitutional Monarchy, under which we have enjoyed so m ny blessings. It was so at the passage of the great Reform Bill of 1832, which laid the foundations of the modern electorate. It was so in the Repeal of the Corn Laws in 1846, and in the Extension of the Franchise in 1884. Once again it is the old cause of freedom and progress that is being fought for, though this time not only among the hills of West Derbyshire but in the devastating world war.

Most English people are proud of the past of their country, and feel that in those old days we blazed the trail which modern Parliamentary democracy in many lands is following or trying to follow ; and also that in olden times were formed those noble and indomitable impulses and sentiments which, in this war, have enabled us not only to save ourselves but, in no small degree, to save the future of the world.

You have obtained a short spell of leave from the Coldstream Guards in order to present yourself to your friends and neighbours in the constituency which is your home, and ask them to make you their member of Parliament before you leave for the impending battles. I earnestly hope they will confer upon you this honour, and, in making this appeal to them, I act with the full authority of and in association with the responsible official leaders of all parties in the State—Conservative, Labour, Liberal, Liberal National. In this election no party or sectional interests are or ought to be involved. A success here for the National Government candidate will be a definite service to our fighting men wherever they may be, and may play a recognizable part in bringing this war to a victorious end at the earliest possible moment.

In ordinary times by-elections do not matter very much, and all kinds of local feelings and class and party quarrels may have their fling. But now we must be strong and united and set a high standard to all our Allies. It would indeed be a disaster if Britain, after the great things she has done, went to pieces and fell into petty squabbles in the very year when her supreme efforts must be made. These by-elections are therefore symbolic, and electors by their votes can prove the heroic temper of our island in these tremendous days.

To party men I say this : Liberal and Labour Ministers are working together in our National Government and are laying the foundations for the prosperity and happiness of our people in years which I shall not see. All these men are as loyal and helpful colleagues to me in my work as my own immediate supporters. Follow their example. Give us your aid, for it will be welcome. Victory is sure, and it will belong to all who have not faltered or flinched or wearied on the long road.

Yours very sincerely,
WINSTON S. CHURCHILL.

RED ARMY ANNIVERSARY

A message to Marshal Stalin on Red Army Day. February 23, 1944.

On this, the twenty-sixth anniversary of the Red Army, I send to you and all ranks this expression of my profound admiration of their glorious record. Inspired and guided by your leadership, and by their love of the soil of Russia, trusting their skilful and resolute commanders, they will go forward to victory, and through victory to peace with honour.

SALUTE THE SOLDIER

A message to the National War Savings Committee in support of the " Salute the Soldier" campaign. March 20, 1944.

I wish the " Salute the Soldier" Campaign every success. It provides an opportunity for the whole nation to demonstrate the pride and affection we all feel for the men in the British Armies. During this year they will be engaged in nearly every theatre of war throughout the world in what we hope may prove to be the decisive stages in this great conflict. I have no doubt that through this Campaign we shall proclaim once more the whole-hearted devotion of the people of Great Britain united in support of those ideals for which our men go out to fight.

THE SPIRIT OF GREECE

A message to M. Tsouderos, President of the Greek Council of Ministers, on Greek Independence Day. March 25, 1944.

All Greeks look back with pride to the War of Liberation when Greece regained freedom after long years of foreign rule. On this anniversary, when Greece is again struggling against alien domination, I send you in the name of the people of Great Britain a message of sympathy for the Greek people in their present sufferings and of hope and encouragement for the future.

Since March last year success has attended the Allied armies in all theatres of war, and in the victories which have been won the Greek armed forces, and especially the Royal Hellenic Navy, have played an honourable part.

I have read with pleasure of the agreement signed by the guerrilla leaders on February 29th. Now that they have composed their differences I trust that they will direct all their efforts against the common enemy. The Germans have already learned on the Pinios river what they can do, and other such blows will I hope follow until the last Nazi has been expelled from Greece.

Amongst the mass of the Greek people the spirit of resistance has throughout remained unbroken, and I am convinced that in spite of the savage oppression of the German invaders this spirit will not fail. The day of liberation is approaching, and all lovers of Greece hope to see her once again united and free.

In the victory which will surely be won I am confident that the long-standing friendship between Great Britain and Greece will be maintained and strengthened.

BRITISH EMPIRE WAR CASUALTIES

The Prime Minister was asked by a Member of Parliament to state the total casualties among British forces since the outbreak of the war, and he did so in the following written answer on April 4, 1944:

FOLLOWING is a tabular statement giving the casualties sustained by all ranks of the British Empire Forces during the first four years of the war. There are also the figures of casualties sustained by the British Merchant Navy during the same period, and the comparable figures for civilian casualties in the United Kingdom, which have been considerable.

War Casualties

Casualties to all ranks of British Empire forces during the first four years of war
(Excluding deaths from natural causes)

	United Kingdom*	Canada	Australia	New Zealand	South Africa	India†	Colonies	Total British Empire
Killed‡	120,958	9,209	12,298	5,622	3,107	5,912	1,635	158,741
Missing	29,469	2,745	11,887	884	279	17,810	15,130	78,204
Wounded	93,622	3,383	29,393	11,315	6,473	13,230	1,803	159,219
Prisoners of War	143,947	4,360	20,760	7,896	13,966	72,848§	7,218	270,995
Total	387,996	19,697	74,338	25,717	23,825	109,800	25,786	667,159

* Including Overseas personnel serving in these forces, in particular from Newfoundland and Southern Rhodesia.
† Including casualties to the Hong Kong and Singapore Royal Artillery.
‡ Including died of wounds or injuries.
§ Including 58,221 officers and other ranks missing but presumed to be prisoners of war.

Note :—(a) The casualty figures are net, *i.e.*, they exclude missing personnel who subsequently rejoined, and repatriated prisoners of war.
(b) Prisoners of war include Service internees in neutral countries.

Casualties to Merchant Seamen on British Ships During the First Four Years of War

Deaths (including deaths presumed in missing ships)		26,317
Internees		3,997
	Total	30,314

Note.—These figures include nationals of the Dominions, India, and the Colonies serving on British registered ships, but do not include any losses that may have been sustained in ships registered outside the United Kingdom.

Civilian Casualties in the United Kingdom During the First Four Years of War

Killed		49,730
Injured and detained in hospital		59,371
	Total	109,101

Note.—These figures exclude casualties at sea.

" SPIRIT OF THE EMPIRE "

A Speech to the House of Commons during a Debate on
Empire Unity
April 21, 1944

March 28.   *Russians captured Nikolaev, Black Sea port at the mouth of the Bug.*

March 29.   *Powerful U.S. naval forces attacked Palau Island, 1,350 miles south of Japan.*

March 30.   *Russians captured Cernauti and caused German retreat in the Lower Bug.*

        R.A.F. lost 94 bombers in a great raid on Nuremberg.

March 31.   *It was revealed that Major-General O. C. Wingate had been killed in a Burma plane crash.*

April 1.   *Russians advanced rapidly on Odessa.*

April 4.   *It was officially announced that in the first four years of the war British Empire casualties were 667,159, including 158,741 killed.*

        Russian troops under Marshal Koniev penetrated well into Rumania, while Bucharest, the capital, was heavily attacked by Allied bombers.

April 5.   *Russian troops captured Razelnaya, thus cutting the main escape route to Rumania for the German troops at Odessa.*

        Allied bombers struck at Ploesti, Rumania's oil refinery.

April 8.   *Russian troops reached the borders of Czechoslovakia on a front of 125 miles.*

        U.S. air operations over Germany cost the Luftwaffe 92 fighters.

April 9.   *Advancing Russian armies captured 200 places in Rumanian territory.*

April 10.   *Russians captured Odessa, major Black Sea port, and launched an offensive for the reconquest of the Crimea.*

April 11.   *Russians made further big advances in the Crimea and Rumania.*

April 12.   *Five hundred bombers based on Italy made a heavy assault on German aircraft works in Austria.*

April 13.   *Russian troops made three big captures in the Crimea— Simferopol, Eupatoria, and Feodosia.*

April 14.   *Two Russian armies linked up in the Crimea, where the enemy suffered enormous losses. Many ships in which Germans were trying to evacuate were sunk.*

        The death of the Russian General Vatutin was announced.

April 15.   *Allied bombers struck heavy blows at the coastal strip north of Rome.*

April 17.   *Russian troops opened a drive for the Galatz Line guarding the Ploesti oil fields.*

     To safeguard invasion plans the British Government took the unprecedented step of restricting the privileges of Ambassadors and Envoys.

April 18.   *Russians captured Balaclava and advanced on Sebastopol.*

     R.A.F. dropped a record weight of more than 4,000 tons of bombs on railway centres in France.

April 19.   *Russia's Black Sea Fleet took part in the operations against Sebastopol.*

April 20.   *Venice was bombed for the first time.*

[*April* 21, 1944.

WHEN we planned this Debate together through the usual channels, it was well understood that its main purpose was to enable the House to express its opinion, and that the Government would have no far-reaching declaration of policy to make. Indeed, it has been everywhere recognized that for us to commit ourselves to hard-and-fast lines of policy, or even to the advocacy of particular suggestions or proposals, would not be appropriate on the eve of the first meeting we have been able to arrange—after many attempts— of all the Dominion Prime Ministers since the war began. Thus viewed, I think it will be almost universally admitted that the Debate has been a great success, and has been of far-reaching usefulness; that there is an all-party agreement on most fundamentals; and that the level of the discussion has been worthy of the breadth of the subject, and has been distinguished by speeches of a statesmanlike character, for I can use no other word for speeches such as I heard yesterday from my hon. Friend the Member for Seaham (Mr. Shinwell), and to-day from my right hon. Friend the Member for Devonport (Mr. Hore-Belisha) and the Noble Lord the Member for Horsham and Worthing (Earl Winterton)—although, after the very kind compliment the Noble Lord has just paid me, I was not quite sure whether I had not better leave him out. I must regret that I could not hear all the speeches which have been made, but I sat up till half-past two this morning reading the full report of every speech, and I crave the indulgence of the House for not having been constantly on the Bench during this Debate, on account of some other things which, hon. Members may know, it is my duty to look after.

What has struck me most about the speeches which I have listened to or have read or upon which I have been kept well informed, has been the great number of enormous topics, some of which have formerly been matters of heated controversy, and may be again, which Members have found it necessary, indeed have found it inevitable, to take for an airing. A great number of these questions concern our future, and they have been raised directly or indirectly. What changes are to be made in the political, economic, and defence structure of the British Commonwealth and Empire? In what way will an ever more closely knitted British Commonwealth and Empire become also, at the same time, more closely associated with the United States? How will this vast bloc of States and Nations, which will walk along together, speaking, to a large extent, the same language, reposing on the same body of common law, be merged in the Supreme Council for the maintenance of world peace? Should we draw closer to Europe —there is another question—and aim at creating, under the Supreme World Council, a living union, an entity in Europe, a United States of Europe? Or, again, should we concentrate upon our own Imperial and Commonwealth organization, or upon our fraternal association with the United States, and put our trust in the English Channel, in air power, and in sea power?

Other more familiar topics than these—because it is easy to see, from the recurrence of these topics in so many speeches, the way in which the modern mind of the House is moving—have been raised, like Free Trade versus Protection, Imperial Preference versus greater development of international trade, and international currency in relation to the policy of the United States and the existence of a vast sterling area. One even sees the gold standard peering around the corner, and, of course, British agriculture is close at hand. My hon. Friend the Member for Eye said yesterday that the sole, or the main, lesson of the war was that the world was one and indivisible. I should myself have thought that the main obvious fact before our eyes is that the world is very seriously divided, and is conducting its controversies in a highly acrimonious manner. Certainly it seems sufficiently divided to give the peacemakers quite a considerable task to weld it into one common mutually-loving whole at the peace table. I cannot pretend to have provided myself with the answers to all these questions, with answers which would give satisfaction to all parties here at home, and cause no complications in our relations with foreign States, but I bid the House to take comfort from the fact that, great as our responsibilities are, no reasonable person could expect us to solve all the problems of the world while we are fighting for our lives. We must be generous, we must be fair to the future, we must leave something to be done by our descendants, if any.

My hon. Friend the Member for West Renfrew (Mr. Wedderburn), whose laudable desire to probe into the distant past is not always accompanied by historical precision, quoted—and I make no complaint of it—a speech which I made forty years ago against Mr. Joseph Chamberlain's policy of Protection and Imperial Preference which certainly does not, whatever else may be thought about it, reveal me as a very ardent supporter of those policies, and certainly makes it very odd that I should have, for the time being, the honour of leading the Conservative Party. I have no intention of passing my remaining years in explaining or withdrawing anything I have said in the past, still less in apologizing for it; but what I am concerned to do is to show to the House, and also to Members of my own Party, how strictly I have, during my stewardship, safeguarded the structure of Imperial Preference, which has arisen out of the controversies and achievements of the last forty years, against any danger of being swept away in the tumult of this war. At my first meeting with the President of the United States, at Argenta in Newfoundland, at the time of the so-called Atlantic Charter and before the United States had entered the war— a meeting of very anxious and critical importance—I asked for the insertion of the following words, which can be read in that document :

" With due respect for their existing obligations."

Those are the limiting words, and they were inserted for the express purpose of retaining in the House of Commons, and the Dominion Parliaments, the fullest possible rights and liberties over the question of Imperial Preference. Again, in February, 1942, when the United States was our closest ally, I did not agree to Article 7 of the Mutual Aid Agreement without having previously obtained from the President a definite assurance that we were no more committed to the abolition of Imperial Preference than the American Government were committed to the abolition of their high protective tariffs. The discussion as to how a greater volume and a more harmonious flow of trade can be created in the immediate post-war years in agreement, leaves us, in every respect, so far as action is concerned, perfectly free. How could it be otherwise, when Parliament itself would not only have to debate the matters, but would have to legislate upon them, when they were brought before it ? I am convinced myself that there should be a careful, searching, far-ranging discussion on the economics of the post-war world, and a sincere attempt made to reconcile conflicting interests wherever possible. There must be a whole-hearted endeavour, begun in good time, to promote the greatest interchange of goods and services between the various communities of the world, and to strive for that process of betterment of standards of life in every country without which, as the hon. Member for Seaham (Mr. Shinwell) pointed out, expanding markets are impossible, and without which world prosperity is a dream which might easily turn into a nightmare.

My right hon. Friend the Member for Devonport (Mr. Hore-Belisha) made a remark which I particularly liked, when he said that the Empire is not a sick body. I cordially agree. But even I can look back to the days when it was considered to be moribund. There were, when I was young, some statesmen whose names are honoured, who spoke of the Colonies as burdens, and of the Dominions as fruit which would fall from the tree when ripe. I did not live myself in the days when those speeches were made, but I remember well times of great anxiety about the Empire, at the end of the last century. I remember the South African war, and how shocked the War Office was when Australia and New Zealand actually wanted to send contingents to fight, and how they eventually overcame their reluctance by adopting the immortal compromise " unmounted men preferred." My right hon. Friend, who is not here, has made great improvements since then. I have never thought myself that the Empire needed tying together with bits of string. I agree with my right hon. Friend the Member for Devonport that natural development, natural forces, mysterious natural forces, will carry everything before them, especially when those forces are fanned forward, as they will be, by the wings of victory in a righteous cause.

Then came another phase. Looking at the British Empire, say, 30 years ago, in 1914, on the eve of the first Great War, all foreign opinion, especially German opinion, was convinced that this vast structure of Empire, created and coming into full life in Victorian times, had reached a condition of ricketiness and looseness when a single violent shock would bring it clattering down and lay it low for ever. Then came upon the world a most frightful war, incomparably greater than anything we had ever known, with slaughter far greater than any, thank God, we have suffered in this struggle. I remember coming out of the Cabinet meeting on an August afternoon in 1914, when war was certain, and the Fleet was already mobilized, with this feeling : " How are we to explain it all to Canada, Australia, South Africa and New Zealand ; nay, how are we to explain it all to our own people in the short time left ? " But, when we came out from the fierce controversy of the Cabinet room into the open air, the whole of the peoples of the British Empire, of every race and every clime, had already sprung to arms. Our old enemies, recent enemies, Generals Botha and Smuts, were already saddling their horses to rally their commandos to the attack on Germany, and Irishmen, whose names I always bear in my memory with regard, John Redmond and his brother, and others of the old Irish Parliamentary Party, which fought us for so many years in this House, pleading the cause of Ireland with great eloquence and Parliamentary renown ; there they were, making these speeches of absolute support and unity with this country until everybody said everywhere "The brightest spot in the world is Ireland." It may be that a grand opportunity was lost then. We must keep our eyes open. I always keep mine open on the Irish question.

We had a pretty dreary time between these two wars. But we have great responsibilities for the part we played—so we have, all of us—and so have the Americans in not making the League of Nations a reality and in not backing its principles with effective armed forces, and in letting this deadly and vengeful foe arm at his leisure. But underneath, the whole Empire and ourselves in these islands grew stronger and our resources multiplied. Little was said about our growth. Little was visible of our closer union ; while the forces which had sent the Anzac Corps to the Dardanelles, and afterwards to the Hindenburg Line, and carried the Canadians to Vimy Ridge, were all growing, unseen, unnoticed, immeasurable, far below the surface of public life and political conflict. These are the natural processes to which my right hon. Friend so aptly referred. Then, this war broke out. The Mother Country—I must still ask leave to use this name ; anyhow, I think it is rather dangerous to plunge into new nomenclature, and I am not sure that anything like "The Elder Sister Country" would be a very great success. There was that old song which I remember in my youth, "A Boy's Best Friend is his Mother," and which seems to me to be sometimes worth humming again. The Mother Country, I say, was geographically involved, once again, in the struggles of Europe, and found it right and necessary to declare war upon Germany because Germany had violated Poland and we had guaranteed to defend Poland. Instantly, from all parts of the British Empire, with one lamentable exception, about which we must all search our hearts, came the same response. None of the disillusionments that had followed "the war to end wars," "the homes for heroes" and so forth—all good slogans in their day—none of the disillusionments which we had gone through, with the ups and downs of unemployment and great privations, none of these had affected in any way the living, growing, intensifying inner life of the British Commonwealth and Empire. When the signal came, from the poorest Colony to the most powerful Dominion, the great maxim held : "When the King declares war, the Empire is at war." The darkest moment came. Did anyone flinch ? Was there one cry of pain or doubt or terror ? No, Sir, darkness was turned into light, and into a light which will never fade away.

What is this miracle ? I think the word was used by some hon. Gentleman yesterday. What is this miracle, for it is nothing less, that called men from the uttermost ends of the earth, some riding twenty days before they could reach their recruiting centres, some armies having to sail 14,000 miles across the seas before they reached the battlefield ? What is this force, this miracle which makes governments, as proud and sovereign as any that have ever existed, immediately cast aside all their fears, and immediately set themselves to aid a good cause and beat the common foe ? You must look very deep into the heart of man, and then you will not find the answer unless you look with the eye of the spirit. Then it is that you learn that human beings are not dominated by material things, but by ideas for which they are willing to give their lives or their life's work. Among the various forces that hold the British Empire together is—and I certainly do not object to the expression which my hon. Friend the Member for Seaham used—"enlightened self-interest." That has a valuable and important part to play, but I am sure he would not make the mistake of placing it in front of those deeper and more mysterious influences which cause human beings to do the most incalculable, improvident, and, from the narrow point of view, profitless things. It is our union in freedom and for the sake of our way of living which is the great fact, reinforced by tradition and sentiment, and it does not depend upon anything that could ever be written down in any account kept in some large volume.

We have had the Statute of Westminster, which some thought would involve the breaking of ties. There was a lot to be said about that on either side. It has not impeded in the slightest degree the onward march of the Commonwealth and Empire. It has not prevented the centripetal forces of our vast organization from exerting their full strength. Here, after our failures—we are not the only nation which had failures between the two wars—here, after the Statute of Westminster, here, after getting into this war, and dragging in the Empire so unprepared—here, amid the wreck of empires, states, nations, and institutions of every kind, we find the British Commonwealth and Empire more strongly united than ever before. In a world of confusion and ruin, the old flag flies. We have not got to consider how to bind ourselves more closely. It would pass the wit of man to do so. It is extraordinary what a poor business it has become to sneer at the British Empire. Those who have tried it in the United States have been discredited. Those who have tried it in the Dominions have found no public backing, although there is free speech for all opinions. Those who decry our Commonwealth of Nations and deride the Mother Country have very little support.

The question before us is, How can we make things better ? How can we gain greater results from our already close ties ? I do not think we should embark upon that task with a sort of feeling that if we do not do something, everything is going to crash. I do not understand that. I do not feel like that. The forces underlying our unity are superior to any temporary shortcomings for which any of us may become responsible. We have to consider practical steps, and to consider these coolly and sagely. The world is in crisis. The British Commonwealth and Empire was never more united within itself. Rudyard Kipling, that refreshing fountain of British Imperial ideas, wrote of the Dominions :

> " Daughter am I in my mother's house,
>   But Mistress in my own."

We have to take a step beyond that now. There is a family council. Methods must be devised, without haste and without rest, to bring the nations of the British Empire into intimate and secret counsel not only during this war—because that is done with great labour and efficiency—but after the war, so that they may know fully our position and we theirs in regard to the march of events and the action which may have to come from them. My right hon. Friend the Member for Devonport spoke wisely and suggestively of " functional unity " within the Empire. The question has been raised : Should we have a permanent machinery like the Committee of Imperial Defence, only on a larger scale, a kind of lively extension of the principle which is embodied in the name of the Chief of the Imperial General Staff, which Lord Haldane created by a far-seeing decision, a sort of continuance, in an Imperial form, of the machinery which I, at present, direct as Minister of National Defence—should we set up something like this to be a standing and perpetual committee of the British Empire ? This would be no more than an expansion on a much greater scale and in much more precise detail of the work hitherto done by the Committee of Imperial Defence, which my right hon. Friend mentioned. But should it extend into the sphere of maritime affairs, of economic affairs and of financial affairs, and how far ?

These are obviously matters which we must begin to explore together when we meet informally our colleagues from the great Dominions. There are some who would clothe the machinery of union with Ministerial authority, there are others who would have it extended to both economic and military affairs. I must say, speaking for myself, I see very little difficulty about the first point, about international bodies being developed with more vigour. We have, of course, representatives of the Dominions on the bodies which function under the Minister of Defence now. I see very little difficulty about the first ; I see very great advantage in the second, namely, Ministerial contact. There must be frequent meetings of the Prime Ministers, and they must be attended by those they choose to bring with them, to discuss all aspects of Imperial policy and Imperial safety. Here as in so many cases time marches forward with a friendly step. The vast developments of air transport make a new bond of union, and there are new facilities for meeting, which will make the councils of the British Commonwealth of Nations a unity much greater than ever was possible before, when the war is over and when the genius of the air is turned from the most horrible forms of destruction to the glories of peace.

It will be quite easy to have meetings of Prime Ministers or Imperial Conferences, whatever you like to call them, every year or more often, on every serious occasion, when we get to the times of peace, and we shall encourage them at any time in the period of war. It is not necessary that these meetings should always take place in London. They may take place in other great centres of our United Empire. Although I am still old-fashioned enough to consider Cockney London as the heart of the Empire, I am quite willing that we should take wing in the future. In this war we have already held, quite apart from the conferences with the President of the United States, a conference in Quebec where I sat for several days with the Dominion Cabinet, and we were all the guests of Canada, which I may say is a very agreeable thing to be. It is very likely, as the sombre marches of the war succeed one another, when Hitler and Hitlerism are finished and blasted from the face of the earth, we shall have conferences of the British Empire and the United States in Australia about all these matters—and there are certainly some in which we find cause of complaint against the Japanese. When peace returns, and we should pray to God it soon may, the Conferences of the Prime Ministers of the Dominions, among whom we trust India will be reckoned and with whom the Colonies will be associated, will, we hope, become frequent and regular facts and festivities of our annual life.

One last word before I sit down. Some assume that there must be an inherent antagonism between a world order to keep peace, and the vast national or federal organization which will eventually be in existence. I do not believe this is true. Both the world order and this great organization may be so fashioned as to be two parts of one tremendous whole. I have never conceived that a fraternal association with the United States would militate in any way against the unity of the British Commonwealth and Empire, or breed ill-feeling with our great Russian Ally, to whom we are bound by the twenty years treaty. I do not think we need choose this or that. With wisdom, and patience, and vigour and courage, we may get the best of both. We have often said of our own British Empire : " In my Father's house there are many mansions." So in this far greater world structure, which we shall surely raise out of the ruins of desolating war, there will be room for all generous, free associations of a special character, so long as they are not disloyal to the world cause nor seek to bar the forward march of mankind.

EMPIRE PRIME MINISTERS MEET

A Speech at the opening of the Conference of Empire
Prime Ministers at 10, Downing Street
May 1, 1944

April 22. *Allied air attacks across the Channel reached a new pitch of intensity after a week in which 17,000 tons of bombs were dropped.*

April 23. *British troops in Burma made a firm stand at Kohima and Imphal to check the Japanese invasion of India.*

April 24. *The Kohima garrison was relieved.*
Allied forces landed at three new points in N.E. New Guinea.

April 25. *Chaos spread through French railway system and air-fields following seven days of non-stop air attack.*

April 28. *The German Navy was reported to have taken up action stations to meet invasion threat.*
Russian troops crossed the River Pruth at a new point below Jassy.

April 30. *Marshal Stalin declared that Germany could be completely crushed only by a combined blow from Russia, Britain and America.*

May 1. *First war-time Conference of Empire Prime Ministers opened in London.*

[May 1, 1944.

I DESIRE to extend to the representatives from overseas a most hearty and cordial welcome to these shores. This meeting is undoubtedly one of the most important events that have taken place since the outbreak of the war. Here in the most deadly climax of the conflict of the nations, at a time when, although we need no longer fear defeat, we are making the most intense efforts to compel an early victory, there are gathered together representatives of all the self-governing Dominions, together with their advisers, military and civil, to take stock of our affairs. I do not expect that we shall reach complete solutions of all the problems that confront the British Empire and vex mankind. We can hardly expect to do so in the heat of war. But it is high time that we got round a table to exchange views and ideas. These ideas are, I think, convergent. But it should be our duty to seek and to find where divergences, or potential divergences, exist, and to see how they can be adjusted while they are still small. I am sure we shall do so in this friendly atmosphere.

And there is a second major reason for these conversations. The British Commonwealth and Empire now have fighting on their side very powerful allies. The Empire has been joined in the struggle against Germany by the mighty force of the Soviet Union and by the great Republic of the United States. It is right that the British Empire in its collective united aspect should put itself solidly on the map, and make all the watching world realize that it stands together, woven into one family of nations capable of solving our common problems in full loyalty to the supreme cause for which we have drawn the sword, and which we shall not cease to pursue until complete victory has been won.

BRITISH EMPIRE'S AID TO RUSSIA

A STATEMENT TO THE HOUSE OF COMMONS
MAY 10, 1944

May 2.   *Spain agreed to Anglo-American demands to restrict supplies of wolfram to Germany.*

May 3.   *Germans reported that the Red Army had launched a new attack west of Jassy, Rumania.*
      Bucharest was bombed by aircraft based on Italy.
      R.A.F. made heavy attacks at night on German troops concentrated at Mailly and Montdidier.

May 4.   *Rehabilitation schemes for Europe after invasion were examined by Dominion Prime Ministers.*

May 5.   *R.A.F. bombers smashed the Pescara Dam in the Adriatic sector of the Italian front.*
      British troops on the Burma front attacked at all points in the Kohima section.

May 6.   *More than 500 bombers based on Italy attacked oil and rail targets in Rumania.*

May 8.   *Russians announced that in a two-days offensive they had broken the main defences of Sebastopol.*
      Bucharest, Berlin and Brunswick were heavily attacked day and night by allied bombers.

May 9.   *Red Army captured Sebastopol, liberating the whole of the Crimea.*

[*May 10, 1944.*

I AM circulating to-day a full statement on the materials and munitions of war supplied to Russia by Great Britain and the Empire countries. The House may, however, like to know that between October 1st, 1941, and March 31st, 1944, we have supplied to the Soviet Union 5,031 tanks, of which 1,223 were from Canada. We have supplied 6,778 aircraft, including 2,672 aircraft sent from the United States of America. These latter were sent on United States Lend-Lease to the Soviet Union as part of the British commitment in exchange for the supply of British aircraft to United States Forces in the European theatre. We have also sent over £80,000,000 worth of raw materials, foodstuffs, machinery, industrial plant, medical supplies and comforts.

I need hardly remind the House that a considerable portion of these supplies has been fought through to Russia along the Arctic route. These operations have been under the general direction of successive Commanders-in-Chief, Home Fleet, and almost all losses of warships have fallen upon the Royal Navy. In merchant ships, on the other hand, the Allied Nations, and particularly the merchant ships of the United States of America, have borne the heavier loss. Many brave men have fallen into icy waters, but our Russian Allies have had some of the help and comfort they needed and deserved.

I should also add that in making this statement I am merely responding to a wish that the facts should be published, as they ought to be. I am not in the slightest degree boasting invidiously about our efforts as compared with those of our Ally, the United States, nor making out any counter-claims against the heroism and glorious military exploits of the Soviet Armies.

The statement circulated by the Prime Minister was as follows :

I am glad of this opportunity to make known details of the very substantial contribution made by the United Kingdom in aid of our Soviet Allies. Not only has this aid been considerable, but it has only been possible to furnish it at heavy cost in lives of our seamen and ships which have been lost on North Russian convoys.

The great bulk of these supplies has been furnished directly by or manufactured in the United Kingdom. Some of the items contain a proportion, small but unascertainable, of raw materials or component parts which we ourselves have received on Lend-Lease terms from the United States, and without which it would not have been possible to make these supplies available to Soviet Union.

The figures also include some supplies made available to the United Kingdom under Canadian Mutual Aid and some procured from Canada by the United Kingdom, partly with the help of the Canadian Billion Dollar Gift. Of the help thus given I should like to take this opportunity of expressing His Majesty's Government's appreciation. Since July 1st, 1943, supplies from Canada have also been going forward by direct arrangement between Canada and the U.S.S.R. and are not included in the present statement.

A list is appended below, setting out the main items dispatched to the U.S.S.R. from October 1st, 1941, to March 31st, 1944. Owing to the wide variety of their nature, specific reference has not been made to all categories of supplies, but this list shows the scale on which aid to the U.S.S.R. has been going forward over the last two and a half years.

SUPPLIES TO U.S.S.R. DISPATCHED BETWEEN OCTOBER 1ST, 1941, AND MARCH 31ST, 1944

1. MILITARY SUPPLIES.

(a) *Armaments and Military Stores.*

Tanks : Since October, 1941, 5,031 tanks have been supplied, of which 1,223 were Canadian built.

Vehicles (includes lorries and ambulances) : 4,020.

Machinery lorries : 216.

Bren Carriers and Starters and Chargers : 2,463 (including 1,348 from Canada).

Motor Cycles : 1,706.

Weapons :

800 P.I.A.T. with ammunition.
103 Thompson sub-machine guns.
636 2-pdr. anti-tank guns.
96 6-pdr. anti-tank guns.
3,200 Boys anti-tank rifles.
2,487 Bren guns.
581 7.92 mm. Besa guns.

Ammunition :

85,000 rounds P.I.A.T.
19,346,000 rounds .45-in. machine gun.
2,591,000 rounds 2-pdr. anti-tank gun.
409,000 rounds 6-pdr. anti-tank gun.
1,761,000 rounds .55 in. Boys anti-tank rifle.
75,134,000 rounds .303-in. rifle.
51,211,000 rounds 7.92 mm. tank gun, Besa.

G.L. Equipment :

(*a*) Mark II : 302 sets.
(*b*) Mark III : 15 sets British ; 29 sets Canadian.

Cable : 30,227 miles telephone cable.

(b) *Naval Supplies :*

9 Mine-sweeping trawlers.
3 Motor mine-sweepers.
102 Asdics.
3,006 Mines.
50 Vickers 130 mm. guns.
603 Anti-aircraft machine guns.
40 Submarine Batteries.

(c) *Aircraft* (Fighters).—Total dispatched 6,778 aircraft, including 2,672 aircraft sent from U.S.A. These were sent on United States Lend-Lease to U.S.S.R., as part of the British commitment, in exchange for a supply of British aircraft to U.S. forces in the European theatre.

2. Raw Materials, Foodstuffs, Machinery and Industrial Plant.

(a) *Raw Materials.*—The greater part of these supplies have been bought from Empire sources. Over the last 2½ years we have sent :

30,000 tons of aluminium from Canada [£3,038,000].
2,000 tons of aluminium from United Kingdom [£720,000].
27,000 tons of copper from Canada [£1,431,000].
10,000 tons of copper from United Kingdom [£620,000]
$4,672,000 worth of Industrial Diamonds, mainly from African production [£1,168,000].
80,924 tons of jute from India [£3,687,000].
81,423 tons of rubber from the Far East and Ceylon [£9,911,000].
8,550 tons of sisal from British East Africa [£194,000].
3,300 tons of graphite from Ceylon [£160,000].
28,050 tons of tin from Malaya and United Kingdom [£7,774,000].
29,610 tons of wool from Australia and New Zealand [£5,521,000].

Total Value of these and other raw materials :
£39,115,000.

(b) *Foodstuffs.*—These include : Tea from Ceylon and India ; Cocoa beans, palm oil and palm kernels from West Africa ; groundnuts from India ; cocoanut oil from Ceylon ; pepper and spices from India, Ceylon and British West Indies.

Total Value of all foodstuffs supplied : £7,223,000.

(c) *Machine Tools, Industrial Plant and Machinery.*—These form the principal direct contribution from United Kingdom production to civil supplies for the U.S.S.R. Since the entry of Russia into the war, the following have been provided :

Machine Tools—£8,218,000.
Power Plant—£4,250,000.
Electrical Equipment—£3,314,000.
Miscellaneous Industrial Equipment—£1,980,000.
Various types of Machinery—£3,019,000 (e.g. Telephone equipment, food-processing plant, textile machinery, port and salvage equipment).

Total Value of (c) : £20,781,000.

Grand Total of Civil Stores made available to U.S.S.R. including (a), (b) and (c) and certain other Items by the United Kingdom from all sources : £77,185,000.

3. MEDICAL SUPPLIES AND COMFORTS.—The public have contributed some of the funds for these supplies. Since October, 1941, £3,047,725 has been spent through charitable organizations on surgical and medical items and clothing. In addition, His Majesty's Government have made a grant of £2,500,000 for clothing, nearly all of which has been spent.

TRIBUTE TO MR. CURTIN

[May 18, 1944.

THIS is an occasion which, even amid the stresses of war, might well be called one of rejoicing. We have here, presiding over our proceedings, the Duke of Gloucester, Governor-General designate of the Commonwealth of Australia. Presently he will go to take up his great task, and the desire, which is manifest throughout the Commonwealth, that he should go there and preside over the constitutional working of their affairs—that he, a brother of the King, should go there—is in itself a most agreeable and significant event.

These are the days when in other countries ignorant people are often disposed to imagine that progress consists in converting oneself from a monarchy into a republic. In this country we have known the blessings of limited monarchy. Great traditional and constitutional chains of events have come to make an arrangement, to make a situation, unwritten, which enables our affairs to proceed on what I believe is a superior level of smoothness and democratic progress.

I had not previously met Mr. Curtin, except in correspondence during the present struggle, but I have met him now, and joined the right hand of friendship with that most commanding, competent, wholehearted leader of the Australian people in all the vicissitudes and mortal terrors through which they have now, I think I might venture to say, safely passed.

Other struggles lie ahead, perhaps long struggles, in the Pacific theatre. I am sure the Australian people will never forget the immense services which have been rendered to Australia by the armed forces and Government of the United States.

We divided the spheres of responsibility with the United States at the beginning of 1942. We did our part in the Atlantic, and they undertook with their strong arm to ward off the menace of Japan and aid Australia to develop her full strength. The whole story is one eminently satisfactory, eminently creditable to the English-speaking peoples all over the world, and will never be made the subject of invidious comparison.

Mr. Curtin has certainly made a great impression on all who have been brought in contact with him, especially in matters of serious business. I trust he will go back safely over the long distances which must be passed before he regains his country. I know he will speak a good word for us wherever he goes. My feeling is that we had made on him an impression about the state of our affairs in our Island which will perhaps be confirmed by history, and is at present expressed in the well-known and never to be too much known words of Macaulay:

> Then none was for a party;
>   Then all were for the state;
> Then the great man helped the poor
>   And the poor man loved the great;
> Then lands were fairly portioned
>   And the Huns were fairly sold;
> The Britons were like brothers
>   In the brave days of old.

A WORLD SURVEY

A SPEECH TO THE HOUSE OF COMMONS
MAY 24, 1944

May 11.   *Allied bombers continued their great day-and-night air assault on the Continent of Europe with attacks in ever-mounting strength.*

May 12.   *The Fifth and Eighth Armies, having been regrouped, launched a great offensive in Italy and crossed the Rapido and Garigliano rivers. General Alexander stated that it was the first of the blows which would finally destroy the Nazis.*

      Four synthetic oil plants in Germany and one in Czechoslovakia were attacked by very strong forces of American bombers.

May 13.   *Bombers cut the Brenner Pass railway, main lifeline of the German armies in Italy.*

      San Angelo and Castelforte were captured in fighting for the Gustav Line.

May 14.   *Fourteen enemy bombers were destroyed in raids on Britain.*

May 15.   *The Gustav line in Italy was smashed everywhere except at Cassino by the advancing Fifth and Eighth Armies.*

      Three strong Japanese positions near Kohima, on the Burma front, were captured.

May 17.   *Dominion Prime Ministers, at their Conference in London, announced full agreement on strategy and foreign policy.*

May 18.   *Cassino and the Monastery were captured when the Gustav Line in Italy was wiped out and outskirts of the Hitler Line taken.*

      In Burma, American and Chinese troops captured an airfield south of Myitkyina.

May 19.   *It was officially announced that 47 R.A.F. and Allied Air Force officers had been shot in Germany while attempting to escape.*

      German troops in Italy retreated in disorder under powerful thrusts by the Fifth Army.

May 20.   *In the Far East Allied warships and aircraft attacked Sourabaya, naval base in Java.*

May 21.   *Allied troops in Italy made powerful inroads on the Hitler defence line.*

      Nearly 5,000 fighters and fighter-bombers attacked the enemy transport system in France and the Low Countries.

May 22.　*The air assault on the enemy transport system was maintained. Kiel was also bombed.*

May 23.　*The Fifth Army struck out from the Anzio beachhead, and a similar drive was made by the Eighth Army to enlarge the breach in the Hitler Line.*

May 24.　*German troops in Italy began a general retreat after a total defeat on the main front and the Anzio beachhead. Tanks poured through the Hitler Line and Terracina was occupied.*

[*May 24, 1944.*

THE meeting of Dominion Prime Ministers, which covered the best part of three weeks, has now concluded, and very full statements to Parliament and the public have been made, individually by the Prime Ministers themselves, and collectively by the declaration to which we have all subscribed. I could not pretend that we have arrived at hard and fast conclusions or precise decisions upon all the questions which torment this afflicted globe, but it can fairly be said that, having discussed a great many of them, there was revealed a core of agreement which will enable the British Empire and Commonwealth to meet in discussion with other great organisms in the world in a firmly-knit array. We have advanced from vague generalities to more precise points of agreement, and we are in a position to carry on discussions with other countries, within the limits which we have imposed upon ourselves.

But this is a Debate upon Foreign Affairs, and nothing was more remarkable than the cordial agreement which was expressed by every one of the Dominion Prime Ministers on the general conduct of our Foreign Affairs and on the principles which govern that conduct, and, I should add, on the skill and consistency with which they have been treated by my right hon. Friend the Foreign Secretary. The utmost confidence was expressed in him and in his handling of all those very difficult affairs, in spite of the complications by which they are surrounded, and, in spite of the need for prompt action which so often arises—for prompt action by the Mother Country before there is time to have full consultation. In spite of all these difficulties, the fullest confidence and pleasure was expressed in the work which my right hon. Friend has done. We therefore embark upon the present Debate with the backing of good will from all these representatives of the Commonwealth and Empire—the word " Empire " is permitted to be used, which may be a great shock to certain strains of intellectual opinion. And we embark upon the present Debate not only with this

backing of hearty goodwill, but with the feeling that this meeting o
Prime Ministers from all over the Empire and the representatives o
India in the midst of a second deadly war is in fact the highest pinnacl
which our world-wide family association has yet reached. At thi
time, in policy and in war, our objective is the same, namely, to bea
the enemy as soon as possible ; and I am not aware of any action or o
any studied inaction for which His Majesty's Government are respon
sible that has not been directly related to that single and dominan
purpose.

The duty of all persons responsible for the conduct of Foreig
Affairs in a world war of this deadly character, and of all who, i
different ways, exercise influence, is to help the fighting men to perforn
the heavy tasks entrusted to them and to ensure them all possibl
ease in execution and advantage in victory. Everyone in a positio
to guide opinion, like Members of this House or of another place, o
newspaper editors, broadcasters, calumnists or columnists—
remember a tendency to throw the accent forward—and others—al
of these should keep this very clear duty before their eyes. The
should always think of the soldier in the battle and ask themselve
whether what they say or write will make his task easier or harder
We long for the day to come when this slaughter will be over, and the
this additional restraint which imposes itself on every conscientiou
man in war-time can be relaxed or will vanish away entirely.

I must make my acknowledgments, first of all, to the very grea
degree with which these precepts are followed among those who accep
the task of guiding public opinion, and especially in the House o
Commons, which is always so careful of the public interest and whicl
in other ways has shown itself to be possessed of those steadfast an
unyielding qualities in the face of danger and fatigue for which i
has always been renowned, but never more renowned than now.
shall try to practise what I have been preaching in the remarks
have to make, and I am sure the Committee will remember how man
different audiences I have to address at the same moment, not onl
here but out of doors, and not only in this Island, but throughout th
Empire, not only among our Allies, great and small, west or east, bu
finally among our enemies, besides, of course, satellites and neutral
of various hues. I must, therefore, pick my way among heated plough
shares, and in this ordeal the only guides are singleness and simplicit
of purpose and a good or, at any rate, a well-trained conscience.

Since I last spoke here on Foreign Affairs, just about three month
ago, almost all the purposes which I mentioned to you have prospered
severally and collectively. First of all, let us survey the Mediterranea
and the Balkan spheres. The great disappointment which I had las
October, when I was not able to procure the necessary forces fo

gaining the command of the Aegean Sea following upon the collapse of Italy and gaining possession of the principal Italian islands, has, of course, been accompanied by an exaggerated attitude of caution on the part of Turkey. The hopes we cherished of Turkey boldly entering the war in February or March, or at least according us the necessary bases for air action—those hopes faded. After giving £20,000,000 worth of British and American arms to Turkey in 1943 alone, we have suspended the process and ceased to exhort Turkey to range herself with the victorious United Powers, with whom she has frequently declared that her sympathies lie, and with whom, I think, there is no doubt that her sympathies do lie. The Turks at the end of last year and the beginning of this year magnified their dangers. Their military men took the gloomiest view of Russian prospects in South Russia and in the Crimea.

They never dreamed that by the early Summer the Red Army would be on the slopes of the Carpathians, drawn up along the Pruth and Sereth Rivers, or that Odessa and Sebastopol would have been liberated and regained by the extraordinary valour, might and energy of the Soviet onslaught. Consequently the Turks did not measure with sufficient accuracy what might have occurred, or would occur, in Rumania and Bulgaria or, I may add, Hungary, what would be the result on all those countries of these tremendous Russian hammer blows struck, even in months which are particularly unsuitable for operations in these regions and which normally would be devoted to the process of replenishing the advancing front for future action. Having over-rated their dangers, our Turkish friends increased their demands for supplies to such a point that, having regard to the means of communication and transport alone, the war would probably be over before these supplies could reach them.

We have, therefore, with great regret, discontinued the process of arming Turkey, because it looks probable that, in spite of our disappointment in the Aegean, the great Allies will be able to win the war in the Balkans and generally throughout South Eastern Europe without Turkey being involved now at all, though naturally the aid of Turkey would be a great help and acceleration of that process. This, of course, is a decision for Turkey to take. We have put no pressure upon them, other than the pressure of argument and of not giving the supplies we need for ourselves and other nations that are fighting. But the course which is being taken, and has been taken so far, by Turkey will not, in my view, procure for the Turks the strong position at the peace which would attend their joining the Allies.

I must, however, note the good service and significant gesture rendered to us by the Turkish Government quite recently, and it is said that it has been rendered to us on the personal initiative of Turkey's honoured President, General Inonu, namely the complete cessation of all chrome exports to Germany. It is not too much to expect that the assistance given us in respect of chrome will also shortly be extended to cover other commodities, the export of which, even if of less importance than chrome, is of material assistance to the enemy. If so, we shall endeavour to compensate the Turkish people for the sacrifice which their co-operative action might entail by other means of importation.

Turkey and Britain have a long history. The Turks entered into relations with us before the war when things looked very black. They did their best through difficult times. I have thought it better to put things bluntly to-day, but I cannot conclude, notwithstanding anything I have said in criticism, without saying that we hope with increasing confidence that a still better day will dawn for the relations of Turkey with Britain and, indeed, with all the great Allies. Always in recent decades there has been in the Mediterranean a certain tension between Turkey and Italy on account of Italian ambitions in the Greek Islands, and also, possibly, in the Adana Province of Turkey. The Turks could never be sure which way the Italian dictator would turn his would-be conquering sword. On that score Turkish anxiety has certainly been largely removed.

The fate of Italy is indeed terrible, and I personally find it very difficult to nourish animosity against the Italian people. The overwhelming mass of the nation rejoiced in the idea of being delivered from the subtle tyranny of the Fascists, and they wished, when Mussolini was overthrown, to take their place as speedily as possible by the side of the British and American Armies who, it was expected, would quickly rid the country of the Germans. However, this did not happen. All the Italian forces which could have defended Italy had either been squandered by Mussolini in the African desert or by Hitler amid the Russian snows, or they were widely dispersed combating, in a half-hearted way, the patriots of Yugoslavia. Hitler decided to make great exertions to retain Italy, just as he has decided to make great exertions to gain the mighty battle which is at the moment at its climax to the South of Rome. It may be that after the fall of Mussolini our action might have been more swift and audacious. As I have said before, it is no part of my submission to the House that no mistakes are made by us or by the common action of our Allies ; but, anyhow, here is this beautiful country suffering the worst horrors of war, with the larger part still in the cruel and vengeful grip of the Nazis, and with a hideous prospect of the red-hot rake of the battle-line being drawn from sea to sea right up the whole length of the peninsula.

It is clear that the Germans will be driven out of Italy by the Allies, but what will happen on the moving battle fronts and what the Germans

will do on their way out in the way of destruction to a people they hate
and despise, and who, they allege, have betrayed them, cannot be
imagined or forecast. All I can say is that we shall do our utmost to
make the ordeal as short and as little destructive as possible. We have
great hopes that the city of Rome may be preserved from the area of
struggle of our Armies. The House will recall that when I last spoke on
foreign matters I expressed the view that it would be best that King
Victor Emmanuel, and above all Marshal Badoglio, should remain
at the head of the Executive of the Italian nation and armed forces
until we reached Rome, when it was agreed by all that a general review
of the position must be made.

Such a policy naturally entailed differences of opinion, which were
reflected not only among the Allied Governments but inside every
Allied country. However, I am happy to say that after various unexpected happenings and many twists and turns the situation is now
exactly what I ventured to suggest and as I described it to the House
three months ago. In addition, far beyond my hopes, an Italian
Government has been formed, of a broadly based character, around the
King and Badoglio, and the King himself has decided that on the
capture of Rome he will retire into private life for ever and transfer
his constitutional functions to his eldest son, the Prince of Piedmont,
with the title of Lieutenant of the Realm.

I have good confidence in this new Italian Government which has
been formed. It will require further strengthening and broadening,
especially as we come more closely into touch with the populous
industrial areas of the North—that is essential—but at any rate it is
facing its responsibilities manfully and doing all in its power to aid
the Allies in their advance. Here I may say we are doing our best to
equip the Italian forces who are eager to fight with us and are not in the
power of the Germans. They have played their part in the line on
more than one occasion. Their fleet is discharging a most useful and
important service for us not only in the Mediterranean but in the
Atlantic; and the loyal Italian Air Force has also fought so well that
I am making special efforts to supply them with improved aircraft of
British manufacture. We are also doing our best to assist the Italian
Government to grapple with the difficult financial and economic
conditions which they inherited from Fascism and the war, and which,
though improving, are still severe behind the lines of the Army. It
is understood throughout Italy, and it is the firm intention of the
United Nations, that Italy, like all other countries which are now
associated with us, shall have a fair and free opportunity, as soon as
the Germans are driven out and tranquillity is restored, of deciding on
whatever form of democratic Government, whether monarchical or
republican, they desire. They can choose freely for themselves. I

emphasize, however, the word " democratic," because it is quite clea
that we should not allow any form of Fascism to be restored or set up
in any country with which we have been at war.

From Italy one turns naturally to Spain, once the most famous
Empire in the world, and down to this day a strong community in a
wide land, with a marked personality and a culture distinguished among
the nations of Europe. Some people think that our foreign policy
towards Spain is best expressed by drawing comical or even rude
caricatures of General Franco ; but I think there is more to it than that
When our present Ambassador to Spain, the right hon. Gentleman
the Member for Chelsea (Sir S. Hoare), went to Madrid almost exactly
four years ago to a month, we arranged to keep his airplane waiting
on the airfield, as it seemed almost certain that Spain, whose dominant
party were under the influence of Germany because Germany had
helped them so vigorously in the recently-ended civil war, would
follow the example of Italy and join the victorious Germans in the war
against Great Britain. Indeed, at that time the Germans proposed to
the Spanish Government that triumphal marches of German troops
should be held in the principal Spanish cities, and I have no doubt that
they suggested to them that the Germans would undertake, in return
for the virtual occupation of their country, the seizure of Gibraltar
which would then be handed back to a Germanized Spain. This last
would have been easier said than done.

There is no doubt that if Spain had yielded to German blandish
ments and pressure at that juncture our burden would have been
much heavier. The Straits of Gibraltar would have been closed, and
all access to Malta would have been cut off from the West. All th
Spanish coast would have become the nesting-place of German U-boats
I certainly did not feel at the time that I should like to see any of those
things happen, and none of them did happen. Our Ambassador
deserves credit for the influence he rapidly acquired and which con
tinually grew. In this work he was assisted by a gifted man, Mr
Yencken, whose sudden death by airplane accident is a loss which
am sure has been noted by the House. But the main credit is un
doubtedly due to the Spanish resolve to keep out of the war. They ha
had enough of war, and they wished to keep out of it. [An Hon
Member : " That is a matter of opinion."] Yes, I think so, and tha
is why my main principle of beating the enemy as soon as possibl
should be steadily followed. But they had had enough, and I thin
some of the sentiment may have been due to the fact that, lookin
back, the Spanish people, who are a people who do look back, coul
remember that Britain had helped Spain to free herself from th
Napoleonic tyranny of 130 years ago. At any rate the critical momen
passed ; the Battle of Britain was won ; the Island power which wa

expected to be ruined and subjugated in a few months was seen that very winter not only intact and far stronger in the homeland, but also advancing by giant strides, under Wavell's guidance, along the African shore, taking perhaps a quarter of a million Italian prisoners on the way.

But another very serious crisis occurred in our relations with Spain before the operation designated "Torch," that is to say the descent of the United States and British forces upon North-West Africa, was begun. At that moment Spain's power to injure us was at its very highest. For a long time we had been steadily extending our airfield at Gibraltar and building it out into the sea, and for a month before zero hour, November 7th, 1942, we had sometimes 600 airplanes crowded on this airfield in full range and in full view of the Spanish batteries. It was very difficult for the Spaniards to believe that these airplanes were intended to reinforce Malta, and I can assure the House that the passage of those critical days was very anxious indeed. However, the Spaniards continued absolutely friendly and tranquil. They asked no questions, they caused no inconveniences.

If, in some directions, they have taken an indulgent view of German U-boats in distress, or continued active exportations to Germany, they made amends on this occasion, in my view, so far as our advantage was concerned, for these irregularities, by completely ignoring the situation at Gibraltar, where, apart from aircraft, enormous numbers of ships were anchored far outside the neutral waters, inside the Bay of Algeciras, always under the command of Spanish shore guns. We should have suffered the greatest inconvenience if we had been ordered to move those ships. Indeed, I do not know how the vast convoys could have been marshalled and assembled. I must say that I shall always consider a service was rendered at this time by Spain, not only to the United Kingdom and to the British Empire and Commonwealth, but to the cause of the United Nations. I have, therefore, no sympathy with those who think it clever, and even funny, to insult and abuse the Government of Spain whenever occasion serves.

I have had the responsibility of guiding the Government while we have passed through mortal perils, and I therefore think I have some means of forming a correct judgment about the values of events at critical moments as they occur. I am very glad now that, after prolonged negotiations, a still better arrangement has been made with Spain, which deals in a satisfactory manner with the Italian ships that have taken refuge in Spanish harbours, and has led to the hauling-down of the German flag in Tangier and the breaking of the shield over the Consulate, and which will, in a few days, be followed by the complete departure of the German representatives from Tangier, although they apparently still remain in Dublin. Finally, it has led to the agreement about Spanish wolfram, which has been reached without any affront to Spanish dignity, and has reduced the export of wolfram from Spain to Germany during the coming critical period to a few lorry-loads a month.

It is true that this agreement has been helped by the continuous victories of the Allies in many parts of the world, and especially in North Africa and Italy, and also by the immense threat by which the Germans conceive themselves to be menaced, by all this talk of an invasion across the Channel. This, for what it is worth, has made it quite impossible for Hitler to consider reprisals on Spain. All his troops have had to be moved away from the frontier, and he has no inclination to face bitter guerrilla warfare, because he has got quite enough to satisfy him in so many other countries which he is holding down by brute force.

As I am here to-day speaking kindly words about Spain, let me add that I hope she will be a strong influence for the peace of the Mediterranean after the war. Internal political problems in Spain are a matter for the Spaniards themselves. It is not for us—that is the Government—to meddle in such affairs——

A member interrupted to ask why, if the Government would not allow a Fascist Government in Italy, they would allow one in Spain ? The Prime Minister continued :

The reason is that Italy attacked us. We were at war with Italy. We struck Italy down. A very clear line of distinction can be drawn between nations who go to war with us, and nations who leave us alone.

I presume we do not include in our programme of world renovation forcible action against any and every Government whose internal form of administration does not come up to our own ideas, and any remarks I have made on that subject referred only to enemy Powers and their satellites who will have been struck down by force of arms. They are the ones who have ventured into the open, and they are the ones whom we shall not allow to become, again, the expression of those peculiar doctrines associated with Fascism and Nazism which have, undoubtedly, brought about the terrible struggle in which we are engaged. Surely, anyone can see the difference between the one and the other. There is all the difference in the world between a man who knocks you down and a man who leaves you alone. You may, conceivably, take an active interest in what happens to the former in case his inclination should recur, but we pass many people in the ordinary daily round of life about whose internal affairs and private quarrels we do not feel ourselves called upon to make continual inquiry.

Well, I say we speak the same words to the Spaniards in the hour of our strength as we did in the hour of our weakness. I look forward to increasingly good relations with Spain, and to an extremely fertile trade between Spain and this country which will, I trust, grow even during the war and will expand after the peace. The iron from Bilbao and the North of Spain is of great value to this country both in war and peace. Our Ambassador now goes back to Spain for further important duties, and I have no doubt he goes with the good wishes of the large majority of the House and of all thoughtful and unprejudiced persons. I am sure that no one more than my hon. Friend opposite [Mr. Shinwell] would wish that he should be successful in any work for the common cause. My hon. Friend has been often a vigilant and severe critic of His Majesty's Government, but as a real Opposition figure he has failed, because he never can conceal his satisfaction when we win—and we sometimes do.

I am happy to announce a hopeful turn in Greek affairs. When I spoke last on this I described them as the saddest case of all. We have passed through a crisis of a serious character since then. A Greek brigade and a large proportion of the Greek Navy mutinied, declaring themselves, in one way or other, on the side of the organization called E.A.M., the Greek freedom movement, and, of course, against the King and his Government. The King of Greece, who was in London, was advised by nearly everyone concerned in Cairo not to go back, and warned that his life would be in danger. He returned the next day. The situation was then most serious. The Greek brigade was encircled by British forces some 30 miles away from Alexandria, and the Greek ships which had mutinied in Alexandria harbour were lying under the guns both of the shore batteries and of our superior naval forces, which had rapidly gathered. This tension lasted for nearly three weeks. In due course the mutinies in the Fleet were suppressed. The disorderly ships were boarded by Greeks, under the orders of the Greek Government, and, with about 50 killed and wounded, the mutineers were collected and sent ashore. The mutinous brigade in the desert was assaulted by superior British forces, which captured the eminences commanding the camp, and the 4,000 men there surrendered. There were no casualties among the Greeks, but one British officer was killed in the attack upon the eminences. This is a matter which cannot be overlooked. The greatest patience and tact were shown by the British military and naval authorities involved, and for some weeks past order has been firmly established, and the Greek forces who were misled into evil deeds by subversive movements have been interned for the time being.

The then Prime Minister, M. Tsouderos, had already tried, before these things happened, to arrange a meeting of representatives of all Greek opinion, and to construct his administration so as to include them. He acquitted himself with dignity, and was helped by M. Venizelos, the son of the great Venizelos whom we all esteemed so highly in the first world war. At this moment there emerged upon the scene M. Papandreou, a man greatly respected, who had lived throughout the war in Athens and was known as a man of remarkable character and one who would not be swayed by party interests, his own party being a very small one. M. Papandreou became the King's new Prime Minister, but before forming his Government he called a conference which met last week in the Lebanon. Every party in Greek life was represented there, including E.A.M., the Communists and others—a dozen parties or more. The fullest debate took place and all expressed their feelings freely.

This disclosed an appalling situation in Greece. The excesses of E.L.A.S., which is the military body operating under E.A.M., had so alienated the population in many parts that the Germans had been able to form security battalions of Greeks to fight the E.A.M. These security battalions were made up of men of whom many would far rather have been out in the hills maintaining the guerrilla warfare. They had been completely alienated. At the same time, the state of hostility and suspicion which led last autumn to an actual civil war existed between E.A.M. and the other resistance organizations, especially the E.D.E.S. under Colonel Zervas, a leader who commands the undivided support of the civilian population in his area and has always shown the strictest compliance with the orders sent him from G.H.Q., Middle East, under whom all his forces have been placed. Thus it seemed to be a question of all against all, and no one but the Germans rejoicing.

After prolonged discussion complete unity was reached at the Lebanon Conference, and all parties will be represented in the new Government, which will devote itself to what is after all the only purpose worthy of consideration, namely the formation of a national army in which all the guerrilla bands will be incorporated, and the driving, with this army, of the enemy from the country or, better still, destroying him where he stands.

On Monday there was published in the newspapers the very agreeable letter which I received from the leaders of the Communists—that is more than I have ever received from the hon. Member for West Fife (Mr. Gallacher) ; perhaps he might write me one, to tell me that he confirms it—and the extreme Left wing party. There is published to-day in the papers the letter I have received from M. Papandreou, and another to my right hon. Friend expressing the hopes which he has for the future of his Government, and thanks for the assistance we have given in getting round these troubles—what I call the diseases of defeat, which Greece has now a chance of shaking off. I believe that the present situation—I hope and pray that it may be so—indicates that a new and fair start will come to Greece in her struggle to cleanse her native soil from the foreign invader. I have, therefore, to report to the House that a very marked and beneficial change has occurred in the situation in Greece, which is more than I could say when I last spoke upon this subject. There was trouble with the destroyer we were giving the Greeks here, and while matters remained so uncertain, we were not able to hand her over, but I have been in correspondence with the Admiralty, and I hope that as a result of this reconstructed Government, and the new start that has been made, this ship will soon be manned and go to strengthen the Greek Navy as it returns to discipline and duty.

I gave some lengthy account last time of the position in Yugoslavia and of our relations with the different jurisdictions there. The difficulty and magnitude of this business are very great, and it must be remembered that not only three strongly-marked races—the Serbs, Croats and Slovenes—are involved, but farther south, the Albanians are also making a bold bid for freedom from German rule. But they, too, at the present time are split into several competing and even antagonistic groups. Nothing is easier than to espouse any one of the various causes in these different countries, with all their claims and counter-claims, and one can find complete satisfaction in telling the tale from that particular standpoint. The best and easiest kind of speech to make is to take a particular cause and run it home on a single-track line without any consideration of anything else ; but we have to think of policy as well as oratory, and we have to consider the problem as a whole, and also to relate our action to the main purpose which I proclaimed at the beginning of my speech, namely, beating the enemy as soon as possible, and gathering all forces for that purpose in priority to any other.

I can only tell the Committee to-day the further positions which have been reached in Yugoslavia as the result of the unremitting exertions of our foreign policy. They are, in my opinion, far more satisfactory than they were. I have received a message from King Peter that he has accepted the resignation of Mr. Puric and his Cabinet, and is in process of forming a new and smaller Cabinet with the purpose of assisting active resistance in Yugoslavia and of uniting as far as possible all fighting elements in the country. I understand that this process of forming the new Government involves the severance from the Royal Yugoslav Government of General Mihailovitch in his capacity as Minister of War. I understand also that the Ban of Croatia is an important factor in the new political arrangements, around whom, or beside whom, certain other elements may group themselves for the purpose of beating the enemy and uniting Yugoslavia. This, of course, has the support of His Majesty's Government. We do not know what will happen in the Serbian part of Yugoslavia.

The reason why we have ceased to supply Mihailovitch with arms and support is a simple one. He has not been fighting the enemy, and moreover, some of his subordinates have made accommodations with the enemy from which have arisen armed conflicts with the forces of Marshal Tito, accompanied by many charges and counter-charges, and the loss of patriot lives to the German advantage. Mihailovitch certainly holds a powerful position locally as Commander-in-Chief, and his ceasing to be Minister of War will not rob him of his local influence. We cannot predict what he will do or what will happen. We have proclaimed ourselves the strong supporters of Marshal Tito because of his heroic and massive struggle against the German armies. We are sending, and planning to send, the largest possible supplies of weapons to him and to make the closest contacts with him. I had the advantage on Monday of a long conversation with General Velebit, who has been over here on a military mission from Marshal Tito, and it has been arranged among other things that the Marshal shall send here a personal military representative in order that we may be kept in the closest touch with all that is being done and with the effects of it in Yugoslavia. This is, of course, additional to the contacts established with Marshal Tito at General Wilson's headquarters in Algiers, and will, of course, be co-ordinated therewith.

It must be remembered, however, that this question does not turn on Mihailovitch alone ; there is also a very large body, amounting to perhaps 200,000, of Serbian peasant proprietors who are anti-German but strongly Serbian, and who naturally hold the views of a peasant-owner community in regard to property, and are less enthusiastic in regard to communism than some of those in Croatia or Slovenia. Marshal Tito has largely sunk his communist aspect in his character as a Yugoslav patriot leader. He repeatedly proclaims that he has no intention of reversing the property and social systems which prevail in Serbia, but these facts are not accepted yet by the other side. The Serbians are a race with an historic past ; it was from Serbia came the spark which fired the explosion of the first world war : we remember their historic retreat over the mountains. Our object is that all forces in Yugoslavia, and the whole united strength of Serbia, may be made to work together under the military direction of Marshal Tito for a united independent Yugoslavia which will expel from their native soil the Hitlerite murderers and invaders, and destroy them until not one remains. The cruelties and atrocities of the Germans in Greece and in Yugoslavia exceed anything that we have heard, and we have heard terrible things, but the resistance of these heroic mountaineers has been one of the most splendid features of the war. It will long be honoured in history, and I am sure that children will read the romance of this struggle and will have imprinted on their minds that love of freedom, that readiness to give away life and comfort, in order to gain the right to live unmolested on their native heath, which their fathers are showing now.

All I can say is that we must be given a little reasonable latitude to work together for this union. It would be quite easy, as I said just now, to take wholeheartedly one side or the other. I have made it very plain where my sympathies lie, but nothing would give greater pleasure to the Germans than to see all these hearty mountaineers engaged in intestine strife against one another. We cannot afford at this crisis to neglect anything which may obstruct a real unity throughout wide regions in which at present upwards of 12 German divisions are gripped in Yugoslavia alone and 20 in all—that is another eight in the Balkans and the Aegean Islands. All eyes must be turned upon the common foe. Perhaps we have had some success in this direction in Greece. At any rate it sums up our policy towards Yugoslavia, and the House will note that all questions of monarchy or republic or Leftism or Rightism are strictly subordinated to the main purpose which we have in mind. In one place we support a king, in another a Communist—there is no attempt by us to enforce particular ideologies. We only want to beat the enemy, and then, in a happy and serene peace, let the best expression be given to the will of the people in every way.

For a long time past the Foreign Secretary and I have laboured with all our strength to try to bring about a resumption of relations between the Soviet Government and the Polish Government which we have always recognized since the days of General Sikorski. We were conscious of the difficulty of our task, and some may say we should have been wiser not to attempt it. Well, we cannot accept that view. We are the Ally of both countries. We went to war because Germany made an unprovoked attack upon our Ally, Poland. We have signed a 20-year treaty with our Ally, the Soviet Union, and this Treaty is the foundation of our policy. Polish forces are fighting with our armies and have recently distinguished themselves remarkably well. Polish forces under Russian guidance are also fighting with the Soviet army against the common enemy.

Our effort to bring about a renewal of relations between the Polish Government in London and Russia has not succeeded. We deeply regret that fact, and we must take care to say nothing that would make agreement more difficult in the future. I must repeat that the essential part of any arrangement is regulation of the Polish eastern frontier, and that, in return for any withdrawal made by Poland in that quarter, she should receive other territories at the expense of Germany, which will give her an ample seaboard and a good, adequate and reasonable homeland in which the Polish nation may safely dwell. Nothing can surpass the bravery of our Polish Allies in Italy and elsewhere daily on the sea and in the air, and in the heroic resistance of the underground movement to the Germans. I have seen here men who came a few days ago out of Poland, who told me about it, and who are in relation with, and under the orders of, the present Polish Government in London. They are most anxious that this underground movement should not clash with the advancing Russian Army, but should help it, and orders have been sent by the Polish Government in London that the underground movement should help the Russian Armies in as many ways as possible. There are many ways in which guerrillas can be successful, and we must trust that statesmanship will yet find some way through.

I have the impression—and it is no more than an impression—that things are not so bad as they may appear on the surface between Russia and Poland. I need not say that we—and I think I may certainly add, the United States—would welcome any arrangement between Russia and Poland, however it were brought about, whether directly between the Powers concerned, or with the help of His Majesty's Government, or any other Government. There is no question of pride on our part, only of sincere good will to both, and earnest and anxious aspirations towards a solution of problems fraught with grave consequences to Europe and the harmony of the Grand Alliance. In the meantime our relations, both with the Polish and the Soviet Governments, remain regulated by the public statements which have been made and repeated from time to time from this bench during the present war. There I leave this question, and I trust that if it is dealt with in Debate those who deal with it will always consider what we want, namely, the united action of all Poles with all Russians against all Germans.

We have to rejoice at the brilliant and skilful fighting of the French Moroccan and Algerian Divisions, and the brilliant leading they have had from their officers in the heart-shaking battle to which I have referred, and which is now at its climax. The French Committee of National Liberation in Algiers has the credit of having prepared these troops, which were armed and equipped by the United States under President Roosevelt's personal decision. The French Committee also places at the full service of the Allies a powerful Navy including, in the *Richelieu*, one of the finest battleships in the world. They guide and govern a vast Empire, all of whose strategic points are freely placed at the disposal of the United Nations. They have a numerous and powerful underground army in France, sometimes called the Maquis, and sometimes the French Army of the Interior, which may be called upon to play an important part before the end of the war.

There is no doubt that this political entity, the French Committee of National Liberation, presides over, and directs, forces at the present time which, in the struggle against Hitler in Europe, give it the fourth place in the Grand Alliance. The reason why the United States and Great Britain have not been able to recognize it yet as the Government of France, or even as the Provisional Government of France, is because we are not sure that it represents the French nation in the same way as the Governments of Britain, the United States and Soviet Russia represent the whole body of their people. The Committee will, of course, exercise leadership in establishing law and order in the liberated areas of France under the supervision, while the military exigency lasts, of the supreme Allied Commander; but we do not wish to commit ourselves at this stage to imposing the Government of the French Committee upon all of France which might fall under our control, without more knowledge than we now possess of the situation in the interior of the country. At the same time I must make it clear that we shall have no dealings with the Vichy Government, or any one tainted with that association, because they have decided to follow the path of collaboration with our enemies. Many of them have definitely desired, and worked for, a German victory.

In Norway and the Low Countries it is different. If we go there we shall find that the continuity of lawful government is maintained by the Governments which we recognize, and with which we are in intimate relations. The Governments of King Haakon and Queen Wilhelmina are the lawfully-founded Governments of those States, with perfect and unbroken continuity, and should our liberating Armies enter those countries we feel we should deal with them and also, as far as possible, with the Belgian and Danish Governments, although their Sovereigns are prisoners, but with whose countries we have the closest ties. On the other hand, we are not able to take a decision at this time to treat the French Committee of National Liberation, or the French Provisional Government, as it has been called, as the full, final, and lawful embodiment of the French Republic. It may be that the Committee itself may be able to aid us in the solution of these riddles, and I must say that I think their decree governing their future action constitutes a most forceful and helpful step in that direction. With the full approval of the President of the United States, I have invited General de Gaulle to pay us a visit over here in the near future, and my right hon. Friend the Foreign Secretary has just shown me a telegram from Mr. Duff Cooper in Algiers, saying that he will be very glad to come. There is nothing like talking things over, and seeing where we can get to. I hope he will bring some members of his Government with him so that the whole matter can be reviewed.

As this war has progressed, it has become less ideological in its character, in my opinion. The Fascist power in Italy has been over-thrown and will, in a reasonable period of time, be completely expunged, mainly by the Italian democracy themselves. If there is anything left over for the future we will look after it. Profound changes have taken place in Soviet Russia. The Trotskyite form of Communism has been completely wiped out. The victories of the Russian Armies have been attended by a great rise in the strength of the Russian State, and a remarkable broadening of its views. The religious side of Russian life has had a wonderful rebirth. The discipline and military etiquette of the Russian Armies are unsurpassed. There is a new National Anthem, the music of which Marshal Stalin sent me, which I asked the B.B.C. to play on the frequent occasions when there are great Russian victories to celebrate. The terms offered by Russia to Rumania make no suggestion of altering the standards of society in that country, and are in many respects, if not in all, remarkably generous. Russia has been very patient with Finland. The Comintern has been abolished, which is sometimes forgotten. Quite recently, some of our represen-tatives from the Ministry of Information were allowed to make a considerable tour in Russia, and found opportunities of seeing for themselves whatever they liked. They found an atmosphere of candid friendliness and a keen desire to see British films, and hear about our country and what it was doing in the war. The children in the schools were being informed about the war on the seas, and of its difficulties and its perils, and how the Northern convoys got through to Russia. There seemed a great desire among the people that Britain and Russia should be friends. These are very marked departures from the con-ceptions which were held some years ago, for reasons which we can all understand.

We have no need to look back into the past and add up the tale and tally of recrimination. Many terrible things have happened. But we began thirty years ago to march forward with the Russians in the battle against the German tyranny of the Kaiser, and we are now marching with them, and I trust we shall until all forms of German tyranny have been extirpated. As to Nazism, the other ideology, we intend to wipe that out utterly, however drastic may be the methods required. We are all agreed on that in this House, whatever our political views and doctrines may be. Throughout the whole of the British Dominions and the United States, and all the United Nations, there is only one opinion about that ; and for the rest, whatever may be said as to former differences, there is nothing that has occurred which should in any way make us regret the twenty years' Treaty which we have signed with the Russians, and which will be the dominating factor in the relations which we shall have with them.

I see that in some quarters I am expected to-day to lay out, quite plainly and decisively, the future plan of world organization, and also to set the Atlantic Charter in its exact and true relation to subsequent declarations and current events. It is easier to ask such questions than to answer them. We are working with 33 United Nations and, in particular, with two great Allies who, in some forms of power, far excel the British Empire. Taking everything into consideration including men and money, war effort, and expanse of territory, we can claim to be an equal to those great Powers, but not, in my view, a superior. It would be a great mistake for me, as head of the British Government, or, I may add, for this House, to take it upon ourselves to lay down the law to all those different countries, including the two great Powers with which we have to work, if the world is to be brought back into a good condition.

This small Island and this marvellous structure of States and dependencies which have gathered round it will, if we all hold together, occupy a worthy place in the vanguard of the nations. It is idle to suppose that we are the only people who are to prescribe what all other countries, for their own good, are to do. Many other ideas and forces come into play, and nothing could be more unwise than for the meeting of Prime Ministers, for instance, to attempt to prescribe for all countries the way they should go. Consultations are always proceeding between the three great Powers and others, and every effort is being made to explore the future, to resolve difficulties, and to obtain the greatest measure of common agreement on levels below the Ministerial level in a way which does not commit the Government.

A few things have already become quite clear and very prominent at the Conference which has just concluded. The first is that we shall all fight on together until Germany is forced to capitulate and until Nazism is extirpated and the Nazi party are stripped of all continuing power of doing evil. The next is that the Atlantic Charter remains a guiding signpost, expressing a vast body of opinion amongst all the Powers now fighting together against tyranny. The third point is that the Atlantic Charter in no way binds us about the future of Germany, nor is it a bargain or contract with our enemies. It has no quality of an offer to our enemy. It was no invitation to the Germans to surrender. If it had been an offer, that offer was rejected. But the principle of unconditional surrender, which has also been promulgated, will be adhered to so far as Nazi Germany and Japan are concerned, and that principle itself wipes away the danger of anything like Mr. Wilson's Fourteen Points being brought up by the Germans after their defeat, claiming that they surrendered in consideration of them.

I have repeatedly said that unconditional surrender gives the enemy no rights but relieves us from no duties. Justice will have to be done, and retribution will fall upon the wicked and the cruel. The miscreants who set out to subjugate first Europe and then the world must be punished, and so must their agents who, in so many countries, have perpetrated horrible crimes, and who must be brought back to face the judgment of the population, very likely in the very scenes of their atrocities. There is no question of Germany enjoying any guarantee that she will not undergo territorial changes, if it should seem that the making of such changes renders more secure and more lasting the peace of Europe.

Scarred and armed with experience, we intend to take better measures this time than could ever previously have been conceived in order to prevent a renewal, in the lifetime of our children or our grandchildren at least, of the horrible destruction of human values which has marked the last and the present world wars. We intend to set up a world order and organization, equipped with all the necessary attributes of power, in order to prevent the breaking-out of future wars, or the long planning of them in advance by restless and ambitious nations. For this purpose there must be a World Council, a controlling council, comprising the greatest States which emerge victorious from this war, who will be under obligation to keep in being a certain minimum standard of armaments for the purpose of preserving peace. There must also be a World Assembly of all Powers, whose relation to the World Executive, or controlling power, for the purpose of maintaining peace I am in no position to define. I cannot say what it will be. If I did, I should only be stepping outside the bounds which are proper for us.

The shape of these bodies, and their relations to each other, can only be settled after the formidable foes we are now facing have been beaten down and reduced to complete submission. It would be presumption for any one Power to prescribe in detail exactly what solution will be found. Anyone can see how many different alternatives there are. A mere attempt on our part to do so, or to put forward what is a majority view on this or that, might prejudice us in gaining consideration for our arguments when the time comes.

I shall not even attempt to parade the many questions of difficulty which will arise and which are present in our minds. Anyone can write down on paper at least a dozen large questions of this kind—should there be united forces of nations, or should there be a world police, and so on. There are other matters of a highly interesting character which should be discussed. But it would be stepping out of our place in the forward march for us to go beyond the gradual formulation of opinions and ideas which is constantly going on inside the British Commonwealth and in contact with our principal Allies. It must not be supposed, however, that these questions cannot be answered and the difficulties cannot be overcome, or that a complete victory will not be a powerful aid to the solution of all problems, and

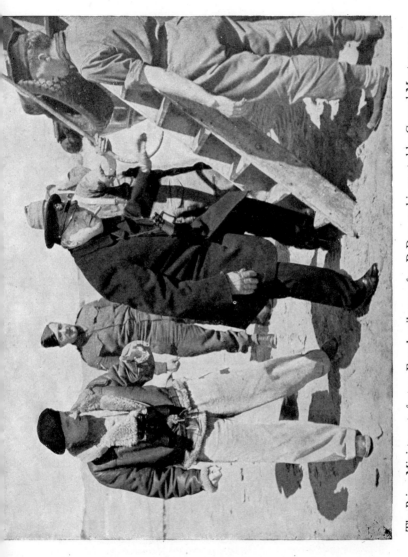

The Prime Minister sets foot on French soil soon after D-Day, and is greeted by General Montgomery

Armistice Day in Liberated Paris

that the good will and practical common sense which exist in the majority of men and in the majority of nations will not find its full expression in the new structure which must regulate the affairs of every people in so far as they may clash with another people's. The future towards which we are marching, across bloody fields and frightful manifestations of destruction, must surely be based upon the broad and simple virtues and upon the nobility of mankind. It must be based upon a reign of law which upholds the principles of justice and fair play, and protects the weak against the strong if the weak have justice on their side. There must be an end to predatory exploitation and nationalistic ambitions.

This does not mean that nations should not be entitled to rejoice in their traditions and achievements, but they will not be allowed, by armed force, to gratify appetites of aggrandisement at the expense of other countries merely because they are smaller or weaker or less well prepared, and measures will be taken to have ample Armies, Fleets and Air Forces available to prevent anything like that coming about. We must undoubtedly in our world structure embody a great part of all that was gained to the world by the structure and formation of the League of Nations. But we must arm our world organization and make sure that, within the limits assigned to it, it has over-whelming military power. We must remember that we shall be hard put to it to gain our living, to repair the devastation that has been wrought, and to bring back that wider and more comfortable life which is so deeply desired. We must strive to preserve the reasonable rights and liberties of the individual. We must respect the rights and opinions of others, while holding firmly to our own faith and con-victions.

There must be room in this new great structure of the world for the happiness and prosperity of all, and in the end it must be capable of bringing happiness and prosperity even to the guilty and vanquished nations. There must be room within the great world organization for organisms like the British Empire and Commonwealth, as we now call it, and I trust that there will be room also for the fraternal asso-ciation of the British Commonwealth and the United States. We are bound as well by our twenty-year Treaty with Russia, and besides this—I, for my part, hope to deserve to be called a good European—we have the duty of trying to raise the glorious Continent of Europe, the parent of so many powerful States, from its present miserable condition as a volcano of strife and tumult to its old glory as a family of nations and a vital expression of Christendom. I am sure these great entities which I have mentioned—the British Empire, the conception of a Europe truly united, the fraternal association with the United States—will in no way disturb the general purposes of the world organization. In fact, they may help powerfully to make i run. I hope and pray that all this may be established, and that we may have the strength and the will to secure those permanent and splendid achievements which alone can make amends to mankind fo. all the miseries and toil which have been their doom, and for all the heroism and sacrifice which have been their glory.

THE INVASION OF FRANCE

STATEMENTS TO THE HOUSE OF COMMONS ON THE LIBERATION OF
ROME AND THE INVASION OF FRANCE
JUNE 6 AND 8, 1944

May 25. After advancing 60 miles in 14 days the Fifth Army in Italy linked up with the Anzio forces.

May 26. Another great day of successes for the Fifth and Eighth Armies. Berlin admitted that Kesselring had been forced to retire at all the main points of attack.

May 27. Thousands of bombers and fighters from Britain and Italy struck at Germany and Occupied Europe throughout the day and night.

May 29. The Germans organized resistance South of Rome, but their counter-attacks were repulsed.

More than 2,000 U.S. aircraft attacked factories in Poland and Belgium.

May 30. The battle for Rome began, and Allied troops made substantial progress.

June 1. The Eighth Army captured Frosinone, the New Zealanders took Sora, and the Americans in the Fifth Army almost surrounded Velletri, key point on the Appian Way.

June 2. It was announced that during May U.S. Air Forces in Europe had dropped 63,000 tons of bombs and the R.A.F. 37,000 tons.

June 3. British and U.S. Air Forces increased their terrific pounding of military targets in Northern France.

June 4. The Fifth Army entered Rome.

The Allied air offensive against Northern France was continued.

June 5. The King of Italy signed a decree transferring his powers to his son the Prince of Piedmont.

JUNE 6. D-DAY.

Allied Navies and Air Forces, operating in tremendous strength, put the first waves of the Invasion Army on French beaches.

Massed landings of airborne troops were made behind the enemy's lines.

Allied forces penetrated several miles inland and there was heavy fighting in Caen.

Mr. Churchill announced that operations were proceeding well and that the sea passage was made with far less loss than had been expected.

June 7.   *Bayeux, 15 miles north-west of Caen, was captured.   Th*
           beachheads were cleared and some of the landing partie
           linked up.   An enemy tank attack near Caen was repulsed.
June 8.   *Fierce fighting along the whole Normandy front.   Beachhea*
           forces were steadily built up and further air-borne landing
           were made.

[*June 6, 1944.*

THE House should, I think, take formal cognisance of the liberatio⟩
of Rome by the Allied Armies under the Command of Genera
Alexander, with General Clark of the United States Service and Genera
Oliver Leese in command of the Fifth and Eighth Armies respectively
This is a memorable and glorious event, which rewards the intens
fighting of the last five months in Italy.   The original landing, made o⟩
January 22nd at Anzio, has, in the end, borne good fruit.   In the firs
place, Hitler was induced to send to the south of Rome eight or nin
divisions which he may well have need of elsewhere.   Secondly, thes
divisions were repulsed, and their teeth broken, by the successfu
resistance of the Anzio bridgehead forces in the important battle whic⟩
took place in the middle of February.   The losses on both sides wer
heavy—the Allies losing about 20,000 men, and the Germans abou
25,000 men.   Thereafter, the Anzio bridgehead was considered by th
enemy to be impregnable.

Meanwhile, the great regrouping of the main Army had to take plac
before the attacks could be renewed.   These attacks were at firs
unsuccessful, and Cassino still blocked the advance.   On May 11th
General Alexander began his present operation, and after unceasing an
intense fighting by the whole of the Armies, broke into the enemy⟩
lines and entered the Liri Valley.   It is noteworthy that, countin⟩
from right to left, the whole of the Polish, British Empire, French, an⟨
United States Forces broke the German lines in front of them b⟩
frontal attack.   That has an important bearing on other matter⟨
which I shall come to before I sit down.

At what was judged the right moment the bridgehead Force, whic⟩
by this time had reached a total of nearly 150,000 men, fell upon th⟩
retiring enemy's flank and threatened his retreat.   The junction ⟨
the main Armies with the bridgehead forces drove the enemy off hi⟩
principal lines of retreat to the North, forcing a great part of his arm⟩
to retire in considerable disorder with heavy losses, especially i⟩
material, through mountainous country.   The Allied Forces, wit⟩
great rapidity, were regrouped, with special emphasis on their lef
flank, which soon deployed against Rome after cutting the importan⟨

ighway. The American and other Forces of the Fifth Army broke through the enemy's last line and entered Rome, where the Allied troops have been received with joy by the population. This entry and liberation of Rome mean that we shall have the power to defend it from hostile air attack, and to deliver it from the famine with which it was threatened. However, General Alexander's prime object has never been the liberation of Rome, great as are the moral, political and psychological advantages of that episode. The Allied Forces, with the Americans in the van, are driving ahead, northwards, in relentless pursuit of the enemy. The destruction of the enemy army has been, throughout, the single aim, and they are now being engaged at the same time along the whole length of the line as they attempt to escape to the North. It is hoped that the 20,000 prisoners already taken will be followed by further captures in future, and that the condition of the enemy's army, which he has crowded into Southern Italy, will be decisively affected.

It would be futile to attempt to estimate our final gains at the present time. It is our duty, however, to pay the warmest tribute of gratitude and admiration to General Alexander for the skill with which he has handled this Army of so many different States and nations, and for the tenacity and fortitude with which he has sustained the long periods when success was denied. In General Clark the United States Army has found a fighting leader of the highest order, and the qualities of all Allied troops have shone in noble and unjealous rivalry. The great strength of the Air Forces at our disposal, as well as the preponderance in armour, has undoubtedly contributed in a notable and distinctive manner to the successes which have been achieved. We must await further developments in the Italian theatre before it is possible to estimate the magnitude and quality of our gains, great and timely though they certainly are.

I have also to announce to the House that during the night and the early hours of this morning the first of the series of landings in force upon the European Continent has taken place. In this case the liberating assault fell upon the coast of France. An immense armada of upwards of 4,000 ships, together with several thousand smaller craft, crossed the Channel. Massed air-borne landings have been successfully effected behind the enemy lines, and landings on the beaches are proceeding at various points at the present time. The fire of the shore batteries has been largely quelled. The obstacles that were constructed in the sea have not proved so difficult as was apprehended. The Anglo-American Allies are sustained by about 11,000 first-line aircraft, which can be drawn upon as may be needed for the purposes of the battle. I cannot, of course, commit myself to any particular details. Reports are coming-in in rapid succession.

So far the Commanders who are engaged report that everything is proceeding according to plan. And what a plan ! This vast operation is undoubtedly the most complicated and difficult that has ever taken place. It involves tides, wind, waves, visibility, both from the air and the sea standpoint, and the combined employment of land, air and sea forces in the highest degree of intimacy and in contact with conditions which could not and cannot be fully foreseen.

There are already hopes that actual tactical surprise has been attained, and we hope to furnish the enemy with a succession of surprises during the course of the fighting. The battle that has now begun will grow constantly in scale and in intensity for many weeks to come, and I shall not attempt to speculate upon its course. This I may say, however. Complete unity prevails throughout the Allied Armies. There is a brotherhood in arms between us and our friends of the United States. There is complete confidence in the supreme commander, General Eisenhower, and his lieutenants, and also in the commander of the Expeditionary Force, General Montgomery. The ardour and spirit of the troops, as I saw myself, embarking in these last few days was splendid to witness. Nothing that equipment, science or forethought could do has been neglected, and the whole process of opening this great new front will be pursued with the utmost resolution both by the commanders and by the United States and British Governments whom they serve.

Later in the day the Prime Minister made a further statement as follows :

I have been at the centres where the latest information is received, and I can state to the House that this operation is proceeding in a thoroughly satisfactory manner. Many dangers and difficulties which at this time last night appeared extremely formidable are behind us. The passage of the sea has been made with far less loss than we apprehended. The resistance of the batteries has been greatly weakened by the bombing of the Air Force, and the superior bombardment of our ships quickly reduced their fire to dimensions which did not affect the problem. The landings of the troops on a broad front, both British and American—Allied troops, I will not give lists of all the different nationalities they represent—but the landings along the whole front have been effective, and our troops have penetrated, in some cases, several miles inland. Lodgments exist on a broad front.

The outstanding feature has been the landings of the airborne troops, which were on a scale far larger than anything that has been seen so far in the world. These landings took place with extremely little loss and with great accuracy. Particular anxiety attached to them, because the conditions of light prevailing in the very limited period of the dawn—just before the dawn—the conditions of visibility made all the difference. Indeed, there might have been something happening at the last minute which would have prevented air-borne troops from playing their part. A very great degree of risk had to be taken in respect of the weather.

But General Eisenhower's courage is equal to all the necessary decisions that have to be taken in these extremely difficult and un-controllable matters. The air-borne troops are well established, and the landings and the follow-ups are all proceeding with much less loss —very much less—than we expected. Fighting is in progress at various points. We have captured various bridges which were of importance, and which were not blown up. There is even fighting proceeding in the town of Caen, inland. But all this, although a very valuable first step—a vital and essential first step—gives no indication of what may be the course of the battle in the next days and weeks, because the enemy will now probably endeavour to concentrate on this area, and in that event heavy fighting will soon begin and will continue without end, as we can push troops in and he can bring other troops up. It is, therefore, a most serious time that we enter upon. Thank God, we enter upon it with our great Allies all in good heart and all in good friendship.

On June 8 the Prime Minister made the following brief reference to the fighting in France :

I do not propose to make any statement about the battle to-day, and shall not do so unless something exceptional turns up. As a matter of fact, I think that all the points which have occurred to me are very fully met in the excellent reports furnished by our able and upright Press. But I would say this, that if this is the last time I speak to the House before the week-end I earnestly hope that when Members go to their constituencies they will not only maintain morale, so far as that is necessary, but also give strong warnings against over-optimism, against the idea that these things are going to be settled with a run, and that they will remember that although great dangers lie behind us, enormous exertions lie before us.

GENERAL DE GAULLE

A STATEMENT TO THE HOUSE OF COMMONS IN REPLY TO A SERIES
OF QUESTIONS REGARDING GENERAL DE GAULLE AND BRITAIN'S
RELATIONS WITH FRANCE
JUNE 14, 1944

June 9.   *British and Canadian forces linked up in the Caen sector and gained ground after heavy fighting. U.S. troops captured Ste. Mère Eglise.*

June 10.   *It was announced that Spitfires were fighting from bases in France.*

         The enemy rout in Italy continued and Allied Command officially stated : " A catastrophe has befallen Kesselring's forces."

June 11.   *The front in Normandy was 51 miles wide and 15 miles deep. British tanks thrust south-east of Bayeux, while the Americans took Lison.*

         Marshal Stalin announced an offensive in the Karelian Isthmus which had broken through the Finnish defences and advanced 15 miles on a 25-mile front.

June 12.   *Mr. Churchill visited Normandy. The Germans lost Carentan, keypoint of the Cherbourg Peninsula. All Allied advances continued.*

         Flying bombs were used by the enemy in attacks on London and Southern England.

June 13.   *British troops in France made a powerful armoured drive to outflank Caen and the three enemy armoured divisions fighting there.*

June 14.   *Germans counter-attacked strongly east of Caen, and west of the town a British armoured thrust reached Caumont and Villers-Bocage.*

         General de Gaulle visited Normandy.

[*June* 14, 1944.

THERE are seven Questions on the Order Paper on this subject, to which I can make only one answer. I do not consider that this matter can be dealt with satisfactorily by a number of separate answers at Question Time. On the other hand, I must advise the House most seriously that a Debate on this matter would have very great dangers. One tale is good till another is told. His Majesty's Government take great trouble over their conduct of business, and on the whole it may be said that it has been conducted with success. When you look at the advance in Italy and the extraordinary achievement of the cross-Channel landing in France, a fair-minded man would consider that the Administration had a right to the confidence of the House when they said they did not wish a particular subject discussed. This is not because we are not prepared to discuss it in all detail, and if need be in all severity ; but the result of such a discussion might well be to emphasize any differences which exist with the French Committee of National Liberation, headed by General de Gaulle. I should be sorry to see these issues prematurely forced to a decision, and I therefore ask from the House a measure of leniency and forbearance in their treatment of this matter.

If, however, there is a desire on the part of a large number of Members to bring these matters to a head, then the rights of the House must clearly be met, and a suitable occasion for a debate will be found. I should advise strongly against this now. In addition to our relations with the French Committee of National Liberation, headed by General de Gaulle, we have also to consider our very close relations with the United States and their relations with the body I have just mentioned. I think it would be better to allow the relations prevailing between General de Gaulle and the United States to proceed further before we have a formidable debate on these questions, which might well be of comfort to the enemy. I, therefore, appeal to the House not to disregard my counsel.

Answering further questions, the Prime Minister continued :

In this last week of great success, I should think as large a proportion of our time was given to the discussions about General de Gaulle and his affairs and his Committee as to any other subject. I can assure the House that it is not that these matters are not engaging the attention of His Majesty's Government. They are, very much indeed. But I am reluctant to bring them to a head at present, and I hope that a better solution will be achieved than would be the case if there had to be a quite definite threshing-out of the matter in the House of Commons. With regard to the financial point, it is rather technical. The President made a statement last night, which is published, I believe, in this morning's papers, but I have not had a chance of reading that statement. I could not commit myself to anything about finance—a statement about which might well be made by the Chancellor of the Exchequer—until we know what it is that the President has said on the subject. It seems to me, however, quite clear that if notes are given out to the French population in return for livestock and other services, the responsibility for meeting them, in the first instance at any rate, would lie with the Governments issuing them.

As for the general question of whether there is entire agreement throughout the country and in the House on all the ways in which the different foreign policies, as affecting all the various countries, have been handled, I can assure the House that I have never aimed at so high an ideal, and, when I think of some of the persons who would have to be converted, I am very glad that I never set my aim so high.

I do not think it would be a good thing to have a Debate in the House now. I am certain it would do more harm than good, and might lead to things being said which afterwards were found to have very serious repercussions, because, if attacks are made, answers will be given, whenever required. Therefore, I still adhere to my request to the House, and my advice to the House—it can only be advice ; I am entirely in their hands—that they will not raise this matter at this time. But I assure the House that it is my earnest desire to give them the fullest account of all these matters, when that can be done without prejudice to such hopes as remain in respect to such matters in the future.

Replying to a member who said there was great anxiety in the House, in the country and in the Press concerning the matter, the Prime Minister said :

I do not at all agree that there is great and widespread anxiety. It certainly deserves careful and unremitting attention, but I think that if there is great and widespread anxiety in this matter, it will be, and should be, properly directed to our gallant soldiers who are striking down the enemy in France and advancing continually, and to the great operations which are in progress, and which give hope as well as anxiety. It seems to me very lacking in proportion for hon. Members to press us, and I am earnestly hoping that we shall not be pressed at this time. If I had no hopes of a better solution than I could announce at the present time, I would not ask for the delay.

As to the question of peace in Europe after the war, we have a long way to go before we can be sure what is going to jeopardize peace. We have also some way to go before we can say what is going to be done to stop peace being jeopardized.

RIGHTS OF SMALL NATIONS

A Speech at a Luncheon given in honour of the Prime Minister
by the Mexican Ambassador
June 15, 1944

[June 15, 1944.

I MUST express my sincere gratitude for the extremely kind terms in which His Excellency the Ambassador has proposed this toast to me, and for the evident lack of repugnance with which you have supported it.

It is a great moment in the history of the world, and it may be that events will occur in the next few months which will show us whether we are soon to be relieved of the curse which has been laid upon us by the Germans. Whether it be this year or next, the British and American peoples will never falter or withdraw their hands from the task which they have undertaken. Together with our other Allies we shall go on to the end, and the end will be the more terrible for our foes the longer their struggle continues and the longer this war is protracted.

It is a very important thing that there should be gathered around this table, thanks to His Excellency, representatives of that famous Conference in Rio de Janeiro in January, 1942, where Latin America associated itself with the United States in their stand against the Axis. I am glad to see here the Ambassadors of the United States and Brazil, whose countries played leading rôles at the Conference. Your Excellency's Foreign Minister was also there, and the general opinion is that the Conference was swayed by the speech of Senor Ezequiel Padilla, Foreign Minister of Mexico, who carried away the honours by his statements.

Time has passed, and after the initial attack launched by an enemy, after a long scheme of rearmament and of aggressive plans with well-prepared armies, and the natural suffering at the outset, we have moved on from that to a band of brother States all over the globe, all gathered against this enemy and showing that peaceful peoples, if they have time, can, with their industries and their heart, produce all the weapons and equipment of war necessary for this fight. Here we are now, free peoples who have shown to the world that they can put into the field men well trained and equipped with all the necessary weapons of war.

It gives great pleasure to me and to my colleagues to be here at

III

your table to-day to express in a definite form the great regard which the peoples of the British islands, the British Empire, and the British Commonwealth of Nations—the very warm regard we feel towards Mexico, and I drink with the greatest pleasure the toast to your esteemed and honoured President. I have never been to Mexico —I hope I shall be able to do so in the span of life left to me—but all I have seen and heard about her attracts me as one of the most beautiful parts of the world, with all her old traditions of history, and with a climate where one has much more sunshine than your Excellency is likely to experience during your stay here.

I am afraid that our friends in the Diplomatic Corps have suffered very much inconvenience from the ban which we thought it necessary to impose. We thought it was absolutely necessary, so that we could say afterwards that nothing had been left undone to keep the secret of military preparations, and therefore we had to put you to this inconvenience. But we know that you share our interest to a very high degree that this secret should be kept. There is no doubt that secrets can be kept. The secret of the landing in North Africa was kept, although several thousands were aware of it. Many more have been aware of this one. In both cases tactical surprise of the enemy was achieved, and he had no idea until he saw the ships coming out of the mists of the morning, when he was going to be hit, how he was going to be hit, or where he was going to be hit. This great struggle in which the lives of a million men may be engaged now on both sides requires extraordinary precautions.

Of course, we have not embarked on this great adventure without being in full accord with our Russian Allies and the decisions taken in Teheran, and, although the execution of the plans adopted there is far from being complete, it is being steadily unrolled, and the months of this summer may, by the victories of this Allied campaign, bring full success to the cause of freedom.

Your Excellency, it is a great pleasure for us to come here and to express to your country, Mexico, warm regard and respect. We are prevented by the exigencies of the war from carrying on trade and offering to your country many of those products which we supplied previously, but immediately after the war is over we hope to resume and increase the trade between this country and Mexico.

We know no fear; we stand together; we have our American brothers fighting side by side with us, as if we were one country and not only Allies, each respecting and helping the other. Even during this war, in the strife in Normandy, far away in the jungles of Burma, in Italy, and in the Pacific Ocean, an effort is being made to achieve a permanent co-operation and to build up an organization which after this war will strengthen the bands between all our nations and will succeed in preserving peace—an organization which will not exclude innocent and fruitful arrangements between individual nations, nor the relations within the American continent, nor the relations of the British Commonwealth, nor the internal relations of Europe. We look forward to a future in which the rights of small nations will be upheld and protected, and in which the strong will use their power under the law for the defence of the weak.

BRITISH CASUALTIES IN ITALY

A Statement in the House of Commons
June 27, 1944

June 15.   *Tokio was bombed by American "Super-Fortresses," flying 1,000 miles from China.*

    The Germans increased their flying-bomb attacks on Southern England, but Mr. Herbert Morrison, the Home Secretary, stated that the damage done was relatively small.

June 16.   *The King visited the battle areas in Normandy.*

    Flying-bomb attacks on Southern England were increased.

June 17.   *A strong force of bombers and fighters attacked the flying-bomb installations across the Channel.*

June 18.   *American troops cut the Cherbourg Peninsula, isolating large forces of Germans.*

    In Italy the Allies reached the outskirts of Perugia.

    In Russia the Red Army broke through the Mannerheim Line, third line of the Finnish defences.

June 19.   *It was disclosed that the flying-bombs were jet-propelled and carried an explosive charge equivalent to a one-ton bomb.*

    American troops reached to within eight miles of Cherbourg.

    French forces occupied Elba.

June 20.   *Americans reached the outskirts of Cherbourg.*

    Allied forces captured Perugia on the central sector of the Italian front.

    The Red Army stormed Viborg, seaport key to Finland.

June 21.   *More than 1,000 American bombers attacked targets in Berlin and flew on to land in Russia.*

    A record number of Allied aircraft flew over the Straits of Dover and attacked the flying-bomb bases.

June 22.   *One of the heaviest air attacks of the war was made on the flying-bomb bases in the Pas de Calais.*

    It was announced that a great blow had been struck at the Japanese Navy, fourteen enemy ships, including a large aircraft carrier, being sunk or damaged by American carrier-borne aircraft.

June 23.   *The Russians launched a great new offensive against Vitebsk on the central front.*

June 24.   *British naval forces smashed a German attempt to escape from Cherbourg by sea, as the city's defences were crumbling.*

June 25. *The Germans admitted the fall of Cherbourg.*

It was announced that during an attack on a convoy in the Arctic Circle three U-boats and six enemy aircraft were destroyed.

June 26. *British Forces advanced in the Caen sector*

Marshal Stalin announced the capture of Vitebsk.

June 27. *On the German Commander's formal surrender, the whole of Cherbourg was occupied by the Americans.*

Four Russian armies swept across White Russia to envelop Minsk.

[*June 27,* 1944.

ON February 16th I informed the House that up to February 12th the following casualties had been sustained by the British Armies in Italy, including Dominion and Indian troops :

Killed	..	..	..	..	..	.. 7,635
Wounded	..	..	..	..	..	.. 23,283
Missing	..	..	..	..	..	.. 5,708
Total	..	..	..	...	..	.. 36,626

Between that date, and the entry into Rome these Forces sustained the following further casualties :

Killed	..	..	..	..	..	.. 6,696
Wounded	..	..	..	..	..	.. 24,683
Missing	..	..	..	..	..	.. 5,117
Total	..	..	..	..	..	.. 36,496

Our total casualties, therefore, from our landing in Italy to the fall of Rome amount I grieve to say to :

Killed	..	..	..	..	..	.. 14,331
Wounded	..	..	..	..	..	.. 47,966
Missing	..	..	..	..	..	.. 10,825
Total	..	..	..	..	..	.. 73,122

I should explain these figures are for Army casualties only, Navy and Air Force losses being excluded, because this is the basis on which the earlier figures were given in February, it having been found impossible to give a figure for the other two Services exclusively relating to operations in Italy, as distinct from the other operations of the Navy in the Mediterranean and of the Air Force over the Mediterranean, Germany, Central and Eastern Europe and the Balkans.

ANSWERS IN THE HOUSE OF COMMONS

PARLIAMENTARY PROCEDURE

Asked if he would set up a Committee to consider any changes that may be necessary in Parliamentary procedure, the Prime Minister said on April 4:

NO, Sir. Not at the present time. The rules are the result of very long experience. They are extremely difficult and it takes a very long time to learn them. If they are kept continually in a fluid state, through the advice of a Committee, I think it would add to the difficulties of Members in finding their way about our procedure. On the whole, I look with a critical eye upon the setting up of a Committee of this kind, but I am quite ready to follow the wishes of the House, after a free debate has taken place. It must be remembered that the function of Parliament is not only to pass good laws, but to stop bad laws.

GATHERING WISDOM

Asked if he had seen a certain " informative article " in *The Times*, the Prime Minister said on April 6:

I always endeavour to assimilate information from the public Press and to gather wisdom wherever I can.

Asked whether he always considered *The Times* a well-informed newspaper, Mr. Churchill replied:

It is far from my duty to give out bouquets or the reverse to the newspapers.

BRITISH AND GERMAN TANKS

Asked by Mr. Stokes, M.P. for Ipswich, to arrange for members to inspect a German Mark VI Tiger tank and a British A.22 tank in view of the interest in the comparative merits of these machines, the Prime Minister said on April 18:

Sir, after this year's campaign has reached a suitable phase, it might be possible to parade not only the two tanks mentioned, but all the tanks to be used in the forthcoming battles and specimens of those we shall capture from the enemy.

Mr. Stokes then asked whether the reason for refusal was that if the request were granted members would realize the untruthfulness of statements that have been made as to the relative merits of the two tanks. Mr. Churchill replied:

Since the word " untruthfulness " has been used, no one has been a greater contributor than the hon. Member.

CIVIL AVIATION

Asked to make a statement about the Anglo-American discussions on civil air transport after the war, the Prime Minister said on April 18 :

The conversations referred to were informal and exploratory. They had for their primary purpose an exchange of views on the desirability of holding an international Conference and on the form of co-operation which each country would advocate on such an occasion. I am glad to say that sufficient agreement was reached for both countries to support the holding of a Conference in the expectation that final dispositions could then be achieved. Concessions were made by both the United Kingdom and the United States of America, but they related only to the basis on which discussions will be launched at an International Conference. It would not be appropriate or useful for me to make any detailed statement in advance of the Conference, which both His Majesty's Government and the Government of the United States hope will be held this year.

I do not think we are in a position to advocate a particular policy at this particular moment. We must give our negotiators a chance, and it is better for us to see what other countries will put forward before we unfold it all. Yet, on the other hand, I can also imagine that it might be an occasion for the House to debate the matter in a general way without pinning our delegates down to any exact particulars.

We are keeping the Russian Government fully informed on this matter, and not only on this matter but on a very wide range of subjects.

UNITED NATIONS' POLICIES

Asked what consultations had taken place between Britain and America regarding an international organization for the maintenance of peace, referred to in Mr. Cordell Hull's broadcast on April 9, the Prime Minister said on April 18 :

Preliminary exchanges of information on post-war questions are constantly taking place between various members of the 34 United Nations, but I cannot hold out expectations that any agreed statement upon the subject will be made in the near future. It is a topic which will not suffer at all from thought or well-considered discussion.

Asked whether there were plans which would conflict with the League of Nations Covenant, Mr. Churchill said :

I think that a great many people agree that Mr. Hull's speech was most helpful in that direction. There is undoubtedly a common building-up of thought between Britain and the United States, and we have every intention of keeping other nations informed. I have to be careful to mention that, because these are all matters for discussion, and will be decided only at the end of the war. I referred to this matter myself rather more than a year ago, and gave some indication that, so far as the British view is concerned, the great body of work achieved by the League of Nations and embodied in the League of Nations ought not to be lost.

I think that if the League of Nations had been properly backed up things might have been different.

NAVAL BASES

Questioned regarding a report that the naval sub-committee of the U.S. House of Representatives had recommended that bases in the Western Hemisphere leased by Britain to America should pass permanently into the possession of the United States the Prime Minister said on April 26:

I am aware that there has been a Press report to this effect. The House may rest assured that there have been no developments calling for a review by the Government or the House of the existing position in this matter, which remains unchanged.

There is not the slightest question of any cession of British territory —not the slightest.

DISORDERS IN GREEK FORCES

Asked to make a statement regarding disorders among Greek forces in the Middle East, the Prime Minister said on April 26:

The disorders which recently broke out in the Greek Army and Navy have now been almost completely cleared up. It is for the Greek Government to decide what measures shall be taken against those who were responsible for these deplorable incidents in their Forces. It must be remembered that a British officer was killed.

In the hope of putting an end to political disunity the King of Greece has already declared his intention of forming a Government as representative as possible, made up of all trends of patriotic opinion, with the exclusion only of those who have collaborated with the enemy against their fellow countrymen acting in the common cause. His Majesty's Government are in full agreement with this policy, and will give the King of Greece and his Government all possible support in its execution.

We shall certainly try to get representatives in that Government of those who are really fighting the enemy. Some of them seem to be more busy fighting their own countrymen. With regard to the future of Greece, it has been repeatedly stated that we shall not interfere with the decision of the Greek people, once normal conditions have been more or less restored.

GREEK NAVAL UNREST

Asked why British forces were used to disarm Greek ships in a British port after 95 per cent. of their officers and men had signed a memorandum urging the creation of a National Greek Government of Resistance, the Prime Minister said on May 9 :

I presume the hon. Member is referring to the recent removal of a number of Greek seamen from one of H.M. destroyers in a United Kingdom port. This ship had seen active service in the Royal Navy, but after being refitted was to have been transferred to the Royal Hellenic Navy. In view, however, of recent disturbances in the Mediterranean, and of unrest among the officers and men detailed to take over the ship, the Admiralty were unable to allow her to be commissioned with a Greek crew. The Greek parties on board were accordingly withdrawn, and it is quite incorrect to speak of a Greek ship having been disarmed in a British port. It was with regret that the Admiralty decided to withhold this ship from the Greek Navy. It is out of the question, however, for so valuable a ship to be commissioned, particularly at this critical juncture, with a crew whose trustworthiness cannot be assured.

When a member suggested that the seamen could be fully trusted to defend Greece but objected to defending the Greek King, Mr. Churchill replied :

I think that is a very improper and reckless question, when there is so much difficulty in different parts of the world, and we are all doing our best to concentrate our forces on the common enemy.

NEWFOUNDLAND

When a member drew attention to the importance of Newfoundland as an air terminus and asked the Prime Minister to " see that the rights and interests of the whole Empire are safeguarded," Mr. Churchill said on May 10 :

That seems to be a proposition to which I could certainly give support.

A member then asked the correct pronunciation of " Newfoundland " and Mr. Churchill replied :

I was always brought up to call it New*found*land, but I am not absolutely sure that *New*foundland is not more correct.

ON SALUTING

Asked if he would consider an order that would make it not a breach of discipline not to salute when off duty, the Prime Minister replied on May 16:

No, Sir. A salute is an acknowledgment of the King's Commission and a courtesy to Allied officers, and I do not consider it desirable to attempt to make the distinction suggested.

If my hon. friend had an opportunity during the war of visiting Moscow he would find the smartest saluting in the world. The importance attached to these minor acts of ceremony builds up armies which are capable of facing the greatest rigours of war.

COMMONWEALTH

When a member asked the Prime Minister to discourage the application of the term " Commonwealth " to the British Empire, as the word denoted an interregnum in British history during which the country was under the dictatorship of a regicide, which was denounced by Scotland and finally rejected by all Britain, the Prime Minister said in reply, on May 25:

The term " British Commonwealth of Nations " has been generally accepted since the date of the Report of the Imperial Conference of 1926, associated with the name of Lord Balfour, as describing the relations of the self-governing parts of the British Empire. History takes very varying views both of the conduct of Oliver Cromwell and of Scotland during the tumultuous period referred to by the hon. and gallant Member. Even the name " Commonwealth " is used in varying connections at the present time. I doubt very much whether any advantageous guidance on the subject can be obtained either from ancient or modern examples.

REPARATIONS

When a member reminded the Prime Minister of the harm done to British ship-building, engineering and other industries through the reparations exacted from Germany after the last war and asked that after the present war there might be no reparations that would cause unemployment in Britain, the Prime Minister said on June 8:

That is most fully in our minds. I am sure that the mistakes of that time will not be repeated ; we shall probably make another set of mistakes.

GERMAN INVASION

Asked to state "as a matter of historical interest" whether the Germans ever set in motion the apparatus of a sea-borne invasion of Britain in 1940, the Prime Minister said on June 20:

I do not know what my hon. and gallant Friend means by "set in motion." "Set in motion" in the sense of crossing the Channel, no; "set in motion" in the sense of making very heavy concentrations, both of troops and ships, to cross the Channel, yes.

Asked whether any of the enemy shipping emerged from ports across the Channel, Mr. Churchill replied:

Not to my belief. A great deal of it was smashed in the ports, and then they changed their minds.

WORLD PEACE PLANS

Asked whether it was intended that all the Allies should consider a world plan for post-war peace and whether such a plan would be laid before Parliament before being adopted, the Prime Minister said on June 27:

It is our hope that the arrangements to be made for the maintenance of international peace and security after the war will be the subject of consultation at the appropriate time between all the United Nations. The reply to the second part of the Question is "Yes."

Asked to see that the British Parliament would not be under a disadvantage in discussing these problems by reason of what was happening in Washington, Mr. Churchill answered:

Certainly, Sir. I do not see why the British Parliament should be under any disadvantage compared with any other legislature.

THE FUTURE OF GREECE

A message to M. Papandreou, the Prime Minister of Greece. May 1, 1944.

I AM very glad you have shown the firmness of character required to act as Prime Minister of Greece during this period when her light among the nations has been dimmed. His Majesty's Government will give you all support in your supreme task and duty of directing all Greek forces against the common foe, who may, at any time, begin to reel or retreat. We have made our position as the Ally of Greece, and one of her oldest friends, abundantly clear. The Nazi tyrant must be destroyed or expelled from the country.

After this has been done and reasonable tranquillity restored, at the earliest moment the Greek nation, free from foreign interference of all kinds, will choose the form of democratic government under which they wish to live, whether it be a monarchy or a republic. The King is the servant of his people. I am sure he has no wish to force himself upon the Greek nation. Having begun the war against Italy in a victorious manner, he is now bound in honour to fight it through to the end against the Germans. No one has a constitutional right to stand between him and this duty.

We are responsible during the war for maintaining good relations with the Egyptian sovereign Power whom we have protected against all German and Italian assaults. In the advent of solemn events in the military field, we cannot allow sporadic disorders to break out among the Greek forces in Egypt, who have been constitutionally placed under the Supreme Allied Commander in the Mediterranean. We shall not hesitate to take any measures necessary for the performance of our duty. It is the Greek nation, not small bodies of soldiers, sailors and politicians resting under our shield, who will decide the future. A free, independent, prosperous and happy Greece would be dear to the British heart. We judge every Greek of every class and party according as they help to rescue the soil of Greece from the Hitlerite foe.

You have set yourself to face the perils and the toils of leading as Prime Minister a renewed attack by Greece on Germany whereby those ancient glories which were revived so recently as 1941 shall not cease to shine. In this task you will have our persevering and powerful support. Your watchwords should be "The union of all against the common foe," "The cleansing of the land from foreign butchers," "Free choice by the Greeks themselves of the government under which they wish to live."

DEATH OF COLONEL KNOX

A message to President Roosevelt on the death of Colonel Knox, Secretary of the U.S. Navy. May 1, 1944.

I have learned with great sorrow of the sudden death of Colonel Knox. If you will allow me to say so, His Majesty's Government and especially the Admiralty feel his loss acutely, for no one could have been more forthcoming and helpful in all our difficult times than was this distinguished American statesman and war administrator. The War Cabinet have desired me to express their sympathy with you in losing so invaluable a colleague, to which I add my own expressions of sincere sorrow.

AN AIR TRANSPORT RECORD

A message to Commodore Gerald d'Erlanger, Commanding Officer of Air Transport Auxiliary, the civilian organization responsible for ferrying new aircraft from factories to R.A.F. stations. May 28, 1944.

I am much impressed by the achievement of the Organization under your command in making more than 200,000 aircraft ferryings on behalf of the Royal Navy and the Royal Air Force during the past four years ; this is indeed a wonderful record.

That this formidable task should have been performed with so low an accident-record redounds greatly to the credit of both your pilots and ground staff. It was not to be expected that operations of this magnitude could have been undertaken without incurring casualties, and I note with regret and sympathy that 113 pilots have lost their lives in the course of their ferrying duties.

The time may come when many of your pilots will be delivering aircraft to the R.A.F. bases that are to be established on the Continent, and I am confident that this important task, which is being entrusted to the Organization under your command, will be carried out with the same efficiency and devotion to duty as has been shown by the personnel of the Air Transport Auxiliary since its inception.

Please convey to all my thanks for, and appreciation of, their past services, and my best wishes in the task that lies before them.

A TRIBUTE TO WEST POINT

A letter to Major General F. B. Wilby, Superintendent of the United States Military Academy, West Point, for the Corps of Cadets. May 29, 1944.

I well remember in the winter of 1895, now quite a long time ago, being shown over the whole Academy at West Point by high authorities, and being enormously impressed with the efficiency of the teaching and the smartness of the cadets. As I had not long before come from Sandhurst, I considered myself an expert upon these points. I was particularly struck by the rule that all West Pointers must always show a crease down the hollow of their back. I do not know whether you have kept this up. Anyhow I am very glad it was not thought of by the British War Office during the time I was at Sandhurst. Certainly it seems to have had very fine results on your side of the Atlantic.

I send best wishes to you and to all at a moment when the grand feats and brotherhood in arms of our Armies are clearing so much evil and tyranny from the world.

TO DR. BENES

A message to the President of Czechoslovakia on his sixtieth birthday. May 29, 1944.

The anniversary of your sixtieth birthday falls at a momentous crisis in human affairs. I am glad to think that at such a moment the Czechoslovak people, united and resolute under your leadership, despite their long, terrible suffering, are ready to play their part with us in close collaboration with our Allies in the West and in the East in compassing a final overthrow of the German tyranny. I am happy to convey to your Excellency on behalf of his Majesty's Government, as well as in my own name, the warmest congratulations on this auspicious occasion, which will, I trust, herald your return to a liberated Prague at no very distant date.

LOYAL NEW ZEALAND

A telegram to Mr. Fraser, Prime Minister of New Zealand, in reply to a message of congratulation on the successful launching of the invasion of Western Europe. June 11, 1944.

I was deeply touched by the telegram which you so kindly sent me on behalf of yourself and the Government and people of New Zealand. Throughout this long struggle New Zealand has never failed us, and her steadfastness and loyalty have helped to sustain us all during the darkest days. Now that victory over all our enemies is with God's help assured, I am confident that the ties which bind us so closely will grow even stronger, and that our unity of purpose will ensure a just and permanent peace.

UNITED NATIONS DAY

A message issued by the Prime Minister on June 14:

On June 14th we honour the cause of the United Nations. This is the cause of good men throughout the world. It is the cause which inspires the energies and claims the loyalties of the greatest Alliance that history has ever assembled to do battle against the powers of evil. As we draw towards the final victory for which we long, it is fitting that we should emphasize the unity which alone can make it possible. Divided, we can await nothing but confusion and ruin ; united, we have brighter hopes than have ever cheered mankind.

INSPIRATION OF GENERAL SIKORSKI

A message read at a meeting in London to commemorate the first anniversary of the death of the Polish Prime Minister and Commander-in-Chief. July 5, 1944.

General Sikorski's name will long be remembered in history. His faith sustained Poland's spirit in her darkest hour. His courage inspired the Polish people to continue their long and relentless struggle against the German invader. His statesmanship had always in view Allied unity in common action against Germany, and the restoration of Poland's independence and greatness. So long as his memory is cherished the accomplishment of the great work for which he gave his life will be assured.

THE FLYING BOMB

June 28.   *In Normandy the Germans' crack Panzer forces were engaged in the greatest tank battle of the invasion.*

    The Russians forced the Dnieper river on a front of 70 miles.

June 29.   *The Germans appeared to be facing disaster in White Russia. The Red Army captured Bobruisk and the enemy retreated in disorder from Minsk.*

June 30.   *Many flying-bombs launched against Southern England were brought down by fighter-planes and other defensive measures.*

    British troops established a salient and bridgehead across the River Odon and repulsed strong enemy attacks.

July 1.   *New assault on Caen began with a great tank battle.*

July 2.   *Russians cut railway line from Minsk to Vilna and advanced over the 1939 Polish border.*

July 3.   *Red Army captured Minsk, capital of White Russia.*

    American troops launched a new offensive southwards from the Cherbourg Peninsula.

    French troops in Italy captured Siena.

July 4.   *Russians captured Polotsk, key railway junction in the Germans' Baltic defences.*

July 5.   *Canadians smashed heavy German counter-attacks against their newly-won positions in Carpiquet village. The Americans fought their way into La Haye.*

July 6.   *Field-Marshal von Rundstedt, Germany's supreme commander in Western Europe, was replaced by Field-Marshal von Kluge.*

    Mr. Churchill revealed that 2,754 flying-bombs had been launched against Britain and that 2,752 people had been killed.

[July 6, 1944.

I CONSIDER that His Majesty's Government were right in not giving out a great deal of information about the flying bombs until we knew more about them and were able to measure their effect. The newspapers have in an admirable manner helped the Government in this, and I express my thanks to them. The time has come, however, when a fuller account is required and a wider field of discussion should be opened, and in my opinion such a discussion is no longer hampered by the general interest. I would at the same time enjoin upon hon. Members and the public outside to watch their step in anything they say, because a thing which might not strike one as being harmful at all might give some information to the enemy which would be of use to him and a detriment to us. Still, a very wide field of discussion will be open henceforth.

Let me say at the outset that it would be a mistake to underrate the serious character of this particular form of attack. It has never been underrated in the secret circles of the Government. On the contrary, up to the present time the views which we formed of the force and extent of the danger were considerably in excess of what has actually happened. The probability of such an attack has, among other things, been under continuous intense study and examination for a long time. During the early months of 1943 we received, through our many and varied Intelligence sources, vague reports that the Germans were developing a new long-range weapon with which they proposed to bombard London. At first our information led us to believe that a rocket weapon would be used. Just over a year ago the Chiefs of Staff proposed to me that the Joint Parliamentary Secretary to the Minister of Supply, my hon. Friend the Member for Norwood (Mr. Sandys), should be charged with the duty of studying all the intelligence as it came in and reporting what truth, if any, there was in these reports and advising the Chiefs of State and the War Cabinet as to counter-measures. Long before this time my right hon. Friend the Home Secretary, whose vigilance has been unceasing, had begun to strengthen the street shelters generally, and he now intensified this work so that these shelters are by no means ill adapted to withstand the blast effects of the bombs at present being used.

The House will realize that the enemy took all possible precautions to conceal his designs from us. Nevertheless, as the result of searching investigations by agents and by reconnaissance, we had by July, 1943, succeeded in locating at Peenemunde, on the Baltic, the main experimental station both for the flying bomb and the long-range rocket. In August last the full strength of Bomber Command was sent out to attack those installations. The raids were costly, on account of the great distances into Germany which had to be flown, but very great damage was done to the enemy and his affairs, and a number of key German scientists, including the head scientist, who were all dwelling together in a so-called Strength-Through-Joy establishment, were killed. This raid delayed by many months the development and bringing into action of both these weapons.

About this time we had also located at Watten, in the Pas de Calais, the first of the large structures which appeared to be connected with the firing of a long-range rocket. This site was very heavily attacked as long ago as September, and has been under continual treatment since by the heaviest weapons borne by the British and American Air Forces. We also carried out a most thorough air reconnaissance of the whole of North-West France and Belgium. This was an immense task, and not without its cost, but in the result we discovered in October last that in addition to the large structures of the Watten type other structures, in greater numbers, were being erected all along the French coast between Havre and Calais. I meditated at that time whether I should make a statement to the House in Secret Session on the subject, but on the whole, everything being in such a hypothetical condition, I thought that might cause needless alarm, and that we had better proceed step by step till we had greater assurances as to what we could say.

The reconnaissance which we carried out was an immense task, but it yielded very important information. Eventually we found that about 100 of these rather smaller sites all along the French coast between Havre and Calais were being erected, and we concluded that they would be the firing-points for a jet-propelled projectile much smaller than the rocket to which our thoughts had first been turned. All these hundred firing-points were continuously bombed since last December, and every one of them was destroyed by the Royal Air Force, with the wholehearted assistance of the growing United States air power. If it had not been for our bombing operations in France and Germany, the counter-preparations in which we indulged, the bombardment of London would no doubt have started perhaps six months earlier and on a very much heavier scale. Under the pressure of our counter-measures, the enemy, who felt, among other impulses, the need of having something to boast about and carrying on a war of nerves in order to steady the neutrals and satellites and assuage his own public opinion, developed a new series of prefabricated structures which could be rapidly assembled and well camouflaged, especially during periods of cloudy weather. It is from those comparatively light and very rapidly erected structures that the present attack is being made.

What is the scale of this attack? The hundred firing-sites which were destroyed, assuming that the enemy's production of the missiles was adequate, could have delivered a vastly greater discharge of H.E. on London per day than what we have now. I think it is only just to the British and American Air Forces to record that diminution by their untiring and relentless efforts in the scale of the attack to which we are now exposed. The new series of firing-points, like the first, have been heavily and continuously bombed for several months past. As new sites are constructed or existing ones repaired, our bombing attacks are repeated. Every effort is used to destroy the structures, and also to scatter the working parties and to deal with other matters concerned with the smooth running of this system of attack. The total weight of bombs so far dropped on flying bomb and rocket targets in France and Germany, including Peenemunde, has now reached about 50,000 tons, and the number of reconnaissance flights now totals many thousands. The scrutiny and interpretation of the tens of thousands of air photographs obtained for this purpose have alone been a stupendous task discharged by the Air Reconnaissance and Photographic Interpretation Unit of the R.A.F.

These efforts have been exacting to both sides, friend and foe. Quite a considerable proportion of our flying power has been diverted for months past from other forms of offensive activity. The Germans, for their part, have sacrificed a great deal of manufacturing strength which would have increased their fighter and bomber forces working in conjunction with their hard-pressed armies on every front. It has yet to be decided who has suffered and will suffer the most in the process. There has, in fact, been in progress for a year past an unseen battle into which great resources have been poured by both sides. This invisible battle has now flashed into the open, and we shall be able, and indeed obliged, to watch its progress at fairly close quarters.

To the blood-curdling threats which German propaganda has been making in order to keep up the spirit of their people and of their satellites, there have been added the most absurd claims about the results of the first use of the secret weapon. I minimize nothing, I assure the House, but I think it right to correct those absurdities by giving some actual facts and figures, knowledge of which, although they may not be known to the enemy, will do him very little good, in my opinion and in the opinion of my advisers. Between 100 and 150 flying bombs, each weighing about one ton, are being discharged daily, and have been so discharged for the last fortnight or so from the firing-points in France. Considering the modest weight and small penetration-power of these bombs, the damage they have done by blast effect has been extensive. It cannot at all be compared with the terrific destruction by fire and high explosives with which we have been assaulting Berlin, Hamburg, Cologne, and scores of other German cities and other war manufacturing points in Germany.

This form of attack is, no doubt, of a trying character, a worrisome character, because of its being spread out throughout the whole of the 24 hours, but people have just got to get used to that. Everyone must go about his duty and his business, whatever it may be—every man or woman—and then, when the long day is done, they should seek the safest shelter that they can find and forget their cares in well-earned sleep. We must neither underrate nor exaggerate. In all up to six a.m. to-day, about 2,750 flying bombs have been discharged from the launching-stations along the French coast. A very large proportion of these have either failed to cross the Channel or have been shot down and destroyed by various methods, including the great deployment of batteries, aircraft and balloons which has been very rapidly placed in position. Batteries move to any position in which they are required and take up their positions rapidly, but once on the site great improvements can be made in the electrical connections and so forth; and the Air Force, confronted with the somewhat novel problem of chasing a projectile, has found new methods every day.

Therefore, I say, a very large proportion of those that were discharged from the other side has been shot down and destroyed by various methods. Sometimes shooting them down means that they explode upon the ground. Therefore the places where they should be shot down are better chosen where successful hits do not necessarily mean explosions in a built-up area. I am very careful to be vague about areas. The weather, however, during the month of June has been very unfavourable to us for every purpose. In Normandy it has robbed us in great part of the use of immense superiority. These battles in Normandy are being waged without that extraordinary and overwhelming, exceptional aid of the vast Air Force we had collected for the purpose. When the weather improves a new great reinforcement will come into play. In Britain the bad weather has made more difficult the work and combination of the batteries and aircraft. It has also reduced the blows we strike at every favourable opportunity at the launching-stations or suspicious points on the other side of the Channel.

Nevertheless, the House will, I think, be favourably surprised to learn that the total number of flying bombs launched from the enemy's stations have killed almost exactly one person per bomb. That is a very remarkable fact, and it has kept pace roughly week by week. Actually the latest figures are 2,754 flying bombs launched and 2,752 fatal casualties sustained. They are the figures up to six o'clock this morning. Well, I am bound to say I was surprised when, some time ago, I perceived this wonderful figure. This number of dead will be somewhat increased by people who die of their injuries in hospital. Besides these there has been a substantially larger number of injured, and many minor injuries have been caused by splinters of glass. A special warning of this danger was issued by the Ministries of Home Security and Health, and in giving wide publicity to the recommendations for reducing this risk the newspapers have also rendered a most useful service.

As this battle—for such it is—may be a somewhat lengthy affair,

I do not propose to withhold the number of casualties. I will give the number because I believe the exaggerated rumours and claims that are made are more harmful than the disclosure of the facts. I will now give the casualties up to date, and thereafter they will be given in the usual form, at monthly intervals, by the Minister of Home Security. The total number of injured detained in hospital is about 8,000. This does not include minor injuries treated at first-aid posts and out-patients' departments of hospitals, and not needing detention at the hospital even for a single day. Of those detained in hospital a large proportion has, in fact, been discharged after a few days. Here let me say that the casualty and first-aid services of Greater London are working excellently. This machine has been well tested in the past, and it has been continually reviewed, kept up to date, and improved in the light of experience. It is not at all strained beyond its capacity and, naturally, we draw from other parts of the country which are not affected to strengthen the central machine.

So far as hospital accommodation is concerned, we prepared for so many more casualties in the Battle of Normandy than have actually occurred so far that we have, for the present, a considerable immediate emergency reserve in which to disperse patients. The injured are speedily transferred to hospitals in safer districts, and I am glad to say that penicillin, which up to now has had to be restricted to military uses, will be available for the treatment of all flying bomb casualties. Here I must say a word about our American friends and Allies in London, from the highest official to the ordinary soldier whom one meets, who have, in every way, made common cause with us and been forthcoming as helpers, wardens and assistants of every kind. No one can visit a bombed site where an explosion has recently taken place without seeing how very quickly they are, in large numbers, on the scene and running any risk to give a helping hand to anyone in distress. And the same is true of the great headquarters under General Eisenhower, where they are conducting this great battle, and where, apart from that, every conceivable assistance is given to our Forces and aid services. It will be another tie, I think, between our two peoples, when they see something of what we go through in London and take a generous part in bearing our burden. A very high proportion of these casualties I have mentioned—somewhat around 10,000—not always severe or mortal, have fallen upon London, which presents to the enemy—now I have mentioned it the phrase " Southern England " passes out of currency—a target 18 miles wide by, I believe, over 20 miles deep, and it is, therefore, the unique target of the world for the use of a weapon of such gross inaccuracy.

The flying bomb is a weapon literally and essentially indiscriminate in its nature, purpose and effect. The introduction by the Germans of such a weapon obviously raises some grave questions upon which I do not propose to trench to-day.

Slight repairs to buildings are being done as quickly as possible. As a temporary measure these are usually rough protective repairs to roofs and windows. A large force of building workers is engaged on this work. Copious reinforcements have been brought in, and are being brought in, from the provinces by the Minister of Labour, and are arriving here daily. Repairs to a very large number of houses have already been carried out, but there are areas where the blast damage is at present somewhat ahead of our growing repair forces. This will be remedied as time goes on.

As to evacuation, as I have said, everyone must remain at his post and discharge his daily duty. This House would be affronted if any suggestion were made to it that it should change its location from London. Here we began the war, and here we will see it ended. We are not, however, discouraging people who have no essential work to do from leaving London at their own expense if they feel inclined to do so by the arrangements they make. In fact, they assist our affairs by taking such action at their own expense. We do not need more people in London than are required for business purposes of peace and war. For people of small means, who are not engaged in war work and wish to leave, registers have been opened and arrangements will be made for their transfer as speedily as possible to safer areas. Children are already being sent at their parents' wish out of the danger areas, which are by no means exclusively confined to the Metropolis. There is, of course, the bomb highway over which the robots all pass before reaching that point of Southern England which I have ventured to particularize this morning. Children are being sent if their parents wish out of the danger areas, and in all cases mothers with small children, or pregnant women, will be given full facilities by the State. And we do not propose to separate the mother from the child except by her wish, but a terrible thing happened last time. Mothers were separated from children of two or three years of age, and, after a period, when they had saved up money and got time to go down and see them, the children hardly knew them. I hope now with our growing strength, reserves and facilities for removal, we shall be able to say to a mother with three or four children, " If you wish to leave, it is perfectly possible. Arrangements will be made to take you into the country with your children. If you wish them to go by themselves and you wish to stay here with your husband, or because of your job, then arrangements can be made that way too." We do not consider that the scale of attack under which we lie at present justifies Governmental compulsion in any case. In order to speed these arrangements, the Minister of War Transport, Lord Leathers, has arranged that the railways should provide a larger service of trains from the London stations.

All these matters and many others are reviewed daily, or almost daily, certainly whenever necessary, by the Civil Defence Committee over which the Minister of Home Security has so long presided. He has presided over it since those dark days when he took over the care of London, especially, which he knew so well, in the old original blitz. Upon this Committee sit either the heads or the representatives of every single Department concerned, and the War Cabinet is always available to confirm any decision which involves high policy. There is no delay. Matters are settled with very great speed, but a very great power is given to this Committee, and questions about what I may call the social side of the flying bomb, the social reactions, should be addressed either to the Minister of Home Security, who will answer them himself, or to the Minister of Health, who has a great sphere of responsibility.

A good many questions can be asked, but the House, I am sure, would wish to have a check-up on them beforehand, because a perfectly innocent and proper question might have some connection which would tell the enemy more than we need tell him. After all, the Germans keep large Intelligence services, always prying about and trying to find out everything they can, and really we ought to leave them something to do. I can see lots of questions that could well be discussed here, and if there were some particular kind of question we wanted to talk over among ourselves, such procedure is always available to the House. I am not going to attempt to parade to the House the many difficult matters that have been settled. I have mentioned a good many of them. I could give a complete list, and if I have left anything out, that is a thing that can be reserved for a future day. We can with confidence leave our civil organization to do its work under the watchful supervision of the House of Commons. We have had many periods in the war in which the Government have relied on the House of Commons to keep them in close touch with the people and the populations affected, and we have welcomed many helpful suggestions. I think that we can have great confidence in our civil organization, for it has immense experience and has handled machinery which has stood far greater strains than this.

On the operational side, a Special Committee has been set up to review, concert and advise upon all counter-measures, both offensive and defensive, to deal with the flying bomb. This Committee consists of the Joint Parliamentary Secretary to the Ministry of Supply as Chairman ; Air Marshal Hill, who is in charge of A.D.G.B. (Air Defence of Great Britain) ; General Pile, who has been our highly competent Commander-in-Chief of the Ack-Ack Command since the beginning of

the war; the Deputy Chief of the Air Staff; and a representative of
the Deputy Allied Commander, Air Marshal Tedder. This Committee
have at their disposal a great number of able scientists and engineers
who are studying from the technical standpoint the improvement of
our counter-measures. The Committee report to me personally, to the
Chiefs of Staff, and, finally, to the War Cabinet. There is an organization for getting quick decisions from all the authorities concerned.

The House will ask, What of the future? Is this attack going to
get worse, or is it going to be beat like the magnetic mine, or beat
like the attempted destruction of Britain by the aeroplane, or beat
as the U-boat campaign was beat? Will new developments, on the
other hand, of a far more formidable character, come upon us? Will
the rocket bomb come? Will improved explosives come? Will
greater ranges, faster speeds, and larger war-heads come upon us? I
can give no guarantee that any of these evils will be entirely prevented
before the time comes, as come it will, when the soil from which these
attacks are launched has been finally liberated from the enemy's grip.
In the meantime I can only say that when I visited various scenes of
bomb explosions on Saturday, only one man of many hundreds whom
I saw asked a question. The question was, "What are you going to
do about it?" I replied, "Everything in human power, and we have
never failed yet." He seemed contented with the reply. That is the
only promise I can make.

I must, however, make it perfectly plain—I do not want there to be
any misunderstanding on this point—that we shall not allow the battle
operations in Normandy or the attacks we are making against special
targets in Germany to suffer. They come first, and we must fit our
own domestic arrangements into the general scheme of war operations.
There can be no question of allowing the slightest weakening of the
battle in order to diminish in scale injuries which, though they may
inflict grievous suffering on many people and change to some extent
the normal, regular life and industry of London, will never stand
between the British nation and their duty in the van of a victorious
and avenging world. It may be a comfort to some to feel that they
are sharing in no small degree the perils of our soldiers overseas, and
that the blows which fall on them diminish those which in other forms
would have smitten our fighting men and their Allies. But I am sure
of one thing, that London will never be conquered and will never fail,
and that her renown, triumphing over every ordeal, will long shine
among men.

A member asked what facilities there would be to bring to the attention of Ministers
points affecting the lives of the people, their welfare and safety, and the Prime Minister
replied:

I would venture to make a suggestion on the spur of the moment.

That is, that the Minister of Home Security should depute someone to whom Members could refer, and, if they did not get satisfaction in that way, they could take such other measures as are open. I feel that there will be questions, small questions, but in some cases very painful questions, and I am anxious that the House should keep in close touch with the Government in this affair, which we are all in together, as in so many others. But it seems to me that it would be a good thing if my right hon. Friend deputed someone who was a member of his Committee to see Members who were anxious about this matter. I did something like this myself 25 years ago during demobilization after the last war, and it gave great satisfaction. At that time questions amounted to several hundreds a day. If there is any better way of doing it, I will talk it over with my right hon. Friend, and he will make some statement to the House.

A member raised the question of the opening of deep shelters, and the Prime Minister said :

I am afraid that I overlooked that in my speech. We always regarded these deep shelters as a reserve, and it has now been decided to make use of them. The Home Secretary is much to be congratulated in having these up his sleeve, and we must make use of them in the manner which is most effective to further our general plans, not merely as places where particular individuals can camp out indefinitely, but as part of the general movement and life of London.

Questioned about evacuation, the Prime Minister said :

The case of the old and infirm must be considered and will be considered. This is one of the first matters to which my right hon. Friend will give his attention, but I think the children are the first consideration.

When another member urged the need for a public debate, the Prime Minister replied :

That might easily do something which the hon. Gentleman would be the last to wish. Something might be said which might help the enemy. Every word is read and eagerly scanned in order to try to make up a case. A debate in public very often consists of criticism, quite naturally, because those who are satisfied remain silent. I am not sure that we need unduly stress the troubles we have to face and mean to conquer, by a public debate during which at any moment it might be necessary for the Minister to say that we ought to go into Secret Session.

It would be better to do what has been promised, that is, have a discussion without the enemy listening. I know a good deal about all this business. I have very good advisers who check, I can assure hon. Members, what I say, so that I do not inadvertently let out something detrimental ; but hon. Members have not the same opportunity. A perfectly well-meaning speech might be resented by the troops when it got around and make them say : " Well, they have said this in the House of Commons." We must be careful, and therefore I should not recommend a full public Debate.

A member said he had received many letters urging reprisals, and the Prime Minister replied :

I have said deliberately that that is a subject which raises grave considerations and upon which I do not intend to embark. That, I am sure, is the best way in which to leave it. Might I appeal to the House not to pursue unduly these interrogatories to-day ? I weighed my words very carefully, and I should like them to represent what we have to put before the House and the people.

Mr. Edgar Granville, M.P. for Eye, asked about the effect of blast on glass, whether tape should be used and whether the Prime Minister would give instructions for doors of shelters to be open. The Prime Minister replied :

Really, these are not questions for me to answer.

Mr. Granville : " They save people's lives. Apparently that does not matter to some hon. Members." The Prime Minister replied :

The hon. Gentleman has no right to suggest that other hon. Members do not care about saving people's lives, or that he has any monopoly of human charity—or any marked pre-eminence in human genius.

Asked to inform Members of the House what Government Departments were responsible for dealing with the various questions arising out of the flying bomb attacks, the Prime Minister made the following statement on July 25 :

The following statement shows the Civil Departments principally concerned and the main fields of responsibility of each Department. Any necessary co-ordination of the regional activities of the civil Departments mentioned is effected by the Regional Commissioner. Civil problems arising from flying-bomb attacks are dealt with by the Civil Defence Committee, which is a Ministerial Committee, on which all Departments concerned are represented under the Chairmanship of the Home Secretary and Minister of Home Security.

Home Office and Ministry of Home Security :
    Police.
    National Fire Service.
    Civil Defence Services (other than First Aid Posts and Ambulances).
    Fire Guards.
    Demolition and clearance.

Salvage and storage of furniture.
Provision of air raid shelters.
Glass protection.
Public warning and industrial alarm system.
Casualty statistics.

Ministry of Health :
Casualty services (First Aid Posts, ambulances and hospitals).
Evacuation of priority classes.
Rest Centres, billeting and care of the homeless.
General supervision and direction of first aid repairs by local
authorities to house property.
Restoration of sewers and water services.
Equipment and management of air raid shelters.
Health and comfort of shelterers.

Ministry of Food :
Emergency feeding arrangements.

Board of Education :
Air raid shelter in schools.
Education of evacuated children.

Ministry of Works :
Allocation of all labour engaged on various classes of first aid work,
according to requirements.
Control of use of building materials, and allocation and distribu-
tion of first aid repair materials and necessary plant.
Assisting local authorities' first aid repair of houses with the
Special Repair Service and contractors who are being brought in
from outside.

Ministry of Labour and National Service :
Supply of all classes of labour.

Board of Trade :
Claims in respect of insurable commodities under the War Risks
Insurance Act or private chattels or business equipment under
the War Damage Act.

Ministry of Fuel and Power :
Restoration of Gas and Electricity supplies.

General Post Office :
Repairs to telecommunications.

Ministry of Aircraft Production (Emergency Services Organization) :
Repairs to war production factories.

War Damage Commission (Questions should be addressed to the Chancellor of the Exchequer) :
  Claims in respect of war damage to land and buildings.

Assistance Board (Questions should be addressed to the Minister of Labour) :
  Relief of distress Schemes.

Ministry of Pensions :
  Claims for injuries, etc.

Ministry of Information :
  Press censorship.
  Communication of information to the public, otherwise than as provided by the Department concerned.

Ministry of War Transport :
  General transport services.

SERVICE PAY AND ALLOWANCES

A STATEMENT CIRCULATED BY THE PRIME MINISTER WITH THE OFFICIAL
REPORT IN REPLY TO QUESTIONS BY TWO MEMBERS WHO DREW
ATTENTION TO ANOMALIES IN SERVICE PAY AND ALLOWANCES
JULY 11, 1944

A S promised in the House, careful consideration has been given
by the Departments concerned to the various questions raised
in the course of the informal discussions which took place following
the debate of March 2nd. It has been decided to make certain further
changes in addition to the major alterations in pay, family allowances
and war pensions which were announced in the recent White Paper
(Command 6521).

Following a review of the present scheme of dependants' allowances,
the conditions which govern eligibility for an allowance, and the amount
of any allowance granted, have been modified. Hitherto no allowance
has been payable if the household income, after payment of rent and
rates, and after allowing for various " disregards," amounted to an
average of 17s. or more a week for each member of the household
(children under the age of 14 counting as half units). This rule has
now been abolished. Moreover, no allowance has hitherto been payable
which would raise the net average income for each member of the
household, including the allowance, above 21s. a week. This limit has
now been raised to 23s. a week. In addition, payment of the maximum rate of allowance of 25s. a week will no longer be confined to cases
where the dependant's household has no other income. The effect
of these changes is to increase both the field of dependants eligible
for an allowance, and the number of eligible dependants who will
qualify for the higher rates of allowance, including the maximum rate
of 25s. a week.

In addition to the improvements in War Service Grants already
announced, a relaxation has now been made in the rule (set out in
Command 6318 of 1941) under which, in addition to the qualifying
allotment, a soldier was expected to contribute to the support of his
family four-sevenths of the amount by which his pay exceeded 4s. a
day. This limit was later raised to 4s. 6d. a day, and now it has been
decided to raise it to 5s. 6d. a day. The broad effect of this change
will be that no soldier below the rank of corporal will in future be
expected, for the purposes of war service grants, to supplement his
qualifying allotment from his pay unless he is on special or trade rates.
The closer approximation of the schemes of qualifying allotment to

a common pattern has enabled this 5s. 6d. point to be taken for war service grants purposes in the case of all three Services alike.

The rates of ration allowance for women members of the Forces, when not provided with Service rations, have hitherto been at four-fifths of the corresponding men's rates, in view of the lower scale of provision in kind which experience shows to be suitable in the case of women. It has now, however, been decided that where women members of the Forces are under the necessity of buying their own meals, for instance in catering establishments, this distinction should no longer be drawn, and the women's rates of ration allowance have accordingly been brought up to the rates payable to men in corresponding circumstances. It has moreover been decided, as a war measure for meeting present conditions in this country, that where A.T.S. and W.A.A.F. officers are on the lodging list or billeted and unable to be dining members of a mess, a special supplementary board and lodging allowance of 2s. a day shall be granted. This increase in the allowances available for their board and lodging takes account of the considerations that while their expenses on board and lodging are much the same as those of men officers, the pay of women officers is lower than that of men officers, that their normal contribution from their pay to their expenses when in mess is generally less, and that they are not eligible for servant allowance. The naval system of lodging and provision allowance is different, but a suitable adjustment will be made there also.

The present rates of outfit allowance granted to officers on first appointment to a commission are £55 and £45 according to whether they are required to possess two suits of service dress, or only one suit of service dress with one suit of battle dress. It has been decided to ease the position of newly commissioned officers by making an all-round increase of £5 in these rates. This increase of £5 will apply also to A.T.S. and W.A.A.F. officers on first appointment. Further consideration is being given to the position of W.R.N.S. officers in view of the special circumstances of that Service.

Sympathetic consideration has been given to the representations which have been made regarding some aspects of the present rules for the compensation of officers in respect of the loss of kit from Service causes. It is hoped to introduce certain improvements on the present provision in the near future.

It has been represented that hardship is sometimes occasioned to personnel who are granted compassionate leave for urgent private reasons, and who have hitherto had to pay their own fares through having exhausted their annual entitlement of four free leave travel warrants. It has now been decided that where compassionate leave is granted and the annual entitlement to free warrants has been exhausted, an additional free warrant may be granted in suitable cases. This concession applies to junior officers as well as to other ranks.

The rules under which officers relinquish acting and temporary rank have been reviewed. The general principle governing the grant of acting or temporary rank in the Army in time of war is that an officer should receive the pay of the rank in which he is employed. It follows that unless two (or more) officers are to be paid for the same job, acting or temporary rank must be relinquished when the officer ceases to perform the duties of the rank in question. Approval has nevertheless already been given for the retention by an Army officer of temporary rank, notwithstanding that he has been replaced in an appointment, on being posted overseas until he joins his new unit; or for a period of three months while absent from duty on account of wounds; or for a period of two months during other sickness; or on courses of instruction. In addition, acting rank may be retained during absence from duty on account of sickness up to 28 days, or on account of wounds for a period of three months. Army officers will in future be allowed to retain paid acting or temporary rank for a maximum period of four months when absent from duty on account of either wounds or sickness. The rules in the Navy and R.A.F., which are not exactly the same as the Army rules, will be amended so as to ensure that officers of all three services participate equally in this concession.

These changes complete the special review of service conditions which has just been undertaken, though, as indicated by the Secretary of State for War in the Debate of March 2nd, conditions of service in general are kept under close study by the responsible Departments, and by the Ministers in charge of those Departments, with a view to making such adjustments as may appear necessary or desirable from time to time.

THE WAR SITUATION

July 7.   *Red Army advanced on a 400-mile front from White Russia to the south of Kovel.*

        R.A.F. bombers launched a 2,000-tons attack on Germans massed north of Caen.

July 8.   *British troops broke into Caen after a great armoured thrust.*

July 9.   *British and Canadian forces completed the capture of Caen and the Americans took La Haye.*

July 11.   *Heavy fighting in France between the Orne and the Odon. U.S. troops advanced towards St. Lo.*

        President Roosevelt announced the recognition by the U.S. of de Gaulle's French Committee of National Liberation.

July 12.   *Heavy counter-attacks by the Germans in France were thrown back.*

July 13.   *The Red Army captured Vilna.*

        In Normandy the enemy was pressed back between La Haye and St. Lo.

July 14.   *Red Army captured Volkovysk and Pinsk and reached to within 15 miles of the East Prussian frontier.*

July 15.   *Russians launched a new offensive into Southern Poland aimed at Lvov.*

July 16.   *Grodno, a fortress covering the approaches to East Prussia, was captured by the Red Army.*

        The Eighth Army captured Arezzo, pivot of the German line in the Italian central sector.

July 17.   *British troops broadened the Odon salient and strong forces of aircraft attacked enemy supply routes over a wide area in France.*

July 18.   *After a period of comparative lull the great battle of France began. British and Canadian troops and tanks crossed the River Orne and broke through the German front. The Americans captured St. Lo.*

        Tojo, Japanese Premier, resigned his post as Chief of the General Staff.

July 19.   *British troops captured Cagny five miles south-east of Caen.*

        In Italy Leghorn and Ancona were taken by the Allies.

July 20.   *It was officially announced in Berlin that an attempt had been made to assassinate Hitler by means of a bomb. Hitler broadcast that a group of army officers were responsible and stated that Himmler had been given the task of " ruthlessly exterminating the usurpers."*

American forces landed on Guam Island in the Pacific.

July 21. *A thousand arrests were made by the Gestapo in Berlin following the attempt on Hitler.*

July 22. *Germany was in a ferment and Hitler appealed to the troops for loyalty.*

July 23. *The Red Army captured Pskov and cut the railway north of Dvinsk.*

The King arrived in Italy on a visit to the troops.

Mr. Churchill returned from a three days' tour of Normandy.

July 24. *Lublin, the stronghold covering the approaches to Warsaw, was captured by the Russians.*

Berlin announced that two German Generals had died from wounds received when the attempt was made on Hitler's life.

The Nazi salute was made compulsory in all the German armed forces.

July 25. *Hitler decreed the total mobilization of every part of Europe under German control.*

Supported by 3,000 aircraft, American troops attacking west of St. Lo broke into the enemy lines on a wide front.

July 26. *The Red Army reached the Vistula west of Lublin.*

While British and Canadian infantry held heavy counter-attacks on the Caen-Falaise road, U.S. armoured columns penetrated enemy positions west of St. Lo.

July 27. *The Red Army took six strongholds—Bialystok, Stanislavov, Dvinsk, Rezekne, Lvov and Shavli.*

Sabang, Japanese-held naval base in the East Indies, was heavily shelled by the Allied Eastern Fleet.

July 28. *The Allies scored their first major victory in France. The Germans' Western Normandy Army was crippled and 4,000 prisoners taken in three days of attack.*

Four more major bases fell to the Russians—Kovno, Brest Litovsk, Przemysl and Yaroslav.

July 29. *Spearheads of American forces advanced towards Brehal.*

July 30. *The Americans continued their advance in the western sector of the Normandy front. The British launched a new attack from Caumont.*

July 31. *In a swift thrust American tanks entered Avranches while the British advanced in the Caumont area.*

August 1. *British troops gained ten miles south of Caumont and American troops crossed the River Selune into Brittany.*

  President Ryti of Finland resigned and was succeeded by Marshal Mannerheim.

August 2. *Mr. Churchill, reviewing the war, told the House of Commons: " I no longer feel bound to deny that victory may come perhaps soon."*

[August 2, 1944.

I HAVE, upon the whole, a good report to make to the House. On every battle front all over the world the arms of Germany and Japan are recoiling. They are recoiling before the armed forces of the many nations which in various groupings form the Grand Alliance. In the air, on the sea and under the sea, our well-established supremacy increases with steady strides. The losses by U-boats since the beginning of 1944, compared to former years, are almost negligible. The vast fleets of the Allies have sailed the seas and oceans from January to June with less than half the losses we have inflicted upon the small, dwindling, and largely immobile naval resources of the enemy, both in the East and in the West. It is always possible that there may be a return of the U-boat war. There is talk of Germany trying to make U-boats faster under the water : there are various tales, and it is never well to discount these matters. It is always possible that the Germans may gain some temporary relative advantage in their aircraft. For these reasons we must be very careful not to relax unduly either our precautions or our exertions in order to turn our strength to other channels. Naturally, we wish to turn our strength increasingly to other channels : when one danger is removed a new opportunity presents itself ; but we must be very careful, in view of the possibility of unexpected and usually unpleasant things turning up in future. But at this moment, throughout the world there is no theatre in which Allied mastery has not become pronounced.

At Washington in January, 1942, it was decided that Germany was the prime enemy, and that only the minimum of forces necessary for the safeguarding of vital interests should be diverted to operations against Japan. Our joint resources, British and American, however, increased so rapidly that it became possible to wage the two wars simultaneously with offensive vigour. In the Pacific the immense armadas of the United States, equipped with aircraft and every conceivable form of craft needed on the sea for amphibious warfare, all on the largest scale, armed with science and led with commanding skill both on sea and on land, under both Admiral Nimitz and General

MacArthur, who commands not only the American but also the powerful Australian and New Zealand Forces, have gained important and expanding success. New Guinea has been dominated, the Marshalls and Saipan have been taken, the fleets and other forces of the United States have already advanced through the far-flung outer defences of Japan, and in some parts they have pierced through the inner defences, thus opening to us the prospect of a much more speedy climax in the Far East. Many scores of thousands of Japanese have been by-passed, and are starving to death in islands and jungles, with only such aid from Japan as can be given by submarines which have to be diverted from their normal warlike use.

The reverberations of these events in Japan, the sense of growing weakness on the sea and in the air, the sense of the vain dispersal of their forces and of economic tribulation at home, have produced the fall of Admiral Tojo, the chief war leader of Japan, whose accomplice and close colleague Admiral Yamamato, declared at one time that he would dictate his terms of peace to the United States in Washington. It is not easy for us here to measure the character of the seismic forces which have produced this remarkable political and military convulsion in Japan, but it can hardly arise from a conviction among the Japanese that Admiral Yamamato's programme is being realized as fully as he and Admiral Tojo had expected. I must repeat that I am increasingly led to believe that the interval between the defeat of Hitler and the defeat of Japan will be shorter—perhaps much shorter—than I at one time had supposed.

In the Indian theatre, coming a step nearer home in this long-distance war, the campaign in Burma has been difficult to follow in detail because of the ceaseless fighting and the intricate character of the country. Broadly speaking, it may be said that at Quebec last year we planned advances into Northern Burma with the object of giving greater security to the immense American air highway into China. I may mention that the American highway carries far more tonnage than was ever delivered, or likely to be delivered in a measurable time, over the old Burma Road. It carries it over what is called the hump —the vast mountain range of the Himalayas—and deals with an immense tonnage every month. This, of course, is of the greatest assistance to General Chiang Kai-shek and the Chinese in their long and hard-driven struggle. The House may imagine what a vast effort this achievement by the United States, indispensable to the life of China, has involved.

We placed our hopes at Quebec in the new supreme commander, Admiral Mountbatten, and in his brilliant lieutenant Major-General Wingate, who alas has paid the soldier's debt. There was a man of genius who might well have become also a man of destiny. He has gone, but his spirit lives on in the long-range penetration groups, and has underlain all these intricate and daring air and military operations based on air transport and on air supply.

This forward move which had been decided on at Quebec involved rather more than 250,000 British and Imperial troops, with many more upon the long and precarious communications stretching back into India. This move met at an early stage a Japanese movement in the opposite direction, which had for its object the invasion of India and the cutting of the American air highway. Thus these two opposing forces came together in collision at many points along a 1,200-mile front, in the early part of February, and they have been locked in engagements of intense fierceness ever since, with the result that the Japanese have been flung backward at every point. At the same time important centres in the north of Burma were captured by brilliant operations conducted by General Stilwell from the North, with the participation of Chinese troops and with the invaluable support of the British long-range penetration groups operating against the enemy's rear. The thanks of the country should go out to the British 14th Army, which has done some of the hardest service in the whole of this war, and must not be forgotten because of the violence and vividness of larger and nearer events at home.

But there are many others besides the 14th Army whom we should not forget. When we think of the Fighting Forces, we naturally think first of all those who are fighting on the main war fronts, but we should be wrong not to remember all those men who loyally serve our cause in distant lands and remote garrisons all over the world, whose steady and unspectacular work does not often get into the newspapers, men who in many cases have not had the stimulus of engagement in battle, men who have not seen their families or their homes for four years or five years, or more. They may be far away, but their work is an essential part of the pattern of victory, and, as such, it rests for ever in our hearts.

To return to Burma, Admiral Mountbatten and his commanders fought a successful and vigorous campaign in these unprofitable jungles and swamps in which our duty lies. The Japanese, everywhere driven back, sustained losses far exceeding our own. India has been successfully defended from invasion for another year, the air line to China strengthened and maintained, and danger warded farther off its necessary bases. In addition, Admiral Somerville, now at the head of a powerful British Eastern fleet, which includes fine French and Dutch units, has shown enterprise in his attack upon Sebang and Sourabaya and other Japanese points in the Dutch East Indies. Our Fleet in Eastern waters will be greatly strengthened at the end of the year. It is probable, however, that the Japanese Navy will have its time fully taken up with the Navy of the United States, which is already double the size of the fleet of that presumptuous, ambitious and treacherous Oriental Power. I thought it right to bring the Burma scene before the House, because our men out there are cheered by the fact that the House of Commons follows with attentive eyes their fortunes and their achievements.

Now I come to a larger matter. A volume would be required to recount the story of the crossing of the Channel and the landing of the Armies of Liberation upon the soil of France. I have only a few minutes, and therefore I must practise the selective art as far as possible. In April, 1943, General Morgan, of the British Army, became the head of the British and American Planning Staff, which surveyed the whole project by the decision of the Combined Chiefs of Staff Committee. They made a plan, which I took with me last year to Quebec, where it was submitted to the President and the Combined British and American Chiefs of Staff. This plan selected the beaches for the attack and presented the outlines of the scheme, together with a mass of detail to support it. It received, in principle, complete agreement. It is rather remarkable that a secret of this character, which had to be entrusted from the beginning, to scores, very soon to hundreds and ultimately to thousands of people, never leaked out either in these Islands or the wide expanses of the United States.

At Teheran, we promised Marshal Stalin we would put this plan, or something like it, into operation at the end of May or the beginning of June, and he for his part promised that the whole of the Russian Armies would be thrown, as indeed they have been, into general battle in the East. In January of this year, the commanders were appointed. The Mediterranean had a British commander, General Wilson, and General Eisenhower assumed the command of the Expeditionary Force gathered in Britain. No man has ever laboured more skilfully or intensely for the unification and goodwill of the great forces under his command than General Eisenhower. He has a genius for bringing all the Allies together, and is proud to consider himself an Allied as well as a United States Commander. The names of all the distinguished commanders are already familiar to the House and the country.

General Eisenhower forthwith appointed the Commander-in-Chief of the British Expeditionary Army, General Montgomery, to the command of all the invading troops, British and American. For more than a year past, American stores, equipment and men have been moving steadily into these Islands, and we ourselves have selected from the British Armies here an expeditionary force which was practically as large as that of the United States in the opening stage. Great reinforcements which flow in from America have already altered, and will continually alter that balance, but in the great adventure we

were practically equal. The training of all these troops was under
taken in a most strenuous fashion. The plan also provided for the
successive landings which were to be made in relation to the major
thrust. The great episode seemed to every one to be the crossing of
the Channel, with its stormy waters, swift currents and 18-foot rise
and fall of the tide, and above all the changes of weather, which when
an operation as big as this has to be undertaken might easily cut a
portion of the Army off upon the shore for several days without anyone
being able to get to them to reinforce them or even to withdraw them
and thus leave them at the mercy of a superior enemy. That was the
element, this possible change in the weather, which certainly hung like
a vulture poised in the sky over the thoughts of the most sanguine.

In all these matters, the work of the Combined Operations Head
quarters, founded in 1940 under Admiral Keyes for the purpose of
amphibious warfare, and developed since 1942 by Admiral Mount
batten, proved its value. As is well-known, I was opposed to making
this great invasion across the Channel in 1942, and thereafter it was
plainly impossible in 1943, owing to our having chosen the Mediter
ranean and our amphibious resources all being concentrated there.
Now we were all agreed, and the Commanders took the vast mass of
knowledge which had been accumulated and put their own stamp upon
it, improving the plan in many ways and animating and training
their troops to fit in to its different phases and features.

I do not believe myself that this vast enterprise could have been
executed earlier. We had not the experience. We had not the tackle.
But, before we launched the attack in 1944 we had made five successful
opposed landings in the Mediterranean, and a mass of wonderful craft
of all kinds had been devised by our services and by our United
States colleagues on the other side of the ocean. The bulk of these
had to be constructed in the United States, although our yards were
strained and gorged to the utmost. There are more than 60 variants
of these landing craft and escort vessels, and they provide for the
landing, not only of an Army, but of everything that an Army can
need.

For instance, I myself saw a few days after the landing was complete
six of these large landing craft—I should say, medium landing craft
vessels of considerable size—charge up in line together till they were
stopped by the sloping sandy beach ; down fell their drawbridges, out
poured their vehicles, and in five minutes an entire heavy battery was
drawn up in column of route ready for immediate, or almost immediate
action. I had this timed, because I certainly thought it would be a
matter of hours, but in less than 15 minutes these heavy craft had
pushed themselves off the shore and were returning to England for
another consignment. This is a new atmosphere, a new light upon

the possibility of an invasion across the Channel, which I hope will not be altogether lost upon our own people in the days when many of us have handed over our burdens to others. The marvellous American invention spelt D.U.K.W., is a heavy lorry which goes at between 40 and 50 miles an hour along the road, and can plunge into the water and swim out for miles to sea in quite choppy weather, returning with a load of several tons, coming ashore and going off to wherever it is specially needed.

An immense system of harbours, breakwaters and landing stages was also prepared which, as soon as the foothold was gained, could be disposed in their appropriate places to give large sheltered water space. In less than a month, harbours had been created compared with which Dover seems small. At these harbours, and on the beaches they protect, a very large Army, with the entire elaborate equipment of modern armies, which have about one vehicle for every four or five men, was landed, and by the end of June, in spite of the worst June gale for 40 years, a solid base had been created which gave us the certainty of being able to conduct an offensive campaign on the largest scale against any Forces which, according to our calculations, the enemy was likely to bring.

These operations were protected and supported by a considerable British Fleet, assisted by a strong detachment of the American Fleet, the whole under Admiral Ramsay. In spite of gales, in spite of mines, in spite of more than 100 German submarines waiting baffled in the Biscay Ports, and a swarm of E-boats and other marauders, ceaseless traffic has been maintained over the 100-miles stretch of channel, and General Eisenhower, with his lieutenant, General Montgomery, now stands at the head of a very large and powerful Army, equipped as no Army has ever been equipped before.

Overwhelming air power was, of course, as indispensable as sea power to the carrying out of such an operation. The strategic bombing by the combined British and American Bomber Forces, and the use of the medium bomber and fighter forces, was the essential prelude to our landing in Normandy. Preparations definitely began for the battle in April, and, not only at the point of attack, for that would have revealed much, but necessarily impartially all along the coast and far in the rear. Thus when our ships crossed the Channel, unseen and unmolested, half the guns that were to have blown them out of the water were already dismantled or silent, and when the counter-attack began on the land and under the sea, the Tactical and Coastal air forces held it back while our foothold on shore and our sea-lanes were being firmly established.

These deeds of the Air Force were not done without losses, which, in killed and in proportion to the number of flying personnel, far

K

exceeded those of any branch of the Services. If we take April 1 as the opening of the air campaign and from then till June 30, over 7,000 men of the Home Command from the R.A.F. alone have been killed or are missing. United States losses are also most severe. The devotion of the pilots and the air crews of both countries was sublime.

Since those days we have been in constant battle, General Omar Bradley clearing the Cherbourg Peninsula, and General Dempsey occupying the area around Caen. We have inflicted losses on the enemy which are about double those we have suffered ourselves. It is remarkable considering we were the challengers, and unusual compared with the experiences of the last war. We have been hampered continually by the most unseasonable weather, which by its early mists and low clouds has day after day put off operations by rendering impossible the avalanche of fire and steel with which our air power prepares for an attack. Now at last we are gaining that space in which to deploy which is necessary for armies of the size that we are using.

I must confess that the latest news seems to me extremely good. The first American Army advancing down the Atlantic coast has reached the line of the River Selune, and may well be approaching the important railway centre of Rennes, about half-way across the base of the Brest Peninsula. Farther to the East the Americans have by-passed the town of Villedieu-le-Poeles and have captured Brecey. The British attack has also made very great progress and has advanced in the centre about 12 miles. On the Canadian front South of Caen we attacked yesterday, and heavy fighting is in progress. We are largely superior to the enemy in men, in armour and in the air, and I have little doubt in mobility also once the front is widened out.

It is the wish and also the desire of General Eisenhower that the battle for Normandy should be viewed as a whole and as one single set of operations conducted by an Allied Force, linked in brotherhood and intermingled in every manner that may seem convenient. But this should certainly not prevent the British House of Commons from expressing its unstinted admiration for the splendid and spectacular victories gained by the United States troops under General Bradley, both at Cherbourg and in the southward march, now become almost a gallop down the peninsula. The Germans have certainly had remarkable opportunities of revising the mocking and insulting estimate which they put upon the military value of the American Army at the time they declared war upon the great Republic.

We British and Canadians too have taken our full share in these fierce and prolonged conflicts. We have fulfilled the indispensable part which was assigned to us by the Supreme Commander and, under him, by General Montgomery. If General Eisenhower as supreme

Commander or General Montgomery, as his lieutenant in the field, had ever in the slightest degree had to consider whether they would employ British or American or Canadian troops in this way or in that, here or there, on any grounds other than military, those officers would have been hampered in a most grievous manner. But lest our enemies should suggest upon their wireless that the burden of the struggle has been unfairly shared or make invidious comparisons of any kind, let me say that the losses of the British and Canadian Forces together are about equal to those of the larger United States Army in proportion to their relative strength. It has been share and share alike, in good fortune and bad, all along the front.

So far as it has gone, this is certainly a glorious story, not only liberating the fields of France after atrocious enslavement but also uniting in bonds of true comradeship the great democracies of the West and the English-speaking peoples of the world. That is all I wish to say of the actual operations across the Channel to-day. Members would be well advised to follow them with the closest attention. Very full and excellent accounts are given in the Press. Very often they are ahead of the official news, and they are not incorrect, because more care has to be taken about anything that is said officially. A most lively and true picture is given by the Press at the present time, in the accounts we have of this fighting so near home.

I promised some weeks ago to refer to the question of the British tanks before the end of the Session, and, with the permission of the House, I will make a short divagation from my theme, as this is the last opportunity.

I have told the House how at the time of the fall of Tobruk the President gave the first 350 Sherman tanks which had already been issued to the American army, and we all know that they played a key part in the Battle of Alamein. When I went back to America a year after, I found that there was an ample supply of these tanks, formerly so precious and rare, from the flow of American mass production which had got into its stride, and they were able to offer us 3,000 or 4,000 more of those invaluable weapons. This was of great advantage to us. We were able to carry through the further redisposition of our tank programme and to reduce the scale of our production, thus releasing man-power and materials for making other instruments of war which we urgently required. We were able also to carry through the development of the Cromwell, the Churchill and other types in an orderly manner, freed from fear of a shortage of tanks in the hands of the troops. The Sherman tank has maintained its reputation gained in Africa at every stage in the battles in Italy and Normandy. It is of course essentially a cruiser tank, like the Cromwell, which is the largest type of British cruiser tank. Both these tanks are

reported to be excellent and trustworthy for the purposes for which
they were designed. As the House knows, we succeeded in mounting
the 17-pounder gun in the Sherman, a remarkable feat, and many
hundreds of these are either in action in Normandy or moving thither
in a steady stream.

General Montgomery has written as follows about the recent battle

" In the fighting to date we have defeated the Germans in battle
and we had no difficulty in dealing with the German army once w
had grasped the problem. In this connection British armour ha
played a notable part. The Panther and Tiger tanks are unreliabl
mechanically, and the Panther is very vulnerable from the flank
Our 17-pounder guns will go right through them. Provided ou
tactics are good we can defeat them without difficulty."

Well, they say the customer is always right.

The Cromwell, of course, possesses superior speed, which will b
specially effective when and if we come as we may into more ope
country. As to the Sherman, I saw with my own eyes last week an
example of the work of the 17-pounder. It was on the approaches t
Caen. There was an expanse of large fields of waving corn out o
which a grey stone village rose. Generals Montgomery and Dempse
brought me to this spot and invited me to count the broken-dow
Panther tanks which were littered about. I counted nine in the spac
of about 1,000 yards square. The general then told me that all thes
nine had been shot with a 17-pounder from one single British Sherma
tank from the side of the village wall. One cannot help being impresse
by these things when one sees them with one's own eyes. Of cours
you will never get the same armour in a 30-ton tank as you will i
one of 60 tons. But mobility, speed and manœuvrability also coun
high, and when the 17-pounder gun is added to all these qualities, n
one has the right to say that these lighter tanks are not fitted i
every way for their task and are not a wise and far-seeing employmer
of our war power.

I am afraid all this must be causing pain and sorrow to the hor
Member for Ipswich (Mr. Stokes).

Mr. Stokes interjected : " That is not the whole story." The Prime Minist
continued :

The hon. Member had better pull himself together, because there
worse to come. The notorious Churchill tank, the most thick-skinne
weapon in Europe, also won commendation. This tank was originall
conceived in 1940, for fighting in the lanes and in the enclosed countr
of this Island, and in spite of every form of abuse as well as the difficult
attendant upon haste in design and construction, it is now once agai

coming into its own as it did for a short while in Northern Tunisia in 1942. It is coming into its own because the conditions of the war in France and in the parts of Italy where we are now fighting are extremely suitable to its climbing and manœuvrable qualities and heavy armour. No particular type can be perfect. The Tiger and the Panther are, essentially, weapons of defence, whereas the Cromwell and the Sherman belong to the offensive. The Churchill can be either defensive or offensive as circumstances may require. I pass from these technical details. General Oliver Leese reports as follows about the fighting in Italy:

" It may interest you to know of the fine performance of the Churchill tanks, which supported the Canadian Corps when they attacked and broke through the Adolf Hitler line last month. They stood up to a lot of punishment from heavy anti-tank guns. Several tanks were hard hit without the crews being injured. They got across some amazingly rough ground. Their 6-pounder guns made good penetration and were quick to load and aim."

I saw also that in the recent fighting in France similar distinction had been gained by these weapons in the assault in some of these wooded hills and in this very thickly enclosed country in which our centre is now moving.

But there is one more general feature which has emerged in the fighting in Normandy to which I must draw the attention of the House. No new tank weapon or type of ammunition has been employed by the enemy. They have brought out nothing new so far, whereas we have put into operation for the first time in these operations the Sherman tank mounting the 17-pounder, the latest Churchill tank, and the new Cromwell tank, and we have also a number of interesting variants of very great ingenuity, which I cannot tell the House about to-day, because we do not know whether the enemy have had an opportunity of testing them and tasting them. It is only when I know they know that the secrets can be unfolded. One has to be very careful, because people object very much indeed if anything is revealed which seems to take away any chance that our troops may enjoy in this country and with our Allies.

In leaving this subject of equipment, I am going to do something that has never been done before, and I hope the House will not be shocked at the breach of precedent. I am going to make public a word of praise for the War Office. In all the forty years I have served in this House I have heard that Department steadily abused before, during, and after our various wars. And if my memory serves me aright I have frequently taken part in the well-merited criticism which was their lot. But when I last saw General Montgomery in the field he used these words, which he authorized me to repeat if I chose. He said : " I doubt if the British War Office has ever sent an Army overseas so well equipped as the one fighting now in Normandy." That is what he said, and I must say I think it is a well-justified statement.

The punctual movement and supply of our large armies in so many varied theatres, the high standard of training imparted to the troops, the smoothness with which arrangements of all kind are fitted together, the meticulous care bestowed upon equipment in all its forms, the efficiency of the hospitals, the large share taken by officers in the Army in the devising of every instrument of amphibious warfare, the whole manner in which the affairs of the millions of men now with the Colours at home and abroad have been handled, reflect high credit upon the War Office, with all its innumerable branches and its enormous staff, military and civilian. They all deserve credit, and none more than the Chief of the Imperial General Staff, that great officer Field Marshal Sir Alan Brooke, and also my right hon. Friend the Secretary of State for War. Indeed I may say that not only in the War Office, but throughout the Service departments, the whole method and execution of war policy stand, I believe, at this moment at a higher level than they have ever reached before, and at a level which compares not unfavourably with similar organizations in any other country, whether friend or foe. War is a hard school, but the British, once compelled to go there, are attentive pupils. To say this is by no means inconsistent with any criticisms that it may be necessary to put forward from time to time.

I must now turn to the campaign of General Alexander in Italy. When I spoke about this in February, how different was the scene ! The army seemed to be frustrated, dammed up in the defiles and caves of Cassino ; the landing force which we had at Anzio, and which we had hoped would resolve the deadlock, was itself penned-in and had, indeed, to fight for its very existence, and on the turn of a card depended the life of that strong force ; our very heavy losses ; other operations apparently being delayed ; the capture of Rome continuously postponed ; the enemy sending reinforcements down, and so forth—an effect of standstill. Criticisms came, as they do whenever success is absent, of those responsible. But now the scene is changed. By a series of very rapid and brilliant manœuvres based upon a victory of sheer hard fighting, sheer dogged ding-dong fighting, the whole scene is changed ; the army made contact with the Anzio bridgehead ; it flung its encircling claws round Rome, protecting the city from all danger. It is absolutely free from all danger now. The Air Force guards it from attack from without. General Alexander's army rolled forward, rapidly pushing the enemy before it, taking

50,000 or 60,000 prisoners, up the whole of the long leg of Italy, and now stands before Florence. It has gained the valuable ports of Leghorn and Ancona, as well as bringing forward its railhead in the centre into much closer proximity.

We have had, of course, to move up this Italian peninsula with very unsatisfactory lines of supply; but with the command of the sea and the ports and the advance of the railhead, the position of that army becomes very greatly strengthened. We may hope that operations of the utmost vigour will be continued by General Alexander and his army through the summer and autumn. What an extraordinary army it is! There has never been anything like it, and there is nothing which could so bring home to one how this is a war of the United Nations. You have the British and the United States troops, the New Zealanders, the Greeks are coming—some are already there—a Brazilian force is already beginning to take its place upon the field, the French are there, the South Africans are there, the Poles have greatly distinguished themselves, and, of course, bearing a most important part, our gallant Indian troops. There are also powerful Canadian forces. I was not reading this out from a list, but it is really a most extraordinary parade of all the nations advancing to cleanse the Italian soil. There are Italians also, because respectable Italian forces, in strength, have been fighting well, and we are going to increase their numbers.

Things are going very well in Italy. I must say that in talking about all these various campaigns that are going on at once all over the world, I have left the obvious, essential fact till this point, namely, that it is the Russian armies who have done the main work in tearing the guts out of the German army. In the air and on the oceans we could maintain our place, but there was no force in the world which could have been called into being, except after several more years, that would have been able to maul and break the German army unless it had been subjected to the terrible slaughter and manhandling that has befallen it through the strength of the Russian Soviet armies.

I salute Marshal Stalin, the great champion, and I firmly believe that our twenty years' treaty with Russia will prove one of the most lasting and durable factors in preserving the peace and the good order and the progress of Europe. It may well be that the Russian success has been somewhat aided by the strategy of Herr Hitler—of Corporal Hitler. Even military idiots find it difficult not to see some faults in some of his actions. Here he now finds himself with perhaps ten divisions in the North of Finland and 20 or 30 divisions cut off in the Baltic States, all of which three or four months ago could have been transported with their material and their weapons to stand between Germany and the Russian advance. It is far too late for him to achieve that at the present time. Altogether, I think it is much better to let officers rise up in the proper way.

I have tried to give the House what cannot be more than a sweeping glance of this world-wide war as it approaches the end of its fifth year, and also as it approaches perhaps its closing phase. I naturally end my military survey at home here in famous and mighty London—in London which, with the surrounding counties, particularly those upon what may be called the bomb-highway, has now been under almost continual bombardment for seven weeks. In all, by our calculations —and I procured the latest for the House—5,735 of these robots have been launched upon us, killing 4,735 persons, with 14,000 more or less seriously injured. There are also many slightly injured. The result has been a sad tale of human sorrow and suffering, and a whole-sale destruction of homes, with all the difficult circumstances attaching to that for people who have lost all the little articles on which their memories and affections centre. We are sure that our defences are gaining in power. We press to the utmost our counter-offensive measures. The patience and courage of our people at a time when they might have thought that for London these trials were past has been wonderful. We are sure that their strength will hold to the end.

I fear greatly to raise false hopes, but I no longer feel bound to deny that victory may come perhaps soon. If not, we must go on till it does. How long it will be we do not know, but there will be unfading honour for all the brave hearts that never failed. The working of all the Civil Defence services, men and women, has been a model. About 17,000 houses have been totally destroyed and about 800,000 have received damage. One can judge the efficiency and vigour of the measures taken by the Ministries involved—Labour, Health and Works—and the strength of our building and repair resources throughout the country, from which volunteers have come forward in large numbers, by the fact that three-quarters, or upwards of 600,000, have already been made at least habitable again, and in the last two weeks the rate at which repairs have been overtaking new damage has very sensibly increased.

Nearly a million people who have no war business here, among them 225,000 mothers with children, have been encouraged and assisted to leave London and, thanks to the hospitality and kindness of those in areas not affected, have been welcomed and comforted. There have been a few exceptions, but they are not worth recording beside the good spirit which has prevailed. They are not worth recording except for the purpose of reprobation. A large number of extra trains were laid on to meet this considerable outward move. It is remarkable, as showing the outlook of the people of this country, that many of these trains—including sometimes the extra relief trains—have come back to London nearly as full as they went out. While a daring and adventurous spirit is to be commended, this kind of needless risk and movement will be discouraged in every way. I only mention it now because it gives the lie in the most effective manner to the fantastic German stories of London being in panic under a perpetual pall of smoke and flames. If the Germans imagine that the continuance of this present attack—which has cost them dear in many ways in other branches of production—will have the slightest effect upon the course of the war, or upon the resolve of the nation or the morale of the men, women and children who are under fire, they will only be making another of those psychological blunders for which they have so long been celebrated.

The only result of the use of this indiscriminate weapon, as far as they are concerned, will be that the severity of the punishment which they will receive after their weapons have been struck from their hands by our fighting men will be appreciably increased. There is no question of diverting our strength from the extreme prosecution of the war, or of allowing this particular infliction to weaken in any way our energetic support of our Allies. Every effort in human power is being made to prevent and mitigate the effects of this bombardment. Hundreds of the best expert brains we have are constantly riveted upon the problem. An hon. Member was not right when, in an earlier discussion, he threw out the suggestion that it was all makeshift and improvisation. Very careful plans had been prepared, for instance, for the artillery—the great gun belt—but it is not always possible to foresee accurately what form the attack will take or how things will go.

At the same time as these preparations were made, a quite different disposition of the guns had to be made to guard the invasion ports from which our convoys to France were to start, and we expected that very likely the flying bombs would begin at the same time as we landed in order to cheer up the German people. But there was a slight interval, and it was convenient in that interval that we were able to make a quick redistribution of the batteries. It was a very complicated matter, and I am glad that Members of the House have attended the various meetings addressed by the Home Secretary and by the Joint Parliamentary Secretary to the Ministry of Supply, and have been able to ask them questions. (Here I must say that I cannot understand why anybody should think that there is any constitutional issue involved in any Member or any number of Members taking a Committee Room and talking to each other on any conceivable subject. It is likely that a grave constitutional issue would arise if Members were to be hampered and obstructed in taking counsel with one another. I think it would be unfortunate if a kind of gulf were fixed between Ministers and other Members, as if they were a sort of élite of the House and were not free to mingle with their Parliamentary colleagues. I think there are a good many arguments I could use to free us of the charge of having infringed the constitution.) As I was saying, hundreds of the best brains we have are riveted on the problem, but I can hold out no guarantee that it will be completely solved until we have occupied the region from which these bombs are launched, as we shall no doubt do before the unconditional surrender of the enemy has been received. But even that will be good enough.

As long ago as February 22nd, I warned the House that Hitler was preparing to attack this country by new methods, and it is quite possible that attempts will be made with long-range rockets containing a heavier explosive charge than the flying bomb, and intended to produce a great deal more mischief. London, we may expect, will be the primary target on account of the probable inaccuracy of the rocket weapon. We therefore advise the classes for whom evacuation facilities have been provided by the Government, and others with no war duties here who can make their own arrangements, to take the opportunity of leaving the capital in a timely, orderly and gradual manner. It is by no means certain that the enemy has solved the difficult technical problems connected with the aiming of the rockets, but none the less I do not wish to minimize the ordeal to which we may be subjected, except to say that I am sure it is not one we shall not be able to bear.

I have finished with this, and as a grim comment on all I have said this fact must be added. The hon. Member for Eye (Mr. Granville) put a Question to the Secretary of State for Air, the answer to which I thought might come in here, so he kindly consented to defer his Question. The weight of flying bombs launched against this country from the night of June 15th to the night of July 31st is estimated to be some 4,500 tons. During the same period the Allied Air Forces dropped approximately 48,000 tons of high explosive bombs on Germany. Of course we try in the main to aim at important military objectives, and consequently it may be that there is less loss of life in particular places than when a weapon is used which has no other object than the indiscriminate slaughter of the civilian population.

I have trespassed a good deal on the House, but I think I must take a little more time, especially in view of the decision which the House has properly taken to have an interval in our labours. I now approach, not without natural anxiety, the delicate subject of Foreign Affairs. I still hold to the view which I expressed last time that as the war enters its final phase it is becoming, and will become, increasingly less ideological. Confusion was caused in some minds by mixing ideology with idealism, whereas in fact there is quite a notable difference between them. While I cherish idealism as a cheerful light playing over the thoughts and hopes of men and inspiring noble deeds, ideology too often presents itself as an undue regimentation of ideas, and may very likely be incompatible with freedom. I have rejoiced to see the Fascist ideology overthrown, and I look forward to its complete extirpation, in Italy.

I rejoice in the prospect, now becoming sure and certain, that the Nazi ideology, enforced in a hideous manner upon a vast population, will presently be beaten to the ground. These facts and manifestations, which I see taking place continually as the world war crashes onwards to its close, make me increasingly confident that when it is won, when the hateful aggressive Nazi and Fascist systems have been laid low, and when every precaution has been taken against their ever rising again, there may be a new brotherhood among men which will not be based upon crude antagonisms of ideology but upon broad, simple, homely ideals of peace, justice and freedom. Therefore, I am glad that the war is becoming less an ideological war between rival systems and more and more the means by which high ideals and solid benefits may be achieved by the broad masses of the people in many lands and ultimately in all.

Since I spoke last on the general position to the House, marked improvements have occurred in several quarters. Foreign affairs are powerfully influenced by the movements of the war situation. The successes I have been recounting to the House have carried all our affairs into a more favourable condition. Among the first symptoms is the great improvement in the relations of the French National Committee headed by General de Gaulle with the Government of the United States. This arose in part from the careful spadework done over here by the Foreign Secretary, and from the great success which attended General de Gaulle's visit to the President of the United States. In these last four years I had many differences with General de Gaulle, but I have never forgotten, and can never forget, that he stood forth as the first eminent Frenchman to face the common foe in what seemed to be the hour of ruin of his country, and possibly, of ours; and it is only fair and becoming that he should stand first and foremost in the days when France shall again be raised, and raise herself, to her rightful place among the great Powers of Europe and of the world. For forty years I have been a consistent friend of France and her brave Army; all my life I have been grateful for the contribution France has made to the culture and glory of Europe, and above all for the sense of personal liberty and the rights of man which has radiated from the soul of France. But these are not matters of sentiment or personal feeling. It is one of the main interests of Great Britain that a friendly France should regain and hold her place among the major Powers of Europe and the world. Show me a moment when

I swerved from this conception, and you will show me a moment when I have been wrong.

I must confess that I never liked Trotsky, but there is one thing he said at the time of the brutal German treaty of Brest-Litovsk which stuck in my mind. He said to the German bullies:

" The destiny of a great nation has never yet been settled by the temporary condition of its technical apparatus."

So it will be with France, struck down in a few weeks of agony, and deprived thereafter of the power of self-expression and almost of the right of existence. But the soul of France did not die. It burned here and there with exceptional brightness. It burned over wider areas with a dim but unquenchable flame.

Our landing in Normandy, the course of the war, the whole tide of events, show quite clearly that we shall presently once again have to deal with the problem of France and Germany along the Rhine, and from that discussion France can by no means be excluded. It is evident from what I have said that I look forward to the closest association of the British Empire, the United States and the Russian and French representatives in the settlement of these important European problems. We are an alliance of united, peace-loving nations who have been forced to take up arms to defend our fundamental rights, and we must not fail in the hour of victory to make the arrangements necessary to perpetuate the peace that we shall have so dearly bought. I must pay my tribute to the House for the wise forbearance that it exercised seven weeks ago in discouraging the Debate on British, French and American relations. That was a time much more critical than this, and the fact that the House, which is all-powerful in these matters, deliberately abstained from discussing a question in which interest ran high on all sides was extremely helpful to the conduct of affairs by the Foreign Secretary, and I think furthered the smooth deployment of our policy.

Everyone should bear in mind the unusual complexities which attend the foreign policy of this Island in the world coalition of which we are members. We have first the Dominions to consider and consult, and then there are the three great Powers. We have two valiant and trusted allies who are larger and in some respects more powerful than we are. We all mean the same thing on fundamentals and essentials, but to reach precise agreement from day to day on diplomatic tactics and details is necessarily an elaborate business. Here we enter a field of triangular diplomacy where we all have to telegraph to each other, and when two are agreed, the third often has further amendments to propose, and when all are agreed very often the subject has ceased to be of interest. How would you have it otherwise, with all the different viewpoints, characteristic, historic, and national, from which these matters have to be approached ? I have said before that if the heads of the three Governments could meet once a month, there would be no problems between us which would not be swiftly and I trust sensibly solved. Geographical difficulties thrust their obstructive hands between us and such constant reunions, and correspondence, however faithfully conceived, is not a substitute for meeting round a table. The three principal Allies have to deal from day to day with all kinds of burning issues arising in eight or ten vanquished, occupied, or neutral States, two or three of which have quite healthy civil wars either in prospect or in progress. When I recall and survey all the complexities of arriving together at united agreements, I must say I think the Governments of the United States, Great Britain and Soviet Russia have done pretty well. But great patience and an unceasing desire to understand each other's point of view are necessary between the great Powers, and the House of Commons can help everyone by taking a broad and tolerant view.

This in my opinion is a hopeful moment for Poland, for whose rights and independence we entered the war against Germany. We therefore did our best, my right hon. Friend and I and others, late into the night, to promote the visit of M. Mikolajczyk and other members of his Cabinet to Moscow, where Marshal Stalin was willing to receive them. The President of the United States was also favourable. How could it be otherwise in these matters, considering his deep interest in the Polish question ? The Russian Armies now stand before the gates of Warsaw. They bring the liberation of Poland in their hands. They offer freedom, sovereignty and independence to the Poles. They ask that there should be a Poland friendly to Russia. This seems to me very reasonable, considering the injuries which Russia has suffered through the Germans marching across Poland to attack her. The Allies would welcome any general rally or fusion of Polish Forces, both those who are working with the Western Powers and those who are working with the Soviet. We have several gallant Polish Divisions fighting the Germans in our Armies now, and there are others who have been fighting in Russia. Let them come together. We desire this union, and it would be a marvellous thing if it could be proclaimed, or at least its foundations laid, at the moment when the famous capital of Poland, which so valiantly defended itself against the Germans, has been liberated by the bravery of the Russian Armies.

Conditions in Yugoslavia have sensibly improved since I last dealt with this topic in the House. The lawful King of Yugoslavia, who came to us under our advice in his distress, has gathered round him under the Ban of Croatia a Government in friendly contact with Marshal Tito. Representatives of the fighting administration of the

Partisans have taken their seat in the new Government, and we have General Velebit, a remarkable and accomplished soldier and thinker, who is the liaison between the King's Government and the Forces led by Marshal Tito. We are working for unity here and elsewhere for one purpose alone—namely, the gathering together of the whole united strength of Yugoslavia—Serbians, Croats, Slovenes—and the cleansing of their soil from the foul German invader. This union and this hurling-out, I can assure the House, have good chances of being accomplished before long.

The Foreign Secretary made a statement last week about Greece which had the full assent of the War Cabinet and marks the line that we are taking in Greece. On this line we intend to fight, so far as may be needful, in the House. By fight in this case I mean argue and then, if necessary, vote. We have a clear view of the policy we intend to pursue, and we shall do our best to carry it through even if we have not the satisfaction of unanimous agreement. In the Eastern Mediterranean it has fallen to us to handle most of the business. We lost about 30,000 men in Greece. We have unbreakable ties with that historic land. We keep our Allies constantly informed of everything that we do, and we endeavour, and with good fortune in the main, to carry them with us. A measure of success has, I think, attended our recent handling of events. The Greek Navy is once again at sea. A Greek brigade will soon take its place in the line of battle in Italy. The Greek air squadrons are also doing useful work. The Government of M. Papandreou is broadly representative of all the main forces of Greece, and this new figure who has sprung upon the stage seems to recall in many ways the vigour and courage which won such wide acclaim in the personality of the great Venizelos, whose son is also associated with the Greek Government.

It seems to me that Rumania must primarily make its terms with Russia, whom they have so outrageously assaulted, and at whose mercy they will soon lie. Russia has offered generous terms to Rumania, and I have no doubt they would be accepted with gratitude by the Rumanian people, if only the Rumanian leaders had not got a Prussian automatic pistol pressed pretty closely against their breast or at the nape of their neck. The same applies to Bulgaria. Thrice thrown into wars on the wrong side by a miserable set of criminal politicians, who seem to be available for their country's ruin generation after generation, three times in my life has this wretched Bulgaria subjected a peasant population to all the pangs of war and chastisements of defeat. For them also, the moment of repentance has not passed, but it is passing swiftly. The whole of Europe is heading, irresistibly, towards new and secure foundations. What will be the place of Bulgaria at the judgment seat, when the petty and cowardly part she has played in this war is revealed, and when the entire Yugoslav and Greek nations, through their representatives, unfold at the Allies' armistice table the dismal tale of the injury the Bulgarian Army has done their countries as the cruel lackeys of the fallen Nazi power?

In the Mediterranean theatre of war, I mentioned that we have recently had the satisfaction of welcoming as our comrades in arms a finely-equipped expeditionary force from Brazil, and there are more legions to come from this great land which, for a long time, has been rendering valuable war service to the Allied cause both in the air and on the sea. As an Englishman, I may be pardoned at this moment for thinking of another South American country with which we have had close ties of friendship and mutual interest since her birth to liberty and independence. I refer to Argentina. We all feel deep regret and also anxiety as friends of Argentina, that in this testing time for nations she has not seen fit to take her place with no reserve or qualification upon the side of freedom, and has chosen to dally with the evil, and not only with the evil, but with the losing side. I trust that my remarks will be noted, because this is a very serious war. It is not like some small wars in the past where all could be forgotten and forgiven. Nations must be judged by the part they play. Not only belligerents, but neutrals, will find that their position in the world cannot remain entirely unaffected by the part they have chosen to play in the crisis of the war.

When I last spoke I made some observations about Turkey which the House may perhaps remember. I have a great regard for the Turks, and there is a current tradition in the British Army of sympathy and alliance with them. In the last war they were turned against us by the influence of a handful of men and the arrival of a single ship-of-war. We must not forget that Turkey declared her alliance with us before the present war when our arms were weak and our policy pacific. I visited Turkey in February of last year and had a lengthy conference with President Inonu and his Prime Minister, Mr. Sarajoglu. We had further conferences after Teheran when we met near the Pyramids. I am well aware of the difficulties of Turkey. When the war began she felt herself a strong military power. She looked out on the ranks of her brave army, her unrivalled infantry and cavalry, and she felt herself a strong military power and was resolute in her goodwill towards England and France.

Presently there appeared an entirely new set of weapons—aircraft, tanks, self-propelled artillery and mechanization in every form, which altered the relative strength of Armies and seemed to be the only means by which victory could be procured. The Turkish Army was by no means modern. It was very much as it had come out of the last war or series of wars. I understand plainly the feelings of military prudence which made the action of Turkey less strong when these new facts became apparent to them all of a sudden at the opening of great battles. These difficulties have to a considerable extent been removed. The German power is falling under the mighty Allied flail, and with the contribution we and the United States are making in Italy and France, and with the advance of Russia in the region of the Black Sea, I feel that the Turks are in a more secure position than they have ever been since the war began, and that they will not be committing themselves to dangers against which they have no shield if they come forward on the side of their friends.

I have the authority of the Turkish Government to announce here to-day in the House of Commons that on the basis of the Anglo-Turkish Alliance Turkey has broken off all relations with Germany. This act infuses new life into the Alliance. No one can tell whether Germany or Bulgaria will attack Turkey. If so, we shall make common cause with her and shall take the German menace as well as we can in our stride. Turkish cities may receive the kind of bombardment we have never shrunk from here. Herr von Papen may be sent back to Germany to meet the blood bath he so narrowly escaped at Hitler's hands in 1934. I can take no responsibility for that. It was the policy of Mustapha Kemal to bring about close unity of action between the Russian and Turkish peoples. The elements were all there, and he endeavoured to bring about an end to an antagonism of centuries. I hope this new step will contribute to the friendship between Turkey and Russia.

The ordeal of the House is very nearly at an end, and I hesitate to inflict myself on it any further; but there are so many important things to say that if you start to give an account of what is going on in this war and leave out anything important, great complaints are made.

At the present time, no speech by a prominent politician in any of the victorious countries would be deemed complete without a full exposition of the future organization of the world. I was severely reproached last time for not having dealt methodically with this considerable topic. One of my difficulties is that it does not rest with me to lay down the law for all our Allies. If it were the general wish, I could certainly make one or two suggestions; but, odd as it may seem, countries like the United States and Soviet Russia might wish to have their say in the matter, and might not look on it from exactly the same angle or express it in exactly the same terms as would gain the loudest applause in this House. I am sorry about this, because nothing would have given me greater pleasure than to devote a couple of hours to giving my personal ideas about the general layout; but it would be very troublesome to all of us here if I made a great pronouncement on this subject and found myself contradicted and even repudiated by our most powerful Allies. From time to time a

great many very eloquent statements are made on the future organization of the world by the most eminent people. In spite of all demands
that we should take the lead in laying down the law, I personally
should prefer to hear the opinions of other powerful nations before
committing our country to too many details.

Can we not be content with the broad declaration upon which we
are all agreed, that there is to be a World Council to preserve peace
which will, in the first instance, be formed and guided by the major
Powers who have gained the war, and that thereafter other Powers,
and eventually all Powers, will be offered their part in this world
organization ? Can we not be content with that, and concentrate
our efforts on winning a victory, bearing ourselves so prominently
in the conflict that our words will receive honoured consideration
when we come to the organization of the peace ?

In the meanwhile, as the House will be aware, important discussions
on the official level are shortly to begin in Washington, and when those
are completed we shall have a very much better idea where we stand.
As I have said, it is vain and idle for any one country to try to lay
down the law on this subject or to trace frontiers or describe the
intricate instruments by which those frontiers will be maintained
without further bloodshed ; it is vain, and it is even unwise. The
man who sold the hyena's skin while the beast lived was killed in
hunting it—if I might venture to make a slight emendation of the
poet's words.

Not only are those once proud German armies being beaten back on
every front and by every one of the many nations who are in fighting
contact with them, every single one, but, in their homeland in Germany,
tremendous events have occurred which must shake to their foundations the confidence of the people and the loyalty of the troops. The
highest personalities in the German Reich are murdering one another,
or trying to, while the avenging Armies of the Allies close upon the
doomed and ever-narrowing circle of their power. We have never based
ourselves on the weakness of our enemy, but only on the righteousness
of our cause. Therefore, potent as may be these manifestations
of internal disease, decisive as they may be one of these days, it is not
in them that we should put our trust, but in our own strong arms and
the justice of our cause.

Let us go on, then, to battle on every front. Thrust forward every
man who can be found. Arm and equip the Forces in bountiful
supply. Listen to no parley from the enemy. Vie with our valiant
Allies to intensify the conflict. Bear with unflinching fortitude whatever evils and blows we may receive. Drive on through the storm, now
that it reaches its fury, with the same singleness of purpose and inflexi-
bility of resolve as we showed to the world when we were all alone.

WITH THE TROOPS IN ITALY

EXTRACTS FROM BRIEF SPEECHES TO THE MEN OF THE FIFTH AND
EIGHTH ARMIES IN ITALY
AUGUST 19 AND 20, 1944

August 3.	Rennes fell to American forces advancing into Brittany.
	Moscow announced the crossing of the Vistula and an advance of another 15 miles.
August 4.	Hitler decreed a purge of his armies, and a " Court of Honour " expelled a Field Marshal and four Generals at its first sitting.
August 4.	Tremendous progress was made in France by the British, American and Canadian armies.
	Myitkyina, in Northern Burma, fell to Allied troops after an 80 days' siege.
August 5.	American troops passed Rennes and penetrated deep into Brittany.
August 7.	Brest Peninsula was sealed-off by a sensational American advance, while the British Second Army occupied the whole of the right bank of the Orne.
	Allied naval forces destroyed an enemy convoy off Brittany.
August 8.	A thousand British bombers pounded the German line south of Caen.
August 9.	The Germans lost 107 tanks in an abortive counter-attack at Mortain in France. British and Canadian troops drove a wedge five miles deep into the German line.
	Mr. Churchill paid another visit to Normandy.
	Field-Marshal von Witzleben and seven other high German officers were condemned and hanged by Hitler's " Court of Honour."
August 10.	General Eisenhower moved his Headquarters to France. U.S. troops captured Le Mans.
August 11.	U.S. armoured column reported in Chartres area 50 miles from Paris.
	In Italy the Germans abandoned Florence.
	Supreme Allied Headquarters announced formation of new Anglo-U.S. Air-borne Army.
August 12.	It was revealed that Mr. Churchill had arrived in Italy to visit the troops.
	In France General Montgomery called on his forces to finish once and for all " this powerful German force."

August 13.   *The Germans fell back in France following devastating blows from the air.*

       In Italy Mr. Churchill met the Yugoslav Prime Minister and Marshal Tito.

       Field-Marshal von Paulus, German commander who was captured at Stalingrad, appealed to the Germans to get rid of Hitler.

August 14.   *Heavy air attacks along the Riviera.*

       It was announced that General Leclerc and a French armoured division were in action.

August 15.   *Allied forces, under the command of General Sir Henry Maitland Wilson, invaded the South of France, taking* 100 *miles of coastline between Nice and Marseilles.*

August 16.   *Allied landings continued in the South of France and troops penetrated to a depth of eight miles.*

       In the North of France the German armies speeded-up their withdrawal.

August 17.   *U.S. armoured columns occupied Chartres and Orleans and were reported to be* 23 *miles from Paris. Many towns in the South of France were also occupied by Allied forces.*

August 18.   *Allied troops continued to make progress in both Northern and Southern France. It was reported that Pétain, Laval and other Vichy leaders had fled to Metz.*

       President Roosevelt said that Allied troops would occupy Germany and Japan.

August 19.   *There were landings by Allied air-borne troops east of the Seine.*

August 20.   *General de Gaulle arrived at Cherbourg.*

       U.S. troops were operating south-east of Paris, near Versailles and Fontainebleau.

I CANNOT predict an early end to the war. But I can give no guarantee that it will not end sooner than we have so far allowed ourselves to hope. The Battle of Normandy promises to bring the end of the war much nearer.

*   *   *   *   *

Though you have done great deeds in the past, and may well be proud of what you have achieved, I come here to-day to tell you that greater ventures and greater achievements are now ahead of you.

You will be playing a constant and absolutely vital part in the long, hard struggle for whose speedy end we all strive, and for whose speedy end we all pray.

We have here in Italy one of the finest armies in the world. The combination of the Fifth Army and the British Eighth Army bind two veteran armies in a bond of brotherhood and comradeship of arms.

No operation could have been more fruitful in this theatre than the work you have done in drawing away perhaps two dozen or more enemy divisions down into Italy, where they have been torn to pieces

You aided notably and most effectively the great battle now proceeding to a victorious climax on the fields of France.

* * * * *

In a brief address to the troops of the Brazilian Expeditionary Force, the Prime Minister said :

Hitler's tyranny we shall break. We shall shatter the sources from which its evil powers are derived, and which will be so obliterated and blasted that for many hundreds of years none will dare do the like again

ENCOURAGEMENT FOR THE ITALIANS

ON leaving the shores of Italy after a profoundly interesting and instructive visit, I should like to send a few words of encouragement and hope to the Italian people.

I am most deeply touched by the extraordinary kindness with which I was welcomed in all the villages and small towns through which I have driven in traversing the entire front. There is no doubt that in the zone of the armies the relations of the Italians with the British, American, and other Allies are of a most friendly and co-operative character.

Of course, owing to the hard conditions of war and the disorganization caused by the demolitions of the enemy and the shortage of shipping and transport, much hardship may arise in particular places. I have given directions to the British representatives on the various international bodies concerned to do their utmost, in harmony with their colleagues, to meet these difficulties, and I am sure their efforts will be warmly supported by our Allies.

Italy suffered a long period of governmental tyranny under the Fascist régime, which terminated in the frightful disaster and most cruel suffering which has befallen the Italian people. She would be very unwise to let herself again fall into the clutches of this Fascist totalitarian system in any guise in which it might present itself.

Such systems of Governmental tyranny breed in the conditions of social dislocation, economic hardship, and moral depression which follow in the wake of war and defeat. It is at such a crisis in their history that peoples should be most on their guard against unscrupulous parties seeking after power, and most zealous in the preservation of their liberties.

When a nation has allowed itself to fall under a tyrannical régime, it cannot be absolved from the faults due to the guilt of that régime; and naturally we cannot forget the circumstances of Mussolini's attack on France and Great Britain when we were at our weakest, and people thought that Great Britain would sink for ever—which, in fact, she has not done.

But in the main, speaking for the British—although the other victorious Allies would have a say in this—I believe that the British nation will be happy to see the day when Italy, once again free and progressive, takes her place among all the peace-loving nations.

It has been said that the price of freedom is eternal vigilance. The question arises, " What is freedom ? " There are one or two quite simple, practical tests by which it can be known in the modern world in peace conditions—namely :—

Is there the right to free expression of opinion and of opposition and criticism of the Government of the day ?

Have the people the right to turn out a Government of which they disapprove, and are constitutional means provided by which they can make their will apparent ?

Are their courts of justice free from violence by the Executive and from threats of mob violence, and free of all association with particular political parties ?

Will these courts administer open and well-established laws which are associated in the human mind with the broad principles of decency and justice ?

Will there be fair play for poor as well as for rich, for private persons as well as Government officials ?

Will the rights of the individual, subject to his duties to the State, be maintained and asserted and exalted ?

Is the ordinary peasant or workman who is earning a living by daily toil and striving to bring up a family free from the fear that some grim police organization under the control of a single party, like the *Gestapo*, started by the Nazi and Fascist parties, will tap him on the shoulder and pack him off without fair or open trial to bondage or ill-treatment ?

These simple practical tests are some of the title-deeds on which a new Italy could be founded.

The first duty of all is to purge the soil of Italy from the foul German taint. This can only be done by hard fighting. I rejoice that large new Italian forces will soon join the Allied Armies.

Hard work, a strong resolve, high inspirations, and above all true unity will all be needed if Italy is to nourish her people and resume her place among the leading Powers of Europe. Political excitement and the clash of many parties will not achieve those simple joys and rights which the mass of the people so desire. Italy must recapture the ideals of freedom which inspired the Risorgimento.

May this thought rest with you through your troubles, and may your friends, both in England and across the ocean, see their hopes rewarded.

QUEBEC PRESS CONFERENCE

A Statement during a joint Press Conference with President
Roosevelt at the Citadel, Quebec, Canada

[*September* 16, 1944.

I HAVE been urging the President for several weeks to let us have another meeting. Our affairs are so intermingled, our troops are fighting in the line together, and our plans for the future are so interwoven that it is not possible to conduct these great affairs and to fulfil these large, combined plans without frequent meetings between the principals, between the heads of the Governments, and also between the high officers on each side. It is nearly nine months since we were together in Cairo, and I felt that a further Conference was much overdue.

It is a year since we met here. Well, no one can say that the Conference last year was simply of an idle and agreeable character. Out of it came decisions which are now engraved upon the monuments of history. Out of it came arrangements by which our vast armies were hurled across the sea, forced their way on shore in the teeth of the enemy's fire and fortifications, broke up his armed strength, and liberated, almost as if by enchantment, the dear and beautiful land of France, so long held under the corroding heel of the Hun.

All this took its being in our meeting last year, and was carried to a higher and finer point by the subsequent conversations at Teheran, in which our Russian Ally took part.

This Conference has met under happier auspices than any other we have had. We cannot but feel that one large part of our task is steadily and surely approaching completion. The completion of that task leads to other problems of a military and quasi-military character, which have to be understood in common by the two great Western powers, in order that the events which will follow the suppression of all resistance by Germany may seem to wear the same aspect of design as have the military operations themselves.

But that is not the whole nor even the main part of our work. We have had to consider the extraordinarily complicated processes by which, after the downfall and unconditional surrender of the Nazi power, the enormous forces now gathered in Europe can be applied in as large a degree as possible, with as much shrewdness as possible, and as soon as possible, to the reduction of the fighting capacity of Japan, and to bend that evil and barbarous nation to the will of those they have outraged, and at whose feet they will presently be suppliant.

A curious feature in this Conference has struck me. I read some of the papers when I am over here, these great big papers about an inch thick—very different from the little sheets with which we get on in Great Britain. I read these papers, and I see from time to time suggestions that the British wish to shirk their obligations in the Japanese war, and to throw the whole burden on the United States. And that astonished me very much, because as a matter of fact, the Conference has been marked by exactly the opposite tendency. If there was any point of difference which had to be adjusted, it was that we undoubtedly felt that the United States meant to keep too much of it to themselves. But I am glad to say we have arrived at a thoroughly amicable agreement, and that Great Britain with her fleet and her air force and, according to whatever plans are made, her military forces, all that can be carried by the shipping of the world to the scene of action, will be represented in the main struggle with Japan. And we shall go on to the end.

And of course, Mr. Mackenzie King and the Dominion of Canada came up and said that they insisted on having their part assigned to them too. And that is the feeling. It is not a question of people shirking an awkward and painful job. It is a question of a stern resolve of all parties to assert their right to be in at the death, with forces proportionate to their national strength. So that, I think, may be given full publicity.

As to the plans we have made, we did not tell you about them from day to day as we were making them, because we thought you would rather hear from us at the Press Conference at the end of our meetings, that we should not be able to tell you about them at all. I sympathize very much, as an old former journalist and war correspondent, with the many able representatives of the Press who waited here from day to day, but I know they understood. All these matters have to be secret, and there cannot be any detailed information given here from day to day, or even at the end of the proceedings. The enemy will learn soon enough, in due course, all that we have decided here. I think we said this last year, now I come to think of it—almost those very words. Well, they have learned. What was then secret is now public. What was then concealed is now apparent. What was then in egg is now afoot. What was then a tender sprout has become a gigantic forest tree. What was then a design has become a blow, a mortal blow to the greatest of the military powers which have ranged themselves up against civilization and the progress of the world. So let it be with this Conference, and let it carry with it the seeds of a future victory, a victory which I earnestly trust may be achieved within the shortest limit of time. But as to that, no one can tell.

This is a struggle, not only against the Japanese, but over the vast distances of the Pacific Ocean and the continent of Asia. But just in the same way as we worked out, with our able staffs, all the details of the liberating invasion of Europe, so that it went like a piece of clockwork, I cannot doubt that our careful planning and our material and mechanical resources will be capable of confronting Japan with problems even more painful and even more difficult than those which Hitler and his lieutenant Rommel failed so conspicuously to solve. The main object of this Conference has been the focusing, with the utmost rapidity, of all the resources of the Grand Alliance of the Western democracies upon Japan. That guilty and greedy nation must be stripped of the power to molest and disturb the peace of the world, and must be forced to take a place where neither their virtues nor their vices can inflict miseries upon their fellow men.

I asked Mr. Eden, the Foreign Secretary, to come out and see me, and I see a lot of speculation has arisen upon that point, but I do not know why it should. People have said, " Oh, we thought it was going to be a purely military conference, and here the President brings up the Secretary to the Treasury, and the Prime Minister asks the Foreign Secretary to fly out to see him. What *is* all this ? " But the business of government, in these times, is all one, and when I have the rare and fortunate chance to meet the President of the United States, we are not limited in our discussions by any sphere. We talk over the whole position in every aspect—the military, economic, diplomatic, financial. All is examined. And obviously that should be so. The fact that we have worked so long together, and the fact that we have got to know each other so well under the hard stresses of war, make the solution of problems so much simpler, so swift. What an ineffectual method of conveying human thought correspondence is—even when it is telegraphed with all the rapidity and all the facilities of modern intercommunication ! They are simply dead blank walls compared to personal contacts. And that applies not only to the President and the Prime Minister of Great Britain, it applies to our principal officers, who at every stage enter in the closest association and have established friendships which have greatly aided the tasks and the toils of our fighting troops.

Now I cannot pretend to be talking to you in a humble frame of mind. Thank God, we have been blessed with so much good fortune, far more than we deserve ; but the fact remains that we have conducted successful war, beginning from small beginnings and at great disadvantage, against the most powerful embattled forces. We have conducted successful war on a scale—and I cannot refrain from saying with a measure of success—which certainly you must go far to match and farther still to surpass.

Do not fear about the future. The same processes that have led us from the dark days of Dunkirk, and the Americans from the dark days of Pearl Harbour, to our present situation when the skies are clearing and when the remaining objectives are becoming singularly plainly isolated and defined—those same processes can be applied, and will bring the toiling millions of the world the quicker out of this burden of trial. Then, indeed, there will be happiness, when the long strain of the heavy burden of war is ended, and when we turn also with prevision and preparation to the task of rebuilding, and when the human heart, relieved from the burdens of anxiety for the loss of dear ones, will have a resurgence of hope which cannot but repay the toil and sacrifices we have undergone.

I have enjoyed this Conference very much. It has been conducted in a blaze of friendship. I never have seen more close and complete unity, apart from that little friction about our having our proper share. Apart from that, which is very satisfactorily adjusted, it has been the most agreeable of all the Conferences which I have ever attended. And may I say that I hope that if we should meet here again in another year, we shall be able to tell you more about the plans we have made than it is open to us to do on the present occasion.

AT THE CITADEL, QUEBEC

A Speech on receiving an Honorary Degree from
McGill University, Canada
September 16, 1944

[September 16, 1944.

THIS is a high honour which I have received at your hands, and one which I greatly value. It is hard to think of any more striking setting in which such dignities could be conferred. War-time has justified you in making this new departure in creating these new degrees, but it is war-time that governs all our affairs at the present. I think this gathering here may well be a unique spectacle, and an episode by itself, in the long and honourable history of McGill University.

I need not say, also, how much I feel the compliment and pleasure of being associated in this honour with my august friend and war-time comrade*—our friendship has grown under the hammer-blows of war—in being the recipient of all these academic distinctions. It has been an added pleasure and an added thrill to me.

Your spokesman has been altogether too kind in his statement of the reasons which have justified the University in taking this step, so far as I am concerned.

We are living in a great age, of which it will always be said that this present generation, in Britain and in the United States, had cast upon them burdens and problems without compare in the history of the world. Under the severest stresses, and under the most hard and searching trials, they have shown themselves not unequal to these problems. On the contrary, they have triumphed over them, and thus cleared the way to the broad advance of mankind to levels they have never yet attained, and to securities of which they will never be deprived.

---

*President Roosevelt

THE QUEBEC CONFERENCE

A Joint Statement issued by Mr. Churchill and
President Roosevelt
September 17, 1944

THE President and Prime Minister and Combined Chiefs of Staff held a series of meetings during which they discussed all aspects of the war against Germany and Japan.

In a very short space of time they reached decisions on all points both with regard to the completion of the war in Europe now approaching its final stages, and the destruction of the barbarians of the Pacific.

The most serious difficulty with which the Quebec Conference has been confronted has been to find room and opportunity for the marshalling against Japan of the massive forces which each and all of the nations concerned are ardent to engage against the enemy.

A REVIEW OF THE WAR

A Speech to the House of Commons
September 28, 1944

August 21.   American columns crossed the Seine south-east of Paris and established a bridgehead at Mantes.

General Koenig was appointed Military Governor of Paris.

August 22.   The Germans were in full retreat in Northern and Southern France.

The Allies reached to within three miles of Marseilles.

The Russian armies launched a new offensive in Rumania. They captured Jassy and advanced to within 70 miles of the Danube.

August 23.   It was announced that Paris had been liberated by the French underground forces after an " armistice " with the Germans still in the city.

Rumania accepted an armistice offered by Great Britain, Russia and America, and ceased hostilities.

U.S. columns reached 55 miles east of Paris.

Marseilles was reported to have been partially captured by the French forces.

August 24.   It was reported that the liberation of Paris was complete, but fierce fighting continued between French patriots and Germans in the city. Allied forces endeavoured to link up with the French inside Paris.

The King sent messages of congratulation to General Eisenhower and General de Gaulle.

German troops in Toulon continued to offer desperate resistance, but the city was heavily attacked by Allied troops.

Nearly 2,000 American bombers attacked oil targets in Germany and Czechoslovakia.

The Russians reported the capture of Kishinev, capital of Moldavia.

August 25.   It was announced that the Germans had moved more troops into Paris and that fighting was continuing.

British air-borne troops landed in the Seine Estuary near Le Havre.

Soviet armies raced to Galatz Gap in Rumania. Russia told Rumania she must liquidate German forces in her country before Russia could cease military operations.

August 26. *General de Gaulle headed a Victory procession through Paris, and was shot at by snipers but not hit.*

August 27. *General Eisenhower entered Paris. Allied forces crossed the Seine at four points.*

In the Rhone Valley the Allied advance continued and Avignon was taken.

August 28. *Allied forces crossed the Marne at Meaux, and U.S. troops drove into Château-Thierry.*

Flying-bomb sites in the Pas de Calais were again pounded by R.A.F. bombers.

August 29. *General Patton's Third U.S. Army captured Soissons. It was estimated that 92,000 prisoners had been taken by the Allies between August 10 and 25, and 30,000 Germans killed in the same period.*

The Prime Minister arrived back from Italy.

The Russians captured Constanza, Black Sea naval base.

August 30. *British reached Beauvais on the way to Amiens.*

The Red Army captured Ploesti oil fields in Rumania.

August 31. *U.S. forces crossed the Meuse and reached the outskirts of Sedan. British Second Army seized Amiens and the Canadians entered Rouen. The enemy retreat was becoming a rout.*

General Montgomery was made a Field-Marshal.

September 1. *U.S. troops captured Verdun.*

Eighth Army in Italy penetrated the outer defences of the Gothic Line.

The Red Army reached the borders of Bulgaria.

September 2. *The Allies entered Belgium, and big German forces straggled back to the Siegfried Line.*

In Italy the Gothic Line was broken and Pisa was captured.

September 3. *The fifth anniversary of the outbreak of war.*

American patrols crossed the Moselle river, and, in the South of France, American and French troops entered Lyons.

September 4. *Finland withdrew from the war.*

Allied troops captured Antwerp.

September 5. *All the Channel ports were cut off and British and American forces linked up in Belgium.*

Russia declared war on Bulgaria.

September 6.	*Relaxation of the black-out in Britain was announced.*
	Russian troops reached the borders of Yugoslavia.
September 7.	*Bulgaria asked the Russians for an armistice and declared war on Germany.*
September 8.	*Ostend and Liége were captured and British troops crossed the Albert Canal.*
	Russian troops entered Bulgaria without opposition.
September 9.	*Hostilities ceased between Russia and Bulgaria.*
	The American First Army reached to within 15 miles of the Siegfried Line.
September 10.	*Mr. Churchill arrived in Canada for a conference with President Roosevelt.*
	British and American troops converged on Aachen.
September 11.	*American forces crossed the German frontier north of Trier. The British Second Army entered Holland.*
	Luxemburg was captured.
	During a heavy American air-raid on Germany, the enemy lost 175 fighter planes.
September 12.	*Second crossing of the German frontier at Eupen by the Americans. Le Havre surrendered to the Canadians.*
September 13.	*First Siegfried Line fort stormed by the Americans.*
	Roetgen, 10 miles south-east of Aachen, was captured.
	It was announced that the American Ninth Army had arrived in France.
	Nearly 3,000 British and U.S. bombers attacked Germany.
September 14.	*Outposts of the Siegfried Line were breached.*
	Praga, in the outskirts of Warsaw, was captured by the Russians.
	It was officially announced that 501 Japanese planes and 173 Japanese ships had been destroyed in a week.
September 15.	*The Siegfried Line was broken east of Aachen.*
	U.S. forces landed on the Palau Islands 550 miles east of the Philippines.
September 16.	*Fierce fighting continued along the Moselle.*
September 17.	*Allied First Airborne Army landed in great strength in Holland.*
	Twenty thousand Germans surrendered to U.S. troops near Orleans.
September 18.	*Further air-borne reinforcements were landed in Holland and established contact with the British Second Army.*
	General Eisenhower announced the establishment of Allied military government in German territory.

September 19.   *British Second Army advanced 50 miles across Holland to near Nijmegen, on the Waal (Rhine).*

        U.S. troops crossed into Germany near Sittard.

        Russia and Great Britain signed an armistice with Finland.

September 20.   *Allied armoured corridor established across Holland and British Second Army reached the south bank of the Waal.*

        The Home Secretary announced big reductions in Civil Defence Services.

September 21.   *British tanks crossed the Waal at Nijmegen and drove northwards in an effort to join air-borne forces at Arnhem.*

        The Government issued a White Paper giving details of the scheme for partial demobilization.

September 22.   *German garrison commander and staff surrendered at Boulogne.*

        British Eighth Army captured Rimini in Italy.

        Tallinn, capital of Estonia, was captured by the Russians.

September 23.   *Germans launched a strong attack in an effort to cut Allied supply corridor through Holland but were defeated.*

        Russian troops entered Hungary.

September 24.   *British troops penetrated a mile into Germany south-east of Nijmegen and captured Beek.*

September 25.   *Reinforcements reached air-borne troops around Arnhem, but their position was considered critical.*

        Mr. Churchill returned to England from Quebec.

September 26.   *Two thousand men, the survivors of the Air-borne Division, were withdrawn from Arnhem. Second Army's supply corridor from Holland was widened.*

        Soviet reported the occupation of all Estonia.

September 27.   *Second Army again widened its corridor through Holland and progressed towards the Maas.*

        The Eighth Army crossed the Rubicon in several places

September 28.   *Canadian troops captured the citadel of Calais.*

        Mr. Churchill reviewed the progress of the war in a speech to the House of Commons.

[September 28, 1944.

LITTLE more than seven weeks have passed since we rose for the summer vacation, but this short period has completely changed the face of the war in Europe. When we separated, the Anglo-American Armies were still penned in the narrow bridgehead and strip of coast from the base of the Cherbourg Peninsula to the approaches to Caen, which they had wrested from the enemy several weeks before. The Brest Peninsula was untaken, the German Army in the West was still hopeful of preventing us from striking out into the fields of France, the Battle of Normandy, which had been raging bloodily from the date of the landing, had not reached any decisive conclusion. What a transformation now meets our eyes! Not only Paris, but practically the whole of France, has been liberated as if by enchantment. Belgium has been rescued, part of Holland is already free, and the foul enemy, who for four years inflicted his cruelties and oppression upon these countries, has fled, losing perhaps 400,000 in killed and wounded, and leaving in our hands nearly half a million prisoners. Besides this, there may well be 200,000 cut off in the coastal fortresses or in Holland, whose destruction or capture may now be deemed highly probable. The Allied Armies have reached and in some places crossed the German frontier and the Siegfried Line.

All these operations have been conducted under the supreme command of General Eisenhower, and were the fruit of the world-famous battle of Normandy, the greatest and most decisive single battle of the entire war. Never has the exploitation of victory been carried to a higher perfection. The chaos and destruction wrought by the Allied Air Forces behind the battle front have been indescribable in narrative, and a factor of the utmost potency in the actual struggle. They have far surpassed, and reduce to petty dimensions, all that our Army had to suffer from the German Air Force in 1940. Nevertheless, when we reflect upon the tremendous fire-power of modern weapons and the opportunity which they give for defensive and delaying action, we must feel astounded at the extraordinary speed with which the Allied Armies have advanced. The vast and brilliant encircling movement of the American Armies will ever be a model of military art, and an example of the propriety of running risks not only in the fighting—because most of the armies are ready to do that—but even more on the Q. side, or, as the Americans put it, the logistical side. It was with great pleasure that all of us saw the British and Canadian Armies, who had so long fought against heavy resistance by the enemy along the hinge of the Allied movement, show themselves also capable of lightning advances which have certainly not been surpassed anywhere.

Finally, by the largest airborne operation ever conceived or executed, a further all-important forward bound in the North has been achieved. Here I must pay a tribute, which the House will consider due, to the superb feat of arms performed by our First Air-borne Division. Full and deeply-moving accounts have already been given to the country and to the world of this glorious and fruitful operation, which will take a lasting place in our military annals, and will, in succeeding generations, inspire our youth with the highest ideals of duty and of daring. The cost has been heavy ; the casualties in a single division have been grievous ; but for those who mourn there is at least the consolation that the sacrifice was not needlessly demanded nor given without results. The delay caused to the enemy's advance upon Nijmegen enabled their British and American comrades in the other two air-borne divisions, and the British Second Army, to secure intact the vitally important bridges and to form a strong bridgehead over the main stream of the Rhine at Nijmegen. " Not in vain " may be the pride of those who have survived and the epitaph of those who fell.

To return to the main theme, Brest, Havre, Dieppe, Boulogne and Antwerp are already in our hands. All the Atlantic and Channel ports, from the Spanish frontier to the Hook of Holland, will presently be in our possession, yielding fine harbours and substantial masses of prisoners of war. All this has been accomplished by the joint exertions of the British and American Armies, assisted by the vehement and widespread uprising and fighting efforts of the French Maquis.

While this great operation has been taking its course, an American and French landing on the Riviera coast, actively assisted by a British air-borne brigade, a British Air Force, and the Royal Navy, has led with inconceivable rapidity to the capture of Toulon and Marseilles, to the freeing of the great strip of the Riviera coast, and to the successful advance of General Patch's Army up the Rhone Valley. This army, after taking over 80,000 prisoners, joined hands with General Eisenhower, and has passed under his command. When I had the opportunity on 15th August of watching—alas, from afar—the landing at Saint Tropez, it would have seemed audacious to hope for such swift and important results. They have, however, under the spell of the victories in the North, already been gained in superabundance, and in less than half the time prescribed and expected in the plans which were prepared beforehand. So much for the fighting in France.

Simultaneously with that, very hard and successful fighting on a major scale has also proceeded on the Italian Front. General Alexander, who commands the armies in Italy with complete operational discretion, has under him the Fifth and Eighth Armies. The Fifth Army, half American and half British, with whom are serving the fine Brazilian Division, some of whose troops I had the opportunity of seeing—a magnificent band of men—is commanded by the United States General Clark, an officer of the highest quality and bearing, with a proud record of achievements behind him and his troops. The Eighth Army, under General Oliver Leese, whose qualities are also of the highest order, comprises the Polish Corps which fought so gallantly under General Anders, and a Greek Brigade which has already distinguished itself in the forefront of the battle. There is also fighting on this Front a strong force of Italians, who are ardent to free their country from the German grip and taint. This force will very soon be more than doubled in strength. The Lieutenant of the Realm is often with these troops.

The largest mass of all the troops on the Italian Front comes, of course, from the United Kingdom. Not far short of half the divisions on the whole front are from this Island. Joined with them are New Zealand, Canadian, South African and Indian Divisions, or perhaps I should say British-Indian Divisions, because, as is sometimes forgotten, one-third of them are British. The British Army in Italy includes also Palestinian units; and here I would mention the announcement, which I think will be appreciated and approved, that the Government have decided to accede to the request of the Jewish Agency for Palestine that a Jewish Brigade group should be formed to take part in active operations. I know there are vast numbers of Jews serving with our Forces and the American Forces throughout all the Armies, but it seems to me indeed appropriate that a special Jewish unit, a special unit of that race which has suffered indescribable torments from the Nazis, should be represented as a distinct formation amongst the forces gathered for their final overthrow, and I have no doubt they will not only take part in the struggle but also in the occupation which will follow.

A very hard task lies before the Army in Italy. It has already pierced at several points the strong Gothic line by which Kesselring has sought to defend the passage of the Apennines. I had an opportunity of watching and following the advance of the Eighth Army across the Metauro River, which began on August 26th. The extraordinary defensive strength of the ground held by the enemy was obvious. The mountain ridges rise one behind the other in a seemingly endless succession, like the waves of the sea, and each had to be conquered or turned by superior force and superior weapons. The process was bound to be lengthy and costly, but it is being completed, has, in fact, been practically completed. At the same time, General Clark's Fifth Army, advancing from the Florence area, has pierced deep into the mountain ranges, and, having broken the enemy's centre, now stands on the northern slopes of the Apennines at no great distance from Bologna, a place of definite strategic importance. General Alexander has now definitely broken into the basin of the Po, but here we exchange the barriers of mountain ridges for the perpetual interruption of the ground by streams and canals. Nevertheless, conditions henceforward will be more favourable for the destruction or rout of Kesselring's Army, and this is the objective to which all British and Allied Forces will be unceasingly bent. Farther than that, it is not desirable to peer at the present moment.

I am now going to give a few facts and figures about the operations in Europe. These have been very carefully chosen to give as much information as possible to the House and to the public, while not telling the enemy anything he does not already know, or only telling him too late for it to be of any service to him. The speed with which the mighty British and American Armies in France were built up is almost incredible. In the first 24 hours a quarter of a million men were landed, in the teeth of fortified and violent opposition. By the 20th day a million men were ashore. There are now between two and three million men in France. Certainly the progress in the power of moving troops and landing troops has vastly increased since the early days, when we had to plunge into the war with no previous experience. But the actual number of soldiers was only part of the problem of transportation. These armies were equipped with the most perfect modern weapons and every imaginable contrivance of modern war, and an immense artillery supported all their operations. Enormous masses of armour of the highest quality and character gave them extraordinary offensive power and mobility. Many hundreds of thousands of vehicles sustained their movements, many millions of tons of stores have already been landed—the great bulk of everything over open beaches or through the synthetic harbours which I described when last I spoke to the House.

All this constitutes a feat of organization and efficiency which should excite the wonder and deserve the admiration of all military students, as well as the applause of the British and American nations and their Allies. I must pay my tribute to the United States Army, not only in their valiant and ruthless battle-worthy qualities, but also in the skill of their commanders and the excellence of their supply arrangements. When one remembers that the United States four or five years ago was a peace-loving Power, without any great body of troops or munitions, and with only a very small regular Army to draw their commanders from, the American achievement is truly amazing. After the intense training they have received for nearly three years, or more than three years in some cases, their divisions are now composed of regular professional soldiers whose military quality is out of all comparison with hurriedly-raised war-time levies. These soldiers, like our own from Great Britain who have been even longer under arms, are capable of being placed immediately on landing in the battle line, and have proved themselves more than a match for the so-called veteran troops of Germany, who, though fighting desperately, are showing themselves decidedly the worse for wear. When I think of the measureless output of ships, munitions and supplies of all kinds with which the United States has equipped herself and has sustained all the fighting Allies in generous measure, and of the mighty war she is conducting, with troops of our Australian and New Zealand Dominions, over the spaces of the Pacific Ocean, this House may indeed salute our sister nation as being at the highest pinnacle of her power and fame.

I am very glad to say that we also have been able to make a worthy contribution. Some time ago, a statement was made by a Senator to the effect that the American public would be shocked to learn that they would have to provide 80 per cent. of the Forces to invade the Continent. I then said that at the outset of the invasion of France the British and American Forces would be practically equal, but that thereafter the American build-up would give them steadily the lead. I am glad to say that after 120 days of fighting we still bear, in the cross-Channel troops, a proportion of two to three in personnel and of four to five-and-a-half in fighting divisions in France. Casualties have followed very closely the proportions of the numbers. In fact, these troops fight so level that the casualties almost exactly follow the numbers engaged. We have, I regret to say, lost upwards of 90,000 men, killed, wounded and missing, and the United States, including General Patch's Army, over 145,000. Such is the price in blood paid by the English-speaking democracies for the actual liberation of the soil of France.

When this view is extended to cover the entire European scene and the campaigns both in France and Italy, it will be a source of satisfaction to the House to know that after more than five years of war, we still maintain almost exactly the same number of divisions, taking both theatres together, in full action against the enemy as the United States have, by all the shipping resources which can be employed, yet been able to send to Europe. Considering that the population of the Empire—of British race—is only 70,000,000, and that we have sustained many losses in the early years of the war, it certainly is a remarkable effort, and one which was most fully and cordially recognized by our American colleagues, the Chiefs of Staff and others, at the recent Conference in Quebec.

In thus trying to do justice to the British and American achievements, we must never forget, as I reminded the House before we separated, the measureless services which Russia has rendered to the common cause, through long years of suffering, by tearing out the life of the German military monster. The terms in which Marshal Stalin recently, in conversation, has referred to our efforts in the West have been of such a generous and admiring character that I feel, in my turn, bound to point out that Russia is holding and beating far larger hostile forces than those which face the Allies in the West, and has through long years, at enormous loss, borne the brunt of the struggle on land. There is honour for all. It is a matter of rejoicing that we, for our part and in our turn, have struck resounding blows, and it is right that they should be recorded among the other feats of arms so loyally performed throughout the Grand Alliance.

I must again refer to the subject of the campaign in Burma, on which I touched in my last statement to the House. I was somewhat concerned to observe from my reading of the American Press, in which I indulged during my stay on the other side, that widespread misconception exists in the public mind, so far as that is reflected by the newspapers, about the scale of our effort in Burma and the results to date of Admiral Mountbatten's campaign. Many important organs of United States opinion seem to give the impression that the British campaign of 1944 in Burma had been a failure, or at least a stalemate, that nothing much had been done, and that the campaign was redeemed by the brilliant capture of Myitkyina—which I may say is spelt "Myitkyina" but pronounced "Michynaw"—by General Stilwell at the head of an American Regiment of very high-class commando troops and with the assistance of the Chinese. That is the picture, but I must present these matters in their true light. It is well known that the United States have been increasingly engaged in establishing an air route to China capable of carrying immense supplies, and, by astounding efforts and at vast cost, they are now sending over the terrible Himalayas, or the Hump as it is called in the Army, I will not say how many times as much as the Burma Road has ever carried in its palmiest days, or will carry for several years to come; an incredible feat of transportation—over mountains 20,000 or 22,000 feet high in the air, over ground where an engine failure means certain death to the pilot—has been performed by a main effort which the United States have made in their passionate desire to aid the resistance of China. Certainly no more prodigious example of strength, science and organization in this class of work has ever been seen or dreamed of.

Along the Eastern Frontier of India stands the 14th British Imperial Army comprising the main war effort of India, including some of the most famous Indian Divisions from the Middle East and a substantial proportion of United Kingdom troops and Divisions, together with some excellent Divisions from Africa—native Divisions from Africa, West Africa principally. This Army under Admiral Mountbatten—amounting to between 250,000 and 300,000 men, apart from rearward services which, in that theatre of extraordinarily long and precarious communications, are very large—has by its aggressive operation guarded the base of the American air line to China and protected India against the horrors of a Japanese invasion. Once again, India and her vast population have reposed serenely among the tumults and hurricanes of the world behind the Imperial shield. The fact should sometimes be noted that under British rule in the last eighty years incomparably fewer people have perished by steel or firearms in India than in any similar area or community on the globe.

As the population has increased by 50,000,000 in the last ten years, it is evident that the famine which was caused by military conditions last year affecting transport is by no means representative of the administration under which the broad peninsula and triangle of India has met an increase in population exceeding the speed of any increase in any other country throughout the whole world. I think it a very remarkable fact that India has received this shelter and has been this vast harbour of peace, protected by the arms and policy of Great Britain, protected also by the care and attention of this House. In this effort the brave fighting races of India have at all times borne a most honourable and memorable part.

I regret to say the fighting on the Burma Front throughout the year has been most severe and continuous, and there were times when the issue in particular localities appeared to hang in doubt. However, the ten Japanese Divisions which were launched against us with the object of invading India and cutting the air line have been repulsed and largely shattered, as the result of a bloody and very costly campaign which is still being continued in spite of the monsoon conditions. How costly this campaign has been in disease may be judged from the fact that in the first six months only of this present year the 14th British Imperial Army sustained no fewer than 237,000 cases of sickness, which had to be evacuated to the rear over the long, difficult communications and tended in hospital. More than 90 per cent. of these cases returned within six months, but the ceaseless drain upon the Army and the much larger numbers required to maintain a fighting strength, in spite of this drain, in the neighbourhood of a quarter of a million may well be imagined. When you have a loss and drain like that going on, much larger numbers are needed to maintain your limited fighting strength. In addition, there were over 40,000 battle casualties in the first six months, that is to say, to the end of June, and the number has certainly increased by now.

I think these facts ought to be known ; I think they ought to be given wide publicity, as I am sure they will now that I have stated them, because the campaign of Admiral Mountbatten on the Burma Frontier constitutes—and this is a startling fact—the largest and most important ground fighting that has yet taken place against the armies of Japan. Far from being an insignificant or disappointing stalemate, it constitutes the greatest collision which has yet taken place on land with Japan, and has resulted in the slaughter of between 50,000 and 60,000 Japanese and the capture of several hundred prisoners. The Japanese Army has recoiled before our troops in deep depression and heavily mauled. We have often, too, found circles of their corpses in the jungle where each one had committed suicide in succession, the officer, who had supervised the proceedings, blowing out his own brains last of all. We did not ask them to come there, and it is entirely their own choice that they find themselves in this difficult position.

We must expect, however, a renewal of the Japanese offensive as soon as the monsoon is over, and every preparation is being made to meet it with the utmost vigour. Nelson said, "If in doubt, a captain cannot do wrong if he places his ship alongside one of the enemy." The engagement of the Japanese on the largest possible scale on land— and certainly not less in the air—is part of the official wearing-down process which marks the present phase of the war against Japan, and this function our 14th Army has certainly discharged with the utmost fidelity and success in spite of the inordinately heavy toll of disease. I trust that this toll will be markedly reduced in future operations. We have discovered many defences against tropical disease, and, above all, against the onslaught of insects of all kinds, from lice to mosquitoes and back again.

The excellent D.D.T. powder, which has been fully experimented with and found to yield astonishing results, will henceforward be used on a great scale by the British forces in Burma and by American and Australian forces in the Pacific and, indeed, in all theatres, together with other remedies constantly improving, and these will make their effect continually manifest. The Japanese, I may mention, also suffer from jungle diseases and malaria, which are an offset against the very heavy losses which are suffered by our Indian and white and African troops. These remedies will be a help to all the Allies ; indeed, they have been a help. The eradication of lice in Naples by the strict hygienic measures taken may be held to have averted a very grievous typhus epidemic in that city and neighbourhood when we occupied it. I can assure the House that the war against the Japanese and other diseases of the jungle will be pressed forward with the utmost energy.

I must here note with keen regret that in spite of the lavish American help that has been poured into China, that great country, worn by more than seven years of war, has suffered from severe military reverses involving the loss of valuable airfields upon which the American squadrons of General Chennault were counting. This, of course, is disappointing and vexatious. When we survey the present state of the European and Asiatic wars as a whole, the House will, I am sure, wholeheartedly acclaim the skill and enterprise of the generals and the tireless courage and fighting qualities of the troops, and they may even feel disposed to view without any special mark of disapprobation the management, combination and design which it reveals on the part of the Allied staffs, and even on the part of the Governments concerned.

But we must not forget that we owe a great debt to the blunders

—the extraordinary blunders—of the Germans. I always hate to compare Napoleon with Hitler, as it seems an insult to the great Emperor and warrior to connect him in any way with a squalid caucus boss and butcher. But there is one respect in which I must draw a parallel. Both these men were temperamentally unable to give up the tiniest scrap of any territory to which the high watermark of their hectic fortunes had carried them. Thus, after Leipzig in 1813, Napoleon left all his garrisons on the Rhine, and 40,000 men in Hamburg. He refused to withdraw many other vitally important elements of his armies, and he had to begin the campaign of 1814 with raw levies and a few seasoned troops brought in a hurry from Spain. Similarly, Hitler has successfully scattered the German armies all over Europe, and by obstination at every point from Stalingrad and Tunis down to the present moment, he has stripped himself of the power to concentrate in main strength for the final struggle.

He has lost, or will lose when the tally is complete, nearly a million men in France and the Low Countries. Other large armies may well be cut off in the Baltic States, in Finland and in Norway. Less than a year ago, when the relative weakness of Germany was already becoming apparent, he was ordering further aggressive action in the Aegean, and the re-occupation of the islands which the Italians had surrendered, or wished to surrender. He has scattered and squandered a very large army in the Balkan Peninsula, whose escape will be very difficult; 27 divisions, many of them battered, are fighting General Alexander in Northern Italy. Many of these will not be able to recross the Alps to defend the German Fatherland. Such a vast frittering-away and dispersal of forces has never been seen, and is, of course, a prime cause of the impending ruin of Germany.

When Herr Hitler escaped his bomb on July 20th he described his survival as providential; I think that from a purely military point of view we can all agree with him, for certainly it would be most unfortunate if the Allies were to be deprived, in the closing phases of the struggle, of that form of warlike genius by which Corporal Schickelgruber has so notably contributed to our victory. There is a great deal more mopping-up to be done in the Low Countries and in some of the French Atlantic ports, and the harbours have to be cleared and developed on the greatest scale possible before the winter gales. Problems of supply have to be resolved on the morrow of the prodigious British and American advances, and I deprecate very much people being carried away into premature expectations of an immediate cessation of the fighting. It is very hard not to be, when, each day, the papers are filled—rightly filled—with the news of the capture of important places and of advances of the armies; but there is still a great deal to be done in the military sense.

Hitherto, as I have said, during the first four critical months in Europe, we have managed to be an equal, or almost equal, partner with the United States, but now, of course, the great flow of their well-trained divisions from across the Atlantic will, step by step, carry them decisively into the leading position, and, unless organized German resistance collapses in the near future, enormous additional United States forces will be brought to bear on the final struggle. I shall certainly not hazard a guess—it could be no more—as to when the end will come. Many persons of the highest technical attainments, knowledge and responsibility have good hopes that all will be over by the end of 1944. On the other hand, no one, and certainly not I, can guarantee that several months of 1945 may not be required.

There is also a possibility that after the organized resistance of the German Army and State is completely broken, fierce warfare may be maintained in the forests and mountains of Germany by numbers of desperate men, conscious of their own guilt and impending doom. These of course would, at a certain stage, deserve the treatment which the Germans have so ruthlessly meted out to guerrilla movements in other countries. It may be necessary for the Allies to declare at a certain date that the actual warfare against the German State has come to an end, and that a period of mopping-up of bandits and war criminals has begun. No one can foresee exactly what form the death agony of Nazidom will take. For us, the important decision will be to choose the moment when substantial forces can be withdrawn from Europe to intensify the war against Japan. We certainly do not consider that the declared date of the ending of the war against Germany must necessarily be postponed until the last desperado has been tracked down in his last lair.

There is no doubt that surpassing victories gained in common make a very agreeable foundation for inter-Allied Conferences like that which has just finished. It is really very much better and very much more pleasing to share victories than it is to share disasters. We have shared both, and I can tell the House that the former is in every way the more exhilarating process I took occasion to associate Canadian, Australian and New Zealand representatives with our work. I have also, with our Chiefs of the Staff, attended a meeting of the Canadian Cabinet, and have received both from Mr. Mackenzie King and Mr. Curtin the most cordial expressions of satisfaction at the manner in which our affairs were conducted and of agreement in the decisions taken. I have also been in very full correspondence, as I often am, with Field-Marshal Smuts and with Mr. Fraser. Certainly when the President and I with our respective staffs met at Quebec, we had behind us a record of successful war which justified feelings of solemn satisfaction, and warmed the glow of our brotherhood in arms

It is now two years almost to a day since Rommel's final offensive against Cairo was repulsed by the newly-appointed Generals Alexander and Montgomery, a month before their decisive victory at Alamein, and since that time our affairs all over the world, and the affairs of our mighty ally Russia, have proceeded without a single reverse of any kind, except only the loss of Leros and Cos in the Aegean, and even those will ultimately turn out to be a loss to Hitler rather than to the Allies. Such a long and mounting tide of victory is unexampled in history. The principal Governments of the Allies have every right to claim the confidence of the United Nations in the new efforts that will be required from all of us, and in the further designs which have been conceived and shaped and have still to be unfolded in action. Complete agreement on every point was reached at Quebec by the Combined Chiefs of Staff. The President and I have both pursued a policy of making no changes other than those enforced by death, as in the lamented loss of Admiral Pound, in the Chiefs of Staff charged with the conduct of the war.

In this country there have been none of those differences between the professional and the political elements such as were evident in a large measure in the former war. We have worked together in perfect harmony. Our confidence in the Chiefs of Staff—British confidence and the confidence of the War Cabinet—has steadily grown. In consequence of the fact that there have been no changes, the men who met together at Quebec knew each other well, were united in bonds of comprehension and friendship, and had the whole picture and sequence of the war ingrained in their minds and in their very being. When you have lived through all these things you do not have to turn up musty files to remember what happened on particular occasions. Men's minds are shaped from day to day by what they live through ; and discussion on that level between these high officers is very quick and swift.

Obviously, our deliberations were concerned with the successful winding-up of the war in Europe by bringing about the unconditional surrender of Germany at the earliest moment, and also with the new phase of the war against Japan, which will dominate all minds and command all resources from the moment when the German war is ended. On behalf of His Majesty's Government, nearly two years ago, I assured the President that Great Britain would pursue the war against Japan with all her strength and resources to the very end. As I explained to Congress when I last addressed them, we have losses to repair and injuries to repay on the Japanese account at least equal to, if not indeed greater than, those suffered by the United States. We owe it to Australia and New Zealand to help them to remove for ever the Japanese menace to their homelands ; and as they have helped us on every front in the fight against Germany, we shall certainly not be behindhand in giving them effective aid.

Our perseverance in this quarrel is not to be doubted. I offered some time ago to embody this undertaking in a definite treaty, but the President made the courteous reply that the British word was enough. That word we shall certainly make good. Accordingly, we offered to the United States a fine modern British Fleet, and we asked that it should be employed in the major operations against Japan. This offer was at once cordially accepted. A large portion of this Fleet is already gathered in the Indian Ocean. For a year past, our modern battleships have been undergoing a further measure of modernization and tropicalization to meet the rapid war-time changes in technical apparatus. We have already, nine months ago, begun the creation of an immense Fleet train, comprising many vessels, large and medium, specially fitted as repair ships, recreation ships for personnel, provision and munition ships, and many modern variants, in order that our Fleet may have a degree of mobility which for several months together will make them largely independent of main shore bases. A substantial portion of the vessels which we shall use for this purpose have been building in Canada, for it is found better and more economical to adapt new merchant ships while they are building to the exact purpose they have to fulfil than to convert existing vessels, although that process has also been carried very far. Thus we hope to place in the Pacific a Fleet capable in itself of fighting a general action with the Japanese Navy, and which, added to the far greater United States Naval power, should give a Naval command in all these vast ocean spaces and seas of the most complete and decisive character.

One must certainly contemplate that a phase in the war against Japan will be the severe, intense, prolonged and ever-increasing air bombardment to which the Japanese mainland installations and munitions centres will be subjected. In this also we shall bear our part to the utmost limit which the bases will allow. As for the land or amphibious operations which the British Empire will conduct, these must rightly be veiled in mystery. Suffice it to say that the scale of our effort will be limited only by the available shipping. In this, however, we may presently receive a magnificent addition. The end of the U-boat war, when it comes, will allow us to go out of convoy in the Western hemisphere, thus adding at a bound at least 25 per cent. to the efficient carrying capacity of our Mercantile Marine, and a larger percentage to the carrying capacity of tankers.

I must, however, add a word of caution about taking too optimistic views of the speed at which this great transference of forces can be made from one side of the world to the other. Not only will the Allied shipping, vast as it is, and far greater as it is than at the beginning of

the war, be a limiting factor, but the development of bases, the accumu-
lation of stores and supplies, and the construction and protection of
airfields, all impose restraints upon those vivid, imaginative strategists
who carry fleets and armies across the globe as easily as they would
help themselves to a plateful of soup. The huge distances, the tropical
conditions and other physical facts, added to the desperate resistance
of the enemy, make the war against Japan an enterprise of the first
magnitude, and it will be necessary to use to the full the resources
of machinery and science to enable our armies to do their work under
the most favourable conditions and with the least sacrifice of Allied
life. When all these aspects are considered, the House may rest assured
that the entire brain and technical power of Great Britain and the
United States will be ceaselessly employed, and having regard to the
results already obtained in so many directions, one may feel good
confidence that it will not be employed in vain.

I have now reached the close of the military aspect of what I have to
say, and it might be convenient for the House, it certainly would be an
indulgence to, I must not say the speaker, but the orator, if we could
have an interlude for lunch, and I would respectfully ask, I will not
say the Leader of the Opposition but my right hon. Friend opposite,
whether he would be in accord with such proceedings ?

* * * * *

When we were last assembled here I had completed a review of
the military situation which, although not by any means complete or
exhaustive, yet, I trust, gave the general outline of our position at
the present time from the point of view of one who has special opportunities of seeing things in their broad perspective. The foreign
situation has responded to military events. Never was the alliance
against Germany of the three great Powers more close or more
effective. Divergencies of view and interest there must necessarily
be, but at no time have these been allowed to affect in any way the
majestic march of events in accordance with the decisions and agreements at Teheran. One by one, in rapid succession, the satellite
States have writhed or torn themselves free from the Nazi tyranny,
and, as is usual in such cases, the process has not been one from
alliance with Germany to neutrality, but from alliance with Germany
to war. This has taken place in Rumania and Bulgaria. Already
there is fighting between the Finns and the Germans. The Germans,
in accordance with their usual practice and character, are leaving a
trail of burnt and blackened villages behind them, even in the land of
their unhappy Finnish dupes.

Hungary is still in the Nazi grip, but when, as will happen, that grip
is broken by the steel-hammer blows of war, or when it relaxes by reason

of the internal lesions and injuries of the tyrant, the Hungarian people will turn their weapons, with all their remaining strength, against those who have led them through so much suffering to their present ruin and defeat. The armistice terms agreed upon for Finland and Rumania bear, naturally, the imprint of the Soviet will—and here I must draw attention to the restraint which has characterized the Soviet treatment of these two countries, both of which marched blithely behind Hitler in his attempted destruction of Russia, and both of which added their quota of injuries to the immense volume of suffering which the Russian people have endured, have survived, and have triumphantly surmounted.

The Bulgarian armistice terms have not yet been signed. The Soviet intervention in this theatre was at once startling and effective. Their sudden declaration of war against Bulgaria was sufficient to induce her to turn her caitiff armies against the German intruders. Britain and the United States have long been at war with Bulgaria, and have now joined with the Soviets in framing suitable armistice conditions. The Bulgarian people have been plunged by their leaders in the last 35 years into three wrongful, forlorn and disastrous wars, and in this last war we cannot forget the many acts of cruelty and wickedness for which they have been responsible both in Greece and Yugoslavia. They have suffered nothing themselves. No foot has been set upon their soil. Apart from some air bombardment, they have suffered nothing. Some of the worst war criminals are Bulgarians. The conduct of their troops in harrying and trying to hold down, at Hitler's orders, their two sorely-pressed small neighbours, Greece and Yugoslavia, is a shameful page for which full atonement must be exacted. They may want to be treated as co-belligerents. So far as Great Britain is concerned, they must work their passage for a long time and in no uncertain fashion before we can accord them any special status, in view of the injuries that our Allies Greece and Yugoslavia have sustained at their hands. In the meantime, let them march and destroy all the Germans they can find in enemy lands. We do not want them in those of our Allies. This is the only path which will serve them and their interests. The more vigour with which they fall upon the Germans, the more they will be likely to draw the attention of the victorious nations in arms away from their previous misdeeds.

It would be affectation to pretend that the attitude of the British and, I believe, the United States Governments towards Poland is identical with that of the Soviet Union. Every allowance must be made for the different conditions of history and geography which govern the relationship of the Western democracies on the one hand and of the Soviet Government on the other with the Polish nation. Marshal Stalin has repeatedly declared himself in favour of a strong, friendly Poland, sovereign and independent. In this our great Eastern Ally is in the fullest accord with His Majesty's Government, and also, judging from American public statements, with the United States. We in this Island and throughout our Empire who drew the sword against mighty Germany, we who are the only great unconquered nation which declared war on Germany on account of her aggression against Poland, have sentiments and duties towards Poland which deeply stir the British race. Everything in our power has been and will be done to achieve, both in the letter and in the spirit, the declared purposes towards Poland of the three great Allies.

Territorial changes on the frontiers of Poland there will have to be. Russia has a right to our support in this matter, because it is the Russian armies which alone can deliver Poland from the German talons; and after all the Russian people have suffered at the hands of Germany, they are entitled to safe frontiers and to have a friendly neighbour on their Western flank. All the more do I trust that the Soviet Government will make it possible for us to act unitedly with them in the solution of the Polish problem, and that we shall not witness the unhappy spectacle of rival Governments in Poland, one recognized by the Soviet Union and the other firmly adhered to by the Western Powers. I have fervent hopes that M. Mikolajczyk, the worthy successor of General Sikorski, a man firmly desirous of friendly understanding and settlement with Russia, and his colleagues may shortly resume those important conversations in Moscow which were interrupted some months ago.

It is my duty to impress upon the House the embarrassment to our affairs and the possible injury to Polish fortunes which might be caused by intemperate language about Polish and Russian relations in the course of this Debate. It is my firm hope, and also my belief, that a good arrangement will be achieved and that a united Polish Government will be brought into being, which will command the confidence of the three great Powers concerned and will assure for Poland those conditions of strength, sovereignty and independence which we have all three proclaimed as our aim and our resolve. Nothing is easier than to create by violent words a prospect far less hopeful than that which now opens before us. Hon. Members will take upon themselves a very grave responsibility if they embroil themselves precipitately in these controversies and thus mar the hopes we cherish of an honourable and satisfactory solution and settlement. We recognize our special responsibilities towards Poland, and I am confident that I can trust the House not to engage in language which would make our task harder.

We must never lose sight of our prime and overwhelming duty, namely, to bring about the speediest possible destruction of the Nazi power. We owe this to the soldiers who are shedding their blood and giving their lives in the cause at this moment. They are shedding their blood in the effort to bring this fearful struggle in Europe to a close; and that must be our paramount task. Every problem—and there are many; they are as legion; they crop up in vast array—which now faces the nations of the world will present itself in a far easier and more adaptable form once the cannons have ceased to thunder in Europe, and once the victorious Allies gather round the table of armistice or peace. I have every hope that wise and harmonious settlements will be made, in confidence and amity, between the great Powers, thus affording the foundations upon which to raise a lasting structure of European and world peace. I say these words on the Polish situation; and I am sure that our friends on both sides will realize how long and anxious has been the study which the Cabinet have given to this matter, how constantly we see representatives of the Poles, how frequent and intimate our correspondence is with Russia on this subject.

I cannot conceive that it is not possible to make a good solution whereby Russia gets the security which she is entitled to have, and which I have resolved that we will do our utmost to secure for her, on her Western Frontier, and, at the same time, the Polish Nation have restored to them that national sovereignty and independence for which, across centuries of oppression and struggle, they have never ceased to strive.

Turning to another difficult and tangled problem, the House will already have read the joint statement by the President and myself which we drafted together, embodying a very definite and distinct improvement and mitigation in our relations with the Italian Government. During my visit to Italy, I had an opportunity of seeing the leaders of all parties, from the extreme Right to the extreme Communist. All the six parties represented in the Italian Government came to the British Embassy, and I had the pleasure of making the acquaintance of all the different Ministers who are working together, as well as they can, in conditions necessarily difficult and depressing. I had conversations with the Prime Minister, Signor Bonomi, and also with him and Marshal Badoglio together. They are friends. The Marshal has very faithfully observed the conditions imposed by the armistice a year ago. He has done his best to send all Italian forces, particularly naval forces, into the struggle against Germany, and he has worked steadfastly for the improvement of relations between Italy and Britain and between Italy and the Allies. His behaviour on leaving office, in giving cordial support to his successor, is also creditable. Finally, I had the advantage of an interview with the Lieutenant of the Realm, whose sincerity and ardour in the Allied cause and whose growing stature in Italian eyes are equally apparent. I give my opinion, and I dare say it will weigh as much as a mocking giggle.

What impressed and touched me most in my journey through Italy was the extraordinary goodwill to the British and American troops everywhere displayed by the Italian people. As I drove through the small towns and villages behind the line of the armies day after day, the friendliness and even enthusiasm of the peasants, workmen and shopkeepers, indeed of all classes, was spontaneous and convincing. I cannot feel—I make my confession—any sentiments of hostility towards the mass of the misled or coerced Italian people. Obviously, no final settlement can be made with them or with their Government until the North of Italy and its great cities have been liberated and the basis on which the present Government stands has been broadened and strengthened. There are good hopes that this will be achieved, I might say soon, but it would be safer to say in due course. Indeed, it would be a miserable disaster if the Italian people, after all their maltreatment by their former Allies and by the Fascist remnants still gathered round Mussolini, were to emerge from the European struggle only to fall into violent internal feuds. It was for that reason, on leaving Rome, that I tried to set before the Italian nation some of those broad simple, Liberal safeguards and conceptions which are the breath of our nostrils in this country—so much so that we scarcely notice them—and which sustain the rights and freedoms of the individual against all forms of tyranny, no matter what liveries they wear or what slogans they mouth.

We were, all of us, shocked by the horrible lynching outrage which occurred in the streets of Rome a week or so ago. Every measure of precaution and authority must be taken to prevent outbreaks of mob vengeance, however great the provocation may have been, and for this, responsibility rests, not only with the Italian Government, but ultimately with the Allied military power. Punishment for criminals who have committed most cruel, barbarous acts under the orders of the Germans, for men who have made themselves the agents of the betrayal of the 300 or 400 hostages shot *en masse* in the catacombs of Rome—punishment for them there must certainly be, but it must be the punishment of courts of justice, with the strictest adherence to the forms and principles of justice. This shameful incident has been a baffling factor in the Italian scene. Nevertheless, it has not deterred us from issuing the joint statement to which I have already referred, and which, so far as Great Britain is concerned, was, of course, approved by the War Cabinet before I gave my agreement to it.

I turn from the Italian scene. Nothing has given the British nation and the King's Dominions all over the world more true joy than the wonderful spectacle of the rescue of France by British and American arms from the horrible oppression of the Hun under which she has writhed or languished for four hideous years. It is now nearly forty years since I first became convinced that the fortunes of Great Britain and France were interwoven, and that their military resources must be combined in the most effective manner, by alliance and agreement and plan ; and I think I can claim to have pursued this object through all the changing scenes we have witnessed, not only before and during the last war, but in the uneasy interval between the two wars, and not only in years of success, but during the period of blackest disaster, and also during periods when there was friction on other grounds between the two countries.

Bearing in mind some mistakes in our own policy between the wars ; bearing in mind also the failure of the League of Nations, in consequence, largely, of the falling out of America, and other weaknesses for which other Powers are responsible, to give general security to the world ; bearing in mind the withdrawal of the United States from the Anglo-American guarantee against German aggression promised by President Wilson, on the strength of which France relinquished her claims on the Rhine frontier ; bearing in mind, above everything, the loss of nearly two million men which France, with her small and declining population, sustained in bearing the brunt, as she bore it, of the last war, and the terrible effect of this unexampled blood-letting upon the whole heartbeat, the life heartbeat, of France ; bearing all this, and much else, in mind, I have always felt the liveliest sympathy for the French in the years when we watched, supinely, the dreadful and awe-inspiring growth of the German power.

It will be remembered that we told the French Government that we would not reproach them for making a separate peace in the fearful circumstances of June, 1940, provided they sent their Fleet out of the reach and power of the Germans. The terms of the Cabinet offer to France in this tragical hour are also on record. I, therefore, have never felt anything but compassion for the French people as a whole who found themselves deprived of all power of resistance and could not share the good fortune of those who, from our shores or in the French Empire, had the honour and opportunity to continue the armed struggle. What could a humble, ordinary man do ? He might be on the watch for opportunity, but he might be rendered almost powerless. The Maquis have shown one way in which, at the end, and after much suffering, and having overcome all the difficulties of getting weapons, free men may strike a blow for the honour and life of their country ; but that is given to the few, to the young and active, those who can obtain weapons.

For my part, I have always felt that the heart of the French nation was sound and true, and that they would rise again in greatness and power, and that we should be proud to have taken a part in aiding them to recover their place in the van of the nations and at the summit of the cultural life of the world. Long have we looked forward to the day when British and American troops would enter again the fields of France, and, regardless of loss and sacrifice, drive the foe before them from towns and cities famous in history, and often sacred to us for the memories of the last war, and of the dear ones whose memories abide with us and who rest in French soil. Often have we longed to receive, and dreamed of receiving, the gratitude and blessings of the French people as our delivering Armies advanced. This has been given to us in unstinted measure, and it has been indeed a glorious experience to witness, and a glorious experience for the Armies to enjoy, this marvellous transformation-scene, and for us to feel that we have acted up to our duties as a faithful Ally to the utmost limit of our strength.

I have repeatedly stated that it is the aim, policy and interest of His Majesty's Government, of this country of Great Britain, and of the Commonwealth and Empire to see erected once more, at the earliest moment, a strong, independent and friendly France. I have every hope that this will soon be achieved. The French people, working together as they must do for their lives and future, in unity of purpose, with sincerity and courage, have a great chance of building a new and undivided France who will take her rightful place among the leading nations of the world.

In my last statement to the House, I spoke of the importance of including representatives of France in all the discussions affecting the Rhine frontier and a general settlement of West Germany. Hitherto, by force of circumstances, the French Algiers Committee could not be a body representative of France as a whole. Now, however, progress has been made. Naturally, that body has new elements, especially amongst those who formed the Maquis and resistance movements, and among those who raised the glorious revolt in Paris, which reminded us of the famous days of the Revolution, when France and Paris struck a blow that opened the path broadly for all the nations of the world. Naturally, we, and, I believe, the United States and the Soviet Union, are most anxious to see emerge an entity which can truly be said to speak in the name of the people of France—the whole people of France. It would now seem possible to put into force the decree of the Algiers Committee whereby, as an interim stage, the Legislative Assembly would be transformed into an elected body, reinforced by the addition of new elements drawn from inside France. To this body, the French Committee of National Liberation would be responsible. Such a step, once taken, when seen to have the approval of the French people, would greatly strengthen the position of France, and would render possible that recognition of the Provisional Government of France, and all those consequences thereof, which we all desire to bring about at the earliest moment. I close no doors upon a situation which is in constant flux and development. The matter is urgent, however, for those, of whom I am one, who desire to see France take her place at the earliest moment in the high councils of the Allies. We are now engaged in discussing these matters both with the French and with other Allied governments, and I am hopeful that, in the near future, a happy settlement will be reached to the satisfaction of all concerned.

I should like to take this opportunity to express our gratification and pride at the part played by British troops in the liberation of Belgium. The House will have read of the tumultuous welcome with which our troops were everywhere greeted by the Belgian people. This also I regard as a happy augury for the maintenance and strengthening of the ties of friendship between our two countries. Many hundreds of thousands of our dead sleep on Belgian soil, and the independence of that country has always been a matter sacred to us as well as enjoined by our policy. I should like to acknowledge in this House the many agreeable things that were said about this country in the Belgian Parliament when it re-assembled last week. I trust that the day is not far distant when our Forces will also have completed their task of liberating the territory of our staunch and sorely tried friends and allies in Holland—allies in the war of the Spanish Succession and in all the struggles for the establishment of freedom in Europe. They are also very near to us in thought and sympathy, and their interests at home, and also abroad, command British support and are largely interwoven with our own fortunes.

I have had to deal with these countries one by one. I now come to the broader aspect, as far as I can touch upon it to-day, which can only be in a very tentative and partial manner. Since August 21st conversations between representatives of this country, the United States and the Soviet Union have been taking place at Dumbarton Oaks, in the United States, on the future organization of the world for preventing war. It is expected that similar conversations will follow between the United Kingdom and American delegations with the representatives of China. These conversations have been on the official level only, and do not in any way bind the Governments represented. There has, however, been assembled a body of principles and the outline of the kind of structure which in one form or another it is the prime purpose of the Allies to erect after the unconditional surrender and total disarmament of Germany have been accomplished. His Majesty's Government could have had no abler official representative than Sir Alexander Cadogan, and there is no doubt that a most valuable task has been discharged. The whole scene has been explored, and many difficulties have been not merely discovered, but adjusted. There are, however, still some important questions outstanding, and we ought not to be hurried into decisions upon which united opinion in the various Governments responsible is not at present ripe. It would not be prudent to press in a hurry for momentous decisions governing the whole future of the world. The House must realize— and I am sure it does realize, I can see by the whole attitude of the House to-day that it fully realizes—that it is one thing for us here to form and express our own opinions on these matters, and another to have them accepted by other Powers as great as we are.

There is another warning which I would venture to give to the House, and that is, not to be startled or carried away by sensational reports and stories which emanate from the other side of the Atlantic. There is an election on, and very vivid accounts of all kinds of matters are given by people who cannot possibly have any knowledge of what has taken place at secret conferences. The United States is a land of free speech ; nowhere is speech freer, not even here where we sedulously cultivate it even in its most repulsive forms. But when I see some of the accounts given of conversations that I am supposed to have had with the President of the United States, I can only recall a Balfourian phrase at which I laughed many years ago, when he said that the accounts which were given bore no more relation to the actual facts than the wildest tales of the Arabian Nights do to the ordinary in- cidents of domestic life in the East. I may say that everything depends on the agreement of the three leading European and world Powers. I do not think satisfactory agreement will be reached—and unless there is agreement nothing can be satisfactory—until there has been a further meeting of the three heads of Government, assisted as may be necessary by their Foreign Secretaries. I must say that I think it is well to suspend judgment and not to try to form or express opinions on what can only be partial and incomplete accounts. I earnestly hope it may be possible to bring about such a meeting before the end of the year. There are great difficulties, but I hope they may be overcome. The fact that the President and I have been so closely brought together at the Quebec Conference, and have been able to discuss so many matters bearing upon the course of the war and on the measures to be taken after the Germans surrender and also for the broad future, makes it all the more necessary that our third partner, Marshal Stalin, who has, of course, been kept informed, should join with us in a tripartite Conference as soon as the military situation renders this possible. The future of the whole world, and certainly the future of Europe, perhaps for several generations, depends upon the cordial, trustful and comprehending association of the British Empire, the United States and Soviet Russia, and no pains must be spared and no patience grudged which are necessary to bring that supreme hope to fruition.

I may say at once, however, that it will not, in my opinion, be possible for the great Powers to do more, in the first instance, than act as trustees for the other States, great or small, during the period of transition. Whatever may be settled in the near future must be regarded as a preliminary, and only as a preliminary, to the actual establishment in its final form of the future world organization. Those who try in any country to force the pace unduly will run the risk of overlooking many aspects of the highest importance, and also by imprudence they can bring about a serious deadlock. I have never been one of those who believe that all the problems of the immediate future can be solved while we are actually engaged in a life and death struggle with the German and Nazi Power, and when the course of military operations and the development of the war against Japan must increasingly claim the first place in the minds of those in Britain and the United States upon whom the chief responsibility rests.

To shorten the war by a year, if that can be done, would in itself be a boon greater than many important acts of legislation. To shorten this war, to bring it to an end, to bring the soldiers home, to give them a roof over their heads, to re-establish the free life of our country, to enable the wheels of commerce to revolve, to get the nations out of their terrible frenzy of hate, to build up something like a human world and a humane world—it is that that makes it so indispensable for us to struggle to shorten, be it even by a day, the course of this terrible war.

It is right to make surveys and preparations beforehand, and many have been made and are being made ; but the great decisions cannot be taken finally, even for the transition period, without far closer, calmer, and more searching discussions than can be held amid the clash of arms. Moreover, we cannot be blind to the fact that there are many factors, at present unknowable, which will make themselves manifest on the morrow of the destruction of the Nazi regime. I am sure this is no time for taking hard and fast momentous decisions on incomplete data and at breakneck speed. Hasty work and premature decisions may lead to penalties out of all proportion to the issues immediately involved. That is my counsel to the House, which I hope they will consider. I hope that the House will notice that, in making my statement to-day, I have spoken with exceptional caution about Foreign Affairs, and, I hope, without any undue regard for popular applause. I have sedulously avoided the appearance of any one country trying to lay down the law to its powerful Allies or to the many other States involved. I hope, however, that I have given the House some impression of the heavy and critical work that is going forward and will lie before us even after the downfall of our principal enemy has been effected. I trust that what I have said may be weighed with care and goodwill not only in this House and in this country but also in the far wider circles involved.

ADVICE TO THE GERMANS

Reminded by a member of his advice to the Germans to overthrow their Nazi task-masters and asked what statement he could make to encourage them to do so, the Prime Minister said on July 12 :

I AM very glad to be reminded of that statement, to which I strongly adhere. I think it has been repeated in other forms by the Foreign Secretary and other Ministers. At any rate, it would certainly be a very well-advised step on the part of the Germans.

Asked to see that members of the German underground movement, few though they may be, received better treatment than the mass of the Germans, Mr. Churchill replied :

I have not been able to come into contact with them yet.

EX-SERVICEMEN'S BADGE

Asked to issue a badge to be worn on civilian clothes by men and women who have been honourably discharged from the forces because of wounds, accidents or illness, the Prime Minister said on July 12 :

The King's Badge is issued to those invalided from the Navy, Army and Air Force and the Merchant Navy and Fishing Fleet, through wounds or war disablement attributable to service since September 3rd, 1939. Suggestions that the terms of qualification should include illness not attributable to service have been carefully considered, and it has been decided not to make this alteration in the entitlement rules.

When told by a member that 200 M.P.s had expressed a desire that a badge should be issued to those who were honourably discharged for any reason, Mr. Churchill replied :

I was not aware of it. I have the greatest respect for the opinion of any hon. Member of the House, and especially of two hundred.

IF GERMANY GOES COMMUNIST

Questioned as to the Government's policy in the event of the German people over-throwing the Nazis and establishing a Communist régime, the Prime Minister said on July 18 :

I should not like to go into this matter, but I am quite sure that

German criminals have no right to escape merely by suddenly embracing the Communist faith.

When another member asked whether the Prime Minister could state the exact difference between a Nazi and a Communist régime, Mr. Churchill answered:

I really could write quite a short brochure on the subject.

POST-WAR HOUSING

Asked to appoint a minister to deal with post-war housing, the Prime Minister said on July 18:

I do not underrate the importance of the issue, but I am always doubtful—I am always inclined to be at first sight doubtful—whether particular evils are always cured by adding to the numbers of Ministers of the Crown.

NO POLITICAL CONSCRIPTION

Asked whether he was taking any steps to continue the National Government, which, a member suggested, would be necessary if the economic aims in the Government's Employment policy were to be achieved, the Prime Minister said on July 18:

I am not thinking of bringing the system of compulsory service, or even the power of direction to civilian work, into the political theatre.

GENERAL MIHAILOVITCH

Questioned regarding Britain's representation at the headquarters of General Mihailovitch in Yugoslavia, the Prime Minister said on July 18:

The British liaison officers attached to General Mihailovitch's mission were withdrawn when it became clear that he was not engaged in operations against the enemy, and that some of his lieutenants were directing their efforts against the Partisans.

I have followed with the closest attention, as far as is humanly possible, what is taking place in Yugoslavia, and I am certainly inclined to consider that the decision which we made some time ago, to dissociate ourselves from General Mihailovitch, was in every way justified.

LIBERATED FRANCE

Asked to make a broadcast to France to mark the occasion of the signing of the formal agreement between Great Britain and U.S.A. and the French Committee of Liberation, the Prime Minister said on July 20 :

The Foreign Secretary sent an inspiring message to France on the occasion of the 14th of July. I saw the last parade of the French Army and Empire on the 14th of July, 1939, and I earnestly hope that I shall have the chance to see another. I am always thinking about a good opportunity of making a broadcast to them, but I should like to choose the occasion for myself.

WORLD SECURITY

Asked whether the Government's proposals for the establishment of an organization for world peace would be placed before the House of Commons for discussion before they were adopted, the Prime Minister said on September 26 :

The policy of His Majesty's Government is to join with the Governments of the United States, the Soviet Union, and China in reaching agreement upon a set of proposals for the establishment of an organization to maintain peace and security and to further social and economic co-operation among the peace-loving nations. The first steps are at present being taken in the conversations still in progress at Dumbarton Oaks, near Washington, between officials representing the four Governments. None of the Governments represented is committed at present. If, as I greatly hope, we succeed in framing such joint proposals, they will be communicated to the other Governments concerned, as the basis for discussion at a general Conference of all the United Nations. An appropriate opportunity will be given to the House to consider these proposals before anything is finally settled.

THE RISING IN WARSAW

Asked to make a statement regarding the rising of General Bor's Polish forces inside Warsaw, the Prime Minister said on September 26 :

I welcome this opportunity of paying tribute to the heroism and tenacity of the Polish Home Army and the population of Warsaw, who, after five years of oppression have yet fought for nearly two months to contribute all in their power to the expulsion of the Germans from the capital of Poland.

His Majesty's Government have always made it clear to all concerned that they were too far from the scene to undertake responsibility for ordering or supporting a general rising in Poland. At the same time, they have consistently used their good offices to promote co-operation and co-ordination of plans in regard to such matters between the Polish and Soviet authorities, and, despite the formidable practical difficulties, they have furnished military supplies by air to the Polish Home Army. As soon as His Majesty's Government learned that the rising in Warsaw had begun, they expressed to the Soviet Government their hope that, although such co-ordination had not yet been achieved, they would nevertheless bring such aid to the Polish insurgents as lay in their power. The Soviet armies were at that time engaged in heavy fighting with strong German forces to the East and North-East of Warsaw, but when their operational plans permitted and direct contact had been established with the Polish Commander-in-Chief in Warsaw, they sent supplies to the Polish forces and provided them with air cover and anti-aircraft support. This assistance has been gratefully acknowledged by the Polish Prime Minister and by the Polish Commander-in-Chief in Warsaw.

Meanwhile, the Royal Air Force, despite the very great practical difficulties and in the face of heavy losses, themselves made the long flight from Mediterranean bases to Warsaw with supplies on all occasions when weather conditions permitted. In their statement issued on September 13th, the Polish Government published particulars and expressed appreciation of this assistance. On September 18th a large escorted force of United States heavy bombers carried out a successful operation, which was planned in co-operation with the Soviet High Command, but was unavoidably postponed for several days because of bad weather. This force, after dropping a large quantity of supplies in Warsaw, the bulk of which came from British sources, flew on to bases in Soviet territory escorted by Soviet aircraft.

These successful combined operations have played an important part in sustaining the gallant resistance of the Polish forces and in enabling them to contribute so effectively to the liberation of their country's capital, which will not, I hope, be much longer delayed.

WAR CRIMINALS

The Prime Minister's attention was drawn to a statement by Sir Cecil Hurst (Chairman of the United Nations War Crimes Commission) that if Hitler escaped to a neutral country nothing could be done in the matter by the Allies, and he was asked what action the Government was taking to prevent such evasion of justice. The Prime Minister replied on September 26:

I understand that the remarks attributed to Sir Cecil Hurst in the newspaper report did not represent accurately what he said. This is one of those cases of taking out detached sentences from their context, and not having proper regard to all the necessary limiting and guarding phrases and words which are proper to public statements. His Majesty's Government are resolved to do their utmost to prevent Nazi criminals finding refuge in neutral territory from the consequences of their crimes.

When the questioner then asked that neutrals should be warned that they would not be allowed to shelter Nazi criminals, Mr. Churchill said :

Odd as it may seem, the point has not entirely escaped the notice of the Government. I notice that a number of neutrals have already made satisfactory statements upon the subject, but it is not our intention to allow the escape of these men to be effected without exerting almost every resource which civilized Powers can contemplate.

When another member asked the Prime Minister to remember " the precedent in the case of Napoleon," Mr. Churchill replied :

I do not see that it applies at all. Napoleon gave himself up, and threw himself upon the mercy of Britain, and he was kept for the rest of his life as a prisoner of State.

MESSAGES

A PLEDGE TO CHINA

A message to Marshal Chiang Kai-shek on the seventh anniversary of the outbreak of the war between China and Japan. July 6, 1944.

ON this day, when China embarks on the eighth year of her fight for freedom, I send to you, Mr. President, and to the Chinese people whose spirit you personify, my best wishes and those of all my countrymen. In the West the past twelve months have seen the overthrow of one of the three members of the Tripartite Pact, and an attack on another which I confidently believe will prove to be the beginning of its end. In the East we have subjected our common enemy to steady pressure, though we have not yet been able, with the other calls upon our strength, to bring to our Chinese ally the assistance we could wish. But when victory in the West is won—and victory now seems sure—we shall fulfil our pledge to bring our whole weight to bear on Japan, an enemy whose odious and barbaric conduct has filled the hearts of my countrymen with implacable and remorseless detestation. But I am confident that the long period of suffering which your people have endured with such steadfast courage will meet with its reward in the destruction of Japanese militarism and the establishment in the East, as in the West, of a system based on security, justice and mutual collaboration. When that day dawns China, for so many years delivered to carnage and destruction, will once again be able to play her part as a leader in the civilized development of the world.

TO MR. MACKENZIE KING

A message to the Prime Minister of Canada on the 25th anniversary of his leadership of the Liberal Party in Canada. August 7, 1944.

I learn that you are to-day celebrating the Silver Jubilee of your assumption of the leadership of your Party. In the whole history of free Parliamentary institutions few if any can claim to have led a Party of the State so long and pre-eminently. Throughout these twenty-five years you and we have watched Canada advance along the road of liberty and progress with admiration and pride. Yet never, perhaps, has this country held Canada in higher esteem than in these last five years of bitter conflict, during which, under your inspired guidance as Prime Minister, she has played so splendid a part in the now imminent overthrow of the powers of evil. It is a peculiar pleasure therefore to offer you at this time my warmest congratulations and, if I may, to add my sincere good wishes for a prosperous future.

LIBERATION OF BRUSSELS

A message to M. Pierlot, Belgian Prime Minister. September 5, 1944.

I thank Your Excellency for your telegram and assure you of the deepest gratification which I, in common with every Englishman, feel in the knowledge that British troops are to play a part in the restoration of Belgian independence and the freeing of her soil from the taint of German occupation.

The fates of Belgium and England have always been closely linked, and I know that the two countries will continue in peace the intimate friendship and understanding which comradeship in arms has brought them.

TRIBUTE TO LORD CECIL OF CHELWOOD

A LETTER OF GREETINGS ON THE EIGHTIETH BIRTHDAY of LORD
CECIL OF CHELWOOD, PRESIDENT OF THE LEAGUE OF NATIONS
UNION WHO WAS MINISTER OF BLOCKADE IN THE 1914–1918
WAR CABINET
SEPTEMBER 14, 1944

10, Downing Street,
Whitehall.

My dear Bob—Many happy returns of your eightieth birthday. It
must be a satisfaction to you to see that the great causes of international
peace and justice for which you have so faithfully pleaded are now
being triumphantly vindicated by the sword.

This war could easily have been prevented if the League of Nations
had been used with courage and loyalty by the associated nations.

Even in 1935 and 1936 there was a chance, by making an armed
Grand Alliance under the ægis of the League, to hold in subjection the
rising furies in Germany, or at the very least to enter into armed
conflict on terms far more favourable than those eventually forced
upon us.

We tried our best, and though the road has been one of tragedy and
terror, the opportunity will surely be offered again to mankind to
guard themselves at least for a few generations from such frightful
experiences.

You may be sure that I shall act in accordance with the spirit and
principles of the League, those principles being clothed with the
necessary authority.

You are entitled to mellow reflections even while the storm still
rages. Accept my very best wishes.

Yours very sincerely,

WINSTON S. CHURCHILL.

EPIC OF WARSAW

A Statement to the House of Commons
October 5, 1944

October 1.   *Allied troops south of Arnhem held German counter-attacks.*
             Russians neared the Danube Iron Gates.

October 2.   *U.S. 1st Army drove wedge in the Siegfried Line between*
             Aachen and Geilenkirchen.

October 3.   *R.A.F. flooded German stronghold on the Island of Walcheren*
             and cut the Dortmund-Ems canal.
             Polish patriots in Warsaw capitulated after 63 days'
             resistance.

October 4.   *Germany announced preparations for guerrilla warfare inside*
             the country.

October 5.   *Allied forces landed on the Greek mainland and entered*
             Patras.

[October 5, 1944.

I AM sure that I am expressing the feelings of the House, as well as those of His Majesty's Government, in paying tribute to the heroic stand of the Polish Home Army and of the Polish civilian population at Warsaw. Their resistance to overwhelming odds, under inconceivable conditions of hardship, came to an end on October 3rd, after a fight which lasted 63 days. Despite all the efforts of the Soviet Army, the strong German positions on the Vistula could not be taken, and relief could not come in time. British, American, Polish and Soviet airmen did what they could to succour the Poles at Warsaw, but although this sustained the Polish resistance beyond what would have seemed possible, it could not turn the tide. In the battle for Warsaw, terrible damage has been inflicted upon that noble city, and its heroic population has undergone sufferings and privations unsurpassed even among the miseries of this war.

The fall of Warsaw, at a time when Allied Armies are everywhere victorious, and when the final defeat of Germany is in sight, must come as a very bitter blow to all Poles. At such a moment, I wish to express our respect for all those Poles who fell, fought or suffered at Warsaw, and our sympathy with the Polish nation in this further grievous loss. Our confidence that the days of their tribulation are rapidly drawing to an end is unshakable. When the ultimate Allied victory is achieved, the epic of Warsaw will not be forgotten. It will remain a deathless memory for the Poles, and for the friends of freedom all over the world.

TOWN AND COUNTRY PLANNING BILL

When the Town and Country Planning Bill was being considered in Committee by the House of Commons on October 6, 1944, the Prime Minister intervened unexpectedly in the Debate to urge the House to agree to drop Part II of the Bill, dealing with Compensation, and have instead, at a later date, a Bill dealing with the Compensation Question by itself

[October 6, 1944.

I MUST offer a very considerable apology to the Committee for what must, at first sight, seem a most unwarrantable intrusion on the active and lively course of these Debates. I have not been able to listen to any of them but, of course, behind the scenes, in the preparation of this Measure, I have had over the last year continuous opportunities to acquaint myself, as far as possible, with the general flow of opinion on the controversial questions involved. I hope my apology will be accepted, because I thought it right at this moment to suggest a somewhat unexpected course which I think will be found, when it is carefully considered, helpful to our affairs in general, and also to the particular matters which we have in hand and to which the House has devoted so much attention and thought. Above all, we need to preserve our sense of proportion. There are all sorts of matters which are extremely important upon which we might expend a great deal of energy and pugnacity, but at present we must do our best to keep our pugnacity for export purposes. It seems to me that the Government would be much to blame if it so handled its public business as to bring about unnecessary, or at any rate premature, schisms and disputes between those who have only one object, namely our safe and victorious emergence from our horrible struggle with Germany.

We must not imagine that the situation is not grave because we feel the assurance of victory. A great deal of blood is going to be shed in the next few months. Liberal, Conservative and Labour blood is going to be shed. It is my duty, above all, as far as I can, while pushing forward the great social Measures which have occupied this House, to make sure that no needless cause of difference is raised to an undue height or proportion. It would be a great pity to lose this Bill, but that would be better than having a disagreeable party dispute about it at present. We must have the Bill, because the local authorities have to be many months ahead in their planning. Our towns have been devastated—almost obliterated. There are great areas of devastation, and the hideous spectacle of ruined homes meets the eye on every side. There must be intense thought, among all those concerned in the different localities, directed upon the rebuilding of the houses which have been shattered, and, of course, upon casting the new buildings into a form most likely to be attractive to future generations and respected by those who watch our work. We must have the Bill. I could not think it would be right to lose it. But I would rather lose the Bill than get into a premature squabble about particular points. We have to recognize the limitations within which we have to work under the immense outside pressure of this great war. The appointed day on which the Bill comes into operation must be a good many months hence. Whatever work is done, however energetic, it may be seven, eight or nine months hence before the appointed day can actually be decreed. So I am advised, and others are here to argue points of detail.

I do not want to hamper the rapid passage of this Bill, upon which broad agreement has been reached except in certain quarters, by delaying it until the controversial questions connected with compensation have been settled. That is the point I was going to submit respectfully to the Committee. These compensation issues affect matters far wider than the Bill itself. There is no reason why the Bill should be delayed and hampered, and still less lost, for their sake. We have, at least, several months in hand before the appointed day in which we can deal with the compensation question as a matter by itself in another Bill. I am quite prepared to go into detail on the point that the local authorities will be hampered in making their plans by the fact that the actual basis of compensation has not yet been settled. There is a considerable argument upon that, which my right hon. Friend the Leader of the House will be ready to deploy. I am satisfied that, once this Bill is through without the compensation Clauses, an immense field of forward progress will be open to the local authorities in every part of the country. But it is clear that persistence on Clause 45—to which, Major Milner, I have all the time been endeavouring to come, and which I have now reached, thanks to the forbearance and indulgence of the Committee—persistence on Clauses 45 and 46 would cause a lot of heat which might all be avoided if more time and reflection were given. The word " time " can be used in two senses. There are the hours of the Sittings of the House, about which there may be argument. I do not put it in that sense—we have to sit the hours necessary to do our job. I mean " time " in the sense of opportunity for reflection.

Several attractive suggestions have been made—some I have heard only this morning—which might have a very good chance of uniting us all on a practical work-a-day scheme, but I, as a very old Parliamentary hand, am always shy of adopting last-minute suggestions. I have again and again seen a Government adopt some last-minute suggestion or accept some very specious or even ingenious Amendment, and then, a few minutes or an hour later, some awkward gentleman gets up from a back bench and points out something that has been overlooked which is vital to the whole proposal. This is very bad for a Government. It is always bad for a Government to change its mind, yet it ought to do so from time to time, out of respect to the House of Commons and out of the influence made upon its collective mind by the Debates. But what is still worse is to change your mind and then have to change it again. That is a double disadvantage, and we must certainly avoid that. Therefore, I will not attempt to offer any last-minute solution.

What I venture to propose to the Committee—and I beg at this moment that the Committee will be indulgent to me although I have not been sharing with them the burden and heat of the day—is that we should drop Part II of the Bill, set the local authorities free to get on with their planning of the devastated areas without a day's delay, and that we bring in, in the course of the next few months, a Bill dealing with the compensation question by itself. This would give much the best chance of reaching an agreement under our present conditions of Coalition Government. However, I must make it clear that it is the intention of His Majesty's Government that this Bill pass without Part II, but that it shall, nevertheless, be inseparably linked with the compensation Measure which we shall deal with as soon as our affairs render it convenient and possible. Words will be inserted in the place of Clauses 45 and 46 to make it clear that before the appointed day when this Bill can come into operation, other legislation must be passed—dealt with, of course, by the fullest process of Parliamentary examination and debate—which deals with the question of compensation. I do not want this question of compensation fettered like a cannon-ball to the legs of this Bill, which has to get on its path as soon as possible. We will come along behind and bring the other Bill along as fast as we can.

We do not meet here in the old forms of controversial struggle. The day may come when we shall, but we have to keep together in this crisis of the German war, and we must not let the kind of matters which can ordinarily be fought out between parties get in our way. We must not let them impair the grandeur of our national unity, by which not only we, but countless people throughout the world, have been greatly benefited. In the preparation of this Bill and the preliminary work, very great concessions have been made by some of our Labour colleagues. There was the question of the standard, and the question of the ceiling, and so forth, in which the Minister of Labour himself took a very leading part for the sake of unity. A man is not to be ashamed who takes a part, for the sake of unity at this time, in favour of the standard, which, I am bound to say, was a very essential part of a square deal. There have been great concessions made by our Labour colleagues, but I feel sure that it is necessary now that more thought should be given and more perseverance should be forthcoming in trying to reach agreement on the matters which are in dispute, and which have clearly been shown to be in dispute, during the patient discussions which have taken place.

I say to the Committee frankly that if I thought this was merely putting off an evil day or putting off a day of quarrel, I would rather drop the Bill; but I am sure that that would be detrimental to the needs which people have and which must be met. I do not think we should be justified in doing that. But if I saw no hope of reaching any solution in this Parliament, I would rather drop the Bill. I do see a hope ; I see more than a hope. I cannot believe that after getting over such enormous difficulties among ourselves, and showing an iron front to the whole of the terrors of the world war, we are now going to be baffled by the different points of view which necessarily present themselves when questions of compensation arise, and when the representatives of three parties have to try to agree upon them. I therefore ask the House to consent——

> The Prime Minister was here interrupted by Mr. Aneurin Bevan, M.P. When Mr. Churchill pointed out that Mr. Bevan was not in his place at the beginning of the speech, Mr. Bevan said : " I did not know the right hon. Gentleman was coming in." The Prime Minister continued :

The importance of the Business of this Committee is not affected by my presence. Really, I am not going to have flattery from this quarter. I am trying to talk this matter over in a very friendly manner. I am finishing now. In an inconceivably short space of time I shall be seated, and the hon. Gentleman, if he should catch the Chairman's eye, will then be able to fall upon me with all his pent-up ferocity. For the moment, I just wish to say that I should like the Committee to consent to the omission of these two Clauses, let the local authorities get on with the work of planning, and let us see whether we can, by taking further thought, produce, with good will and perseverance, an overtaking, or at the very worst an intercepting, solution, in the shape of a separate Bill which will be satisfactory to the House.

> Mr. Bevan then asked whether the Prime Minister had informed the Cabinet that he was going to make the statement he had just made. Mr. Churchill replied :

I came—after an interval, I must frankly confess, for physical refreshment—straight from the Cabinet to the Committee to make this statement, and to express their wishes and their views. I am convinced that the right hon. Gentleman the Minister of Labour and I look at this matter at the present moment, and at this solution— reserving all the natural differences which exist between us on so many matters, but proclaiming at the same time all the associations that we have in common—in entire agreement.

After speeches by several other members the Prime Minister spoke again in the debate as follows :

I must say that I am very agreeably impressed with the resolve to face practical difficulties and realities in this matter which has shown itself in the Committee at the present time, but I want to get this Bill. We cannot afford to lose this Bill. I think we are all agreed about that, and therefore I think we are all agreed that, as far as to-day goes, we can postpone these Clauses, because to plunge in upon them will frustrate the desire to get the Bill, and will cause trouble. I am quite ready to say that the Government would rather have the Bill, with the Clauses, in a broadly agreed form, than have the Bill go forward and another Bill come along to overtake it. If we have to choose between that and losing the Bill, we would rather have this cumbersome method of the tank being separated from the engine, and the engine having to go back and catch it. We are all agreed what to do this afternoon. So far as I can make out, it is pretty nearly universal. There is the week-end and Monday, and I certainly think that discussions should proceed, through the usual channels and also in the Cabinet, to see whether we can save this Bill and have an agreed compensation Clause.

It would only be on the supposition that everything else fails that we should go forward on the plan which I have announced. It may be that after the interchanges have taken place, and with the desire to do our work in order to get results which matter to the people— definite results of our labours—some kind of arrangement can be arrived at, and I certainly was attracted by the indication which fell from my right hon. Friend who spoke from the Front Bench opposite upon this issue. By all means, let us, if we can, in the limited time available, make a satisfactory job of work and do a good job all in one piece.

That is what we should like to do, but, if it comes to a question of the Bill being, perhaps, flung over, and we have to delay it to a new Session, I think we shall have to fall back on the much cruder and more cumbrous method which I have felt myself obliged to propose. Therefore, I suggest that we leave out these Clauses now, and see in what way we can realize the hope expressed by the hon. Member for Ebbw Vale (Mr. Bevan) and also by my right hon. Friend the Member for East Edinburgh (Mr. Pethick-Lawrence). After all, we have got to do the job and get the best we can. We must not lose the Bill, and I think the Committee is pretty well agreed about it, and that is the way in which the Government will submit it.

VISIT TO MARSHAL STALIN

A Speech at the Aerodrome before departing from Moscow
October 19, 1944

[October 19, 1944.

MARSHAL STALIN, your Excellencies, ladies and gentlemen, friends and war comrades gathered here, I have now come to the end of a most strenuous and at the same time most agreeable visit to Moscow. We have worked very hard. We have been a council of workmen and soldiers. But the generous hospitality and cordial friendship with which we have been welcomed and sustained has left me and my friend and colleague the Foreign Secretary, Mr. Eden, with the most pleasant memories of these crowded and serious days.

Most of all has it been a pleasure to me and an honour to have so many long intimate talks with my friend and war comrade Marshal Stalin, and to deal with the many difficult questions inseparable from the united forward march of great nations through the many vicissitudes of war.

I hope most earnestly, and I believe with deep conviction, that the warrior statesman and head of Russia will lead the Russian peoples, all the peoples of Russia, through these years of storm and tempest into the sunlight of a broader and happier age for all, and that with him in this task will march the British Commonwealth of Nations and the mighty United States of America.

THE LAST LAP

A Speech on the War Situation. House of Commons
October 27, 1944

October 6.   *Canadian troops opened a general assault towards the south bank of the Scheldt.*

                    Russians advanced 20 miles into Hungary.

October 7.   *Record force of 3,000 British and American heavy bombers raided Germany.*

                    Allied troops in Greece reached the outskirts of Corinth.

October 8.   *Mr. Churchill and Mr. Eden arrived in Moscow for a conference with Marshal Stalin.*

October 9.   *Canadian troops made an amphibious attack behind German pocket on the south bank of the Scheldt.*

October 10.   *Surrender ultimatum issued to the German garrison at Aachen.*

                    Allied troops captured Corinth.

October 11.   *Szeged, second largest city of Hungary, captured by the Russians.*

October 13.   *Germans massed tanks in an attempt to rescue Aachen garrison.*

                    Russians captured Riga.

October 15.   *Germans announced that Admiral Horthy, Regent of Hungary, had been deposed after suing for armistice.*

                    Field-Marshal Rommel's death from wounds was announced by the Germans.

October 16.   *Germans stated they had set up a Government in Hungary and quashed the country's bid for peace.*

October 18.   *Russians captured seven Carpathian passes and advanced 30 miles over Czechoslovakian frontier.*

                    Hitler ordered men between 16 and 60 to join the people's army under Himmler.

October 19.   *Big American forces under General MacArthur landed on the Island of Leyte, in the Philippines.*

October 20.   *Russian forces captured Belgrade, the capital of Yugoslavia.*

                    American troops captured Aachen.

October 22.   *Mr. Churchill arrived home from Moscow.*

                    Russians captured nickel mines of Petsamo on the Norwegian-Finnish border.

October 23.   *Great Britain, United States and Russia recognized General de Gaulle's Provisional Government of France.*

October 24. *The Russians made a big advance into East Prussia.*
October 25. *Two Japanese aircraft carriers and four cruisers were among the 58 ships sunk in a battle with the U.S. fleet off the Philippines. Six American warships were lost.*
October 26. *Princess Beatrice, great-aunt of the King, died. The Archbishop of Canterbury died.*

[*October* 27, 1944.

THE present stage of the war is dour and hard, and the fighting must be expected on all fronts to increase in scale and in intensity. We believe that we are in the last lap, but this is a race in which failure to exert the fullest effort to the end may postpone that end to periods almost unendurable to those who now have the race in their hands after struggling so far. The enemy has two hopes. The first is that by lengthening the struggle he may wear down our resolution; the second, and more important, hope is that division will arise between the three great Powers by whom he is assailed, and whose continued union spells his doom. His hope is that there will be some rift in this Alliance; that the Russians may go this way, the British and Americans that; that quarrels may arise about the Balkans or the Baltic, about Poland or Hungary, which he hopes will impair the union of our councils and, consequently, the symmetry and momentum of our converging advance. There is the enemy's great hope. It is to deprive that hope of all foundation and reality that our efforts must ceaselessly be bent.

You would not expect three great Powers, so differently circumstanced as Britain, the United States and Soviet Russia, not to have many different views about the treatment of the various and numerous countries into which their victorious arms have carried them. The marvel is that all has hitherto been kept so solid, sure and sound between us all. But this process does not arise of itself. It needs constant care and attention. Moreover, there are those problems of distance, occasion and personalities which I have so often mentioned to the House, and which make it extremely difficult to bring the heads of the three principal Allies together in one place at one time. I have, therefore, not hesitated to travel from court to court like a wandering minstrel, always with the same songs to sing—or the same set of songs.

The meeting at Moscow was the sequel to Quebec. At Quebec, the President and I felt very much the absence of Russia. At Moscow, Marshal Stalin and I were deeply conscious that the President was not with us, although in this case the American observer, Mr. Averill Harriman, the accomplished Ambassador of the United States, made us feel at all times the presence of the great Republic. There was a special reason for our dual conference at Quebec. The British and American fighting forces are intermingled in the lines of battle as fighting men of two countries have never been intermingled before. Fighting men have never before mingled so closely and so easily. We must meet ; we must discuss.

As to Russia, Great Britain has many problems in Eastern Europe to solve in common with Russia, and practical issues arise on all these from day to day. We must disperse misunderstandings and forestall them before they occur. We must have practical policies to deal with day-to-day emergencies, and, of course, we must carry with us at every stage the Government of the United States. I am satisfied that the results achieved on this occasion at Moscow have been highly satisfactory. But I am quite sure that no final result can be attained until the heads of the three Governments have met again together, as I earnestly trust they may do before this year is at its end. After all, the future of the world depends upon the united action in the next few years of our three countries. Other countries may be associated, but the future depends upon the union of the three most powerful Allies. If that fails, all fails ; if that succeeds, a broad future for all nations may be assured. I am very glad to inform the House that our relations with Soviet Russia were never more close, intimate and cordial than they are at the present time. Never before have we been able to reach so high a degree of frank and friendly discussion of the most delicate and often potentially vexatious topics as we have done at this meeting from which I have returned, and about which I thought it would be only respectful to the House to make some short statement.

Where we could not agree, we understood the grounds for each other's disagreement and each other's point of view, but over a very wide area, an astonishingly wide area considering all the different angles from which we approached these topics, we found ourselves in full agreement. Of course, it goes without saying that we were united in prosecuting the war against Hitlerite Germany to absolute victory, and in using the last and every resource of our strength and energy in combination for that purpose. Let all hope die in German breasts that there will be the slightest division or weakening among the forces which are closing in upon them, and will crush the life out of their resistance.

Upon the tangled question of the Balkans, where there are Black Sea interests and Mediterranean interests to be considered, we were able to reach complete agreement. I do not feel that there is any immediate danger of our combined war effort being weakened by divergencies of policy or of doctrine in Greece, Rumania, Bulgaria, Yugoslavia, and, beyond the Balkans, Hungary. We have reached a very good working agreement about all these countries, singly and in combination, with the object of concentrating all their efforts, and concerting them with ours against the common foe, and of providing, as far as possible, for a peaceful settlement after the war is over. We are, in fact, acting jointly, Russia and Britain, in our relations with both the Royal Yugoslav Government headed by Dr. Subasic and with Marshal Tito, and we have invited them to come together for the common cause, as they had already agreed to do at the conference which I held with them both at Naples. How much better that there should be a joint Anglo-Russian policy in this disturbed and very complex area, than that one side should be backing one set of ideas, and the other the opposite ! That is a most pernicious state of affairs to grow up in any country, as it may easily spread to corresponding differences between the great Powers themselves.

Our earnest hope and bounden duty is so to conduct our policy that these small countries do not slip from the great war effort into internal feuds of extreme bitterness. We have, as I say, invited them to come together and form a united government for the purpose of carrying on the war until the country itself can pronounce. All this is, of course, only a guide for the handling of matters from day to day, but it is so much easier to enter into arrangements by conversation than by telegram and diplomatic correspondence, however carefully phrased and however lengthily expressed, or however patiently the discussions may be conducted. Face to face, difficulties which appear really insuperable at a distance are very often removed altogether from our path. But these workaday arrangements must be looked upon as a temporary expedient to meet the emergency, and all permanent arrangements await the presence of the United States, who have been kept constantly informed of what was going forward. Everything will eventually come to review at some future conference, or at an armistice or peace table.

There were, of course, a good many serious military questions discussed. I had with me the Chief of the Imperial General Staff, General Ismay, and other officers acquainted with the conduct of the whole of our military affairs and strategy, and we also had the advantage of the assistance, not only of the American Ambassador, but of the very able United States technical representative, General Deane. All these discussions were part of the process of carrying out and following up the great decisions taken nearly a year ago at Teheran, which, I think, may be said without exaggeration to have altered the face of the world war. But naturally, I could not say anything about these discussions or decisions, except that I found them very good, and, indeed, the best that could be devised to lift the cruel scourge of war from Europe at the earliest possible moment.

The most urgent and burning question was, of course, that of Poland; and, here again, I speak words of hope, of hope reinforced by confidence To abandon hope in this matter would, indeed, be to surrender to despair. In this sphere there are two crucial issues. The first is the question of the Eastern frontier of Poland with Russia and the Curzon Line, as it is called, and the new territories to be added to Poland in the North and in the West. That is the first issue. The second is the relations of the Polish Government with the Lublin National Liberation Committee. On these two points, apart from many subsidiary and ancillary points, we held a series of conferences with both parties. We saw them together and we saw them separately, and, of course, we were in constant discussion with the heads of the Soviet Government. I had several very long talks with Marshal Stalin, and the Foreign Secretary was every day working on these and cognate matters with Mr. Molotov. Two or three times we all four met together without anyone else but the interpreters being present.

I wish I could tell the House that we had reached a solution of these problems. It is certainly not for want of trying. I am quite sure, however, that we have got a great deal nearer to the solution of both. I hope Mr. Mikolajczyk will soon return to Moscow, and it will be a great disappointment to all the sincere friends of Poland, if a good arrangement cannot be made which will enable him to form a Polish Government on Polish soil—a Government recognized by all the great Powers concerned, and indeed by all those Governments of the United Nations which now recognize only the Polish Government in London. Although I do not underrate the difficulties which remain, it is a comfort to feel that Britain and Soviet Russia, and I do not doubt the United States, are all firmly agreed on the re-creation of a strong, free, independent, sovereign Poland loyal to the Allies and friendly to her great neighbour and liberator, Russia. Speaking more particularly for His Majesty's Government, it is our persevering and constant aim that the Polish people, after their sufferings and vicissitudes, shall find in Europe an abiding home and resting-place, which, though it may not entirely coincide or correspond with the pre-war frontiers of Poland, will, nevertheless, be adequate for the needs of the Polish nation and not inferior in character and quality, taking the picture as a whole, to what they previously possessed.

These are critical days, and it would be a great pity if time were wasted in indecision or in protracted negotiation. If the Polish Government had taken the advice we tended them at the beginning of this year, the additional complication produced by the formation of the Polish National Committee of Liberation at Lublin would not have arisen; and anything like a prolonged delay in the settlement can only have the effect of increasing the division between Poles in Poland,

and also of hampering the common action which the Poles, the Russians and the rest of the Allies are taking against Germany. Therefore, as I say, I hope that no time will be lost in continuing these discussions and pressing them to an effective conclusion.

I told the House on September 28th of my hope that the re-organization of the French Consultative Assembly on a more representative basis would make it possible for His Majesty's Government, at an early date, to recognize the then French Administration as the Provisional Government of France. The Assembly has now, in fact, been enlarged and strengthened by the addition of many fresh representatives of both the resistance organizations in France, and the old Parliamentary groups. It constitutes as representative a body as it is possible to bring together in the difficult circumstances obtaining to-day in France, and it will be holding its first session in Paris in a few days' time. This development was closely followed by a further step towards the restoration of normal conditions of government in France. The Civil Affairs Agreement concluded by France with Great Britain and the United States last August, after long and patient exertions by the Foreign Secretary, provided for the division of the country into a Forward Zone, in which the supreme Allied Commander would exercise certain overriding powers of control considered necessary for the conduct of military operations, and an Interior Zone, where the conduct of, and responsibility for, the administration would be entirely a matter for the French authorities. For obvious reasons, at the beginning, when for those anxious weeks we stood with our backs to the sea a few miles from the beaches, the whole of France had to be in the Forward Zone; but as the tide of battle moved up to and beyond France's Eastern frontier, General Eisenhower, working in the closest and most friendly co-operation with the French civil and military authorities, found he could safely hand over his special powers except in the areas immediately behind the battle zone, and he felt that these authorities had shown themselves fully capable of undertaking the grave responsibilities which fall to the government of any country on which a vast modern army on active service has to be based.

The French Administration was, accordingly, able to announce on October 20th that, with the concurrence of the Allied High Command, it had established an Interior Zone comprising the larger part of France, including Paris. This marked the final stage of transformation of the Committee of National Liberation into a Government exercising provisionally all the powers of the Government of France, and a Government accepted as such by the people of France in their entirety. The way was thus clear for the formal recognition of the Committee as the Provisional Government, and His Majesty's Ambassador in

Paris was accordingly instructed, on October 23rd, to inform the French Minister for Foreign Affairs of the decision of His Majesty's Government in the United Kingdom, in the Union of South Africa and in New Zealand to accord such recognition. A similar communication was made by the Canadian Government through the Canadian Ambassador in Paris, and by the Commonwealth Government through the French representative at Canberra. The United States and Soviet Governments, with whom we had acted throughout in the closest agreement and concert in this matter, were taking similar and simultaneous action.

Some critics have asked : Why should this step not have been taken earlier ? The reason is very simple. The British and American Armies had something to do with the liberation of France, and the British and United States Governments had, therefore, a responsibility at this particular moment for making sure that the French Government, emerging in part from their military action, would be acceptable to France as a whole, and would not appear to be imposed upon the country from without. It is not for us to choose the Government or rulers of France, but at this particular juncture, for that very reason, we had a very special responsibility. I have been myself for some weeks past satisfied not only that the present French Government, under General de Gaulle, commands the full assent of the vast majority of the French people, but that it is the only Government which can possibly discharge the very heavy burdens which are being cast upon it, and the only Government which can enable France to gather its strength in the interval which must elapse before the constitutional and parliamentary processes, which it has declared its purpose to reinstate, can again resume their normal functions. I also made it clear in my speech on August 2nd that France can by no means be excluded from the discussions of the principal Allies dealing with the problems of the Rhine and of Germany. This act of recognition may, therefore, be regarded as a symbol of France's re-emergence from four dark years of terrible and woeful experience, and as heralding a period in which she will resume her rightful and historic role upon the world's stage.

I said that these remarks would be in the nature of a supplement to the statement I made some time ago. I have but one other subject to mention, and it is one which will cause universal rejoicing. I mean the liberation of Athens and a large part of Greece. I was able, when I visited Italy six or seven weeks ago, to arrange with General Wilson, after very careful discussion, for the necessary measures to be set in train which would enable the Royal Greek Government of Monsieur Papandreou to return to Athens at the earliest possible moment, and as a preliminary to this, I advised that Government to move from

Cairo to Caserta, where they would be in the closest touch with the Commander-in-Chief. I think the arrangements were extremely well made by General Wilson, and to him we entrusted the watching for the exact moment to intervene. He found that moment with very happy discretion, so that hardly any loss of life occurred, and no damage has been done to the immortal capital which is dear to the hearts of so many nations throughout the world.

Vivid and moving accounts have appeared in the Press of the decisive events which have recently taken place, and of the fervid welcome which our Forces received throughout Greece, and above all in Athens. When we were driven out of Greece in 1941 amid so much bloodshed and disaster, with the loss of over 30,000 men, we promised to return, and the Greek people never lost faith in that promise, nor abandoned their belief in final victory. We have returned, and our pledge has been redeemed. The lawful Greek Government sits in Athens. Very soon the Greek brigade, which has distinguished itself in the fighting at Rimini on the Italian front, helping to drive the Germans out of Italy, will return with honour to its native land. The tide of war has rolled far to the northward in Greece. Behind the British troops, the organization of U.N.R.R.A., in which the United States plays so great a part, is already moving to the scene. Ships have been loaded for many weeks past, and the much-needed supplies of food for the sorely-tried Greek population will soon be in process of active distribution, if, indeed, that process has not begun already. We are going to do our best to assist in stabilizing the Greek currency, which has been a special mark of sabotage by the Germans, and highly competent officials from the Treasury are already on their way to Athens, where the Foreign Secretary is at the present time, and where he is remaining, according to my latest information, until he can confer with them and with the Greek Government on this subject.

We are doing our best in every way to bring Greece back to normal. Though, of course, we are actively aiding the Greeks in every sphere to recover from the horrible injuries inflicted on them by the Germans, and are thus adding another chapter to the story of the friendship between our countries, we do not seek to become the arbiters of their affairs. Our wish and policy is that when normal conditions of tranquillity have been restored throughout the country, the Greek people shall make, in perfect freedom, their decision as to the form of Government under which they desire to live. Pending such a decision, we naturally preserve our relations with the Greek Royal House and with the existing constitutional Government, and we regard them as the authority to whom we are bound by the alliance made at the time of the attack upon Greece in 1941. Meanwhile, I appeal to all Greeks of every party and of every group—and there is no lack of parties or of groups—to set national unity above all other causes, to cleanse their country of the remaining German forces, to destroy and capture the last of the miscreants who have treated them with indescribable cruelty, and, finally, to join hands to rebuild the strength and reduce the sufferings of their famous and cherished land.

DEATH OF PRINCESS BEATRICE

A SPEECH TO THE HOUSE OF COMMONS
OCTOBER 31, 1944

[October 31, 1944.

I BEG to move,

" That an humble Address be presented to His Majesty to express the deep concern of this House at the loss which His Majesty has sustained by the death of Her Royal Highness the Princess Beatrice ; and to condole with His Majesty on this melancholy occasion ; and to assure His Majesty that this House will ever participate with the most affectionate and dutiful attachment in whatever may concern the feelings and interests of His Majesty."

The death of Her Royal Highness the Princess Beatrice, youngest and last surviving child of Queen Victoria, closes a chapter in the history of the Royal House, and evokes memories of that famous and placid era of peace and progress which is called the Victorian Age. By the public the Princess will be chiefly remembered for her close association with Queen Victoria ; as a child, in married life, and as a widow, she was the Queen's constant companion on private and public occasions, and it was to her that the Queen bequeathed the manuscript of her private journal. Moreover, she was confirmed in the public regard by the severe personal loss, first of her husband, Prince Henry of Battenberg, who died in the second Ashanti war, and then of her son, Prince Maurice, who died of wounds in France in 1914. The Princess was interested in many works of beneficence, chiefly perhaps in ex-Servicemen, for whom, from her own personal sorrow, she had a keen natural sympathy.

She long held the position of Governor and Captain of the Isle of Wight, in which office she succeeded her husband, and she gained in very great measure the affection and the regard of the whole community in the island, in which she had spent many happy days during her early residence there at Osborne with her mother.

The House will no doubt wish to take this opportunity of expressing their deep sympathy with her children, Her Majesty the Queen Dowager Victoria Eugénie of Spain, and the Marquess of Carisbrooke

The Prime Minister visits General Eisenhower before the invasion of the Continent. General Hodges is on the right.

The Prime Minister goes to see for himself. He watches anti-aircraft guns during the Battle of the Flying-Bomb

American Thanksgiving Day at the Albert Hall, London

PROLONGATION OF PARLIAMENT

A SPEECH TO THE HOUSE OF COMMONS
OCTOBER 31, 1944

October 28.   *General Stilwell, Deputy Supreme Commander in South-*
East Asia and C-in-C of the American forces in India,
Burma and China, was relieved of his command.
An armistice between Bulgaria and the Allies was signed
in Moscow.

October 30.   *Allies made swift progress in South-Western Holland.*
Aircraft of the Royal Navy sank six ships off Norway
and damaged 20 more, including a U-boat.

October 31.   *British captured Capelle and reached the River Maas.*

[*October* 31, 1944.

IN asking for a prolongation of the life of this Parliament for another
year, I doubt very much whether the Parliament will last so long.
There are powerful factors of uncertainty which tell in opposite
directions, or from different angles. The meetings of the various
parties opposing the Coalition are to take place shortly before and
shortly after Christmas, and while we cannot at all forecast what will
occur, we certainly cannot exclude the possibility that a desire to
return to the party system will be strongly expressed. On the other
hand, we cannot tell when the war against Nazi Germany will be
definitely ended or will fall into the guerrilla stage. I am confident
that all organized parties will see that business through to the very
end. This would almost certainly be the view, I believe, of the great
Trade Union movement, where determination to finish Hitlerism is
strong and invincible.

I am very clearly of opinion that the coalition of parties ought not
to be broken before Nazidom is broken. This was the purpose for
which we came together in the present Government, and it is still
the supreme purpose which affects the safety of the nation and the
Empire. As I said the other day, any attempt to estimate the date
when the war with Germany can be officially declared over could be no
more than a guess. A political convulsion in Germany might bring
it to a speedy end at any time, but against that must be set the iron
control of German life in all its forms, including the Army, which has
been established by Hitler's storm troops and secret police. This

P   229

exceeds anything previously known among men. Therefore, we cannot count upon any of the normal reactions of public opinion. From every quarter it seems that the civil population are plunged in a dull apathy, and certainly anyone who stirred against the police would instantly be shot or decapitated. Therefore I simply cannot place any dependence upon political uprisings in Germany.

On military grounds it seems difficult to believe that the war could be ended before Christmas, or even before Easter, although, as I have said, many high military authorities with every means to form a correct judgment have expressed themselves more hopefully, and although every effort is being made, and will be made, against the enemy. The German troops are fighting with the utmost tenacity, although cut off in many places, and in defence of positions evidently forlorn. They have been counter-attacking with vigour, though as yet without success, in Holland and on the Moselle. A great deal of work has still to be done to improve the ports and build up supplies and concentrate forward the ever-growing Allied Army. In Italy the fighting is also of the most obstinate character, and the weather has broken. The Eastern front has shown its main activity on the north and south flanks. Immense successes have rewarded strenuous Russian military efforts and skilful Russian and Allied diplomacy. The distances are however very large, and many hostile defence positions have to be stormed or turned. In all these circumstances I certainly could not predict, still less guarantee, the end of the German war before the end of the spring, or even before we reach the early summer. It may come earlier, and no one will rejoice more than I if it should. Anyhow, I have no hesitation in declaring that it would be a wrongful act, unworthy of our country's fame, to break up the present governing instrument before we know where we are with Hitler's Germany. Those who forced such a disaster, even thoughtlessly, would take on themselves a measureless responsibility, and their action would be fiercely resented by the nation at large. I am thankful to say that there are no signs of any such desire in any responsible quarter.

Let us assume, however, that the German war ends in March, April or May, and that some or all the other parties in the Coalition recall their Ministers out of the Government, or wish to bring it to an end from such dates. That would be a matter of regret, both on public and on personal grounds, to a great many people, but it would not be a matter of reproach or bitterness between us in this Government or in this House once Germany has been defeated.

We are told there must on no account be what is called a coupon election. By that I presume is meant an agreement between the official parties not to oppose each other in most of the seats, and to form a solid front against those who criticize or oppose us. In other words, it would mean that the present Coalition should go to the country and obtain from it a renewal of confidence. I have no doubt they would get it, but there would be some who would say it was too easy. But one must admit that many people would think this would hardly be a fair way of testing opinion in the country, and in fact it would be quite impossible to obtain party agreement to such a course. Many people feel that it would impede the electorate in expressing their free choice. Neither would it be seemly, or indeed practicable, once a dissolution had been announced, for Ministers to go all over the country expressing the utmost distaste for each other's views and records, and yet be together in Cabinet discussing as colleagues all the gravest matters of the hour. Nor again would it be proper for the Ministers who are also in some cases leaders, and whose knowledge is needed to guide the country, to remain silent and apparently indifferent to the fortunes of their parties or of their candidates. I do not find it easy to escape from the weight and force of these arguments.

The announcement of the dissolution would therefore necessarily mark the close of the present Administration. The Conservative party have a majority of more than 100 above all parties and independents in the present House, and it would therefore fall to us to make arrangements for the inevitable General Election. I cannot conceive that anyone would wish that election to be held in a violent hurry or while we were all rejoicing together and rendering thanks to God for our deliverance. There must be an interval. Moreover, we have above all things to be careful that practically everybody entitled to vote has a fair chance to do so. This applies above all to the soldiers, many of whom are serving at great distances from this country. Nothing would be more shameful or more dishonourable than to deny the great mass of the soldiers, and the Service men of the Air Force and of the Navy, a full opportunity of recording their votes. In my opinion they have more right to vote than anyone else in the country, and we should all be ashamed if anything were done which prevented these men, to whom we owe almost everything, from taking their full part in deciding the immediate future of their country. That is not to say that every single man in the most remote station can be certain of being able to vote, but everything in human power will be done to give the fullest possible opportunities for the exercise of the franchise to all in the fighting Services.

It is, however, in fact not legally possible, after the new electoral arrangements have come into force, as they do on the 1st December this year, for polling to take place in less than eight weeks from the issue of the writs. A minimum of six weeks must in fact elapse between the issue of the writs and the nomination of candidates alone. All this has been concerted with a general measure of assent by the House, and with·

the sole view of obtaining the fullest and fairest expression of the national opinion. Besides all this, the partial redistribution authorized by the recent Act has to be carried through. A start will be made immediately, not waiting for the end of the German war, but the process will certainly take several months.

It may therefore be taken as certain that from the moment the King gives his consent to a dissolution a period of between two and three months would be required. This also would be fair to the political parties and candidates, who have to set about one another in the usual lusty manner. Moreover, in the interval there will undoubtedly have to be certain financial arrangements made and other matters of business wound up. It follows therefore that if events should take the course I have indicated, it would seem that, roughly speaking, there is no likelihood of a General Election for from seven to nine months from now. Finally, it is contrary to precedent for Governments to hold on to office until the last moment of their legal tenure, or legally extended tenure, and it would be very unwholesome for any practice of that kind to be introduced. For these reasons we have decided not to accept any proposals or suggestions such as I have seen bruited about to reduce the period in the Bill from twelve months to six months, and I ask to-day, in introducing it, for a twelve months' prolongation of the life of the present Parliament.

We think that we have given good reasons to the House to show that the twelve months' period would be a sensible and proper provision to make at the present time. On the other hand, we must assume that the Japanese war will have to be carried on for an indefinite period after the destruction of the Nazi power. Here again there may be the possibilities of some political upheaval in Japan inducing a sudden surrender, but it would be very foolish to count upon this in a race of men of this desperate and barbarous character, whose whole constitution is dominated by the military and naval hierarchies who dragged them into their mad aggression. When the whole of the Japanese problem is examined, on military grounds alone it would certainly not be prudent to assume that a shorter period than eighteen months after the destruction of Hitler would be required for the final destruction of the Japanese will or capacity to fight, and this period must be continually revised every few months by the combined Chiefs of Staffs.

The prolongation of the life of the existing Parliament by another two or three years would be a very serious constitutional lapse. Even now, no one under 30 has ever cast a vote at a General Election, or even at a by-election, since the registers fell out of action at the beginning of the war. Therefore, it seems to me that, unless all political parties resolve to maintain the present Coalition until the Japanese are defeated, we must look to the termination of the war against Nazism as a pointer which will fix the date of the General Election. I should regret the break-up of the present highly efficient Government, which has waged war with unsurpassed success and has shaped or carried out within the last two years a programme of reform and social progress which might well have occupied a whole Parliament under the ordinary conditions of peace for five or six years. In fact, I may say—and I will indeed be quite candid on this point—that having served for 42 years in this House I have never seen any Government to which I have been able to give a more loyal, confident and consistent support. But while I should regret and deplore the break-up of these forces, so knit together by personal goodwill, by the comradeship of fighting a great cause, and by the sense of growing success arising from that comradeship, yet I could not blame anyone who claimed that there should be an appeal to the people once the German peril is removed. Indeed, I have myself a clear view that it would be wrong to continue this Parliament beyond the period of the German war.

The foundation of all democracy is that the people have the right to vote. To deprive them of that right is to make a mockery of all the high-sounding phrases which are so often used. At the bottom of all the tributes paid to democracy is the little man, walking into the little booth, with a little pencil, making a little cross on a little bit of paper—no amount of rhetoric or voluminous discussion can possibly diminish the overwhelming importance of that point. The people have the right to choose representatives in accordance with their wishes and feelings, and I cannot think of anything more odious than for a Prime Minister to attempt to carry on with a Parliament so aged, and to try to grapple with the perplexing and tremendous problems of war and peace, and of the transition from war to peace, without being refreshed by contact with the people.

I can assure the House that in the absence of most earnest representations by the Labour and Liberal Parties, I could not refrain from making a submission to the Crown in respect of a dissolution after the German war is effectively and officially finished. I am sure this is a straightforward, fair and constitutional method of dealing with what is in many ways an unprecedented situation, though not one which need in any way baffle our flexible British system. Meanwhile, I must confess that the position will not become increasingly easy. The odour of dissolution is in the air, and parties are inclined to look at each other across the House with an increasing sense of impending division.

But we have to be specially careful in such circumstances that nothing shall hamper the vigorous prosecution of the war, and that, I am sure, is the resolve of all parties and also of most of those individuals who are specially interested in bringing the Coalition to an end.

I thought it right to touch upon these matters, because they are after all of very considerable importance to our constitutional procedure, but further than this I find it impossible to form an opinion. Mr. Jorrocks said of fox-hunting that it was the image of war without its guilt, and only five-and-twenty per cent. of its danger. Something like that might be said of a General Election. It is a trial of strength between parties, of which the nation is the arbiter. I have often thought that it is sometimes unwise of generals to try to foresee with meticulous exactness just what will happen after a battle has been fought. A battle hangs like a curtain across the future. Once that curtain is raised or rent we can all see how the scenery is arranged, what actors are left upon the scene, and how they appear to be related to one another. In this case it will certainly be much better to wait till the new situation is fully disclosed.

Meanwhile, as we probably have a good many months of the closest comradeship and hardest work before us, and there will be ample opportunity later for party oratory, which will necessarily occur between the dissolution and the poll, I should deprecate strongly the over-emphasizing of party differences now, and recommend that we all bend ourselves with unflagging energy and unbroken union to the national task.

DEATH OF LORD MOYNE

A SPEECH TO THE HOUSE OF COMMONS ON THE ASSASSINATION OF THE
RESIDENT MINISTER IN THE MIDDLE EAST
NOVEMBER 7, 1944

November 1. *British assault troops landed on the Island of Walcheren.
British troops entered Salonika.*

November 2. *British troops captured Zoulelande on the Island of
Walcheren and most of the town of Flushing.
Two hundred enemy aircraft were destroyed over Germany
by American planes.*

November 3. *German resistance in the Scheldt pocket ended with
surrender, and Belgium was liberated.
Lieut.-General Sir Oliver Leese was appointed to
command the 11th Army Group in South-East Asia.*

November 4. *Field-Marshal Sir John Dill died in Washington.
Germans were driven from the Dutch mainland south of
the River Maas.*

November 5. *Russians reached the outskirts of Budapest.
U.S. Flying Fortresses bombed Singapore.*

November 6. *Lord Moyne, British Resident Minister in the Middle
East, was assassinated in Cairo by Jewish terrorists.*

[*November* 7, 1944.

PARLIAMENT and the nation have suffered a very heavy loss
in the death of Lord Moyne, who died at the hands of foul
assassins in Cairo last night. We have as yet received no official
information which fixes the authorship of the crime or gives us a clue
to its motives. The murderers themselves narrowly escaped lynching
at the hands of Egyptian passers-by, and the Egyptian Government
have stated that they were not Egyptian subjects. Very searching
inquiries will be made into the origins and associations of these strangers
to Egypt, and the House will doubtless require the fullest information
as soon as it has been obtained.

This morning, I speak only a few words of Walter Moyne and of the
grief which all who knew him feel at his loss. I have known him
almost all his life. For over thirty years, mostly in this House, we were
intimate friends. Very young indeed did he succeed in getting out
to the South African War, where he proved his courage and shed his

blood. The bitter party strife which preceded the last world war made no difference to our relations, or to his relations with many of his opponents. He fought in the first world war with distinguished courage, rising to the command of a battalion and passing through the very worst of the fighting year after year, both on Gallipoli and in France and Flanders.

It was a great pleasure to me when I went to the Exchequer to find him appointed as Financial Secretary. He served more than twenty years in the House of Commons before going to the Lords. When the present Government was formed at the beginning of the war, he accepted without the slightest hesitation or demur the post of Under-Secretary of State at the Ministry of Agriculture, although he had formerly for several years been its chief. This was characteristic of his whole conduct towards the public. Everyone must help wherever it was thought that he could help the best, and all service was equally honourable. His work as Secretary of State for the Colonies was admirable, and only the exigencies of political change led to his leaving the Government for a short while.

At the beginning of this year he became Resident Minister in the Middle East, and this I must describe as the great period of his life. During this present year the press of the most difficult, tangled, anxious and urgent problems was thrust upon him, often forcing him to take decisions at the shortest notice and without reference home. These affairs affected not only matters in the Middle East, but the relations with Allied Governments and enemy Governments seeking to surrender, and were of a most complex character.

The dispatches and telegrams which he wrote were a model of clarity and vigour. I was deeply impressed by the expansion of his mind under the stress of responsibility and events. Certainly I can testify, and so can the Foreign Secretary, to the marked impoverishment of our affairs in this theatre resulting from his removal, and to the very great difficulty that will be found in filling the gap. In particular Lord Moyne devoted himself this year to the solution of the Zionist problem, and I can assure the House that the Jews in Palestine have rarely lost a better or more well-informed friend.

I feel sure the House will wish to express its sympathy with the children and relations he has left behind him, and also may I ask, even in this time of cruel sacrifice darkening so many homes, that even those who did not know him will share the pain felt by all his friends at the passing of a charming personality and a good and faithful servant to the State.

THE FRUITS OF 1944

A Speech at the Lord Mayor's Luncheon at the Mansion House, London
November 9, 1944

November 7. *Middelburg, capital of Walcheren, was captured.*
November 8. *Mr. Roosevelt won a decisive victory over Mr. Thomas Dewey in the U.S. Presidential election.*
German High Command announced that their new missile, the V2 rocket, had been used against London.
November 9. *U.S. troops north of Metz established new crossings over the Moselle.*
Mr. Churchill spoke at the Lord Mayor's Luncheon of the need for an early meeting of the leaders of Russia, U.S. and Britain.

[*November 9, 1944.*

WHEN I look back over the war-time years I cannot help feeling that time is an inadequate and even capricious measure of their duration. At one moment they seem so long, at another so short. Sometimes events are galloping forward at breathless speed ; sometimes there are long, hard, anxious pauses which we have to bear. Anniversaries like this seem to recur with extreme rapidity when you get to one and look back at the other. It seems such a very brief span, and yet the intervening months are so packed with incident and so burdened with toil that as you retrace your steps mentally over them you cannot believe that they have not lasted for several years. It is hard to remember how long ago this war began, and one can never be quite sure whether it has lasted a flash or an age.

I had a very shrewd suspicion, my Lord Mayor, when I received your gracious invitation, that you would probably propose the health of His Majesty's Ministers and I must hold myself in readiness for the task of making some reply, and I thought that I would see whether I could get some hint out of what I had said last year, when this agreeable event and festival was also celebrated. I saw that I was then congratulating you upon the year of victory of 1943. I was congratulating the City of London on that memorable and exhilarating year of almost unbroken success, and I was recounting a long succession of places and countries which had been cleared of the enemy—all Africa, Sicily,

Sardinia, Corsica, and one-third of Italy were in the hands of the British and United States armies. The mighty war which the United States was waging in the Pacific had prospered beyond all hope, and in Russia Marshal Stalin's armies were already rolling triumphantly forward to cleanse their native land of the German invader.

But the events of 1943 have been far surpassed by those of 1944. Rome and Athens, Paris and Brussels and Belgrade, all have been rescued, and by their own exertions have largely rescued themselves, from German oppression. All of Hitler's satellites have turned against him. Not only have they been struck down, but they have actually turned their arms upon his baleful coercion. Slaves, driven so far against their interests, against their honour, against, in many cases, their inclination, have had a chance to turn upon the slave-driver, and may now wreak the vengeance which is due as much from them as from any of the free countries which fought from the beginning. Both in the East and in the West the Allied vanguards stand on German soil.

The U-boat menace has for the time being—I always put that sort of remark in, because life is full of changes and hazards in these years —the U-boat menace has for the time being been practically effaced. There was one recent month in which up to the last day they did not sink a single ship. On the last day they got one—therefore the matter was hardly of a character to be specially mentioned. But that great peril which hung over us for so long and at times concentrated the whole attention of the defence organization of this country and of the United States has been effaced, and from the air there rains down on the guilty German land a hail of fire and explosive of ever-increasing fury. We have had our own experience, and we know how severe the ordeal may be ; but I can assure you that we have not suffered one-tenth, and we shall not suffer one-tenth, of what is being meted out to those who first started and developed this cruel and merciless form of attack. Such are some of the fruits—for if I tried to name them all I should indeed vex your patience—of 1944, and no one can be blamed, provided that he does not slacken his or her efforts for a moment—no one can be blamed for hoping that victory may come to the Allies and peace may come to Europe in 1945.

When I was here last year I could not tell you that I was about to start for the meeting of the three great Allies—the heads of the three Governments—at Teheran. There it was that the plans were made and the agreements and decisions taken which were executed with so much precision and with a degree of combination to which Marshal Stalin referred in his wise and weighty speech a few days ago. Now I do not mind saying that it is high time we had another triple conference, and that such a meeting might easily abridge the sufferings of mankind and set a term to the fearful process of destruction which is now ravaging the earth.

The prospects of such a meeting have been vastly improved by the results of the Presidential Election in the United States for which we waited so breathlessly on Tuesday last. I see on looking back on my past records that when I was here last year I appealed both to the British and the American public to be very careful that the electioneering did not in any way ruffle the good will that existed throughout the English-speaking world, and was so great an aid to our Armies.

It is certainly remarkable that the whole of this tremendous turmoil of the United States elections should have been carried through without any stirring of the ancient, moth-eaten and threadbare controversies which are to be found in the history books between Great Britain and her American kinsmen and now brothers in arms. We were very careful ourselves to avoid even the slightest semblance of mixing ourselves up with American political affairs, and I offer my compliments to Parliament, to the Press, and to public men of all parties and of no party—perhaps especially to them—for the care and restraint which have made all potential indiscretions die upon their lips.

Now that the event is over and the results have been declared, there are a few things I should like to say about the American Presidential Election. Let us first of all express our gratitude to both of the great parties in America for the manner in which the interests of the Alliance and the prosecution of the war have been held high above the dust of party conflict. The United States has set an example to the world of how democratic institutions can be worked with the utmost vigour and freedom without injury to the permanent interests of the State. We know that we in Britain have in the Republican Party of the United States vast numbers of friends and well-wishers, and that the upholding of Anglo-American relations is cherished by tens of millions in both the great parties over there.

I am sure that every one will have been moved by the spirited and sportsmanlike manner in which Governor Dewey at the moment of defeat offered his congratulations to his opponent, and pledged himself and his party to work wholeheartedly for the world cause. What a model this should be to those States where political differences are often not soluble by words or votes, where the question of who is to be in and who is to be out may be a matter of life and death, or be settled by violence and intrigue, and where there may be but a short step between being the ruler and being the victim! Here in this country, the forerunner of all the democratic and Parliamentary conceptions of modern times, we in this country, who are very old at the game of party politics hard fought out, have learned how to carry through and debate great fiercely-contested political issues without the severance of national life, and even in most cases without the severance of personal and private friendships. However we may regret it, it seems almost certain that we too in this old Island shall have our General Election in 1945, and I am confident that it will be conducted by all concerned with a liveliness and robust vigour which will gratify the political emotions and the combative instincts of our people at home, without destroying the marvellous underlying unity and sense of brotherhood which have long subsisted in this country and have reached their highest degree amid the perils from which we have been delivered, and in the Government composed of men of all parties who will, I am sure, preserve to their latest day sentiments of warm comradeship in this great episode and tremendous time of trouble which no ordinary political differences will ever be able to disturb.

We have strictly avoided any expression of opinion about party issues in the United States, but at this moment now I feel free to express on personal grounds the very great joy which it gives me to know that my intimate war-time co-operation with President Roosevelt will be continued in the months that lie immediately before us. These are months profoundly interwoven with the future of both our countries, and also, we trust, through the future association of our two countries, interwoven with the peace and progress of the whole world.

I have spoken of the famous capital cities that have been freed by the costly fighting of this stern but very glorious year, and we have in General Koenig, the Governor of Paris, and in the Burgomaster of Brussels, living representatives to bring home to us the splendid events which have so recently taken place.

The attention of the Western Allies and, indeed, of the world has naturally been dominated by the decisive battle in Normandy, in which Anglo-American armies have destroyed or pulverized the structure of German resistance in France. The brilliant exploitation of that victory enabled the Americans to sweep the enemy from France, aided by the audacious and gallant Maquis, and enabled the British to clear the Channel coast and to drive the enemy out of Belgium and out of a large part of Holland.

How many times, when a great battle has been won, have its results been thrown away by tardiness or lack of vigour in pursuit! Here we have seen under General Eisenhower's supreme direction the highest results surely and firmly seized and held at every stage.

It is nearly always right to pursue a beaten foe with all one's strength, and even to run serious risks in doing so ; but, of course, there comes a time when the pursuers outstrip the utmost limits of their own supplies, and where the enemy, falling back on his own depots, is able once again to form a front. This showed itself very plainly in the serious and continuous fighting which broke out on the Moselle and in that neighbourhood, when the American advance, thrust forward with so much impetus and *lan*, came up against a hard core of regathered enemy resistance. A pause in the Allied advance was inevitable, and during the last two months the bringing-up of supplies and reinforcements and the improvement of harbours have been the main preoccupation of the Supreme Allied Command, apart from the heavy fighting I have spoken of on the Moselle. But during these last eight or ten weeks two considerable struggles have been fought by armies under British command, in both of which Canadian and Polish forces were represented, and in both of which a large proportion of United States troops fought with their customary distinction.

The first of these two great operations was in Italy under General Alexander. They have surmounted the terrible barrier of the Apennines and the Gothic line, and this has carried us into the valley of the Po. The progress of the seasons has, however, brought us to very bad weather—quite exceptional weather for this time of the year—and progress there is hard. The forcing of this mountain line, so strongly fortified and held by a hostile German army practically as large as our own, already constitutes a great feat of arms, and has cost us and our Allies very nearly 50,000 casualties.

The second interim battle has been in the Netherlands under Field-Marshal Montgomery. It has opened the Scheldt, and will very shortly place the great port of Antwerp at the disposal of the northern flank of the Allied Armies, which will presently move into Germany for the final struggle. In these two operations—in Italy and in Holland and Belgium—very heavy losses have been sustained, in the greatest proportion by the British and Canadian forces. In both we have been aided by our valiant Allies. In both opportunities have been offered for the display of superb heroism, and deeds have been done which, when they are known and when they can be studied with the attention they deserve, will long figure in song and story and long light the martial annals of our race and nation.

I thought it right to point out in a precise and definite manner these two important and prolonged battles which have been fought—one in the Apennines and one around the Scheldt. They are only the prelude to further great operations which must be conducted in the months to come. I felt that it had not perhaps been realized how very great has been the efforts which we have so largely had the honour to make, and that it was appropriate to place them in their proper setting in the unfolding chain of this hard and obstinate war.

Now we stand on the threshold of Germany, and it will take the full exertions of the three great Powers and every scrap of strength and sacrifice that they can give to crush down the desperate resistance which we must expect from the deadly military antagonist at last so largely beaten back to his own lair. I cannot to-day any more than on the other four occasions when I have been called on to respond to this toast—I cannot offer you an easy future even on the continent of Europe. Supreme efforts must be made. It is always in the last lap that races are either gained or lost. The effort must be forthcoming. This is no moment to slacken.

Hard as it may seem after five long years of war, every man and woman in this land must show what they are capable of doing, and I am sure that our soldiers at the front will not be found incapable of that extra effort which is necessary to crown all that has been attained and, above all, to bring this frightful slaughter and devastation in Europe to an end within the shortest possible period of time. I can assure you that that, at any rate, is the dominant thought of His Majesty's Government.

Although it is our duty to work hard—and we have worked hard—to produce large schemes of social improvement and advance, although it is our duty to make preparations for the change-over from war to peace, from war in Europe to war in Japan, in far distant Asia, although we are bound to work as hard as we can, nothing must be allowed to stand in the way of the prosecution of the war to its ultimate conclusion. If we were to fail in that we should not be worthy either of your confidence or of the kindness which has led you to drink our health this afternoon.

V2 ROCKET

A Statement to the House of Commons
November 10, 1944

[*November* 10, 1944.

LAST February I told Parliament that the Germans were preparing to attack this country by means of long-range rockets ; and I referred again to the possibility of this form of attack in my statement in this House on July 6th.

For the last few weeks the enemy has been using his new weapon, the long-range rocket, and a number have landed at widely-scattered points in this country. In all, the casualties and damage have so far not been heavy, though I am sure the House would wish me to express our sympathy with the victims of this as of other attacks. No official statement about the attack has hitherto been issued. The reason for this silence was that any announcement might have given information useful to the enemy, and we were confirmed in this course by the fact that, until two days ago, the enemy had made no mention of this weapon in his communiqués.

Last Wednesday an official announcement, followed by a number of highly-coloured accounts of the attacks on this country, was issued by the German High Command. I do not propose to comment upon it, except to say that the statements in this announcement are a good reflection of what the German Government would wish their people to believe, and of their desperate need to afford them some encouragement. I may, however, mention a few facts. The rocket contains approximately the same quantity of high explosive as the flying bomb. However, it is designed to penetrate rather deeper before exploding. This results in somewhat heavier damage in the immediate vicinity of the crater, but rather less extensive blast effect around. The rocket flies through the stratosphere, going up to 60 or 70 miles, and outstrips sound. Because of its high speed, no reliable or sufficient public warning can, in present circumstances, be given.

There is, however, no need to exaggerate the danger. The scale and effects of the attack have not hitherto been significant. Some rockets have been fired at us from the Island of Walcheren. This is now in our hands, and other areas from which rockets have been, or can at present be fired against this country will doubtless, be over-run by our Forces in due course. We cannot, however, be certain that the enemy will not be able to increase the range, either by reducing the weight of the war-head or by other methods. Nor, on the other hand, can we be certain that any new launching areas which he may establish farther back will not also, in turn, be over-run by the advancing Allied armies.

The use of this weapon is another attempt by the enemy to attack the morale of our civil population in the vain hope that he may somehow by this means stave off the defeat which faces him in the field. Doubtless the enemy has hoped by his announcement to induce us to give him information which he has failed to get otherwise. I am sure that this House, the Press, and the public will refuse to oblige him in this respect.

THE VISIT TO PARIS

November 11, 1944

A Speech at a Luncheon given in honour of the Prime Minister by General de Gaulle

---

[*November* 11, 1944.

IT is difficult for me to speak on a day such as this, which fills us with emotion. For more than thirty years I have defended the cause of friendship, of comradeship, and of alliance between France and Great Britain. I have never deviated from that policy throughout the whole of my life. For so many years past have these two nations shared the glories of western Europe that they have become indispensable to each other. It is a fundamental principle of British policy that the alliance with France should be unshakable, constant, and effective. This morning I was able to see that the French people wanted to march hand in hand with the British people.

It gave me so much pleasure to see Paris again, this Paris which is a brilliant star shining above the world. I saw the French Army march along the Champs-Elysées just before the war. What a lot of sacrifices have had to be made since then ! What a lot of suffering has had to be endured ! How many good friends have been lost ; what memories remain with us to-day ! It is a privilege for me to be at the side of General de Gaulle. In spite of all the critics, we still believe in the defeat of the enemy.

One night in October, 1940, during the worst of the raids on London, I did not fear to address the French people in French to tell them that a day would come when France would take her place among the great nations and play her part as the champion of liberty and independence. In thanking General de Gaulle for the words he has just spoken I should be lacking in truth and gratitude if I did not pay tribute to the capital part he has played in this transformation which has brought us to a moment in history when all we have to do is to be worthy of our destiny in order to start a new era of vision and of greatness.

A SPEECH AT THE HÔTEL DE VILLE, WHERE THE PARIS LIBERATION
COMMITTEE WELCOMED THE PRIME MINISTER

[November 12, 1944.

MONSIEUR le Préfet de la Seine, Monsieur le Président du
Comité Parisien de la Résistance, Ladies and Gentlemen :
It is with the most vivid sensations that I find myself here this
afternoon. I am going to give you a warning : be on your guard,
because I am going to speak, or try to speak, in French, a formidable
undertaking and one which will put great demands on your friendship
for Great Britain.

To be here in Paris is an extraordinary realization for me. I have
never lost my faith in the citizens of Paris. In the hard years when
you were beneath the yoke of the Huns and we were suffering the
blitz (which was in comparison a minor ill), during all those years I
always had a feeling of unity with the people of Paris, this immortal
city whence great movements for the liberation of the world have
sprung, and which, at every point in its long history, has proved its
faculty for guiding the world's progress. But, Ladies and Gentlemen,
I have never lost my faith in the French Army—never. It may well
be that there are mechanical devices which the enemy can use and
which do not give people a chance of showing their courage, their
devotion, and their skill in military affairs. Things like this have
happened, and we too, if it had not been for the Channel, should have
been put to a hard test had we been attacked by 2,000 tanks without
our having the means to destroy them or tanks to oppose them. I
am sure that if there had been an opportunity of fighting on equal
terms, the French Army would have shown, and was going to show,
qualities which have made its fame imperishable in the pages of
history, under the leadership of the great men of the past, Clemenceau,
Foch and Napoleon, by whose tomb I stood yesterday. Have no
fears for the power of the French Army. I am not speaking only to
you, but I am also expressing the feelings of England and the policy
of her Government in saying that the French Army, a strong army,
and a strong army as quickly as possible, is absolutely necessary to
re-establish a balance in Europe and to provide those elements of
strength and stability which are so greatly desired by this world which
has suffered so horribly.

When I spoke to you in French from London four years ago, four
years almost to a week, I said I had always known for certain that
France would again take her place with the greatest nations and
exercise her power and her influence on the whole development,
cultural, political and military, of the future world.

Then came a great event. I was thrilled when, at the front in Italy, I heard the news that Paris had risen, and I rejoiced with you that Paris had been freed, freed from the Huns by the strong, bold and vigorous effort of her people guided by many of the men and women whom I see here at this moment. It was a great affair, and the Leclerc Division, for the dispatching of which to France I had done my utmost, was there. I could not prophesy what was going to happen, but I did everything in my power to have arrangements made for the transport of that Division by sea and for its equipment with heavy arms. And what a stroke of fortune that they should have been brought here to Paris at the very moment when they could assist the powerful and vigorous effort of the citizens themselves to liberate this great and historic city !

Now most of France is free. Great battles are being joined. I well understand that you wish to take as great a part as possible in the line of battle, and it is essential that you should be helped as far as possible by the Allies. In Italy your soldiers have already given proof of their skill and have struck heavy blows against the Germans. But it is here in France that you wish to be represented by the most powerful force which can be raised and equipped. I assure you that the war cannot be prolonged ; it may be that in six months' time the desperate enemy will be beaten on the field, and that part of the need for a line of modern divisions will have disappeared. Well, we will do our best to enable everything possible to be done so that the forces of France may be actively engaged against the enemy in the months that remain to us in this frightful war.

But there are other battles to win. There are other works to accomplish, and if in your courtesy you will allow me, at this moment when you have arranged in my honour a demonstration which I shall remember to the last moment of my life, I will say these words to you : Unity, unity, stability and solidarity !

This is the moment when the whole might of the nation should be directed to the foundation, on an unshakable basis, of the grandeur and authority of the great French people. Happily, you have at your head an incontestable leader, General de Gaulle. From time to time I have had lively arguments with him about matters relating to this difficult war, but I am absolutely sure that you ought to rally round your leader and do your utmost to make France united and indivisible. This is the moment to forget many things, to remember great things, and it is the moment when France should take her place with the other great Powers and march with them, not only to sweep the Prussians from her territory, not only to tear their name from the book of honour, not only to arrange matters as they must be arranged if we are to be saved from a repetition of the horror which we have twice suffered in my lifetime ; but also in order that France and the genius of France, eminent in so many spheres, may make a united contribution to the great movement of progress which is budding in the hearts of men and women of goodwill in all the countries of the world.

A MESSAGE TO GENERAL DE GAULLE AFTER THE VISIT TO FRANCE

[*November* 16, 1944.

NOW that I am back home, let me express to your Excellency and to your colleagues of the French Government my profound appreciation of the splendid hospitality and innumerable kindnesses and courtesies shown me and my friends during the memorable days which I have just spent in France. I shall always recall as one of the proudest and most moving occasions of my life the wonderful reception which the people of Paris gave to their British guests on this our first visit to your capital after its liberation.

I was also most grateful for the opportunity of seeing for myself something of the ardour and high quality of the French troops which are completing the liberation of their native soil under the skilful leadership of General de Lattre de Tassigny. The welcome extended to us was indeed a happy augury for that continued friendship between our two countries which is essential to the safety and to the future peace of Europe.

LEER FOR OVERSEAS FORCES

[November 17, 1944.

I HAVE a statement to make concerning a scheme which we have been working out for a system of short leave for troops overseas.
On many occasions recently, and from all quarters of the House, there has been pressure to effect some reduction in the present period of overseas service in the Army. The Secretary of State for War has explained the many difficulties of operations, of shipping and of man-power, which stand in the way of reducing, at this juncture, the overseas tour in the Army. I have myself also pointed out quite recently, in relation to this very question, the overriding need for doing nothing which will weaken our effort in the fighting theatres at this climax of the war.

The problem is an intractable one, but it has been approached from every angle, and with all sympathy for the men who have been separated from their families at home for all too long by the exigencies of the war. The limited reductions in the length of the overseas tour in the Army which restrictions of shipping and man-power admit, have recently been stated in the House by the Secretary of State for War. The same man-power difficulty does not arise where men leave the theatre of war for a relatively short period, and return to their units thereafter; and the recent general improvement in the shipping situation has enabled the time taken on the journey to be reduced considerably. The War Office have, therefore, proposed to me that the system of repatriation of men with long continuous service overseas should be supplemented by a leave scheme for the benefit of those who, while not yet qualified for repatriation, have for a considerable length of time overseas borne the burden of campaigns fought often in the most adverse climatic conditions. A plan has been worked out to afford a period of leave at home of about four weeks' duration to a number of men who have borne the main burden of battle in the fighting line, after considerable overseas service. Operational and shipping considerations necessarily restrict the benefits of this scheme to a proportion only of those whom we should like to bring within its scope if these considerations permitted.

A total quota of about 6,000 men per month—if you take 13 four-weekly periods in the year, about 80,000 a year—to come home under this scheme, has been allotted to the following overseas theatres:

Italy and North Africa, Middle East, Persia-Iraq, India, South-East Asia, and East Africa. Within that quota at intervals of every three weeks or so Commanders-in-Chief will select the men to come home. This leave plan must be subject to war needs in each theatre, and the Commander-in-Chief has complete discretion to suspend it on that account if necessary. Again, it will clearly need review when hostilities with Germany come to an end, at which time the claims upon shipping and man-power of the Government release plans, which of course are on a vast scale, would have to claim priority. The application of this scheme to British officers and men in the Indian Army will be the subject of a later announcement. The numbers concerned here are not very great.

Of course the existing arrangements for posting men home on urgent compassionate grounds will continue unaffected by this leave scheme, as will also the entitlement to repatriation of men who have served continuously overseas for those periods which my right hon. Friend indicated in this House on September 26th as the present objective in the reduction of the overseas tour of service in the Army. This is in addition to, and not in substitution for, anything going on now.

No doubt the shortening of the overseas tour in the Army is much better than a system of short leave at home. No doubt also the working of this leave plan will give rise to inequalities as between man and man. Nevertheless, I commend this plan to the House because I feel that the impossibility of achieving any general overall reduction in the Army overseas tour should not preclude all hope of seeing their families for those who cannot be posted home. The Secretary of State for War informs me that a scheme of this nature, although it must for obvious reasons be limited in scope, will be welcomed by the Army overseas as a genuine effort to meet, to some extent, the natural desire for leave of those who have been serving abroad for long periods, and his opinion is confirmed by the strongly-expressed views of Commanders-in-Chief. This I can myself corroborate, as the result of recent talks with General Wilson and General Alexander.

I hope it may prove possible that a contingent of men from the Mediterranean theatre may benefit by this leave scheme in time to be with their families for Christmas. From the more distant theatres, men will arrive home in the early weeks of the New Year. The problem of the British Armies in North-West Europe is different. It may be that within a reasonable time it will be possible to institute some system of short leave to the United Kingdom on the lines enjoyed by our Armies in France and Belgium in the last war. But such plans must turn on events we can none of us foresee. They depend on how the great battles go.

PALESTINE TERRORISM

A Statement to the House of Commons
November 17, 1944

[*November* 17, 1944.

I HAVE now to make a short statement about Palestine. The Foreign Secretary gave the House a full report of the assassination of Lord Moyne. This shameful crime has shocked the world. It has affected none more strongly than those like myself who, in the past, have been consistent friends of the Jews and constant architects of their future. If our dreams for Zionism are to end in the smoke of assassins' pistols, and our labours for its future to produce only a new set of gangsters worthy of Nazi Germany, many like myself will have to reconsider the position we have maintained so consistently and so long. If there is to be any hope of a peaceful and successful future for Zionism, these wicked activities must cease, and those responsible for them must be destroyed root and branch. The primary responsibility must, of course, rest with the Palestine authorities under His Majesty's Government. These authorities are already engaged in an active and thorough campaign against the Stern Gang and the larger, and hardly less dangerous, Irgun Zvai Leumi. In particular, the Palestine police have been loyally and effectively carrying out their duties in the midst of constant danger. A number of persons suspected of active complicity in terrorist activities have been arrested, and on October 19th 251 were deported from the country, where their presence, with the possibility of a large-scale attempt at rescue, only led to increased insecurity. Since then, numerous further arrests have been made, including those of some wanted terrorists.

I am satisfied that the Palestine authorities have all the powers necessary to enable them to deal with the situation. They will, with the help of the military and the close co-operation of the General Officer Commanding in Chief, intensify their activities, but it will be realized that although the primary responsibility rests with the Goverment, full success depends on the wholehearted co-operation of the entire Jewish community. This His Majesty's Government is entitled to demand and to receive. I have received a letter from Dr. Weizmann, President of the World Zionist Organization—a very old friend of mine—who has arrived in Palestine, in which he assures me that Palestine Jewry will go to the utmost limit of its power to cut out this evil from its midst. In Palestine the executive of the Jewish Agency has called upon the Jewish community—and I quote their actual words :

" to cast out the members of this destructive band, to deprive them of all refuge and shelter, to resist their threats, and to render all necessary assistance to the authorities in the prevention of terrorist acts, and in the eradication of the terrorist organization."

These are strong words, but we must wait for these words to be translated into deeds. We must wait to see that not only the leaders, but every man, woman and child of the Jewish community, does his or her best to bring this terrorism to a speedy end.

THANKSGIVING DAY

A Speech at a Royal Albert Hall Concert in celebration of
American Thanksgiving Day
November 23, 1944

[November 23, 1944.

WE have come here to-night to add our celebration to those which are going forward all over the world wherever Allied troops are fighting, in bivouacs and dug-outs, on battlefields, on the high seas, and in the highest air. Always this annual festival has been dear to the hearts of the American people. Always there has been that desire for thanksgiving, and never, I think, has there been more justification, more compulsive need than now.

It is your Day of Thanksgiving, and when we feel the truth of the facts which are before us, that in three or four years the peaceful, peace-loving people of the United States, with all the variety and freedom of their life in such contrast to the iron discipline which has governed many other communities—when we see that in three or four years the United States has in sober fact become the greatest military, naval, and air power in the world—that, I say to you in this time of war, is itself a subject for profound thanksgiving.

We are moving forward in this struggle which spreads over all the lands and all the oceans; we are moving forward surely, steadily, irresistibly, and perhaps, with God's aid, swiftly, towards victorious peace. There again is a fitting reason for thanksgiving.

I have spoken of American thanksgiving. To-night here, representing vaster audiences and greater forces moving outside this hall, it is both British and American thanksgiving that we may celebrate. And why is that? It is because under the compulsion of mysterious and all-powerful destiny we are together. We are joined together, shedding our blood side by side, struggling for the same ideals, until the triumph of the great causes which we serve shall have been made manifest.

But there is a greater Thanksgiving Day which still shines ahead, which beckons the bold and loyal and warm-hearted, and that is when this union of action which has been forced upon us by our common hatred of tyranny, which we have maintained during these dark and fearful days, shall become a lasting union of sympathy and good-feeling and loyalty and hope between all the British and American peoples, wherever they may dwell. Then, indeed, there will be a Day of Thanksgiving, and one in which all the world will share.

" THE TASKS WHICH LIE BEFORE US "

A Speech to the House of Commons
November 29, 1944

November 10.	*Mr. Churchill made a statement in the House of Common. about the V2 rocket attacks on Britain.*
	Eighth Army in Italy captured Forli.
November 11.	*Mr. Churchill observed Armistice Day ceremonie. in Paris and conferred with General de Gaulle.*
	Britain, U.S. and Russia invited France to join European Advisory Commission.
November 12.	*R.A.F. bombers sank Tirpitz, great German battleship.*
	Himmler read a proclamation by Hitler, whose silence caused sensational rumours.
November 14.	*British troops launched a new attack against the enemy west of the River Maas.*
November 16.	*Allies made a slow but steady advance on a 600-mile front in Western Europe.*
November 17.	*Air Chief Marshal Sir Trafford Leigh-Mallory, new Air C-in-C in South-East Asia, was reported missing on the flight to take up his new post.*
November 18.	*Germans retreated along the U.S. Third Army front, and the French liberated Delle.*
November 19.	*British and American forces captured Geilenkirchen.*
	French troops entered Alsace.
	General Eisenhower made an appeal to America for more shells.
November 20.	*French troops reached the Rhine between Mulhouse and the Swiss frontier. Belfort was captured and German resistance in Metz ended.*
November 21.	*British troops advanced in the bend of the Maas west of Venlo.*
November 22.	*Allied troops in Alsace advanced rapidly. Mulhouse was captured by the French.*
November 24.	*American 7th Army reported to have crossed the Rhine near Strasbourg.*
	Tokio was bombed by U.S. Super Fortresses.
November 25.	*U.S. First Army captured Weisweller, on the road to Cologne.*

November 26.   *Field-Marshal Sir Harold Alexander appointed Supreme Commander, Mediterranean Theatre.*

   Germans lost 122 fighters when U.S. bombers attacked oil and railway targets.

November 27.   *Mr. Cordell Hull, U.S. Secretary of State, resigned through ill-health.*

   R.A.F. again breached Dortmund-Ems Canal.

November 28.   *U.S. Third Army captured 13 small towns in the Saar region, and the U.S. Ninth Army reached the banks of the River Roer.*

   Demonstrations in Canada against conscription for overseas service.

November 29.   *The King and Queen opened sixth war Session of Parliament.*

   Russians launched new offensive in Southern Hungary.

November 30.   *Antwerp was reopened to Allied shipping.*

   U.S. Ninth Army launched a new attack north-west of Julich.

[November 29, 1944.

EVERYONE will agree that this has been a long Parliament. We need not embark on historical controversy as to the claims to continuous life which could be put forward on behalf of a Parliament much longer than this, but I am very glad that the closing Session of this long ten years' Parliament should show all due respect for the traditional and ceremonial occasions which ignorant, unthinking people who have not meditated upon these matters or studied the true movement of events and of forces in the human breast might easily regard as meaningless punctilio. Here in the Speech from the Throne and in the Debate on the Address may be seen all the workings of the British Constitution, or all the principal workings. The Sovereign, advised by His Ministers, delivers the Gracious Speech. The House then proceed to express their thanks, but have a perfect right to move Amendments saying that they regret that this or that has been put into or left out of the Gracious Speech, and if they carry such an Amendment, the Government of the day is defeated on a major point of confidence, and it is not easy to conceive a situation in which they could continue to retain their office. I have on another occasion reminded the House that this Debate on the Address is the beginning of what is called "the grand inquest of the nation." A new Session begins, and at this moment and in this process of the Address, there is nothing that can be held back from discussion. Amendments can be moved on any matter, and considerable periods are left by Mr. Speaker, either at the beginning or during the course of the Debate, when the Debate is general and open. There is no time similar to the period of the Debate on the Address when real trials of strength can be brought about in days of party conflict between the Government and the Opposition.

I have always been of opinion that the wishes of the House in respect to the Debate on the Address should be met by the Administration. If the House wish for a few more days to discuss the special Amendments and so forth, the Government should put no obstacle in the way within reason. Of course, we are governed by the end of the year as well as by March 31st, in regard to certain legislation. Perhaps I am trespassing beyond my duty, but I have always rejoiced that the Debate on the general aspects of the Address was a considerable feature, because then is the time when a Member who has got no friends and no group can get up, if he should catch Mr. Speaker's eye, and speak about anything in the world which he thinks will benefit his fellow creatures. This is customary in a Parliamentary sense, a democratic element in our annual procedure.

Of course I must admit, as an aged Member of this House, and as one who has done some forty-two years of service here—unhappily for me there was a break of two years, two Parliaments which lasted for a year apiece—that after all this long experience and service in the House, I find it very unpleasant to have the Debate on the Adjournment one day, and the Debate on the new Session the next. In the high and far-off times when I first entered this building, there was usually a six months' or five months' Recess, between the grouse on the 12th August and the latter part of January or the beginning of February, when the House reassembled. I do not consider those days were without their wisdom. Do not—and this has a bearing on some of the remarks which have recently been made—ever suppose that you can strengthen Parliament by wearying it, and by keeping it in almost continuous session. If you want to reduce the power of Parliament, let it sit every day in the year, one-fifth part filled, and then you will find it will be the laughing-stock of the nation, instead of being, as it continues to be in spite of all the strains of modern life, the citadel as well as the cradle of Parliamentary institutions throughout the world; almost the only successful instance of a legislative body with plenary powers, elected on universal suffrage, which is capable of discharging, with restraint and with resolution, all the functions of peace and of war.

This digression on general topics will, perhaps, be excused by another digression which I find it my duty to make, and this is a more sober and more sombre digression. All our affairs, down to the smallest detail, continue to be dominated by the war. Parliamentary business is no exception. I must warn the House and the country against any indulgence in the feeling that the war will soon be over. It may be ; but do not indulge that feeling, and think that we should now all be turning our thoughts to the new phase in world history which will open at the close of this war. The truth is that no one knows when the German war will be finished, and still less how long the interval will be between the defeat of the Germans and the defeat of the Japanese. I took occasion, some months ago, to damp down premature hopes by speaking of the German war running into January and February. I could see disappointment in several quarters as I looked around the House, and I followed this up quickly by indicating the late Spring or the early Summer as periods which we must take into account as possibilities. My present inclination is not at all to mitigate these forecasts, or guesses. " Guesses " is the right word, for they can be little more. Indeed, if I were to make any change in the duration of the unfolding of events it would be to leave out the word " early " before the word " summer."

The vast battle which is in progress in the West has yielded to us important gains. The enemy has everywhere been thrust back. The captures of Metz and Strasbourg are glorious and massive achievements. The brilliant fighting and manœuvring of the French Army near the Swiss Frontier and their piercing of the Belfort Gap and their advance on a broad front to the Rhine is not only a military episode of high importance, but it shows, what many of us have never doubted, that the French Army will rise again and be a great factor in the life of France and of Europe, and that the French soldier, properly equipped and well led, is unsurpassed among the nations.

I had the opportunity of visiting this Army, and one had hoped to be there at the moment when its attack was delivered upon the Belfort Gap, but in the night twelve inches of snow fell and everything had to be put off for three days. Nevertheless, I had the opportunity of seeing a very large number of the troops who were going to be engaged, if not in the first stage, in the second stage of this battle. For an hour or more they marched past in a swirling snowstorm, and as the light faded I had a good look, at close quarters, at their faces. These are all young men from 18 to 22, average 20. What a fine thing to be a Frenchman, 20 years of age, well-armed, well-equipped, and with your native land to avenge and save ! The light in these men's eyes and their alert bearing give one the greatest confidence that our nearest neighbour and long friend in war and in these great struggles of our lifetime will rise in power and force from the ruins, the miseries, and the disgraces of the past, and will present us once more with a France to be numbered among the Great Powers of the world.

I have spoken of the fighting in the Belfort Gap, and I have mentioned Strasbourg, and, farther to the North, the very great battles which the Americans have gained around Metz. Opposite Cologne and North of it the fighting has been most severe, and it is here that the gains of ground will be most important and consequently are most disputed. The weather, which it is always customary and excusable, even legitimate, to abuse at this season of the year, in these regions has made the tasks of the American troops and those of the British on their left flank extremely difficult. What is called the fourth element in war—mud—has played a formidable part. We have not yet succeeded in driving the enemy back to the Rhine, still less have we established a strong bridgehead across it. The battle there is continuing still with the greatest vigour. Immense losses have been inflicted upon the enemy. The wearing-down process here, burdensome as it has been to the United States and British Forces, has been far greater upon the enemy, and, of course, any large and effective break in the German front in these regions—Cologne and northwards—would have the highest strategic consequences.

I may mention that in the interval between the liberation of France and that of the greater part of Belgium Field-Marshal Montgomery's group of armies, with substantial United States assistance, drove the enemy back to the line of the Maas, or lower Meuse, and established a sure flank guard, a flank barrier, in Holland, protecting the whole line of the main armies operating eastwards. It also opened the great port of Antwerp, which was captured intact, to the reception of large convoys of ocean-going ships, thus making an incomparable sea-base available for the nourishment of the Northern group of British Armies and the various groups of American Armies also deployed. In these operations, including the storming of the islands, which contained episodes of marvellous gallantry, grand feats of arms, the British and Canadian forces suffered about 40,000 casualties—that is, in the interval between the two great battles. In the new battle which runs from General Montgomery's Army, broadly speaking opposite Venlo down to the Vosges Mountains, where the French take up the long line, the whole front is held by the Americans, who are bearing the brunt with their customary distinction and courage.

I am not giving a review of the war situation, I have no intention of doing so ; later on, perhaps when we meet after Christmas, it will be right to review it, and it may be very much easier then than it is now. There may be hard facts and cheering facts to put before the House. The House knows that I have never hesitated to put hard facts before it. I know the British people and I know this House, and there is one thing they will not stand, and that is not being told how bad things are. If ' is humanly possible to do it without ndangering affairs, one is always well-advised to tell people how bad hings are. I remember occasions when I have greatly revived the nergy and ardour of the House by giving them an account of the hocking position we occupied in various quarters, and how very likely hings were to get worse before they would get better.

My motive in doing so was to strengthen the position of the Government. I say that I am not giving a review of the war situation to-day, ut I mention these outstanding, these commanding facts in order to issipate lightly-founded impressions that we can avert our eyes from he war and turn to the tasks of transition and of reconstruction, or till more that we can turn to the political controversies and other liversions of peace, which are dear to all our hearts, and rightly dear o the democracies in action, because without controversy democracies annot achieve their health-giving processes. But I do not think we an look on any of these matters with a sense of detachment from the var issue, which is right over us, which weighs intensely and preonderantly upon us and upon every form of our national life. All lse must be still subordinated to this supreme task. It is on the foe hat our eyes must be fixed, and to break down his resistance demands nd will receive the most intense exertions of Great Britain, of the Jnited States, and of all the United Nations and converted satellites —all forces that can be brought to bear.

This is just the moment not to slacken. All the races which the alendar holds, or nearly all of them, are won in the last lap ; and it is hen, when it is most hard, when one is most tired, when the sense f boredom seems to weigh upon one, when even the most glittering vents, exciting, thrilling events, are, as it were, smothered by satiation, vhen headlines in the newspaper, though perfectly true, succeed one nother in their growing emphasis, and yet the end seems to recede efore us, like climbing a hill when there is another peak beyond— t is at that very moment that we in this Island have to give that extra ense of exertion, of boundless, inexhaustible, dynamic energy that ve have shown, as the records now made public have emphasized in letail. Tirelessness is what we have to show now. Here I must bserve that it is one thing to feel these tremendous drives of energy t the beginning of a war, when your country is likely to be invaded and ou do not know whether you will not all have to die honourably ut soon ; it is one thing to exhibit these qualities, which certainly he House has never been estranged from, at such a moment, and quite nother thing to show them in the sixth year of a war. On the other and we must remember that the enemy whose country is invaded as also those supreme stimuli to which we ourselves responded in he very dark days of 1940 and 1941.

I have said enough to emphasize the preponderance of the war, weighing down upon us all—the German war—and after the German war we must not forget there is the war with Japan. It is on this footing and in this mood that we must address ourselves to the Gracious Speech and to the loyal Address which it is now our duty to present to His Majesty. Compliments have been paid to the Mover and the Seconder of the Address. It has become almost a hackneyed phrase to say that their performances have never been surpassed. In the forty-two King's Speeches—or something like it—which I have heard I think that that phrase must have been used twenty times at least, and it certainly can be used on this occasion. But what is the note that is struck by those two young Members of the House of Commons ? It is Youth, Youth, Youth ; efficient youth marching forward from service in the field or at the coal face, marching forward to take their part in Parliament ; and I am of opinion that those who have toiled and sweated, and those who have dared and conquered, should receive whatever party they belong to, a full share of representation in any new House of Commons that may be called into being. I must say I thought they were extremely good speeches, and I cannot doubt that those two young Members will be real additions for a long period of time, as I trust and pray, to the membership of this House.

Remember we have a missing generation, we must never forget that —the flower of the past, lost in the great battles of the last war. There ought to be another generation in between these young men and us older figures who are soon, haply, to pass from the scene. There ought to be another generation of men, with their flashing lights and leading figures. We must do all we can to try to fill the gap, and, as I say, there is no safer thing to do than to run risks in youth. It is very difficult to live your life in this world and not to get set in old ways, rather looking back with pleasure to the days of your youth. That is quite right, and tradition is quite right. A love of tradition has never weakened a nation, indeed it has strengthened nations in their hour of peril ; but the new view must come, the world must roll forward,

" Let the great world spin for ever down the ringing grooves of change."

as Tennyson said many years ago. Let us have no fear of the future. We are a decent lot, all of us, the whole nation. Wherever you go you need have no fear. I was brought up never to fear the English democracy, to trust the people. We need have no fear in these matters, and those speeches made by those two young Members give one the feeling that there must be rich reserves in the Army, in the industries and in the workshops, of men of assured quality and capacity who, whatever their differing views on political affairs, are none the less absolutely united in maintaining the historic greatness of Britain and of the British Commonwealth of Nations throughout the world.

I have to inform the House that it is the Government's intention to propose a Motion to-morrow to give precedence to Government business, to provide for the presentation of Government Bills only, and to stop the ballot for private Members' Bills—all following the precedents of the last five years, as well as of the last war. I regret to have to ask Members again to forgo their rights and privileges. They have been induced to make this sacrifice readily, if not cheerfully, in the past when our whole energies have been concentrated upon the war. The moment has not yet arrived for us to resume our normal arrangements, and I fear I must ask for the whole time of the House to be put at the disposal of the Government in view of the heavy programmes and the many months of hard work which lie before us, into which a contingent of my hon. Friends on this side are so eager to plunge.

On a previous occasion I gave my reasons for believing that we are entering upon the last Session of the present Parliament. The Gracious Speech contains references to a number of important Measures which we hope to bring forward this Session, in furtherance of the programme of reform and social advancement upon which the Coalition Government embarked two years ago. If events take the course I have previously indicated, if we are to attempt to complete our legislative programme, if we are to make any marked progress with it, we shall require all the available time of the House. In recent Sessions Members have had many opportunities of raising matters of general interest, and we hope most sincerely that such occasions will be available from time to time. The Debate on the Address is supposed to clear a lot of things out of the way, but in Parliamentary usage we have never been reluctant to give to any large number of Members who may request a Debate on a particular topic the opportunity they desire and deserve. Of course, anyone who chooses to learn Parliamentary procedure will see that in the course of a Session there are very few topics that he cannot find occasion to vent, but careful study of the rules of procedure is recommended to those who wish to find these opportunities.

All this may be considered to be preliminary to the very few words I have yet to say. No one can complain that the King's Speech is not heavily loaded with legislation—a more elaborate and substantial King's Speech in regard to legislation has rarely been produced. I have here a paper which sets out all the Bills—of which I think there are twelve, it might easily have been thirteen—which figure in the programme : the great health and national insurance group—the National Health Service Bill, the National Insurance Bill, the Industrial Injury Insurance Bill ; Family Allowances hold a high place ; the Water Bill, the River Board Bill, Reform of Parliamentary Franchise Bill, Local Elections Bill, Public Authorities Loans Bill, Adjustment of Local Government Areas Bill—a topic which lends itself to expansive conversation—Export Credit Bill, Requisitioned Land and War Works Bill, Wages Council Bill, Education (Scotland) Bill—which has already been given a special emphasis by the seconder of the Address—and Colonial Development and Welfare Bill. All these are mentioned, and that is the order in which they are mentioned, in the King's Speech, but not necessarily the order in which they will be taken in our Business procedure.

I myself should like to put in a word for a decision on the Report of the Select Committee on the Rebuilding of the House of Commons, because I think a Resolution from the House on that subject would liberate certain energies, not on a large scale, which might be detached from the war—some very aged lapidaries exist who can be getting on with the work. We really shall need a House to sit in, I can assure hon. Members, after this war is over, when so many great matters will have to be decided on which agreement will not be so perfect and so unanimous as it has been found to be in respect to the general structure of the new Chamber.

We shall proceed with this programme which has been unfolded in the King's Speech. We shall proceed with it as opportunity serves— one cannot do more than that—and we shall proceed with it also in accordance with the time which is left to this Parliament. Our tenure now depends upon the official end of the German war. It is a great inconvenience not to be able to forecast that date. I can only say that we shall press forward perseveringly with the great programme of legislation which this remarkable Coalition has framed, and we shall press steadily forward until the hour of our separation arrives. Hurried legislation is not usually successful; prolonged sittings do not necessarily mean rapid progress. The Dissolution undoubtedly hangs over us, and there is no question of postponing the Dissolution in order to carry a programme of legislation which, with the best will in the world, could not be carried this Session. If, most unhappily, the end of the war in Europe should be unexpectedly deferred, we shall make more progress in the social field, but if it should come to pass at dates which it is reasonable to hope, the summer, the early summer, or earlier if good fortune crowns our arms, then we cannot expect to accomplish more than a small part of what is set down in the Gracious Speech. Much will turn on the result of an appeal to the nation conducted under extraordinary circumstances out of our reverence for democracy, with many difficulties not present in peace time, with an electorate which has not voted for ten years, and with scarcely any voter under thirty years who has had the chance to vote before. I shall not attempt to pierce the veils of the unknown. I see there are already some prophets in the field who know exactly how all these complex forces and circumstances will in the end express themselves.

> Here a member interjected: "One a close friend of yours." The Prime Minister replied:

I should like further and better particulars.

> The member said he was referring to Mr. Assheton, the new Chairman of the Conservative Party. The Prime Minister continued:

I have not had the pleasure of reading in detail his statement, but I was not aware that he had predicted results—results are, of course, often predicted by people who wish to encourage their followers—or the time when the event would take place. It is only natural that one who is responsible for the actual marshalling of the armies should set the time and date a little in front of what may actually prove to be zero hour.

All the same, whatever may be the doubts as to when the election will come, and how it will finish up, and where we shall all find ourselves sitting at the end of it, and what our relations with each other will be—all these are uncertain—there is one thing which is quite certain: all the leading men in both the principal parties—and in the Liberal Party as well—are pledged and committed to this great mass of social legislation, and I cannot conceive that whatever may be the complexion of the new House, they will personally fail to make good their promises and commitments to the people. There may, therefore, be an interruption in our work, but it will only be an interruption, and one which must not be allowed in any circumstance to turn us from the purposes on which our resolves have been taken. This is a matter on which anyone has a right to speak for himself, irrespective of what may be the consequences of the General Election. No one can bind any future Parliament, but some of us, I suppose, will get back, and I cannot believe that any of those who have set their hands to this great social programme—insurance, health, compensation and the other matters that are in it—I cannot believe that any of us, whether in office or in opposition, who have been sponsors of this programme, will fail to march forward along the broad lines that have been set forth.

As I have said, I could not at this stage lay out the exact order of priority of the various legislative Measures which have been set down. The Debate on the Address and the necessary legislation which must be passed before the end of the year will take up our time until we return. There is then a great deal of necessary financial business, sometimes arduous, to be discharged—in getting you, Mr. Speaker, out of the Chair on the Army, Navy and Air Force Votes, and the Civil Service Votes. This will all take time. The Consolidated Fund Bill must be disposed of : here is another opportunity for a great many topics to be raised for which Members come along asking for special days to be given. They should just study the precedents of the past, and see all the things that have been worked in on that Bill. Easter falls early next year. It falls on April Fools' Day. I hope that is not an irreverent thing to say, but in case anybody thinks it is, perhaps I may be allowed to say April 1st. We must have a Budget of a more or less uncontroversial character to tide us over the election period, and as much legislation as possible will be fitted in with these obligatory features of our Parliamentary work. More than that it is premature to define.

There is one matter which was referred to by my right hon. Friend the Member for South-West Bethnal Green (Sir P. Harris). Housing is the most threatened sector in the home front. I have for some time been disquieted by the situation. During the last four or five months I have been continually referring to it by Minute and by personal discussion. The objective is painfully plain, namely, to provide in the shortest time the largest number of weather-proof dwellings in which our people can live through this winter in reasonable comfort. The subject is divided, like ancient Gaul, into three parts— repair, prefabricated, and permanent ; or, using the code names which have become so common in military matters, " repair," " prefab." and " perm." At the summit of this problem sits Lord Woolton and what I will venture to call somewhat disrespectfully " the housing squad," including not only War Cabinet Ministers—it is not usual to give details of Cabinet Committees—but also some who are not ministerial at all. These collect, co-ordinate, and in a great many cases decide, subject to the War Cabinet in the last resort, what is to be done. I have reserved to myself the right to take the chair when and if at any time I think it is necessary or desirable.

That is the function, the relationship, of Lord Woolton to this general scheme. I may say that Lord Woolton has shown a very great deal of energy and grip in trying to meet the difficulties of the past, difficulties which are being continually added to by the fire of the enemy. He has taken a number of steps, but I did not consider that the situation, borne in upon me by Questions and the answers which I have had to give in this House, was such that we did not require to smooth out and make more precise the arrangements for gripping this problem. Naturally, with the war going on, one's mind is drawn to the focusing of the executive forces of an emergency character upon the really serious parts of the problem. On a lower level, but of equal practical importance, an importance which outweighs the superior level, is the great field of emergency executive action. I can say a word—and it is only a word—on this matter of the relations between the Minister of Works and the Minister of Health in this field of London repair. The Ministry of Health is the great ambassador Department which deals with local authorities, and nothing must be done to hamper that long usage. Therefore, the Ministry of Health is the ambassador for the Ministry of Works in respect of the taking-over of areas, streets and so forth that really requires more power than any local authority can bring to bear. For the rest, executive power will increasingly reside in the Ministry of Works, which will have to discharge all the tasks of repair that cannot be undertaken, or are not being effectively undertaken, by the local authorities, and will have to produce the prefabricated houses I spoke of at the beginning of the year, which, although they cannot be produced in the numbers I then mentioned, can still be produced in very great number and of varying types. Further, they have to make, with the assistance of the Board of Trade in the closest liaison, as the military would say, the fittings and parts of all kinds which must be made not only for the repairs and for the " prefabs.," but also for the " perms.," which must get forward as fast as they possibly can under the driving power of the Minister of Health and, of course, the Secretary of State for Scotland. I do not want to go more into this now, because we shall very likely have a special Debate on the subject, either on an Amendment to the Address or on the resumption, if desired, and if Mr. Speaker would permit, of the general Debate on the Address. People sometimes do not like to have an Amendment to the Address, because it must take the form of a Vote of Censure ; but we are in the hands of the House and under the orders of the Chair.

I do not think it is any use for me at this time to enter upon the subject of foreign policy. I have a list of 25 countries on which I am prepared to give information about their tangled politics and their relations with ourselves ; but the House may rest assured that I have no intention of doing so, as no sufficient provocation has been offered to His Majesty's Government to induce me to embark upon this lengthy excursion. After all, a Foreign Affairs Debate can be brought on as part of the Debate on the Address. All I have tried to do at this time is to give a general survey of the tasks which lie before us, of the limitations which may be assigned to our powers to discharge these tasks, of our duty to persevere in all we are pledged and committed to, and of the sense of the overlying obligations which we have to carry the war through in its closing stages with all energy and unity, not only at home among ourselves but among the great united Powers of the Grand Alliance, who, I am happy to say, were never more closely and intimately and comprehendingly united than they are at this time.

FUTURE OF LEND-LEASE

[*November* 30, 1944.

I ASK the House to allow me to read a statement upon the future workings of Lend-Lease. This statement has been carefully agreed with our United States colleagues and friends.

I thought it proper to take this first opportunity of telling the House the outcome of the discussions which have been taking place in the last few weeks in Washington between a British Mission headed by Lord Keynes and the American Administration. The Mission has been occupied in examining the manner in which the continuation of the war, after the defeat of Germany, is likely to affect the best use of our joint resources, and in particular the changes in the programme of supplies which the American Administration feel that it is proper and right for us to have in accordance with the terms of the Lend-Lease Act—an Act which, we must remember, is for the defence of the United States, and is strictly limited to what is necessary for the most effective prosecution of the war by the United States and its Allies.

The end of the war with Germany will make possible large reductions in some of our requirements. We expect that our needs will be met by a programme at a rate not much more than half of what we have been receiving in 1944. All of those supplies and services will be exclusively for the joint war effort against the common enemy. The prolongation of the war, in what will be, for us, the sixth or seventh year, means that certain improvements are essential, if our national economy is to be as fully effective as possible for the prosecution of the war. Fatigue and abstinence carried too far, and endured too long, can impede the effectiveness of a people at war at least as much as more sensational forms of privation. The defeat of Germany must be followed in due course by some release of man-power to increase the supplies available for essential civilian consumption, some improvement in standards and variety of national diet, some devotion of current resources to the provision of emergency housing, and a serious effort to rebuild the export trade, which we deliberately gave up in the extremity of our emergency, but without which we cannot live in future. Those are forms of sacrifice which it is both possible and right to make for a limited period, but which become self-defeating if they are continued too long.

All these matters, both military and economic, have been jointly examined, in the utmost detail, by our representatives in Washington and the heads of the American Departments concerned. We have put at their disposal every particular and every relevant fact in our possession. One part of the relevant material which can safely be published has, moreover, been made available to the public here and in the United States in the White Paper published a few days ago. During the recent brief Recess, our representatives in Washington have been in a position to make a full report to us. I take this opportunity to express our very great appreciation of the practical sympathy with which the realities of the position have been examined, and of the results which have been achieved.

Let me remind the House that it is not within the scope of the Lend-Lease Act to provide general relief, or to prepare for post-war reconstruction, or to aid our export trade. That great Act has stood us and our Allies in good stead, and in recent conversations we have neither asked nor expected any assistance which is not strictly within its terms and provisions. Nevertheless, as the war proceeds, the nature of the aid which forwards its prosecution most effectively, though unchanged in major matters, gradually changes in detail. Accordingly, so that we may play our full part in continuing the struggle, a programme of Lend-Lease aid against Japan, after the defeat of Germany, has now been planned with the American Administration, to maintain our fighting power against Japan. Without any reduction in our proportional effort, we shall be able, along with the United States, to release some of our man-power to produce somewhat more for civilian consumption. Some improvement in the variety of the civilian diet will be made possible. We shall be able to build more temporary and emergency houses. We must necessarily, for the most part, depend on our own efforts in this field; but, in addition to those efforts resulting from the planned and proportional programme, we anticipate aid from American sources, not only in materials but also in complete houses, to meet some of our needs for temporary and emergency houses for war workers in war areas.

These items are being closely examined with the help of experts sent out by the Ministry of Works during the tenure of Lord Portal. It is too soon to say on what scale the possibilities of physical production and of shipping will allow this most generous assistance to be released in practice, but it is not too soon to say that the principle is recognized that the provision of emergency shelter for bombed-out war workers is an essential condition of a fully effective contribution to final victory, and, therefore, a war need eligible for Lend-Lease assistance.

Finally, we have been able to reduce the Lend-Lease programme, so that there will be no obstacle to the efforts which we ourselves must begin at once, and intensify after the defeat of Germany, to increase the export trade which will be absolutely vital to us when, at the termination of the war, the present system of Lend-Lease necessarily and properly comes to an end. This is a matter on which, I am well aware, hon Members are anxious to hear, in some detail, what the position will now be. As I said, the defeat of Germany will make possible reductions in the Lend-Lease programme. In certain fields we have been able to anticipate those changes, and to work on the basis of the new programme from the beginning of 1945. Thus, from that date, we shall no longer receive shipments to this country under Lend-Lease of any manufactured articles for civilian use which enter into export trade, nor of many raw and semi-fabricated materials, such as iron and steel and some non-ferrous metals. Consequently, in accordance with the White Paper of September, 1941, we shall then be free to export a wide range of goods made from those materials.

Naturally, we have not used in export, and do not propose to use, any critically scarce materials, except where the export is essential to the effective prosecution of the war; but till the German war is at an end there can, of course, be no significant release of resources. The defeat of Japan must still continue to have the first call on our resources after that; but after the defeat of Germany, it will be both possible and necessary to turn over an increasing part of our resources to civilian production, including the export trade. As a result of the recent discussions with the United States Administration about our Lend-Lease programme, after the defeat of Germany exporters will be subject only to those inevitable limitations dictated by the needs of the war against Japan.

There is not, of course—and never has been—any question of our re-exporting in commerce any articles which we have received under Lend-Lease. Nor, in general, shall we receive in this country under Lend-Lease finished articles identical with those which we shall export. Such articles will be paid for by us. Where we continue to receive any raw materials, the quantities supplied under Lend-Lease will be limited to our domestic consumption, for the manufacture of munitions and the maintenance of our essential war-time economy. We shall pay cash for any additional supplies which we might wish to take from the United States for export purposes. Thus one uncertainty about future conditions has now been removed. It should be possible for exporters henceforward to make plans with the assurance that they will be able to give effect to those plans with the least possible time-lag, when the defeat of Germany releases man-power, capacity and materials.

I should like to add one word. The White Paper on reciprocal aid lately published, and the President's last Lend-Lease report, provide vivid evidence of the extent to which the community and interdependence of effort between the two great Atlantic communities has now proceeded. Never, I think, has there been a more thorough understanding of the facts of the economic position, and the problems of Great Britain and the United States of America, on both sides, than we have now been able to reach. If men of good will start out from the same premises of agreed fact, they do not necessarily find it impossible to reach the same conclusion.

Everything in this statement was agreed, almost sentence by sentence, with our American colleagues. I must add that I consider the statement I have made is one of a highly satisfactory nature, and gives real hope for the future and the smooth development of economic affairs between the two countries in time to come.

SHELLS FOR BRITISH TROOPS

A REPLY TO A LETTER FROM SIR WALTER CITRINE, SECRETARY OF
THE TRADES UNION CONGRESS, FOLLOWING STATEMENTS BY
PRESIDENT ROOSEVELT AND GENERAL EISENHOWER ABOUT
THE SHELL SHORTAGE CONFRONTING AMERICAN TROOPS
NOVEMBER 30, 1944

AT the beginning of 1943 the products of our shell plants, both forging and filling, were so far ahead of actual consumption that in order to make the best possible use of our resources of manpower we felt that we should slow down production and transfer where possible to other forms of munitions, such as aircraft. This policy clearly enabled us to bring a greater weight to bear on the enemy. By the first quarter of 1944, however, the experience of the battles in Italy and the imminence of the invasion of France made it evident that a time was coming when firing on a much larger scale might be necessary. Consequently, the filling of existing stocks of empty shells from past production was put in hand. Steps were taken to reinstate production of new shells of the three important calibres on a large scale, both in Canada and in this country. These shell plants have been working at a progressively increasing rate ever since. In addition to the regular processes of review by the War Office authorities and the Chiefs of Staff, special conferences on this subject have been presided over by me on April 18, 1944, and October 25, 1944, and a still further increased flow has been arranged for the future.

In addition to this, it is right at this stage of the war to draw to a certain extent upon the large reserves which are available in order not to finish up with unduly large unused supplies. There is no ground for suggesting that there has been the slightest slackening of the effort of those engaged in our plants, and the highest praise is due to all connected with them. British troops at the front have every reason to be satisfied with the work of their comrades, men and women, in the munition factories.

BRITAIN'S PUBLIC SCHOOLS

A Speech to the Boys of Harrow School
December 1, 1944

[*December* 1, 1944.

THE Memorial to those who fell in the last war rises clear and solid, and on it will be graven the names of those who carried on their fathers' work. It is thought that in all the changing circumstances of our social and economic life, it is better to concentrate the Memorial Fund as far as possible upon the life, strength and resources of the school, and on giving Harrow as much as possible of the power to remain this extraordinarily coherent and elevating entity from which so much inspiration has been derived. With Field-Marshal Gort and Field-Marshal Alexander in the military field, you have much to be proud of.

I think no better idea could be devised than to establish a fund which will make it easy for Harrovians who may not otherwise have sufficient money to send their sons here. It shall be made easy, and not unduly expensive for those who might be hampered, as many will be in the changing course of our affairs to come, to carry on in a still further generation the wishes, the hopes, the memories and achievements of their parents. Nothing could be better than that.

You read in the newspapers a great deal about the future of the public schools. I can assure you that during this war great changes have taken place in the minds of men, and there is no change which is more marked in our country than the continual and rapid effacement of class differences. I do not wish to see the public schools fall into desuetude. We cannot afford to pull down the great and beneficent institutions which helped to make us what we were in the last war and to keep us what we are in this. But it is by broadening the intake, and by the schools becoming more and more based upon aspiring youth in every class of the nation and coming from every part of the Kingdom, that you will preserve all the traditions and inspirations which are gathered in the great public schools, and make them the possession of all our fellow countrymen and of lads from all over the land.

It has been said that the prerogatives of the Crown have become the privileges of the people. The public schools have also their gift to give, and I hope and trust that after this war is over, there will not only be a Harrow Fund to help the sons of old Harrovians to come back to the school, but that the institution of scholarships and so forth may from all over the country bring the youth of our nation to enjoy our songs, our amenities, our memories, and all that so many years has centred here.

Some there may be who would go to a place where there is, I believe, a river of some sort [laughter]. But wherever it may be, we are a united nation as we have never been before, and as no other nation is in any part of the world. Let us keep that true sense of unity. Let us feel that brotherhood which knows no barriers.

Very great and glorious is this Island. Far and wide across the surface of the globe there are few in any free community who do not regard us with respect, admiration and even wonder. For a whole year we stood alone against an overwhelming powerful force, a force armed to the teeth, long trained and prepared for war. Now that we are marching to a period of great stress and difficulty, now that you will go forward into a world where problems will be made greater by the victories which have been and will be won, where duty will become more compulsive because of the need to live up to what has happened in the past, you give to me by your voices and your aspect that feeling that there will never lack a youth in Britain capable of facing, enduring, and conquering every evil in the name of freedom and for the sake of their dearly-loved native land.

We are no longer one small island and its Empire opposing the great embattled army of the enemy, but are now in the van of a concord of the greatest nations in the world, numbering more than thirty proclaimed Allies, with the vast majority of the human race setting their hopes on our forward advance and on our final and, as we can certainly say, assured victory.

THE CRISIS IN GREECE

A SPEECH TO THE HOUSE OF COMMONS IN A DEBATE ON AN AMENDMENT
REGRETTING BRITISH INTERVENTION IN GREECE AND OTHER PARTS OF
LIBERATED EUROPE. THE AMENDMENT WAS DEFEATED BY 279 TO 30
DECEMBER 8, 1944

December 1. *United States Third Army reached the River Saar at three points.*
Princess Elizabeth launched Britain's greatest battleship.

December 2. *East African troops entered Kalewa in Burma.*

December 3. *Official stand-down of the Home Guard. The King took the Salute in Hyde Park.*
Athens police fired on Greek demonstrators.

December 4. *British Second Army occupied Blerick, a suburb of Venlo.*
U.S. Third Army reached to within 6 miles of Saar-brücken.

December 5. *British troops were forced to intervene in the fighting in Athens.*
The Eighth Army captured the Italian city of Ravenna.

December 7. *British and Greek regular troops began clearing hostile elements from Athens.*

December 8. *House of Commons by 279 votes to 30 supported the British Government's action in Greece.*
Russian troops reach to within 25 miles of Budapest.

[*December* 8, 1944.

THE value of the speech which has just ended was, I thought, that it showed how extremely complex these Greek politics are. The hon. Gentleman [Sir Richard Acland, leader of the Commonwealth Party] made a very large number of assertions, some of which were accurate, some of which were, according to my information, rather the reverse. At any rate, hours of debate, day after day, would be required if this House were to attempt to emulate the mastery of the details of the position in Greece which he has been able to acquire in spite of other serious preoccupations.

I address myself to the Amendment as a whole, and I must point out that it does not deal only with Greece, but with other parts of Europe. The House, I am sure, will therefore permit me to deal with the whole of this question of our intervention on the Continent, the tone, character, temper and objects of our intervention where we have to intervene, by dealing with other countries besides this one which has been the main focus of the two speeches to which we have listened. Before I come to particular countries and places, let me present to the House the charge which is made against us. It is that we are using His Majesty's Forces to disarm the friends of democracy in Greece and in other parts of Europe, and to suppress those popular movements which have valorously assisted in the defeat of the enemy. Here is a pretty direct issue, and one on which the House will have to pronounce before we separate this evening. Certainly, His Majesty's Government would be unworthy of confidence if His Majesty's Forces were being used by them to disarm the friends of democracy.

The question however arises, and one may be permitted to dwell on it for a moment, who are the friends of democracy, and also how is the word "democracy" to be interpreted? My idea of it is that the plain, humble, common man, just the ordinary man who keeps a wife and family, who goes off to fight for his country when it is in trouble, goes to the poll at the appropriate time, and puts his cross on the ballot-paper showing the candidate he wishes to be elected to Parliament—that he is the foundation of democracy. And it is also essential to this foundation that this man or woman should do this without fear, and without any form of intimidation or victimization. He marks his ballot-paper in strict secrecy, and then elected representatives meet and together decide what government, or even, in times of stress, what form of government they wish to have in their country. If that is democracy, I salute it. I espouse it. I would work for it.

Here a member interjected: "In Spain?" The Prime Minister continued:

I am not at all afraid to go into that discussion, but I have a good deal of ground to cover. It is one of those gross misrepresentations in which a certain class of people indulge that I have spoken praising words about Franco. All I said was that Spanish politics did not merely consist in drawing rude cartoons about him. It is really no use for my hon. Friend to screw his face up as if he were taking a nasty dose of medicine. I expect there are some other nasty gulps to swallow in the course of what, with great respect, I shall endeavour to lay before the House. I must say that I do not wish to be drawn into a discussion of Spain this morning. In the remarks I have made about democracy and the attitude I have taken throughout the time I have been burdened with these high responsibilities, and broadly I believe throughout my life—in the remarks I have made, and in my statements representing the policy of His Majesty's present Government, I stand upon the foundation of free elections based on universal suffrage, and that is what we consider the foundation for democracy.

But I feel quite differently about a swindle democracy, a democracy which calls itself democracy because it is Left Wing. It takes all sorts to make democracy, not only Left Wing, or even Communist. I do not allow a party or a body to call themselves democrats because they are stretching farther and farther into the most extreme forms of revolution. I do not accept a party as necessarily representing democracy because it becomes more violent as it becomes less numerous. One must have some respect for democracy, and not use the word too lightly. The last thing which resembles democracy is mob law, with bands of gangsters, armed with deadly weapons, forcing their way into great cities, seizing the police stations and key points of Government, endeavouring to introduce a totalitarian régime with an iron hand, and clamouring, as they can nowadays if they get the power——

Here there was an interruption, and the Prime Minister continued :

I am sorry to be causing so much distress. I have plenty of time, and if any outcries are wrung from hon. Members opposite I can always take a little longer over what I have to say, though I should regret to do so. I say that the last thing that represents democracy is mob law and the attempt to introduce a totalitarian régime and clamours to shoot everyone—there are lots of opportunities at the present time—who is politically inconvenient as part of a purge of those who are said, very often without foundation, to have sought to collaborate with the Germans during the occupation. Do not let us rate democracy so low, do not let us rate democracy as if it were merely grabbing power and shooting those who do not agree with you. That is the antithesis of democracy.

The hon. Member [Mr. Gallacher] should not get so excited, because he is going to have much the worse of the argument and much the worse of the Division. I was eleven years a fairly solitary figure in this House and pursued my way in patience, and so there may be hope for the hon. Member.

Democracy, I say, is not based on violence or terrorism, but on reason, on fair play, on freedom, on respecting the rights of other people. Democracy is no harlot to be picked up in the street by a man with a tommy gun. I trust the people, the mass of the people, in almost any country, but I like to make sure that it is the people and not a gang of bandits from the mountains or from the countryside who think that by violence they can overturn constituted authority, in some cases ancient Parliaments, Governments and States. That is my general description of the foundation upon which we should approach the various special instances on which I am going to dwell. During the war, of course, we have had to arm anyone who could shoot a Hun. Apart from their character, political convictions, past records and so forth, if they were out to shoot a Hun, we accepted them as friends and tried to enable them to fulfil their healthy instincts.

We are paying for it in having this Debate to-day, which personally I have found rather enjoyable, so far. We are paying for it also with our treasure and our blood. We are not paying for it with our honour or by defeat. But when countries are liberated, it does not follow that those who have received our weapons should use them in order to engross to themselves by violence and murder and bloodshed all those powers and traditions and continuity which many countries have slowly developed and to which quite a large proportion of their people, I believe the great majority, are firmly attached. If what is called in this Amendment the action of " the friends of democracy " is to be interpreted as carefully-planned *coups d'état* by murder gangs and as the iron rule of ruffians seeking to climb into the seats of power without a vote ever having been cast in their favour—if that is to masquerade as democracy, I think the House will unite in condemning it as a mockery. I do not admit—I am keeping to the words of the Amendment—that those popular elements who so " valorously " —in some cases I must say—assisted the defeat of the enemy have the right to come forward and say, " We are the saviours of the nation ; we must therefore henceforward be its rulers, its masters ; that is our reward ; we must now claim to sit in judgment over all "—that is, the vast mass of people in every occupied country who have had to live out their lives as well as they could under the iron rule and oppression of the Germans. These valorous elements are now to rule with dictatorial power gained by a *coup d'état*, by bloody street fighting and slaughter, and are to judge the high, the middle and the poor.

So far I am generalizing on the principles of what democracy should be, and also some of the principles which it should not follow. War criminals, the betrayers of their countrymen, the men who sincerely wished that Germany might win—these may be the objects of popular disgust or boycott, and may in extreme cases be brought before the courts and punished with death ; but I hope those will be courts of law, where fair trial may be had, and not mere expressions of mob fury or political rivalry. But to those who try to establish the point that the men who went out into the hills and were given rifles or machine guns by the British Government have by fee simple acquired the right to govern vast complex communities such as Belgium or Holland—it may be Holland next—or Greece, I say I repulse that claim. They have done good service, but it is for the State, and not for them, to judge of the rewards they should receive. It is not for them to claim ownership of the State.

That is what is being fought out now. However long I laboured I could not hope to convert individual gentlemen opposite to the better course, but I am addressing my remarks not only to them but to other Members in the House, of whom there are quite a large number. I say we march along an onerous and painful path. Poor old England! (Perhaps I ought to say " Poor old Britain! ") We have to assume the burden of the most thankless tasks, and in undertaking them to be scoffed at, criticized and opposed from every quarter ; but at least we know where we are making for, know the end of the road, know what is our objective. It is that these countries shall be freed from the German armed power, and under conditions of normal tranquillity shall have a free universal vote to decide the Government of their country—except a Fascist régime—and whether that Government shall be of the Left or of the Right.

There is our aim—and we are told that we seek to disarm the friends of democracy. We are told that because we do not allow gangs of heavily-armed guerrillas to descend from the mountains and instal themselves, with all the bloody terror and vigour of which they are capable, in power in great capitals, that we are traitors to democracy. I repulse that claim too. I shall call upon the House as a matter of confidence in His Majesty's Government, and of confidence in the spirit with which we have marched from one peril to another till victory is in sight, to reject such pretensions with the scorn that they deserve.

The Amendment on the Paper has particular reference to Greece, but it is a general attack on the whole policy of His Majesty's Government, which is represented as supporting reactionary forces everywhere, trying to instal by force dictatorial government contrary to the wishes of the people. I deal, therefore, not only with Greece. I pin myself at this moment, in the first instance, on to other parts of Europe, because this theme has also to some extent been opened up in the last sentences of an American Press release with which we were confronted a few days ago. It is not only in Greece that we appear to some eyes, to the eyes of those who support this Amendment, to be disarming the friends of democracy and those popular movements which have assisted the defeat of the enemy. There is Italy, there is Belgium.

Let me come to Belgium. Belgium is another case of what the Amendment calls the friends of democracy being disarmed in favour of the organized constitutional Administration. This is a grave case, and deserves scrutiny. At the end of November there was to be what the Germans call a Putsch organized in Belgium in order to throw out the Government of M. Pierlot, which Government was the only constitutional link with the past, and the only link we have recognized during the war with the Belgian Government that was thrown out over four years ago by the Germans in their brutal invasion. This Government has received a vote of confidence of 132 against only twelve, with six abstentions, from the Belgian Parliament, so far as it has been possible to reconstitute it, because some time is needed, after chaos, to set up some authority.

However, the friends of democracy, the valorous assisters in the defeat of the enemy, took a different view. They organized an attack upon the Belgian State. A demonstration, largely attended by women and children, marched up to the Belgian Parliament House, and lorry-loads of friends of democracy came hurrying in from Mons and other places, heavily armed. Here you see the hard-worked Britain, which you are asked to censure to-night. What does this reactionary, undemocratic country do? Orders were sent—I must confess it—to stop the lorries on the way, and to disarm their occupants. Moreover, we British placed light tanks and armoured cars in the side streets near the front of the Parliament House, which the Belgian gendarmerie were defending for the Belgian Government. Here was interference in a marked form. Here was an attempt to stand between the friends of democracy and the valorous, anarchic overthrow of the Belgian State. We British stood in the way of that ; I have to admit these things to you.

But under whose orders, and under whose authority, did we take this action? General Erskine, the British officer, made various proclamations, like those that General Scobie has made, on the needs of the situation. His proclamations had a highly salutary effect, and those concerned in the movement of Allied Forces acted accordingly. Who is General Erskine? He is the British head of the Anglo-American Mission, which has been set up to act as a link between the Supreme Commander of the Allied Expeditionary Force and the Belgian Government and people. He represents, is directly responsible to, and derives his authority from, General Eisenhower, that remarkable American Supreme Commander, whose wisdom and good fellowship we admire, and whose orders we have promised to obey. The following are instances of General Eisenhower's intervention in Belgian affairs.

On 28th October General Erskine handed a letter to M. Pierlot, in which, with the authority of General Eisenhower, he directed that all civilians in Belgium should be disarmed, and asked for the co-operation of the Belgian Government—that is the old Belgian Government, which had been installed in Brussels—in this matter. The letter concluded with the request that the Supreme Commander should receive the immediate assurance that this assistance would be forth-coming, and stated that the Army group commander—in this instance,

Field-Marshal Montgomery—would then be instructed to offer all assistance. On 11th November His Majesty's representative in Brussels reported to the Supreme Commander that he had himself been in Brussels on the previous day, and had met the Belgian Prime Minister and Government. He had reaffirmed his decision to give them all the assistance they required in carrying out the disarmament of the Resistance Forces. On 29th November the Belgian Government received information that armed demonstrators were on their way in lorries from Mons, and intended to attack Government offices. The Belgian Government made an official appeal for Allied support—I am talking about Belgium now, not Greece, because the positions seem so very similar—and the necessary precautions were taken by S.H.A.E.F., and the measures I have described were taken by the British troops and the Belgian gendarmerie.

Personally, as the House will readily guess, I consider that General Eisenhower's decisions were absolutely right, and that they stopped disorder and tumult along the lines of communication. After all, these lines of communication, from Antwerp forward, are those which will sustain several millions of men in their forward march into Germany in this war—which I should be sorry to see go on longer than is necessary. Not only did we obey General Eisenhower's orders, but we thought those orders wise and sensible.

After all, we British, who are now suggested to be poor friends of democracy, lost 35,000 to 40,000 men in opening up the great port of Antwerp, and our Navy has cleared the Scheldt river. The sacrifice of these men has always to be considered, as well as the friends of democracy advancing in lorries from Mons, to start a bloody revolution in Brussels.

> Here Mr. Aneurin Bevan asked: " Is it not a fact that the military authorities in Belgium are satisfied that the Belgian Prime Minister unwarrantedly asked for the intervention of British troops? Does not all the evidence now coming forward go to show that there was no such threat as the right hon. Gentleman pretends?" The Prime Minister continued:

I should think it was hardly possible to state the opposite of the truth with more precision. I back up those who seek to establish democracy and civilization. The hon. Member must learn to take as well as to give. There is no one more free with interruptions, taunts, and jibes than he is. I saw him—I heard him, not saw him—almost assailing some of the venerable figures on the bench immediately below him. He need not get so angry because the House laughs at him: he ought to be pleased when they only laugh at him. As I said, I back up all those who seek to establish democracy and civilization on a basis of law, and also popular, untrammelled, unintimidated, free, universal suffrage voting. It would be pretty hard on Europe if, after four or five years of German tyranny, she were liquidated and degraded and plunged into a series of brutal social wars. If the friends of democracy and its various defenders believe that they express the wishes of the majority, why cannot they wait for the General Election; why cannot they await the free vote of the people —which is our sole policy in every country into which British and American armies are advancing? There is the story of Belgium, which, I submit, with the utmost respect, to the American people, as well as to the House of Commons, carries many lessons which are applicable to other parts of the world.

Now I come to the case of Italy, which is, I gather, oddly enough, embodied in the case of Count Sforza. The Amendment does not specifically mention his name, but other communications which have been given to the world seem to show that in this respect also we have offended against democracy. It is a great mistake, as the Foreign Secretary said, and quite untrue, to say that we have vetoed Count Sforza's appointment to be Prime Minister or Foreign Secretary of the Italian Government. The Allies alone could do that. The Italians, having unconditionally surrendered, have a perfect right to choose anyone they please for any office of State. That, so they say, is one of their fundamental rights, and it belongs naturally to any country which has unconditionally surrendered, after having done most grievous injuries to its conquerors. We have not attempted to put our veto on the appointment of Count Sforza. If to-morrow the Italians were to make him Prime Minister or Foreign Secretary, we have no power to stop it, except with the agreement of the Allies. All that we should have to say about it is that we do not trust the man, we do not think he is a true and trustworthy man, nor do we put the slightest confidence in any Government of which he is a dominating member. I think we should have to put a great deal of responsibility for what might happen on those who called him to power.

> Here a member interrupted to say that Mr. Churchill had said the same about de Gaulle. The Prime Minister continued:

How little helpful it is to the progress of our Debate to fling in other large questions! I am not speaking about France to-day. I certainly never felt about de Gaulle the sentiments which experience has engendered in me about Count Sforza. De Gaulle is a man of honour, and has never broken his word. That is what I am coming to, because these things have to come out. I say that we should have to put a great deal of responsibility on those who called him to power. We are not avid of becoming deeply involved in the politics of the conquered or liberated countries. All we require from Italy is a Government which will guarantee us the necessary protection and facilities for the lines of communication, from Naples to Ravenna, lately taken, and to the North. Our interest in Italy is in the front where we have Armies engaged under General Alexander and General Mark Clark, that daring and skilful American General under whom we have confidently placed an Army at least three-quarters of which is British or British-controlled.

At this point, I will take a little lubrication, if it is permissible. I think it is always a great pleasure to the Noble Lady the Member for the Sutton Division of Plymouth [Viscountess Astor] to see me drinking water.

We have a joint arrangement with the Americans about Italy, and we should be very sorry if it were proved that we had broken away from this joint arrangement, and we have not done so, in any way. When, in the shifting tangles and contortions of Italian politics, with six parties rolling over each other, with all their conflicts of political interests, none of them being hampered by having been elected by anybody, in this confused scene, we were suddenly told that Count Sforza was to become Prime Minister or Foreign Secretary. The British Minister, Mr. Hopkinson, who is under the Ambassador, did undoubtedly say to the Italian inquirer that we did not think this would be a particularly good choice, or words to that effect. We had a perfect right to say this. We could not stop his being chosen, but we had a right to say our say. We were entitled to say that we did not think it would help the conduct of Italian affairs to choose for this office a man with whom Britain, if she counts for anything, would not care to establish cordial relations.

What is the reason for this prejudice on our part ? I should not like to make charges against public men without giving reasons, or one of the essential reasons. Why is it that we, and I particularly, say we have no trust in him, that we do not think he would be the sort of man we should like to have to do business with round the table ? I must go back to the time of the Italian collapse and surrender in 1943.

Count Sforza, who had been living for twenty years in America, was very anxious to get back to Italy. We did not think that this would be a good thing in the extremely disordered and tumultuous state in which Italy was left on the morrow of her revolt against Germany. However, on September 23rd, Count Sforza sent the following message to Marshal Badoglio, and repeated it in a letter to Mr. Berle, from which I have the President's permission to quote :

" I have read with extreme interest the statement of Marshal Badoglio of the 16th September, 1943, unequivocally stating that he considers the defeat of the Germans and their expulsion from Italy to be his primary duty and urging all Italians to join in this struggle.

"In my view, it now becomes the paramount duty of all Italians, irrespective of party or political differences, to support and assist in the struggle to crush German Arms and to drive every German soldier from Italian soil.

"So long as Marshal Badoglio is engaged in that task and is acceptable to the Allies in devoting Italian military resources to that struggle, I consider it criminal to do anything to weaken his position or hamper his work in fighting for the liberation of Italy and the Italian people. I am prepared to offer my full support so long as he is thus engaged, all the more because it is the only way to destroy the last criminal remnants of Fascism.

"Matters of internal politics can, and should, be adjourned for the period of the struggle, and the activities, military and political, of all Italians who seek freedom and the future of their Fatherland should be devoted to supporting the organized forces which are endeavouring to overthrow the common enemy. I pledge my honour to do this myself, and urge this course on my many friends and associates."

As Count Sforza passed through London, I was anxious to ascertain whether this was his sincere resolve or not, because something had appeared in another paper which was of a different tenor. We had a meeting, at which the Minister of State and Sir Alexander Cadogan, of the Foreign Office, were present. I went through this letter with Count Sforza almost line by line, and he assured me that it represented his most profound convictions. No sooner however, had he got back to Italy than he began that long series of intrigues which ended in the expulsion of Marshal Badoglio from office. Many may be very glad of this, but it is not the point I am considering. The point is whether he did not most completely, and without explanation, depart, at a very early day, from the solemn undertaking he gave, and without which we should have had power, I think, to convince our American friends, with whom we act in common, that it would not be a good thing for him to go back.

At this point the Prime Minister was interrupted by three members who referred to statements he had made in 1928 about Fascism in Italy. He continued:

I am not a bit afraid of anything I have said in a long political life. I certainly thought, at that particular time, that the kind of régime which was then set up in Italy was better than a general slump of Italy into the furious Bolshevik civil war which was raging in many other parts of Europe. I never see the slightest good in going back on what one has said.

I have no particular need to defend Marshal Badoglio. It does not arise in the course of the argument, except that we got from him the

Italian Fleet, which came over intact, save for the loss of one ship and 1,700 men ; and there was no moment in his tenure of office when he did not do his utmost to carry out his bond and help to drive the Germans from Italy and keep good order behind the lines. In other words, he helped Italy to work her passage home, which is by no means yet completely accomplished.

Presently, he fell a victim to Count Sforza's intrigues, and a six-party Government was formed under Signor Bonomi. Six parties were in the Government, but none had the slightest electoral foundation. They were merely parties like the Commonwealth party here, and had just about the same claim to represent democracy. We now did our best to help this new Government. I travelled to Italy and interviewed Signor Bonomi and others, and took the greatest trouble to draw up a series of mitigations in the treatment of Italy by the victorious Allies. These I proposed to the President by telegraph, and, when we met at Quebec, and when I stayed with him in his home at Hyde Park, we framed a joint declaration designed to give Italians a good chance of playing their part as co-belligerents, and also to make sure, as far as we could manage it, that the necessities of life were not lacking to the masses of the people.

The six parties have now made another contortion. Signor Bonomi has fallen and I understand he has now formed another Government of four out of the previous six parties. We wish him well. We have no objection at all to his forming a Government of four parties.

Here Mr. Shinwell interjected : "The best men of all parties ?" The Prime Minister continued :

I do not challenge the hon. Gentleman when the truth leaks out of him by accident from time to time.

The House will be glad that I now come to Greece, which forms the mainspring of the Vote of Censure we have to meet to-day. I have taken great responsibilities for our foreign policy towards Greece, and also in respect of what has taken place in Athens, and my right hon. Friend the Foreign Secretary and I have worked in the closest agreement. On or about 16th August, it became evident that the magnificent advance of the Russian Armies—[HON. MEMBERS : "Bolsheviks."] Oh, no. That is a very mischievous remark. Some hon. Members are always trying to entrap me, when we have to have these difficult Debates on foreign affairs, into saying something which would seem to be disrespectful to the splendid patriot armies which have cleansed the soil of Russia.

I say that we have taken great responsibilities, and when in August it became evident that the Russians' advance along the Black Sea shore, and their imminent impact upon Rumania and Bulgaria, taken together with the advance of the British and American Armies up the Italian Peninsula, and also with the growing power of Marshal Tito and his Partisans—whom we have always supported—would make the position of the Germans in Greece untenable, I proposed to the President that we should try to gather forces to enter Greece as and when the German position was sufficiently weakened, and, above all, to save Athens from the anarchy and starvation which threatened it. I pointed out that if there were a long hiatus after the German authorities went from the city before an organized Government could be set up, it was very likely that the E.A.M. and the Communist extremists would attempt to seize the city and crush all other forms of Greek expression but their own.

We had the right to express a point of view on the Greek question, because in an attempt to redeem our pledged word, we had sustained 30,000 casualties in what may, perhaps, be called a chivalrous resolve to share the miseries of Greece when she was invaded by Italy and Germany in 1941. At that time we were ourselves all alone in the world. My honoured friend, the President, was of opinion that we should certainly have plans made, and accordingly, at the Quebec Conference, it was proposed by the combined Chiefs of Staff that the British should prepare a Force to occupy the Athens area and so pave the way for the commencement of relief and for the establishment of law and order, and for the instalment of the Greek Government which we and the great bulk of the United Nations had formally recognized. The Americans and ourselves began to accumulate large masses of food and shipping, and established U.N.R.R.A. U.N.R.R.A. began to grow up in Alexandria, and other organizations for food distribution were actively engaged, and we gathered our much-strained shipping together at the cost of food to this country. A large part of these stores and medical relief as provided by America out of her riches. The rest of the burden fell upon us, and, of course, the diminution of shipping falls heavily upon us.

The proposal of the combined Chiefs of Staff was initialled by the President and me, and on 14th September a directive was sent by the combined Chiefs of Staff to General Wilson, the Supreme Commander in the Mediterranean, with whom I had already consulted on the military aspects. He was instructed to take the necessary action as and when he thought fit. All through 1944 we had had the usual trouble with the Greek Government and Greek troops in Egypt. There were mutinies and disorders; there were repeated resignations of Ministers and repeated returns to office, but out of this emerged a man, Papandreou, who had lived all this time in Greece without being in the slightest degree subservient to the enemy or losing his reputation in any way on such a charge; and when he came out he restored order to the Greek Government, which is the constitutional Government and which can only be displaced by a free vote of the people.

At an hotel in the Lebanon in May, 1944, a long meeting was held between the Papandreou Government and the leaders of all parties in Greece, including E.A.M., whom we brought out by air. An agreement was reached to establish a joint Government which could take over power in Athens when, with or without the help of the Allies, it was freed from the Germans. At the same time we prepared in deepest secrecy our British expedition. We did not think it necessary to tell anyone about it, not even the Greek Government. It was duly authorized by the British and American Chiefs of Staff. Secrecy was all important, and secrecy in this case was also preserved. Mr. Papandreou repeatedly appealed to us in the name of his Government of all parties, including the Communists and E.A.M., to come to the rescue with armed forces, and was much disappointed when I was unable to give him any definite reply. Our first move was to bring the Greek Government from Cairo, where they were living, to Caserta, which was the headquarters in Italy, so that they might be ready to go in should we at any time find it possible to provide the troops, about which we said nothing. When all was in readiness and the right moment came, General Wilson struck by air and by sea, and this enterprise, like so many others, which the House must not forget in judging this afternoon the fate of the National Government, was marked by excellent timing and extreme efficiency, and was also crowned with complete success.

The British troops were welcomed enthusiastically as they entered Athens, and so also was the Greek Brigade, which had mutinied earlier in the year, but had now been freed from the mutinous element. I took great trouble about this Brigade, to give it a chance to redeem its reputation. It not only redeemed its reputation, but won renown for the Greek army by entering Rimini at the head of the Allied Forces and wresting it from the Germans. This Brigade now came back to Athens, having heaped coals of fire upon the Italian heads which had invited the Germans to ruin Greece, by helping the Italians to drive the Germans from Italy itself ; and it was received with a great welcome in the streets of Athens. By this time M. Papandreou had gathered no less than six E.A.M. representatives into his Government, and also the leader of the Liberal Party, Mr. Sophoulis, a veteran and venerable counsellor of 84 or 85 years of age. Mr. Sophoulis was already complaining that too many E.A.M. and Communist representatives were already installed in places of power. M. Papandreou, however, is a man of the Left, a democrat, a Socialist, not a Liberal or anything like that, in fact almost everything that is supposed to be correct nowadays, and M. Papandreou put his trust in those six gentlemen.

Meanwhile, the forces of E.L.A.S., which is the military instrument of E.A.M., were planning a descent on Athens as a military and political operation, and the seizure of power by armed force. E.L.A.S. is a mixed body and it would be unfair to stigmatize them all as being entirely self-seeking in their aims and actions. Nevertheless, during the years of Greek captivity I must say that E.L.A.S. devoted far more attention to beating-up and destroying the representatives of the E.D.E.S., commanded by Colonel Zervas—a man of the Left by our standards, less extreme than E.A.M., a man who was correct according to the current jargon—the wrong element of the E.A.M., I say, devoted themselves more to attacking Zervas and his followers on the West side of Greece than they did to attacking the Germans themselves. For the past two years E.L.A.S. have devoted themselves principally to preparations for seizing power. We may, some of us, have underrated the extremes to which those preparations have been carried or the many privations and cruelties which have been inflicted on the village populations in the areas over which they prevail. I have taken every pains to collect information, and everything I say on fact in these matters has been most carefully examined beforehand by the officials who are thoroughly acquainted with the details.

At this point there were more interruptions, and the Prime Minister said :

I really must be allowed to continue my argument. Of course, in this House we are Conservative, Labour, Liberal and so forth ; we are not E.L.A.S. and E.D.E.S. as some gentlemen seem to imagine. E.L.A.S. did not hesitate on occasion to help the Germans to catch and kill the supporters of E.D.E.S. The German rule in Greece was feeble, and took the form mainly of hideous reprisals upon the unhappy countryside ; and hence by a kind of tacit agreement the Security Battalions, some of which were a kind of local Home Guard of the villages against predatory E.L.A.S. bands, came into being. Other bands were formed which acted in a manner contrary to the interests of the country ; and there was, as we can now see, a fairly well organized plot or plan by which E.L.A.S. should march down upon Athens, seize it by armed force, and establish a reign of terror under the plea that they were purging collaborationists. (How much the Germans knew about this before they left I cannot tell, but a number of them have been left behind and are fighting in the E.L.A.S. ranks.) Faced by this prospect, the Greek Government containing the six E.A.M. Ministers tried to arrange for a general disarmament, to be followed by the creation of a National Army or Home Guard of about 40,000 strong. This met with a ready response in all districts which E.L.A.S. could not dominate, but the formation of this National Army had not advanced to a point where they could offer effective resistance to the organized movement of subversive forces intended to overwhelm the State by violence. Also, the police in Athens, who had lived through the vicissitudes of the German tyranny, were no sure guarantee of stability. While all this was coming to a head, peace and order reigned in the city of the violet crown. Sir David Waley and Treasury experts toiled to save the drachma and to re-establish a stable currency, and the British Navy and merchant ships were landing at the Piræus stores, mainly American, which actually reached a total, I am told, of 45,000 tons in a single week. We came therefore to Greece, with American and Russian consent, at the invitation of the Government of all parties, bearing with us such good gifts as liberty, order, food, and the assurance of an absolute right to determine their own future as soon as conditions of normal tranquillity were regained.

I told the House that I would be frank with them. I have stated our action in detail. I must admit that not everyone agreed with the course we have taken, for which I accept the fullest responsibility. There were those who said, " Why worry about Greece ? " I am not speaking of Cabinet discussions. I come in contact with many streaks of opinion. They said, " Why worry about Greece ? If they have to starve, there are other countries in like plight. Haven't we enough on our hands without being lumbered into this job of International Red Cross, U.N.R.R.A., and maintaining order while the process of liberation and the distribution of food is going on ? Why not let Athens take its chance ? What does it matter to us if it falls under another tyranny when the Germans go, and if its people starve ? We have full occupation for every man that we can call to our service for work against the German foe." Well, these are powerful arguments, especially when put in a more attractive form than I have cast them ; but His Majesty's Government felt that having regard to the sacrifices that they made at the time of the German invasion of Greece, and to the long affection which has grown between the Greek and British people since their liberation in the last century, and having regard also to the decisions and agreements of our principal Allies, we should see what we could do to give these unfortunate people a fair chance of extricating themselves from their misery and starting on a clear road again. That is the only wish and ambition which we had, or anyone in the British Government had, for our entry into Greece and for the action forced upon us there. That is our only wish, and, personally, I am not ashamed of it.

However, events began to move. The carefully-prepared forces of E.L.A.S. began to infiltrate into Athens and into the Piræus. The other bodies began to move down from the Northern hills towards the city. The six E.A.M. Ministers resigned from the Government at this timely moment. One gentleman, I believe, was a little slow, but on being rung up on the telephone and told he would be killed if he did not come out, he made haste to follow the general practice. The intention of the "friends of democracy" who now entered the city was to ovethrow by violence the constitutional Government of Greece, and to instal themselves, without anything in the nature of an election, as the violent expression of the people's will. And here the trouble came to a head. I repudiate, as I have said, the idea that democracy can stand upon a violent seizure of power by unrepresentative men, or that it can be maintained by terrorism and the killing of political opponents. No doubt there are others who have a different view. We, however, were now assured by General Wilson—who is up to the present moment in actual charge of the Mediterranean—that we had ample forces in Greece and on the way. Moreover, we did not feel it compatible with our honour, or with the obligations into which we have entered with many people in Greece in the course of our presence there, to wash our hands of the whole business, make our way to the sea, as we easily could, and leave Athens to anarchy and misery, followed by tyranny established on murder. We may not be level with the strongest Powers in the modern world, but hitherto we have always been ready to risk our blood and such treasure as we have to defend our honour.

In the small hours of Tuesday morning, with the full approval of my right hon. Friend the Foreign Secretary, I informed General Wilson that he was responsible for providing sufficient forces on the spot, and very substantial numbers of highly-trained troops which he had already sent were being reinforced. At the same time I directed General Scobie, who has shown very great qualities of sobriety, poise, and at the same time martial vigour, to assume complete control of Athens and the district around it, and to use whatever force might be necessary to drive out and extirpate the E.L.A.S. bands by which the capital had then become infested. I also directed our Ambassador to do his utmost to prevail upon M. Papandreou, who seemed to wish to resign, to remain in power. I did this because nothing could be more silly or futile or dangerous than to have violent street fighting proceeding all around the Prime Minister's hotel while he was endeavouring to transfer his powers to some other leader, perhaps M. Sophoulis, 84 years of age, and arranging with the five or six principal parties all the details of a new Administration. I thought it would be much better to have calm and peace and order in Athens before any question of political change in the Administration was embarked upon. It is a great pity to have everything in the melting-pot at once, though this is one of the well-known subversive methods by which the undoing of States, great and small, has often been accomplished.

If I am blamed for this action I will gladly accept my dismissal at the hands of the House ; but if I am not so dismissed—make no mistake about it—we shall persist in this policy of clearing Athens and the Athens region of all who are rebels against the authority of the constitutional Government of Greece—of mutineers against the orders of the supreme Commander in the Mediterranean under whom all the guerrillas have undertaken to serve. I hope I have made the position clear, both generally as it affects the world and the war, and as it affects the Government. I have no fear at all that the most searching inquiries into the policy we have pursued in Europe—in Belgium, in Holland, in Italy and in Greece—the most searching examination will entitle any man into whose breast fairness and fair play enter, to accuse us of pursuing reactionary policies, of hampering the free expression of the national will, or of not endeavouring to enable the countries that have suffered the curse of German occupation to resume again the normal, free, democratic life which they desire, and which, as far as this House can act, we shall endeavour to secure for them.

THE FUTURE OF POLAND

A Speech to the House of Commons
December 15, 1944

December 9.   *Heavy fighting continued in Athens.*
               American troops made notable gains on the Saar front.
December 10.   *It was announced that a powerful British Fleet had been*
               formed to operate in the Pacific.
December 11.   *More than 2,000 American heavy bombers and 1,200*
               fighters attacked Germany and Austria.
December 12.   *Field-Marshal Alexander and Mr. Harold Macmillan*
               arrived in Athens, and General Scobie, the British Com-
               mander, presented terms to the Greek insurgents.
December 13.   *Russians captured more ground North-East of Budapest.*
December 14.   *Greek insurgent leaders were reported to be seeking terms*
               for an armistice.
December 15.   *Mr. Churchill declared that Britain supported Russian*
               plans to limit Poland's Eastern frontier to the Curzon
               Line and give her East Prussia in compensation.

[December 15, 1944.

IN opening this Debate I find myself in a position to read to the House again some extracts from the carefully-considered statements that I made to them in February, after I had returned from Teheran, and also in October of the present year. I rely upon those statements, and when I read them over again last night in preparation for this Debate I found it very difficult to improve upon them or alter them in any way. This may accuse me of infertility of mind, but it also gives me some confidence that I have not misled the House or felt myself stultified by the harsh and unforeseeable movement of events. It is not often that one wishes to repeat what one said two months ago, and still less ten months ago, but I propose to do so, because in no other way and in no other words that I can think of can I remind the House and bring home to them the grim, bare bones of the Polish problem.

On 22nd February I said:

" At Teheran I took occasion to raise personally with Marshal Stalin the question of the future of Poland, and I pointed out that it was in fulfilment of our guarantee to Poland that Great Britain declared war upon Nazi Germany, and that we had never weakened in our resolve, even in the period when we were all alone, and that the fate of the Polish nation holds a prime place in the thoughts and policies of His Majesty's Government and of the British Parliament. It was with great pleasure that I heard from Marshal Stalin that he, too, was resolved upon the creation and maintenance of a strong, integral, independent Poland as one of the leading Powers in Europe. He has several times repeated these declarations in public, and I am convinced that they represent the settled policy of the Soviet Union. Here I may remind the House that we ourselves have never in the past guaranteed, on behalf of His Majesty's Government, any particular frontier line to Poland. We did not approve of the Polish occupation of Vilna in 1920. The British view in 1919 stands expressed in the so-called Curzon Line, which attempted to deal, at any rate partially, with the problem. I have always held the opinion that all questions of territorial settlement and readjustment should stand over until the end of the war, and that the victorious Powers should then arrive at formal and final agreements governing the articulation of Europe as a whole. That is still the wish of His Majesty's Government. However, the advance of the Russian Armies into Polish regions in which the Polish underground army is active makes it indispensable that some kind of friendly working agreement should be arrived at to govern the war-time conditions and to enable all anti-Hitlerite forces to work together with the greatest advantage against the common foe.

" During the last few weeks "—I may remind the House that I was speaking on 22nd February—

" the Foreign Secretary and I together have laboured with the Polish Government in London with the object of establishing a working arrangement upon which the Fighting Forces can act, and upon which, I trust, an increasing structure of good will and comradeship may be built between Russians and Poles. I have an intense sympathy with the Poles, that heroic race whose national spirit centuries of misfortune cannot quench, but I also have sympathy with the Russian standpoint. Twice in our lifetime Russia has been violently assaulted by Germany. Many millions of Russians have been slain and vast tracts of Russian soil devastated as a result of repeated German aggression. Russia has the right of reassurance against future attacks from the West, and we are going all the way with her to see that she gets it, not only by the might of her arms but by the approval and assent of the United Nations. The liberation of Poland may presently be achieved by the Russian Armies after these Armies have suffered millions of casualties in breaking the German military machine. I cannot feel that the Russian demand for a reassurance about her Western frontiers goes beyond the limits of what is reasonable or just. Marshal Stalin and I also spoke and agreed upon the need for Poland to obtain compensation at the expense of Germany both in the North and in the West."

I said that nearly a year ago. I have nothing to alter in it from the point of view of His Majesty's Government. On 27th October, more recently, I reported upon my last visit to Moscow, and I said:

" The most urgent and burning question was of course that of Poland, and here again I speak words of hope, of hope reinforced by confidence."

I am afraid this does not hold in the same degree at the present time.

" To abandon hope in this matter would indeed be to surrender to despair. In this sphere there are two crucial issues. The first is the question of the Eastern frontier of Poland with Russia and the Curzon Line, as it is called, and the new territories to be added to Poland in the North and in the West. That is the first issue. The second is the relation of the Polish Government with the Lublin National Liberation Committee. On these two points, apart from many subsidiary and ancillary points, we held a series of conferences with both parties. . . .
" I wish I could tell the House that we had reached a solution of these problems. It is certainly not for want of trying. I am quite sure, however, that we have got a great deal nearer to the solution of both."

—I say that this part is subject to some review in the light of events—

" I hope Mr. Mikolajczyk will soon return to Moscow, and it will be a great disappointment to all the sincere friends of Poland, if a good arrangement cannot be made which will enable him to form a Polish Government on Polish soil—a Government recognized by all the great Powers concerned, and indeed by all those Governments of the United Nations which now recognize only the Polish Government in London. Although I do not underrate the difficulties which remain, it is a comfort to feel that Britain and Soviet Russia, and I do not doubt the United States, are all firmly agreed on the re-creation of a strong, free, independent, sovereign Poland loyal to the Allies and friendly to her great neighbour and liberator, Russia. Speaking more particularly for His Majesty's Government, it is our persevering and constant aim that the Polish people, after their sufferings and vicissitudes, shall find in Europe an abiding home and resting-place, which, though it may not entirely coincide or correspond with the pre-war frontiers of Poland, will nevertheless be adequate for the needs of the Polish nation and not inferior in character and quality, taking the picture as a whole, to what they previously possessed.

"These are critical days, and it would be a great pity if time were wasted in indecision or in protracted negotiation. If the Polish Government had taken the advice we tendered them at the beginning of this year, the additional complication produced by the formation of the Polish National Committee of Liberation at Lublin would not have arisen, and anything like a prolonged delay in the settlement can only have the effect of increasing the division between Poles in Poland, and also of hampering the common action which the Poles, the Russians and the rest of the Allies are taking against Germany. Therefore, as I say, I hope that no time will be lost in continuing these discussions and pressing them to an effective conclusion."

The hopes which I thought it proper, and indeed necessary, to express in October have faded. When Mr. Mikolajczyk left Moscow my hope was that he would return within a week or so with the authority of the Polish Government in London, to agree about the Polish frontiers on the basis of the Curzon Line and its prolongation to the southward called "the Curzon Line A", which comprises, on the Russian side, the city of Lvov. I have several times drawn Mr. Mikolajczyk's attention to the dangers of delay. Had he been able to return after the very friendly conversations which passed between him and Marshal Stalin, and also the conversations which he had with the Lublin National Liberation Committee ; had he been able to return, with the assent of his colleagues, I believe that the difficulties inherent in the forming of a Polish Government in harmony with the Lublin Committee might well have been overcome. In that case he would be at this moment at the head of a Polish Government, on Polish soil, recognized by all the United Nations, and awaiting the advance of the Russian Armies moving farther into Poland as the country was delivered from the Germans. He would also be assured in his task of the friendship and help of Marshal Stalin. Thus he could at every stage have established a good relationship between the Polish underground movement and the advancing Russians, and a Polish Administration would have been set up by him in the newly-delivered regions as they expanded.

I have the greatest respect for Mr. Mikolajczyk, and for his able colleagues who joined us at Moscow, Mr. Romer and Mr. Grabski. I am sure they are more qualified to fill the place of the late General Sikorski than any other of the Polish leaders. After endless discussions, into some of which we were drawn, on Mr. Mikolajczyk's return from Moscow, the Poles utterly failed to obtain agreement. In consequence, on 24th November, Mr. Mikolajczyk, Mr. Romer, and a number of other Polish Ministers, resigned from the Polish Government, which has been almost entirely reconstituted in a form that in some respects I certainly am not able to applaud. Mr. Mikolajczyk and his friends remain, in the view of His Majesty's Government, the only light which burns for Poland in the immediate future.

Just as I said that if the Polish Government had agreed, in the early part of this year, upon the frontier there never would have been any Lublin Committee to which Soviet Russia had committed herself, so I now say that if Mr. Mikolajczyk could swiftly have returned to Moscow early in November, as he hoped and expected to do, with the power to conclude an agreement on the frontier line, Poland might now have taken her full place in the ranks of the nations contending against Germany, and would have had the full support and friendship of Marshal Stalin and the Soviet Government. That opportunity, too, has been, for the time being, suspended. This prospect has vanished like the last. One is reminded of the story of the Sibylline books, in which on every occasion the price remained the same and the number of volumes decreased, until at last they had to be bought on the most unfavourable terms. Mr. Mikolajczyk's ordeal has been a most severe and painful one. Torn between the love of his country and the intense desire to reach a settlement with her mighty neighbour, which was most abhorrent to many of his fellow-countrymen, confronted with the obstinate and inflexible resistance of his London colleagues, whose veto was like the former Liberum Veto, which played so great a part in the ruin of Poland, with these circumstances around him, Mr. Mikolajczyk decided to resign. Almost a month has passed since then, and now I imagine that the prospects of a reconciliation between the Polish Government and the Lublin Committee, with the Soviet Government behind them, have definitely receded; although they might perhaps advance again were Mr. Mikolajczyk able to speak with authority for the fortunes of the Polish nation.

The consequences of this recession of hopes of a working agreement between Russia and the Poles have been masked to British eyes by the fact that the Russian Armies on the long Vistula Front have been motionless; but when they move forward, as move forward they surely will, and the Germans are expelled from large new tracts of Poland, the area administered by the Lublin Committee will grow, and its contacts with the Soviet Government will become more intimate and strong. I do not know what misfortunes will attend such a development. The absence of an agreement may well be grievous for Poland, and the relations and misunderstandings between the advancing Russian armies and the Polish underground movement may take forms which will be most painful to all who have the permanent well-being of Poland and her relations with Russia at heart. The fact that a Prime Minister resigns and that a new Government is formed does not, of course, affect the formal diplomatic relations between States. We still recognize the Polish Government in London as the Government of Poland, as we have done since they reached our shores in the early part of the war. This course has been continued up to the present by all the rest of the United Nations, excepting only Russia, which is the Power most concerned, and the Power whose armies will first enter the heart of Poland. It is a source of grief to me that all these forces could not have been joined together more speedily against the common foe.

I cannot accept the view that the arrangements which have been proposed for the frontiers of the new Poland are not solid and satisfactory, or that they would not give to Poland that " abiding home " of which I spoke to the House in February. If Poland concedes Lvov and the surrounding regions in the South, on the line known as Curzon Line A, which my right hon. Friend the Foreign Secretary will deal with in more detail later on in the Debate—if Poland makes this concession and these lands are joined to the Ukraine, she will gain in the North the whole of East Prussia west and south of the fortress of Koenigsberg, including the great city and port of Danzig, one of the most magnificent cities and harbours in the whole of the world, famous for centuries as a great gathering-place of the trade of the Baltic, and, indeed, of the world. This will be hers instead of the threatened and artificial Corridor, which was built so laboriously after the last war, and Poland will stretch broadly along the Baltic on a front of over 200 miles. The Poles are free, so far as Russia and Great Britain are concerned, to extend their territory, at the expense of Germany, to the West. I do not propose to go into exact details, but the extensions, which will be supported by Britain and Russia, bound together as they are by the twenty years' Alliance, are of high importance. Thus, they gain in the West and the North territories more important and more highly developed than they lose in the East. We hear that a third of Poland is to be conceded, but I must mention that that third includes the vast track of the Pripet Marshes, a most desolate region, which, though it swells the acreage, does not add to the wealth of those who own it.

Thus I have set before the House what is, in outline, the offer which the Russians, on whom the main burden of liberation still falls, make to the Polish people. I cannot believe that such an offer should be rejected by Poland. It would, of course, have to be accompanied by the disentanglement of populations in the East and in the North. The transference of several millions of people would have to be effected from the East to the West or North, as well as the expulsion of the Germans—because that is what is proposed : the total expulsion of the Germans—from the area to be acquired by Poland in the West and the North. For expulsion is the method which, so far as we have been able to see, will be the most satisfactory and lasting. There will be no mixture of populations to cause endless trouble, as has been the case in Alsace-Lorraine. A clean sweep will be made. I am not alarmed by the prospect of the disentanglement of populations, nor even by these large transferences, which are more possible in modern conditions than they ever were before.

The disentanglement of populations which took place between Greece and Turkey after the last war was in many ways a success, and has produced friendly relations between Greece and Turkey ever since. That disentanglement, which at first seemed impossible of achievement, and about which it was said that it would strip Turkish life in Anatolia of so many necessary services, and that the extra population could never be assimilated or sustained by Greece having regard to her own area and population—I say that disentanglement solved problems which had before been the causes of immense friction, of wars and of the rumours of wars. Nor do I see why there should not be room in Germany for the German populations of East Prussia and of the other territories I have mentioned. After all, six or seven million Germans have been killed already in this frightful war, into which they did not hesitate, for a second time in a generation, to plunge all Europe. At the present time, we are told that they have ten or twelve million prisoners or foreigners used as slaves in Germany, who will, we hope, be restored to their own homes and lands when victory is gained. Moreover, we must expect that many more Germans will be killed in the fighting which will occupy the spring and summer, and which we must expect will involve the largest and fiercest battles yet fought in this war.

When these ideas, which arose at the Teheran Conference, were first foreshadowed by me to the House, the British and American armies had not landed on the Continent. France was not liberated. She was powerless, not like now when she is rising with great rapidity to a strong and fine position among the nations of the world. The armies of General Eisenhower did not stand along the Rhine when these matters were discussed. They were still gathering in this Island, not along the Rhine where they are now growing in strength as the waves of American manhood cross the Atlantic and take their places in the crusade and in the line of battle. Nor had the Russians advanced to the Vistula ; vast distances separated them even from the frontiers of Poland. Nor was one large German army cut off in Courland, the peninsula which has Memel and Libau at its base. Nor was there that great position which the Russian armies hold in the extreme North with their right hand, nor was their left hand reaching out beyond Budapest in the South, threatening an advance into the very heart of Austria. Nor had Rome been occupied, nor the Apennines pierced.

In those days, the Poles might well have had some show of reason in asking whether the great Allies would have the power, even if they were so minded, to deliver the new territories to Poland which were to compensate her for what she was giving up in the East; but the situation has changed vastly in favour of the Allies, and it seems to me extremely unlikely that, after the spring and summer campaigns have been fought—if it be necessary to go so far in the business, and we shall go whatever distance is necessary to complete our object— it seems extremely unlikely that the evil and hateful forces in Germany, who plotted, planned and began this war, will have the power to resist the decisions of a peace or armistice Conference at which the principal victorious Powers will be assembled. The prospects of final victory have, in the time that has passed since these matters were first discussed at Teheran, become for the Allies solid and spacious. Therefore, as I say, it has always been said by the Poles, when I have been discussing the matter with them here, " We know what we have to give up; what certainty have we of receiving compensation in other quarters? " They have much more certainty of it now than at this time last year. In fact, I cannot see any doubt whatever that the Great Powers, if they agree, can effect the transference of population.

I find great difficulty in discussing these matters, because the attitude of the United States has not been defined with the precision which His Majesty's Government have thought it wise to use. The friendship of the United States Government for Poland, no less than our own, the large mass of Poles who have made their homes in the United States, and are, or are becoming, American citizens, the constitutional difficulties of the United States in making treaties and foreign agreements of every kind—all these have not enabled the Government of that great nation to speak in the terms which I have thought it my duty, with the assent of my colleagues, to use in this House. We know, however, that the Government and people of the United States have set their hearts upon a world organization to prevent the outbreak of future wars, and that this world organization will be fatally ruptured by a quarrel between any of the three most powerful Empires which compose the Grand Alliance of the United Nations. The President is aware of everything that has passed, and of all that is in the minds both of the Russians and of the British. He had at Moscow, in Mr. Averill Harriman, the U.S. Ambassador, a most accomplished representative, who in the capacity of observer, was present at all, or nearly all, of our Polish talks on the occasion of our last visit. The President has, therefore, been kept fully informed, not only by His Majesty's Government, but also by his own highly competent and distinguished representative, and by all the many sources and channels that are open to the unceasing vigilance of the State Department.

I am particularly careful not ever to pretend to speak in the name of any other Power unless so directed beforehand, and I hope the House will make allowances for the care with which I pick my words upon this point. All I can say is that I have received no formal disagreement in all these long months upon the way in which the future of Poland seems to be shaping itself—or being shaped. No doubt when the time comes the United States will make their own pronouncement on these matters, bearing in mind, as they will, the practical aspect which they assume, and also that failure on the part of the three greatest Powers to work together would damage all our hopes for a future structure, a world Government which, whatever else it may fail to do, will at any rate be equipped with all the powers necessary to prevent the outbreak of further war.

It is asked, why cannot all questions of territorial changes be left over till the end of the war ? I think that is a most pertinent question, and it is, in fact, the answer which I and the Foreign Secretary gave in almost every case that has been presented to us. Well, I understand the argument. The armies, it is said, may move here and there, their front may advance or recede, this country or that may be in occupation of this space of ground or the other, but it is at the peace table alone that the permanent destiny of any land or people will be decided. Why cannot that be said in this case ? It can be said in every case, or almost every case, except in that of Poland. So why should Poland be excepted from this general rule ? It is only for Polish advantage, and to avoid great evils which might occur. The Russian armies—I know nothing of their intentions, I am speaking only of what is obvious to anyone who studies the war map—will probably, during the early part of next year, traverse large areas of Poland, driving the Germans before them. If, during those marches, fierce quarrels and fighting break out between large sections of the Polish population and the Russian troops, very great suffering—which can still be avoided—will infallibly occur, and new poisoned wounds will be inflicted upon those who must dwell side by side in peace, confidence and good neighbourliness if the tranquillity of Europe is to be assured or the smooth working of the world organization for the maintenance of peace is to be created and maintained.

All these matters are among the most serious which could possibly be examined as far as our present lights allow. Our British principle has been enunciated that, as I have said, all territorial changes must await the Conference at the peace table after the victory has been won, but to that principle there is one exception, and that exception is, changes mutually agreed. It must not be forgotten that in the Atlantic Charter there is, I think, inserted the exception that there should be no changes before the peace table except those mutually agreed.* I am absolutely convinced that it is in the profound future interest of the Polish nation that they should reach agreement with the Soviet Government about their disputed frontiers in the East before the march of the Russian armies through the main part of Poland takes place. That is the great gift they have to make to Russia, a settlement now at this time which gives the firm title of mutual agreement to what might otherwise be disputed at the Peace Conference. I must, however, say, because I am most anxious the House should understand the whole position, speaking on behalf of His Majesty's Government in a way which I believe would probably be held binding by our successors, that at the Conference we shall adhere to the lines which I am now unfolding to the House, and shall not hesitate to proclaim that the Russians are justly treated, and rightly treated, in being granted the claim they make to the Eastern frontier along the Curzon Line as described.

The Foreign Secretary and I have laboured for many months, we have spared no labour of travel, no risk of political rebuff and consequent censure, in our effort to bring about that good understanding between the Poland whom we still recognize and the mighty Ally who has so heavily smitten the German military power. We have never weakened in any way in our resolve that Poland shall be restored and stand erect as a sovereign, independent nation, free to model her social institutions or any other institutions in any way her people choose, provided, I must say, that these are not on Fascist lines, and provided that Poland stands loyally as a barrier and friend of Russia against German aggression from the West. And in this task, of course, Poland will be aided to the full by a Russian and British guarantee of assistance, and will also, I cannot doubt, though I cannot declare, be aided by the United States acting at least through the world organization which we are determined to erect—which she and the whole of the United Nations are determined to erect—for the salvation of mankind toiling here below from the horrors of repeated war.

Another great war, especially an ideological war, fought as it would be not only on frontiers but in the heart of every land with weapons far more destructive than men have yet wielded, would spell the doom, perhaps for many centuries, of such civilization as we have been able to erect since history began to be written. It is that peril

* Later in the debate Mr. Eden said that the exception referred to in the Prime Minister's speech was not in the Atlantic Charter, but was part of a statement of policy made by the Prime Minister in September, 1940, when he said : " We have not at any time adopted since this war broke out the line that nothing can be changed in the territorial structures of the various countries. On the other hand we do not propose to recognize any territorial changes which take place during the war unless they take place with the free consent and goodwill of the parties concerned."

which, according to the best judgment of this National Government of all parties, which has so lately renewed its troth to stand together for the duration of the war against Germany—it is that peril that we have laboured and are striving sincerely and faithfully to ward off. Other powerful States are with us on each side, more powerful States perhaps even than the British Empire and Commonwealth of Nations. We can only try our best, and if we cannot solve the problem we can at least make sure that it is faced in all its sombre magnitude while time remains.

I have spoken of fading hopes and of disappointment at the failure to reach a Russo-Polish Agreement, but there has been another disappointment. It has been impossible to arrange any meeting of the three Great Powers. We had good grounds for believing that we might have met before Christmas. Indeed, I confidently expected that we should, but so far, although the prospect is earnestly looked forward to, nothing definite has been settled. Therefore, the strong, authoritative, if provisional decisions which are now required, not only on the Russo-Polish question, but on a host of vital matters, political, international, military and economic, apart from such progress as can be made by correspondence and individual visits, stand at the bar and wait. There ought to be a meeting at least of the three Great Powers at the earliest possible moment. So far as I and the Foreign Secretary are concerned, we can only repeat what has been said so often, that we will proceed to any place, at any time, under any conditions, where we can meet the heads of our two chief Allies, and we should welcome, above all, a meeting in this Island, a meeting in Great Britain, which has waged war from the very outset, and has risked, without flinching, national annihilation in the cause of freedom.

TROOPS WELFARE IN THE FAR EAST

A SPEECH TO THE HOUSE OF COMMONS
DECEMBER 20, 1944

December 16.   *The Germans opened a full-scale offensive on the American section of the Western Front and advanced several miles into Belgium and Luxemburg.*
  Eighth Army in Italy captured Faenza.

December 18.   *The German counter-offensive developed, and deep penetrations were made in the U.S. positions.*

December 19   *British and U.S. heavy bombers attacked German supply lines in an attempt to hold up the counter-offensive.*

December 20.   *Germans claimed to have taken 10,000 prisoners in their Western Front advance.*
  Greek rebels overran R.A.F. H.Q. in Athens.
  It was announced that organized Japanese resistance had ended in Leyte (Philippines).

[December 20, 1944.

I HAVE been asked to make a statement which I have prepared in conjunction with the Ministers at the head of the War Office and the India Office. Many Members of the House have very properly been concerned about the welfare of our Forces serving in the Far East. The Service Departments, and in particular the War Office, who have the greatest interest in this subject, have for many months made preparations in conjunction with the Government of India for the reception of the great Forces which are assembled and assembling in the Far Eastern theatre, and not least among their activities has been the provision of such stores and equipment as may be necessary on a reasonable basis for the well-being and contentment of those Forces. But in my view the time has now come when the influence of the Government machine as a whole, civil as well as military, must be brought to bear upon this important question. For this reason the Under-Secretary of State for the Home Department (Lord Munster) has recently made a tour of India and the Burma Front for the purpose of examining the situation on the spot and reporting to the Government about the improvements which are required. His report is being published as a White Paper, and will be available in the Vote Office before the House rises this evening.

The Government and the House are indebted to him for the manner in which he has discharged this responsible task. His report calls attention to a considerable number of matters in which improvement is urgently required. At the same time, he has rightly recognized the difficulties which have had to be faced by the authorities charged with these matters, and he has presented what is I think a very fair and helpful picture of the situation. It is important, in arriving at a judgment on these matters, to realize that the task of providing suitable amenities for troops serving in the East is far more intricate and harder than for troops serving under European conditions. The great spaces to be covered, the lack of ordinary European amenities of life anywhere except in large towns, and the small numbers of European women who can devote their services voluntarily to the provision of amenities, are great handicaps. The Government of India, since 1942, have had to receive a very large increase in the number of European troops in India, and their resources have been strained to the utmost to provide accommodation and to fulfil military construction programmes essential for operations. A great deal has been done to improve and expand welfare facilities for the British Forces, but clearly more can be achieved if additional resources and personnel can be provided from outside India.

The Government will apply themselves energetically to this problem. The Government of India and the South-East Asia Command have already been asked for a detailed statement of the help they require to make good the deficiencies in the welfare field to which Lord Munster has drawn attention.

One of our first concerns is, naturally, the welfare of the sick and wounded. Lord Munster visited 34 hospitals in the course of his tour. I am glad to say that he reports from a layman's point of view that he is satisfied that the medical facilities are maintained at a high standard of efficiency, in spite of the administrative difficulties of an extended front and poor communications. He has drawn attention to certain shortages of medical personnel in India. These are the reflection of general shortages. Every effort is being made to improve the position, but the Government have to pay regard to the many other claims, both civilian and Service, on the available supply of doctors and nurses. Consideration is being given urgently to his proposal that further numbers of the Voluntary Aid Detachment should be sent out to India, and to the other proposals he makes to improve the present position.

In some directions it will not be possible to achieve what we desire until the defeat of Germany enables greater resources to be diverted to the East. But plans have been made and directions are being given so that when these greater resources become available, they can be diverted without loss of time to the amelioration of the conditions of service of the men and women of the Services and the Merchant Navy who are called upon to continue the fight against Japan. At that stage a greater volume of air transport should become available, and this will render practicable an improvement in the facilities for the conveyance of fresh food and other comforts to the troops in the forward areas, and for the movement of men on urgent compassionate leave and to some extent on ordinary leave from the front. It will also make possible a wider use of air transport for the evacuation of casualties and the improvement of the transport of mails. A plan is being prepared under which the rapidity of mails can be progressively improved and the charges reduced. The immediate target is to carry by air all letter mail to the Far East, and it is hoped to achieve this early in 1945. The Under-Secretary of State for the Home Department has drawn attention in his report to the inadequacy of accommodation in leave centres and static camps in the Far Eastern theatres. A thorough revision of the present scales of accommodation and amenities in these centres and camps has already been ordered. Attention is being given to the adoption of modern methods of construction, the extension of fly-proofing of buildings, and the provision in greater quantities of modern appurtenances, including refrigerators, shower baths, and good furniture. These improvements will proceed as far as resources permit. Special attention is also being given to the provision of a varied diet and up-to-date hygienic systems of preparing and cooking food.

Measures are being taken as a matter of urgency which will in due course improve the supplies of beer available for the Forces in India. Indian production of beer has already been expanded to the fullest extent which is practicable without the import of raw materials and plant, but I hope it will be found possible to increase further both imported supplies and Indian production. Arrangements are also well advanced to produce in India cigarettes of a type more palatable to British troops. Trial brands have already been issued with a view to large-scale production when it is known which type is preferred by the men. Measures are also in hand to accelerate the provision of cinema apparatus and wireless equipment, most of which I should mention can only be obtained from the U.S.A. The value of the work done by British women for the well-being of the troops in India has been proved. Steps are now being taken to encourage more British women, both those who are resident in India now and volunteers from home, to undertake this important and valuable contribution to the welfare of the troops. Canteen services are not the responsibility of N.A.A.F.I. in this theatre, but the Government of India are taking special steps to improve and to enlarge the local organization.

It has also been decided that special consideration will be given to Service men and their families in assessing priorities for the allotment of houses and furniture after the war. The wives and families of Service men engaged in the Far Eastern theatre will, of course, share in this preferential treatment. In order that Service men overseas may keep abreast of important developments in social policy at home, pamphlets explaining new legislation on matters of major importance will be prepared and distributed to Service men and merchant seamen.

The House will have observed that in recent months a good deal more attention has been paid by the general public in this country to the efforts and achievements of our men in the Far East. The Ministry of Information and other authorities concerned recognize that this sympathetic interest must be fed by a service of reliable information as to what goes on there. Both the authorities at home and those in control of information on the spot will continue their efforts to maintain and improve the sources of such a service.

Although it is not a matter referred to in his report, Lord Munster has drawn my attention to the uncertainty which prevails in the minds of the men on the subject of the length of time for which they will be required to serve in the East. The position seems to have been made clear by the Secretary of State for War on 26th September and by me on 17th November. But it will perhaps be useful if I restate the position so far as those serving in India and S.E.A.C. are concerned.

British officers and men of the British Army serving in the East are eligible for posting to the Home Establishment under the Python scheme. This was explained by the Secretary of State for War in his statement. This scheme is not applicable to British officers of the Indian Army, but does apply to British Service officers and men attached to the Indian Army. The intention is to reduce the period of service in the Far East to the shortest period which is practicable, and, generally speaking, priority for posting to the Home Establishment under this scheme is given to those who have served longest away from this country. It is hoped before very long to have posted home all those who have served for more than four years in India and S.E.A.C. In fact the aim is to reduce the qualifying period for repatriation from those theatres to a few months under four years. There may be unavoidable exceptions to this in cases where individuals or specialist personnel cannot be spared for operational reasons, or where trained replacements cannot yet be provided ; but this is the general policy, which will be carried out to the furthest extent that war allows.

In addition there is the 28-day leave scheme which I recently announced to the House. This is designed to give a short period of leave at home to men who have been engaged in exceptionally arduous conditions but who may not come within the scope of the Python scheme for some time. The selection is made at the discretion of the Commanders-in-Chief concerned. But naturally, length of absence will be taken into account. Moreover, the current scheme whereby men are posted back to the United Kingdom on exceptional grounds of compassion will continue to operate. Men who receive leave under the short leave scheme will return again to service in the Far East, but as far as is practicable in present circumstances men repatriated under the Python scheme will not.

British officers and men belonging to the Indian Army are not eligible for posting to this country under the Python scheme. Home posting is impossible, because the Indian Army has no home establishment ; and transfer to the British Army for this purpose would involve the loss to the Indian Army of an officer who has received special training for service with Indian troops. In lieu of the Python schemes a leave scheme has been introduced under which British officers of the Indian Army can receive 61 days' leave at home. There are many officers of the Indian Army with very long periods of oversea services and at present no officer with less than five years' service is considered for leave, as it is obviously equitable that those with the longest service abroad should receive leave first. The short leave scheme also applies to British officers and other ranks of the Indian Army, and they are eligible on the same basis as those of the British Army.

His Majesty's Government are giving constant attention to the needs of the men and women serving in the Far East. I have issued instructions to those concerned on the spot and to Departments here that in relation to operational needs a higher priority must be given to the requirements for welfare and amenities for the Forces in the Far East than hitherto. I have also, at the desire of the Secretary of State for War, appointed Lieut.-General King to be my personal representative in the India and South East Asia Commands for welfare matters. It will be General King's duty to ascertain how matters are progressing and to report to me on difficulties which may arise and on the assistance which is required from this country. He will be concerned with the welfare of all three Services and the Merchant Navy, and will have a staff suitably composed for that purpose. The rapidity with which improvements can be effected must to a large extent depend on the progress of the war in Europe, but we shall press on in the meantime with every measure for which our resources are available.

CONFERENCE IN ATHENS

A Speech at a Conference in Athens attended by
Representatives from all Greek Parties
December 26, 1944

December 21. The German offensive deepened in the Ardennes, but the flanks were held by American troops and Stavelot was recaptured from the enemy.

December 22. German Western Front offensive reported to have been checked. Two hundred enemy tanks were destroyed.

It was officially announced that 250,000 men would be added to the British Army by a new call-up.

December 23. Germans made further progress in their counter-offensive, but Allied resistance strengthened.

In Burma the Japanese showed signs of withdrawal from the area between the Chindwin and the Irrawaddy rivers.

December 24. Over 6,000 sorties were flown by the Allied air forces over the German counter-offensive area.

Eighth Army troops in Italy captured Rosetta.

December 25. Mr. Churchill arrived in Athens to make a personal effort to solve the Greek crisis.

German advance on the Western Front slackened and several small towns were recaptured by Allied troops.

Russians encircled Budapest.

December 26. Mr. Churchill spoke at an All Party Conference in Athens after the discovery of a plot to blow up British H.Q. in that city.

The Germans advanced towards the Meuse, but in other sectors U.S. troops regained ground.

December 27. German armoured columns endeavoured to reach the Meuse but were halted, and the Allies increased pressure on the southern flank of the enemy's advance.

Germans attempted a withdrawal in the Luxembourg sector.

The Russians continued the siege of Budapest, and other Red Army units headed in the direction of Vienna.

December 28. Mr. Churchill left Athens for London and it was announced that he would recommend to the King of the Hellenes the establishment of a Regency.

U.S. troops recaptured more ground in the Ardennes.

It was estimated that since the start of the German offensive 1,088 of their aircraft had been destroyed or damaged.

December 29.   *Mr. Churchill arrived in London and had an immediate Cabinet meeting and a conference with the King of the Hellenes on the Greek situation.*

Germans withdrew on the northern flank of their advance into the Ardennes as Allied bombers continued their attacks on enemy supply lines.

[*December 26*, 1944.

GENTLEMEN, we hold many important matters in our hands.
To-day Greece may become a united nation marching with the other united nations of the world towards victory. To-morrow, if all our efforts fail, we shall have to bend to our hard task, and we British shall be given a large part of the duty of rescuing the city of Athens from the anarchy and miserable conditions now prevailing, and of securing a sufficient area of safety around it to enable the people of Athens to go through their daily life and work, to receive the supplies which are coming in, and to feel that they have peace, that they have safety, and that they have freedom.

It is not because the task which is confronting His Majesty's Government in Great Britain is beyond our strength, or because we shrink from discharging that task, that we have asked this company, all of whose interests are centred in Greece, to assemble here to-day. We hope, however, most earnestly, that as comrades in the common struggle against the Nazi tyrants we may find some way out of all our difficulties.

I hope the representatives of E.L.A.S. will not feel we misunderstand their point of view and their difficulties. We are all in difficulties. There must be responsibility for the future, and there must be comprehension between man and man.

Why is it we British came here ? We came with the knowledge and approval of President Roosevelt and Marshal Stalin. We also thought that at Caserta we had the invitation of all Greeks, including the commander of the E.L.A.S. army. In those days there were Germans to throw out, and it is quite true that we are in a different situation now. That is why we accepted when we were invited to come.

That is why I take the pains to offer the delegates of E.L.A.S. the statement of our position ; that we consider we were invited, and that we came with good hearts and full hands, with no thought in view but the restoration of Greece to her place, won by hard fighting, in the ranks of the Allies when victory is not so distant.

Why is it that we cannot leave ? Since we have been here, very violent and unexpected troubles have arisen, and we have become involved in them through doing what we believed was our duty. That duty we shall discharge inflexibly and faithfully to the end, but do not let anyone have in his mind the idea that Great Britain desires any material advantages from Greece. We don't want an inch of your territory, we seek no commercial advantages save those which are offered by Greece to all the nations of the world. We have not the slightest intention of interfering with the way in which normal and tranquil Greece carries on its affairs.

Whether Greece is a monarchy or a republic is a matter for Greeks and Greeks alone to decide. All we wish you is good, and good for all.

What will enable us to leave Greece ? Naturally, now that all these tragic things have happened, we are bound in honour to bring this matter to a good conclusion. We must, of course, ask the acceptance and fulfilment of General Scobie's terms. We hope there may be established a broad-based Greek Government, representative of the Greek nation, possessed of sufficient armed power in a Greek National Army, and with Greek police to preserve itself in Athens until a fair free general election can be held all over the country, or at any rate over the greater part of the country.

We hope the voice of the Greek people will be fully expressed in the same way as we express our voice in England and America, by the method of elections based on a secret ballot, so that every man, rich or poor, has an equal right to cast his vote of citizenship.

All we want from the Greeks is our ancient friendship. All we seek is that you should live happy and free and become prosperous and take a place in the councils of the United Nations worthy of the Greeks who broke the Italian power and fought so bravely against the overwhelming might of Germany.

I exhort you to believe that I speak on behalf of His Majesty's Government, and that I speak the truth from my heart.

When we came here yesterday we thought it would be a good thing to have a talk around a table. It is better to let every effort be made to remake Greece as a factor in victory, and to do it now. Therefore, we had a talk with Mr. Papandreou, the Prime Minister, who at Lebanon I was led to believe was supported by all parties in Greece, and we proposed to him that there should be a conference like this.

I and Mr. Eden have come all this way, although great battles are raging in Belgium and on the German frontier, to make this effort to rescue Greece from a miserable fate and raise her to a point of great fame and repute. Mr. Papandreou said immediately he would welcome such a conference, and we have all met here now in this city, where the sound of firing can be heard from minute to minute at no great distance.

The next British step was to invite the Archbishop to be chairman of this Greek conference. We do not intend to obstruct your deliberations. We British and other representatives of the great united victorious Powers will leave you Greeks to your own discussions under this most eminent and most venerable citizen, and we shall not trouble you unless you send for us again. We may wait a little while, but we have many other tasks to perform in this world of terrible storm.

My hope is, however, that the conference which begins here this afternoon in Athens will restore Greece once again to her fame and power among the Allies and the peace-loving peoples of the world, will secure the Greek frontiers from any danger from the North, and will enable every Greek to make the best of himself and the best of his country before the eyes of the whole world.

For all eyes are turned upon this table at the moment, and we British trust that whatever has happened in the heat of fighting, whatever misunderstandings there have been, we shall preserve that old friendship between Greece and Great Britain which played so notable a part in the establishment of Greek independence.

THE GREEK SITUATION

A STATEMENT AT A PRESS CONFERENCE IN ATHENS

[*December* 27, 1944.

I ASKED you to come here because I did not want to leave Athens without an interchange of courtesies between us. I have always found that that was a good thing between journalists.

Of course we feel that our policy has been right. There are two questions. One is : Ought the British to have come to Greece ? The second is : What ought we to have done when the civil war broke out ?

I exchanged telegrams with the President, as the result of which he agreed with me that we should come in as quickly as we could on the tail of the Germans, to help push them out of the country and bring in the food and make sure it could be distributed so that things could settle down quietly, as they should in any normal country.

The question was put to Marshal Stalin and he gave his agreement. Obviously it is very desirable to have this part of the world tranquil and beginning to get its living again.

Then there was the military conference at Caserta, when the Germans began leaving the Peloponnese. There we were invited to come in by a Greek Government which represented all the political parties, including the Communists and E.A.M.

We received an invitation from an all-party Greek Government. We held the meeting at Caserta to settle the military aspect, and we had General Sarafis there, representing E.L.A.S., and so we came in.

Then there was an interval of a month or six weeks when the Greek politicians talked and talked and struggled against internal unrest and tried to form some kind of army.

Meanwhile, other people gathered from the North and from the hills and entered the capital. All of a sudden, as you know only too well for me to have to tell you, a situation of great gravity arose here.

It is certainly clear to me that there would have been a massacre in this city if we had not intervened with our troops, few though they then were. How big the massacre would have been, what form it would have taken, what kind of Government would have emerged from it, what personalities, what ideologies, I cannot tell. I have got my view, but everybody can form his own. Certainly in my opinion there would have been a very serious massacre.

There is always a moment of great weakness when the German

tyranny is broken, when public men are few and far between, and when you have to set up something which enables the light of the country to burn again, the ordinary men and women to go about their business and walk the streets in safety. It is that which we have endeavoured to bring.

A tale has been telegraphed all over the world that we were supporting a Fascist Government endeavouring to impose a particular rule on this country, endeavouring to bring back the King, endeavouring to get some advantage or lasting control or influence for ourselves out of it. All those stories are absolutely without the slightest foundation. We seek nothing from Greece. We look for no selfish advantages. We want no territory. We do not require bases or anything like that. As for money, we would rather give it than take it. There is nothing we want of any kind from Greece except her friendship. That is all we want.

I rely on you to give publicity to my absolutely plain statement on these matters, as to why we came, and also as to whether we were right to intervene to prevent what we believe would have been a massacre. Many of you who are on the spot formed your own opinions about that.

Having got into the business, we have contracted many grave responsibilities. We have driven the rebels from the immediate centre of the city. We have enough troops here and on the way to make us complete masters of the City of Athens and the territory of Attica which surrounds it. The sooner the other side sees reason the sooner the fighting will stop. But it will not stop until that result has been achieved, either by friendly negotiations or by increasing use of military weapons. How could we lay aside our task now at this point ?

You have seen yourselves, for instance, that there are thousands of Greeks in Athens who have been formed into regiments of national guards. If we went away and the other side came in, they and all who have shown us friendliness would be liable to be punished by the conquerors with whatever severity they might choose.

When people have come into the open and given you their help you cannot leave them like that, nor will we until there are guarantees that we can believe in, for a fair, decent Government which will not pay off old scores either way. This is a very difficult thing to do. When we came here we thought it best to try to get a conference. The conference assembled last night. We invited E.L.A.S. to come, and their principal leaders came. We brought the Greeks together under the chairmanship of the Archbishop Damaskinos.

After they had been brought together and various speeches made, which, as you have seen, have been published to the world, we left them. We had with us representatives of the United States, of France and of Soviet Russia, as observers. We all then left. Afterwards discussions proceeded between the Greeks alone for a long time, as a result of which they met again. They are now meeting at the Greek Foreign Office.

I do not know exactly what results they will reach. I have had only some partial accounts of what has happened. I cannot tell what has happened, because I do not know, which is a very good reason. But I hope to know before this evening is out what has happened, more or less. Perhaps it will be prolonged till to-morrow, but I am hoping that we shall see our way clear to-night.

We are absolutely determined that the whole of this built-up area must be cleared of armed persons not under the control of any recognized Government, and that a sufficient area all around must be cleared. We shall use whatever force is necessary to obtain that object. Then we must hope that some good sense will come to this tortured people, that they will see that there is some purpose in working together, in giving Greece a chance to regain the glories which she won in repulsing the attack of Italy, and that she must take her place among the United Nations instead of being a society without integration or formation of any kind as she is at present, torn to pieces by passions, jealousies and rivalries to an extent most painful to those who wish her well.

I think that I ought to set before you the very simple reasons which led the Foreign Secretary and me to come at a time when everything is not entirely quiet in Belgium and on the frontiers of Germany, and to see if we could get started some sensible settlement which could easily be reached in any country where people did not feel their politics so intensely that they might ruin themselves thereby. We have done our best to bring them together to abridge the fighting and the misery.

The Prime Minister then answered the following questions put to him by Press representatives:

Question. Is there any question of an amnesty for the E.L.A.S. leaders?

Obviously, if there is a cessation of fighting there ought not to be a proscription either way.

Question. Can you suggest what might happen if no agreement is reached?

If no agreement is reached the guns will go on firing as they are now, the troops will clear this area, we shall establish security and peace and order in Attica. As to whether there could then be some vote taken in the area which would be liberated from disorders and perils of every kind, that would be a matter to be studied. Of course, we must expect that in a not very long time the President and Mr. Stalin and myself, with our advisers, will meet together, and we shall then review this situation, because if you cannot get a satisfactory and trustworthy democratic foundation you may have to have, for the time being, an international trust of some kind or other. We cannot afford to see whole peoples drifting into anarchy.

Question. Having come and seen the situation at first hand, what do you consider to be at the bottom of the present crisis?

I have a very clear idea, but I do not want to use language which might give offence to any section in Greece at the moment. I am hoping they will find some way of solving their difficulties. There is a moment of great danger in every country when it has been under German oppression and passes from that oppression into taking over its own affairs. There are no means of holding fair and free elections of any kind.

Question. Could you enlighten us on the attitude of the King of the Hellenes towards a Regency?

You are very right to mention the King of the Hellenes. If it is established that all the parties, or nearly all the parties, and the principal elements that still constitute what is left of the life of Greece, wish to have a Regency, I should be hopeful that he would take that course. But it is not for me to say what he would do or would not do. Of one thing I am sure, that he will not come back here unless a plebiscite of his people calls for his return.

SOME PARLIAMENTARY QUESTIONS

VOTES FOR OVERSEAS FORCES

Asked to make a statement on the processes by which Service men stationed overseas would be informed of political issues at a general election, the Prime Minister said on October 3:

PERSONNEL—that is jargon for officers and men—are able to keep themselves informed of the broad political trends by listening to the wireless and reading the ordinary newspapers and journals. At the time of a General Election the information given in these ways on political questions will no doubt increase considerably. The short interval between nomination day and polling day will in most cases preclude personnel overseas from receiving in time literature specially prepared in support of particular candidates. This was one of the reasons for the provision made in the Parliament (Elections and Meetings) Act for facilities for voting by proxy.

Everything possible will be done, subject to the limitations of time and space.

I cannot think that an election is impending in the sense of what you would call imminent, but I can assure the House that no one is more anxious than I am that every facility possible and practicable, having regard to the fact that fighting is still going on on an increasing scale, should be given to the troops to understand what are the issues for which the opposing candidates stand, and to record their votes on the largest possible scale. That is our intention. It would be disgraceful if, through any lack of care and forethought on our part, these men, who have in my view the first right to express an opinion, were deprived of their opportunity to do so. I say all this under the reservations which may be imposed by the force of physical events.

REPARATIONS BY GERMANY

Asked whether the Allies have considered the amount of indemnity and reparations Germany will have to pay after her defeat, and how much was paid last time, the Prime Minister said on October 3 :

No decisions have as yet been reached by the Allies on the question of the payment of reparations and indemnity by Germany. We have a considerable mass of experience on record. After the last war the German Government was called upon to pay a fixed annuity of £170,000,000 in gold, and a variable annuity equal to 26 per cent. of the value of German exports, together with further annuities the payment of which was postponed. These figures were afterwards modified and reduced almost to vanishing point. Also, loans of nearly £2,000,000,000 sterling were given to the Germans by the American, and to some extent by the British, public, none of which were repaid, and on balance the Germans did better out of it than the others. We must not imitate that this time.

NAZI WAR CRIMINALS

Asked whether Hitler, Goering, Goebbels and Himmler were on the British and United Nations list of war criminals, the Prime Minister said on October 4 :

So far as the British list is concerned, the parties mentioned are included. It should not be assumed that the procedure of trial will necessarily be adopted. I am not in a position to make any statement about the United Nations' list at the present time.

We have to consider a lot of countries, and are working in touch with a great many countries. All this is very general at the present time. We have not completed our job yet, and I am not able to give full answers respecting international bodies and international procedure.

MEETING OF UNITED NATIONS' LEADERS

Asked to arrange the next meeting between himself, President Roosevelt and Marshal Stalin in this country, the Prime Minister said on November 16 :

This point has occurred to me and my colleagues several times, and I trust that the Question of my hon. and gallant Friend may lend additional force to it ; but I cannot be sure.

I think these matters have to be left to be worked out as best they can. We may have our views in this country, but, working with a great number of powerful Allies, we have to recognize that our views sometimes have to yield to those of other people.

WAR-TIME CONTROLS

Asked to make a statement regarding the continuance of controls after the war with Germany, the Prime Minister said on November 16:

It is not possible to look beyond the end of the Japanese war, and my reply relates to the period between the defeat of Germany and the defeat of Japan. Until Japan has been defeated the war must have first call on our efforts. After the defeat of Germany it will be possible and necessary to turn over an increasing part of our resources to civilian production. Then we must make exertions to restore our export trade and to re-equip our industry. The shortage of houses, both permanent and emergency, must be grappled with as if it were a war-time measure. Active steps must be taken to relieve the shortage of civilian goods.

As stated in the White Paper to be published to-day, the existing system of allocating man-power to the Forces and to the various industries will be maintained. Nevertheless, it is intended to mitigate so far as possible the rigidity of the existing controls over labour. Many of the war-time controls over raw materials, industrial capacity, agriculture, food, transport and so forth will likewise be as necessary in that period as they are to-day. In these fields, also, relaxations will be possible, and will be made whenever circumstances permit and in an orderly manner. Any other course would result in violent disturbances which might well lead to inflation ; would be harmful to the economic life of the country ; and would make it impossible to ensure that the Nation's resources are devoted to essential needs, and are fairly distributed during the periods in which demand will still be without any economic relation to supply.

It is too early to forecast the stages by which control will be relaxed. But the House can rest assured that the whole matter will be dealt with in a severely practical manner, each case being considered not only on its merits but as part of an organized scheme. It is important in this phase that theoretical, ideological or partisan tendencies either way should be excluded, and the governing consideration in every case should be the public interest.

AMMUNITION SUPPLIES

Asked whether the production of shells was adequate to meet the present and anticipated expenditure in Western Europe, the Prime Minister said on November 28 :

Ammunition supply is constantly reviewed. Nine months ago we opened up our shell filling and making plants again on a large scale on account of impending operations and the immense piling-up of reserves which had occurred earlier, and had led to a temporary damping-down. That was nine months ago. Since then further important expansions have been made, and I am prepared to say that, providing factory workers maintain—and they may even improve upon—the present planned output, there is no reason to suppose the British Armies will be short of the necessary ammunition to fight their battles. We have also very considerable reserves, the use of which depends upon the varying estimates made as to the duration of the German resistance.

LEND-LEASE PAYMENTS

Asked to state the nature of the agreement between Britain and America " for the payment of goods and raw materials outwith the Lend-Lease agreement," whether payment would be made out of Britain's foreign assets or whether the United States would accept goods and material, the Prime Minister said on December 5 :

I must thank the hon. Gentleman for making me acquainted with the word " outwith ", with which I had not previously had the pleasure of making acquaintance. For the benefit of English Members I may say that it is translated, " outside the scope of." I thought it was a misprint at first.

It is our wish that our current dollar expenditure, including payment for goods and raw materials not obtained under Lend-Lease, should be met so far as possible out of our current dollar receipts in respect of goods and material produced in this country and otherwise. As a consequence of the arrangements which have been made, I hope that this purpose will, to a large extent, be attained.

When the questioner then said that the Prime Minister's statement required elucidation, adding " the point is whether this is going to be one-way traffic . . . increasing the load of our foreign debt, or whether America will be prepared, in return for goods she sends to this country, to accept goods from us," Mr. Churchill replied :

I think my hon. Friend is going a little outwith the Question which he put.

LOSSES IN GREECE

Asked to state Britain's losses in men, ships and aircraft since the landing in Greece, the Prime Minister said on December 14:

As far as can be ascertained, the total casualties sustained by the Royal Navy, the Royal Air Force and the Imperial Military Forces in Greece since our landing this year, in response to the appeal of the Greek Government, were up to the end of November under 300. This figure includes killed, wounded, missing, and prisoners of war. About 160 additional military casualties—I have not the naval and air figures, but they are not large—of whom 35 are killed, must be added since that date. Eight more minor naval vessels and 32 aircraft have been lost in the same period.

EX-SERVICEMEN'S BADGES

When a member said that men, honourably discharged from the Services with disabilities alleged to be non-attributable to their service, could not obtain a badge to protect them from insults from ignorant members of the public, the Prime Minister replied on December 19:

In present-day conditions of universal national service, no man's patriotism can be challenged because he wears civilian clothes. Moreover, the only persons discharged from the Forces who have not already some outward official mark of their service, for instance, the ribbon of the Africa or 1939–43 Stars, the King's Badge, or chevrons for war service, would be some of those discharged on account of non-attributable disability after service of less than twelve months. It is not proposed to institute a special badge for these.

POLICY IN GREECE

Asked whether there was complete accord between Britain, America and Russia regarding the Government's policy in Greece, the Prime Minister said on December 20:

The burden of attending to the troubles in Greece has fallen upon Great Britain, and we have not so far been able to discharge this task without criticism even here at home, which has added to our difficulties. The three Great Powers are in entire agreement upon the general aims which bind our Alliance, and we have every need to keep in the closest association in this dangerous and momentous phase of the war.

There is complete co-operation, but whether there is complete agreement on every aspect of this matter is another question altogether, I have not the slightest doubt that effective co-operation will go on in all aspects of the war. We had a certain task thrown upon us, and we are discharging it to the best of our ability.

THE WAR AGAINST THE U-BOATS

Statements issued monthly during 1944 by the Prime Minister
and President Roosevelt

[January to December.

[JANUARY]

TOTAL merchant ship tonnage lost by U-boat action in December
was again low despite an extension of operating areas. Fewer
U-boats were destroyed during the month by our air and sea forces
owing to several factors, including increased caution by the enemy.
Our supply routes were, however, well secured against U-boat attack.

In 1943 U-boats sank but 40 per cent. of the merchant ship tonnage
that they sank in 1942. On the other hand, United Nations merchant
ship tonnage constructed in 1943 approximately doubled the tonnage
delivered in 1942.

Nearly half of our tonnage lost for the year 1943 was during the
first three months : 27 per cent. was lost during the second quarter of
1943, and only 26 per cent. was lost during the last six months.

[FEBRUARY]

The year 1944 has opened with a very satisfactory first month for
the Allies in their continued campaign against the U-boat.

In spite of the limited opportunities to attack U-boats owing to the
extreme caution exercised by them, more were destroyed in January
than in December. This has been accomplished by unrelenting
offensive action by our surface and air forces.

The amount of merchant ship tonnage sunk by U-boats during
January, 1944, is among the lowest monthly figures for the whole war.

The German claims should, as usual, be ignored, as they are grossly
exaggerated and issued purely for propaganda purposes.

[MARCH]

In spite of the increase in traffic of the United Nations' shipping in
the Atlantic, February, 1944, was the lowest month as to tonnage of
Allied merchant-shipping losses by enemy U-boat action since the
United States entered the war ; and February was the second lowest
month of the entire war.

Again there were more U-boats than merchant vessels sunk, so the exchange rate remains favourable to the United Nations.

In actual numbers a few more U-boats were sunk in February than in January.

[APRIL]

March was an active month in the war against the U-boats, which operated in widely dispersed areas from the Barents Sea to the Indian Ocean. The enemy has persevered vainly in strenuous endeavours to disrupt our flow of supplies to Russia by the Northern route.

Our merchant-shipping losses were mainly incurred in far distant seas; though a little higher than in February, they were still low, and the rate of sinking U-boats was fully maintained.

The Allied merchant fleet continues to improve both in quantity and quality, but the strength of the U-boat force remains considerable, and calls for powerful efforts by surface and air forces.

[MAY]

In April the United Nations' anti-submarine activity continued at a highly satisfactory level. Again for another month the extraordinary fact continues that the number of enemy submarines sunk exceeds the number of Allied merchant ships sunk by submarines.

[JUNE]

During May our shipping losses have been by far the lowest for any month of the war, and they have in fact been but a fraction of the losses inflicted on enemy shipping by our warships and aircraft, although their merchant shipping is petty compared with that of the Allies.

There has been a lull in the operations of the U-boats, which perhaps indicates preparations for a renewed offensive. The change which has come over the scene is illustrated by the fact that, in spite of the few U-boats at sea, several are now sent to the bottom for each merchant ship sunk, whereas formerly each U-boat accounted for a considerable number of merchant ships before being destroyed.

This is to be ascribed to the vigilance and to the relentless attacks of our Anglo-American-Canadian and other anti-U-boat forces, including the scientists who support them in a brilliant manner.

[JULY]

Hitler's submarine fleet failed on all counts in June, 1944. Not only were the U-boats unable to halt the United Nations' invasion of the Continent, but their efforts to prevent the necessary supplying of our constantly-growing Allied army in Europe were made completely ineffective by our counter-measures.

The U-boats apparently concentrated to the West of the invasion during the month, relatively few of them being disposed over the Atlantic. Their sinking of United Nations merchant vessels reached almost the lowest figure of the entire war. For every United Nations merchant vessel sunk by German submarines, several times as many U-boats were sent to the bottom.

Thousands of Allied ships have been moved across the Channel to Normandy and coast-wise to build up the military forces engaged in the liberation of Europe. No merchant vessel of this vast concourse has been sunk by U-boat, with the possible exception of one ship. In this case doubt exists as to her destruction by U-boat or mine.

This is despite attempts by a substantial force of U-boats to pass up-Channel from their bases in Norway and France. Such attempts were, of course, expected, and United States and British air squadrons of Coastal Command, working in co-operation with the surface forces of the Allied navies, were ready. From the moment that the U-boats sailed from their bases they were attacked by aircraft of Coastal Command. Both aircraft and surface forces followed up sighting reports, hunting and attacking the U-boats with relentless determination.

The enemy was thus frustrated by the brilliant and unceasing work of Coastal Command and the tireless patrols of the surface forces, and has suffered heavy casualties.

[AUGUST]

The number of German U-boats sunk during the war now exceeds 500. It is therefore understandable that the U-boats still operating are extremely cautious. Their efforts have been ineffective during July, a month which has been so important for the success of Continental operations.

The number of U-boats destroyed has been substantially greater than the number of merchant ships sunk. Seventeen U-boats have been sunk while attempting to interfere with our cross-Channel traffic since the first landing of the Army of Liberation.

The U-boat fleet is still of impressive size ; nevertheless the U-boats remain the hunted rather than the hunters. They have been attacked from the Arctic to the Indian Ocean, aircraft playing a great part with the surface forces. This pressure will be maintained until all chances of revival of the U-boat campaign are killed, whatever may be the new devices and methods developed by the enemy.

The Nazi claims of sinkings continue to be grossly exaggerated. For instance, their claim for June, the latest month for which complete figures are available, was an exaggeration of 1,000 per cent.

[SEPTEMBER]

Last month, due to the effectiveness of the Allied operations in France, the principal U-boat operating bases in the Bay of Biscay were neutralized. As a consequence the Germans have been forced to operate their undersea craft from Norwegian and Baltic bases, thereby stretching even thinner their difficult lines of operation. The exchange rate between merchant ships sunk and U-boats destroyed continues to be profitable to the United Nations' cause. While U-boat operations continue, they are sporadic and relatively ineffectual.

[OCTOBER]

During September there has been a lull in U-boat activity, which is possibly seasonal. This year, as last, the enemy may hope to renew his offensive in the autumn and may rely on new types of U-boats to counter our present ascendancy. Shipping losses have been almost as low as in May, 1944, the best month of the war. The rate of destruction of U-boats in proportion to shipping losses remains satisfactory. The U-boat war, however, demands unceasing attention. Only the zeal and vigour of the Allied air and surface forces have procured the comparative safety of our shipping and the enemy's scant success.

[NOVEMBER]

The scope of the German U-boat activities in October was materially below that of any other month of the war ; in consequence the number of United Nations merchant vessels sunk by German submarines was also the lowest of any month of the entire war. Although the number of German U-boats destroyed was less than what has come to be considered a good monthly " bag," it compares very favourably with the number of Allied merchant vessels sunk by U-boats. The Allies continue to supply on schedule their ever-growing armies in Europe.

[DECEMBER]

Shipping losses from U-boat action have again been very small, and the number of U-boats sunk in proportion has again been satisfactory. The enemy has by no means abandoned the struggle, and has introduced new devices, such as the extensible air intake and exhaust which enable U-boats to remain submerged for long periods and so penetrate into areas denied to them for the past three years.

Reports that U-boat construction has been abandoned are probably German-inspired and are untrue. On the contrary, improved types of U-boats may at any time be thrown into the battle, and retention of our present command of the sea will undoubtedly call for un-remitting vigilance and hard fighting.

HOPE FOR 1945

[December 31, 1944.

THE opening of another war-time New Year, which will almost
certainly be an election year, gives me, as your Grand Master,
an opportunity of sending a message of greeting and good hope to the
members of the Primrose League.

On the outbreak of war the members of the League, true to their
principles, devoted themselves with whole-hearted patriotism to the
service of their country. They have continued without looking back
" to scorn delights and live laborious days."

To-day we are entering upon a year that should bring us victory in
Europe. Before many months have passed the evil gang that has too
long dominated that unhappy continent will be wiped out. Until that
end has been achieved there can be no return to our normal habits.
It would be tragic folly to prolong, by any slackening in the last
phase, the agony that a megalomaniac ambition has loosed upon
the world.

The Primrose League was founded to keep green the memory of a
great and wise nineteenth-century statesman, and to uphold the
national ideals and principles that he enunciated. Those principles
have an abiding validity. They have stood the test of time and of
experiences unimaginable in those tranquil Victorian times. The
speeches and writings of Disraeli are a mine of political sagacity. He
loved his country with a romantic passion. He had a profound faith
in the greatness of the English character, and a burning desire to bring
about an improvement in the condition of the people.

It would be easy to select from his speeches, almost at random,
passages that are as apposite to this age as they were to his own.
Let me remind you of but one, spoken at Edinburgh in 1867 :—

In a progressive country change is constant ; and the great question
is, not whether you should resist change, which is inevitable, but
whether the change should be carried out in deference to the manners,
the customs, the laws, the traditions of the people, or in deference to
abstract principles and arbitrary and general doctrines.

If we are to hammer out successfully, in this old country of ours,
new policies to conform with the spirit of the new times into which

we are emerging, we should surely do well to ponder these words of one who was himself a great reformer and a bold innovator.

It is just upon a hundred years since the publication of " Sybil," a work of fiction that was not only a literary but also a political event. Few novels ever made a deeper or more lasting impression upon the political thought of a nation. It was for him a confession of faith from which he never departed. To the Primrose League, when they take up once again their task of promoting the policies and the ideals that will for ever be associated with the name of Disraeli, the celebration of the centenary of " Sybil " will be a landmark and an inspiration.